SPIRIT AND ME!

To Lon God
loves a trier so
keep at it.

SPIRIT AND ME!
(BORN A MEDIUM)

by
Ken Pretty

Con-Psy Publications

ISBN 1-898680-15-9
Published by
Con-Psy Publications
PO Box 14, Greenford, Middlesex UB6 0UF, UK

Printed in England by Booksprint

To all those both in and out of the body who have consciously and or unwittingly contributed to the contents herein, I readily offer up my heartfelt thanks and love.

An anonymous verse runs as follows:

"Why should I say 'tis yet too soon
To seek for Heaven or think of death?
A flower may fade before 'tis noon,
And I this day may lose my breath."

Many years ago, a little more succinct perhaps, I wrote and included the following in the copy when advertising an evening of clairvoyance:

There is no death - just loss of breath;
We only pass as through a door -
Don't be misled - there are no dead,
Investigate yourself - be sure!

The cover picture, the "Winged Wheel", is mainly defined as *Illumination of Mentality*. (Other definitions: *Eternal Progress of the Soul by Light of Spirit And, When Souls aspire for Higher loves, True Wisdom is Attained. Another, according to the Greek Mysteries is: The Interior Form of the True Soul moving incessantly onward towards the Highest*)

This potent symbol hangs in my sanctuary in Spain. I am no artist – yet I painted it! Early on Tuan taught me that in Spirit there are multitudinous entities ready, willing and able to assist us in *any* undertaking. Such appeals though depend more on *trust* than faith and as usual, just letting it lie in that as on so many times before I asked once again, this time requesting the help from an artist.

Then, three or four days later, I heard clairaudiently an American voice telling me I should begin! Placing myself in his hands and told what to do, in no time at all I had drawn the outline in pencil. The whole painting, using acrylic paints, was completed in less than three hours. On completion the "floating helper" identified himself as one Will Gaines. He said that in the body, he had worked in the movie business as a scenic painter and also painted in his spare time. Once again *knowing* that I could receive such help produced what was needed!

Thanks again Will and may your God go with you!

P.S. The poor quality black and white image I have used is just 3 x 1cms while the painting is 104 x 45cms!

CONTENTS

INTRODUCTION

How many of us have read something somewhere or other; a novel, a short story, a magazine, or simply an article in a newspaper. After all, it is often said that "everyone has a story to tell" but really good story-tellers are a very rare species! And even if that statement is wrong, the fact remains that, by comparison to humankind per capita, very few of these actually commit *theirs* to paper! So it is that from the comfort of our armchairs we often critically thrust it aside declaring to the world that *we* could do better. But safely ensconced thus, it is all too easy to make such pronouncements.

Equally, as we dismiss the effort out of hand, most of us are blissfully unaware that however good, bad, or indifferent we thought the piece, it was most unlikely to have been the writer's first effort. Indeed, he or she has probably received more than enough rejection slips to paper the average room but this does not stop them.

So why do they keep on trying? Because, and this is the crux of the matter, they really want to win. By definition, all realised goals whether spiritual or material, mental or physical had to have a catalyst and within the truly ambitious it is a compulsive driving will! Patently obvious, for example, in athletics, politics and show business it is easily seen too that such ambitious endeavour is complemented by an equally obvious enthusiastic on-going motivation. In writing the driven, dedicated scribe will also keep on scribbling until he or she achieves their objective and it is this that makes them so different, and indifferently dismissive to the armchair criticasters.

I too for many years have been going to write a book but "I never found the time" would be too glib an answer in replying to why I did not do so. Intrepid writers would also (quite rightly from their standpoint) simply retort that such comments smack at excuses rather than reasons! And yes of course I *could* have, but it would not have been the right time. So when finally I knew I was receiving the nudge from Spirit, I purchased, (though I knew nothing about them) a computer... And it began...

Initially however, whilst not knowing what I had to write about, I always knew the sort of thing I would *not* write. Far too many psychics and mediums have already subscribed to the "life story" thing yet have hardly begun to live their lives and really have only a miniscual biography anyway.

Friends and family may well applaud we "lesser mortals" and our autobiographies as wonderful. OK but who else, I ask, might consider them to be much more than a passing read? It surely cannot have gone unnoticed that the most successful of these are written by famous film-stars and personalities; sports-persons, prominent politicians and the like? Equally observed is that, compared to their's, a medium's fame is small potatoes, with only, by comparison, really very minor public exposure or acclaim. Nonetheless, it must follow that if one relates incidents that have occurred to one in one's life, the writing of them has to be, in part anyway, autobiographical!

So it was, with certain misgivings, that in late 1995 aged sixty-four I finally sat in front of a blank screen, having absolutely no idea of how or what form the text would take! Then, almost immediately "the penny dropped" and from the very first sentence I knew that I had no need to worry. I quickly realised that, for the most part anyway, what I was about to write was going to be *through me* and not *by* me. It also quickly became evident (thank God for mediumship) which direction the book was to take.

Spirit wanted it to be in three parts: Part One (the easy bit for which I claim almost total authorship) was to be semi-autobiographical. Part Two: God Concepts as taught to me; A Scenario of Mediumship, the Attitudes to it and The Reasons for its and Spiritualism's Slow Progress and The Pathway to Spiritual Development. Finally, Part Three was to be called "The DIY Manual for Budding Mediums" which, of course is self-explanatory.

Accordingly, in Part One I have tried to keep the writing of things that have happened to me to a minimum, the leaning being more towards phenomenon. There have been very many more and some of these were and still are, truly incredible. However, I have deliberately declined to write about these because I do not want to be accused of sensationalist padding.

I cannot claim much of the rest as being my own original ideas and thoughts as these are mostly inspirational. Notwithstanding, I genuinely take *full* personal responsibility for Parts Two and Three. These, in essence, were received either when sitting at the computer keyboard, in sleep-state and or from memories of earlier contacts, communications and communion with those souls no longer in the body.

In simple terms then, apart from my two finger bumbling typing, my contribution has been to allow Spirit to work with me and through me as the instrument (medium, sensitive, channel). Metaphorically speaking, playing the part of the resident "plumber" I have tried to ensure that the thoughts, instructions and explanations of the workings of mediumship, etc. expounded herein have flowed through me uncluttered, like water through a well maintained pipe.

Many times in my life I have been fortunate enough to have had the opportunity to dip into, to take a drink from, and even, on occasions, to "bathe" in the Sea of Perpetual Knowledge. Anyone may partake of this; it requires only a true, strong and healthy desire to join in the search for Truth.

Knowing, not just simply believing, was taught to me by Spirit very early on to be held as a basic tenet. Belief alone they said presupposes that something may not be true! So, at the risk of appearing egocentric or "spiritually obsessive" I repeat that I *know*, I do not *simply believe*! Highly evolved souls are most eager to impart their spiritual knowledge and techniques of communication to any and all on the earth-plane who are prepared to listen. Learn as I have learned, as their pupil; to trust, to have faith in, and to keep faith with, these teachers of Truth and Light. There is no secret here; it has ever been so.

In knowing these lofty souls of whom and to whom I speak on a regular basis, I offer, by way of example (for I also know it is not offensive to them) the following analogy. Like our domestic pets the love of these souls for us is absolute and unfailing, generous in the extreme. In their willingness to accept us for what we are, irrespective of our treatment of *them*, they are totally forgiving of *us* and *our* shortcomings. Without reservations of any kind they always confirm, by their example, their unwavering fidelity, friendship and love. Therefore rest assured for True, Lofty Spirit never imposes on anyone!

Remember then that we learn from Spirit not by command, but from desire! Further I know and avow that these Illumined Souls patiently wait, ever ready, willing and able to instruct us in a fuller understanding of right thought, right speech and right action, probably the three hardest lessons to learn whilst we are still in the body.

"Learn, oh man, to know thyself, and walk with the knowledge of the Spirit within thee." So runs the chant of the Grand Lama and it was something I took to heart in the early days of my psychic quest and development. I still cannot begin to lay claim to a complete knowing of myself but I *surely know* that Spirit is within me. I therefore keep trying, consciously searching, the while asking, sifting and analysing all that I read or receive from whatever quarter.

He who reads, thinks; he who thinks, reasons; and he whom reasons cannot help advancing on the path that leads to the Light. But in your reading take care, for books have four kinds of readers. The sponges, who suck up everything without regard for the quality. The hour glasses that, having received, pour out the "sand" just as quickly, repeating the process over and over, disregarding and or being unaware of the need to move forward. The casuals, who read without learning how the "wine" is produced and think, that because of their size,"the dregs" must be the best part. Retaining these, they lose the pure wine" down the drain! Finally, there are the sieves; these carefully separate, sort and sift the "gold" from the dross, thereby retaining only the best. The choice, as in all things, is of course yours, but I consciously urge you to try to be a sieve, both in your reading and in your quest for knowledge too.

In the early days I also consciously determined to be a sieve. By the exercising of simple logic I quickly saw the obvious flaws to be found in books on the spirit world" (intentional quotation marks). So at the tender age of sixteen or so, in no time at all, finding them wanting, I rejected much of those early works. It seemed to me that they were not only religiously biased but they also leaned more towards fantasy and wishful thinking than logical argument and reason. It was then that I placed myself under the tutelage and guidance of Tuan, my door-keeper. He, over the years has introduced me to many other enlightened beings who have also taught (and continue to teach) me so much.

Charged then with the responsibility of passing on in book-form much of what I have learned, I do so gladly. Of course, I know there will be those who will disagree outright with what is written whilst others will defend these words as truth and a way forward. There will be also be the cynics, challenging my words from an orthodox standpoint. Very well so be it! If our words make you think at all, then at least it will have been worth the effort of writing them! *It is, after all, with the expressed idea of making people think that we have compiled it anyway.*

Consequently, I sincerely hope that you will find the contents of interest. May you also find them of value in your own pursuit of the Spiritual Pathway. Here is found Truth, Light and ultimately, Perfection; that of being absorbed into the Whole, in total At-One-Ment with the God-head. Notwithstanding, whatever your ideas, thoughts and criticism, constructive or otherwise, I hope you at least find the exercise of reading our efforts worthy of yours.

Many people I have taught over the years tell me that I have been most fortunate in receiving such a comprehensive knowledge of Spirit and its workings. Whilst endorsing this perspective I nevertheless have to state that it has not by any means been an easy task. Much time, energy, learning, love, and heart-ache too, has gone into the process. More importantly, I am now (at least in my present earthly incarnation) somewhat in my twilight years. However, I still realise and accept that such things are on-going, so there is bound to be more of the same in my future.

Therefore, although I am truly most grateful for that which I have learned, I caution the student to recognise that the nettle often has to be grasped, so always try to be prepared. And remember what should be your constant endeavour; to *fill your mind with useful knowledge that you do not speak empty words.*

When we are young, life on this plane appears to stretch before us, metaphorically speaking, for ever, but we should remember that time here is of the essence! Asked to describe the relationship between Time (theirs and ours) and Eternity one of the Manna Group (explained within these pages) stated:

"A bird sharpened his beak each week upon a mountain. Eventually, that mountain became worn down becoming as flat as the surrounding plain yet in that time but a second had passed in eternity!"

With such time-scale comparison, so succinctly illustrated by those words, one is immediately acutely aware of just how incredibly and ridiculously short our "three score years and ten" on earth really are!

With regard to what the future will hold, based on the knowledge I have received until now, I know that one day the Voice of Spirit Truth will become the norm. Orthodoxy will finally have learned a bitter lesson; that Spiritual Truth is perpetual and can never be a forgery! Strangely, orthodox religions have never subscribed, at least openly, to the truth; *that religion can only be true when it benefits all humanity!*

In acknowledging other help I thank all those on this side of the veil who have helped me over the years. These, both public and private, range from recipients, patients and fellow "discussionists" to contemporaries in all walks of psychic and mediumistic and spiritual pursuits.

Knowing so little about my relatives and ancestry, the references to them are, in parts, necessarily sketchy, even sparse. I am also unaware as to whether or not they have influenced *my* mediumship in any way. But just in case they have, either from "the other side" or through the genes, (and this is purely speculative, since as yet there is no proof yet that psychic traits are hereditary) or in any other way outside of my knowledge, I want to thank them as well.

Finally, I would like to thank those illumined souls; my Door Keeper, my helpers and The Manna Group for the unselfish help, guidance and love they have given to me in this, my last incarnation. I have tried faithfully to reproduce herein their thoughts and instructions; their do's and don'ts as received by me. These same I subscribe to as being intrinsically theirs so I hope and pray that, having taken on this mantle of responsibility, I have been able to do them justice.

Ken Pretty 1999

PART ONE
About me!

Chapter 1
BEGINNINGS

I was born in a small terraced house in Kerry Road, New Cross, South East London, on the 2nd. March 1931, the seventh of a seventh! Equally, or so I am informed by various astrologers, I have an intriguing and very rare astrological chart which clearly reveals (seven cardinal signs in one house) my psychic and mediumistic abilities. If the old saying is also true then it follows that I automatically possess some "powers". Deliberately placing those words in inverted commas, I believe that all things, from the lowest form of plant and insect life up through the evolution chain to animals and humans, have natural psychic ability (powers) "built in" to a larger or lesser degree in much the same way that we have other talents. Psychic(ship) however is not the same, and does *not* mean mediumship! (But more on this later!)

My father always had a good job and was never out of work. Even in 1928 during the depression, although it meant leaving his family, he still worked. He went to Rangoon, Burma in his capacity as the number one test pile driver for Sir Alexander Gibbs' company. Although he regretted having to go so far away he was very conscious of his responsibilities, the most important being, as far as he was concerned, to provide for his family. But it was worth it! He earned eight pounds per day (a veritable fortune then) over a period of two years. His returning to England ensured my entrance into the world exactly nine months later, my grandmother proclaiming that I must have been "made" in the taxi on the way back from the docks!

He never bought a car nor passed his test until well after the age of sixty! Accordingly, on most fine weekends he would pay a friend who owned a hire-car to take us all out into the countryside. However, his all consuming passion in life was football, so if he had a match on both Saturday and Sunday it meant no day out for the tribe!

He actually played football from a very early age, representing Portsmouth Senior Schoolboys when he was only nine years old! I vividly recall being taken at about six years of age to watch him play. Totally confused, I could not understand why they were playing in freezing cold weather in shorts and thin shirts! Blowing a blizzard, the snow was almost impenetrable! They were hardly able to see their own team never mind the opposition or the ball! Small wonder that I have always considered football a bit of a waste of time and energy! Dad though, continued playing in top amateur leagues until he retired at the age of fifty, no less!

My mother was a great lady with all that this implies. She had a natural elegance about her which no doubt sprang from the genes of her forebears and was always very conscious of the way she appeared to others. She would never venture past the front door without first having fixed her hair and put on a bit of make-up, or "mickie" as she called it. Neighbours on the other hand would think nothing of popping to the shops in their old slippers, their hair in curlers and often even without their false teeth!

Her handbag always held an extra pair of stockings in case the ones she was wearing became laddered. Also, in case she fell ill while she was out anywhere, she would always have on, from top to toe, fresh clean clothes. And for the same reason the first chore of the day after breakfast was bed-making thus ensuring that the bedrooms were tidy in case anyone was brought home ill! I still retain these habits and do the same things regarding cleanliness, underclothes and beds, stockings and make-up, I hasten to add, excepted!

We were not poor, but neither were we rich. Both Mum and Dad were very caring parents and somehow managed to share their love equally between all of their kids. We were never denied, nor short of a cuddle, a sympathetic ear or whatever. All natural "touchers", this probably accounts for the fact that my family is never afraid to embrace anyone and kiss their cheek. (On second thoughts such things, the kissing bit especially, are perhaps left-overs from the French side of the family tree!) During my life this love showed itself many times, an example of which was my mother fondly combing my curly hair, not because it needed it, but because I enjoyed it; for that matter I still do. I have always had a good head of hair and when I was young it was often compared to the advert for Pears soap featuring the famous Bubbles Kid. Indeed I only lost my curly locks because I was evacuated shortly after the declaration of war in 1939.

Hidings were uncommon but when anyone got her wild up, Mum would hit whichever kid was within reach! Many is the time a voice was heard protesting that they had done nothing! Her response invariably was always the same; that it would make up for when you had got away with something and not been caught! (Although I comment later on parents hitting kids because they are angry at themselves and not their kids, I still think that, on the whole, it did none of us any harm and, probably, quite the reverse!)

Until about fourteen years of age she always washed our hair; nobody escaped! She was especially attentive to our ablutions on Friday nights, when everyone took a bath followed by the compulsory dose of syrup of figs and the daily spoonful of cod-liver-oil and malt! The "water-heater" was classic "Heath-Robinson" being an old stone copper with the water heated by a fire beneath it. The bath, made of galvanised iron, when not in use, hung on a nail in the back yard.

Not having the luxury of a bathroom, at other times (until after reaching the age of fourteen and a half, one was permitted to visit the public bath-house) one had to strip-wash in the scullery. The loo, which same (although not hanging on a nail) was also out in the back yard. This often meant if someone needed to "go" and could not wait, they would have to pass one or another who would be trying, but failing somewhat, to hide their "bits" with just a small towel for cover. (Large bath towels only became "every-day" commodities among ordinary folk when, some years after the war, they began taking foreign holidays.) As such there was little regard or place for false modesty in our family! By far the best part of every Friday though was Dad's arriving home from work. On the way he always bought sweets and chocolate for each and every one of us when we would generally stuff ourselves silly for a few hours.

Having given up smoking some twenty odd years ago I find being around smokers totally abhorrent. The exception, perhaps are certain pipe tobaccos and "rollups", which I tolerate probably because it stirs in me the memory of the sweetish tobacco smell on my father's breath. As a small child, taking me on his knee or turning his leg and foot into a "horse" his breath would waft down as he sang "Ride a Cock-horse!"

As you read on, you will find that for various reasons, not the least of which was the interference by Mr. Hitler, I spent many of my formative years outside of and apart from the family circle. I missed out on many things, amongst which was learning about my relatives and ancestors. Normally, one perhaps spends summers or other holidays with grandparents, aunts, uncles, cousins and so on. These generally, at the drop of a hat, will readily talk about the family, but the war and evacuation prevented my gaining much of this information.

Shortly after hostilities ceased "itchy feet" resulted in various family members moving to different parts of the world while I myself went into the Royal Air Force. We do not boast a family "historian" either, so all I really had was recourse to some papers among effects left by my parents. Accordingly, much of what I know I have gleaned from these. So, by adding information told to me by family members, some, but not all, by any means, of the gaps have been filled.

My grandfather left the North of England with my father, who, at the time, was only about three years old and they moved around quite a bit. Grandad finally set down some sort of roots in Southsea, Portsmouth. Years later I discovered that he and his wife's families were Mancunians and that he had left her and a large brood behind. It was never explained to any of us why my grandfather left, nor why he chose to take just one of his children with him! And since my father rarely talked about "the Manchester connection" anyway, it remains, and no doubt always will, another family mystery.

On one occasion Roy and I were evacuated to Bolton in Lancashire for about twelve weeks due to Adolf introducing the V1. We were billeted with a very unkind woman called Mrs. Jessie Crook. Once during our stay we went to Manchester to meet my paternal grandmother and some of my aunts and uncles but, unfortunately, hardly a word passed between us. At thirteen and eleven respectively and uncomfortable at being surrounded by complete strangers (and adults at that) speaking with funny accents, it was no wonder that there was a total lack of communication. On reflection though I guess that they were perhaps just as uncomfortable and tongue-tied as my brother and I! Whatever! The exercise was never repeated! It was not that important to us anyway for, as already stated, Dad had very rarely mentioned his family and after the death of his mother, never again in any detail. Nevertheless, after her death, he did occasionally stay in touch by letter and or telephone with his siblings.

Dad used to talk about his Cornish grandfather who was apparently, during his lifetime, variously a professional smuggler, a horse trader, a paid bare fist fighter and always drank far more than his share of booze! By all accounts it appears that he fought more than one individual who died afterwards as a result of the beatings they received from him. He himself though also clocked up more than his own share of torn muscles, broken bones, lost teeth, cuts and bruises, etc.

At another time in his life he was also charged with murder. It was alleged that he had thrown a customs officer over a cliff to avoid being arrested. At the coroner's inquest however, the finding was that the man had apparently run the wrong way in the dark and that he must have fallen off the cliff, dying in the line of duty. A verdict of accidental death was recorded and Great Granddad, held until then, walked away, a free man. However, shortly after the inquest he apparently left both the smuggling gang and the area and travelled north. Thus, escaping the prospect of swinging from the hangman's noose, he died, years later, from natural causes.

My father had only managed to pick up bits and pieces about his family tree too so he did not really know just how much was fact or fiction. It is obvious however that there have been many of the proverbial skeletons (on both sides) in the family cupboards over the years. Read on and you will see that much of it reads like fiction, but you know what they say about the truth!

I never met either of my grandfathers in the flesh and only briefly the one grandmother, mentioned above, but I did run across Dad's father one evening...

I was demonstrating at West Wickham Spiritualist Church. At the time Ken Marshall, a good medium in his own right, was the president. I saw clairvoyantly three men, each of whom had one leg missing. One of them said he was my grandfather and asked me to speak to a certain woman in the congregation. I relayed that I was getting something about a record but I was not being told why (when Granddad interjected that I would soon). Simply smiling, she said she knew about it!

After the meeting she sought me out and said that she had seen me last when I was a small child. It transpired that the other two were her uncles. On enquiring further she told me her surname was Chalk and we worked out that she was a second cousin. I knew this name was on my father's side of the family and realised that this was the reason for Grandfather showing himself. No, not quite, she continued. The point was that the Chalks and the Pretty families between them held a weird record. The two families combined had actually lost more legs working on the railways than anyone else! (See end of chap. - On proof!)

Descended from French aristocrats, my mother's ancestors fled to England during the French revolution. My great grandparents, virtually paired off by the rich parents on both sides were very wealthy in their own right, owning an extensive estate in Arundel, Sussex. In spite of the arranged marriage they were, apparently, very happy and had a large family. Unfortunately however, Great Grandfather died fairly young leaving Great Grandma to raise the children on her own.

My maternal grandfather, ostracised by his family because he married a "commoner" had his share of the estate cut from the will and on his mother's death he obtained a gun set on demanding his right by force.

A firm of solicitors had controlled the trust fund his father had set up and she brought up the children using only the interest from it (or so she thought). However, upon her death enquiries revealed that excessive mortgages held on the property and lands meant that there was no money left anyway, so Granddad put his gun away!

The eldest son, one of my Great Uncles, was at the time, a chief of police. He investigated the solicitors but came to no conclusion being unable to prove any misdemeanour. He, however, was never poor and died a very wealthy man! It has been suggested since that he may well have been in collusion with the obvious but "unsolvable" fraud carried out by the solicitors but his siblings were never able to proved anything.

Not long after they married, my mother's parents moved to premises in Little Charlotte Street, Portsmouth, long since gone, due to Adolph's bombs and slum clearance schemes. They opened a shop and were soon supplying the naval and merchant ships with various pickled goods. My Grandma used her own recipes and very popular among these were pickled onions and shallots, red cabbage, eggs and soused herring. In no time at all there was a thriving business, very necessary since they too had a great number of mouths to feed!

Usually if one of we kids tried to duck a chore, Mum and or Dad would often repeat the following story.They would tell us that many's the time during their courtship when they would have to go and collect huge blocks of salt and ice. Most times too, before they could even think of going out for the evening, they would have to peel a whole bath of shallots. And this after already doing a day's work that often started at six in the morning!

My Mother went into service at the age of eleven and my Father also left school at the same age. Yet he was still very good at maths, a brilliant speller of words and wrote, in a beautiful hand, intelligent and interesting letters. He also claimed the somewhat dubious distinction of being the first person in England to sell "Cherry Blossom" boot polish, which, I believe, is still around even to-day!

Great Grandma obviously forgave Granddad somewhat for marrying below his station for she occasionally visited with them. Such visits were usually preceded by an urchin, who, on spying her carriage, would race to the shop in order to warn them that the tall lady was coming. His reward would be a couple of pickled onions or a slice of bread and dripping! But what an imposing figure she must have been!

No less than six feet six inches in height and always, apparently, wore tall hats to boot! (See e.of ch. qualify what is received before discarding!)

After some years, with the shop now successful, they had enough put by to purchase a horse and cart. A coal round soon prove profitable and after my grandparents died, Uncle Len, who had run that side of the business, being the eldest, inherited the whole thing. Soon the shop was sold and Stares, Coal Merchants became well known and remained highly successful in Portsmouth and the surrounding areas for many years.

Around that time Dad, lodging with the Chalks, worked in the Woolwich Arsenal, London, making munitions. Each week-end he would go down to Portsmouth to be with Mum, or she would come up to London. My eldest sister, conceived on one such visit, meant that my parents had to bring their marriage forward! So in October 1915, in the parish of Portsea, near Portsmouth, they were hitched!

Immediately removing to London, the story told at the time was "that was where he worked!" I suspect however, that folk counted the months twix marriage and first-born much more carefully in those days, which was a far more obvious reason for leaving one's hometown! They rented the Kerry Rd. house just before their first child was born and stayed there until about 1934 when I was about three and a half years old. We only moved a few hundred yards up the road however, just around around the corner in fact, to the shop and premises at 94, Edward St. Previously this had been a post office, then a chemists shop. Then when Mr. Lamb, the owner died, his wife carried it on for a time and as she was not qualified, it reverted to a general drug store. It was here that "my phenomenas" (deliberate plural) began...

(It is worth mentioning at this point that no discussion on psychic things took place at 94 until the family finally had to admit that there was something extraordinary happening. Therefore I refute any ideas or protestations that may be forthcoming that my experiences at the time could have been in any way due to suggestion by such discussion!)

Years later I discovered that many "happenings" had in fact occurred on both sides of the family. But if, like me, you rapidly become bored looking at other folks' snap-shots, especially when you do not know the places or people presented, then you will understand my reluctance to list all of those "happenings" here. In any event, I am certain that many of you could match, or indeed top my accounts with your own supernormal experiences, not to mention others that you may have heard about!

Once again though, since I have only a sketchy history of my family, there may well have been more psychics in our "tree" than the following. For this reason alone, to those whom I have perhaps inadvertently left out on either side of the veil, I sincerely apologise.

Auntie Sue, a sister of my father was a very well known medium in the North of England and demonstrated for many years in churches throughout that area.

My maternal grandmother ("the pickler" of Little Charlotte Street) used to "read"

22

a candle flame and accurately predicted storms, fires, or a ship being lost at sea and the like. She also had a friendly ghost, a nun, who would awaken her from her sleep, sit on her bed and talk to her. She would warn that someone in the family was going to be ill and even told her of impending deaths too!

Many mysterious things happened at Little Charlotte St. premises, a very striking example of which is the writing that appeared on the wall one day. Tellingly, however many times the words were painted out, whether the paint had dried or not and no matter how dark the colour used, the words always re-appeared within a few hours, as distinct as ever!

Only ever spoken of as "the writing" I never did find out what these words were but since everyone who spoke of it did so almost in a whisper, it may well have been a threat, or even something quite crude! I would love to have held a séance in that house and found out more. I am sure it would have been most intriguing whatever they read, but, more importantly, I may well have found out who wrote them!

My mother's sister Millie was also psychic and some of her more profitable gigs were at the naval base at Gosport. There, for the amusement of the officers' wives at dances and other functions she would tell fortunes. She employed a crystal ball and whilst some swore by her, calling her brilliant, there were others who claimed that she was simply a clever manipulator and a charlatan to boot!

Whatever, she invariably returned home by taxi with both a bag full of money and her spirits too, though it must be said that ninety-nine point nine per cent of these came out of a bottle! Mum said that many times she had seen her demonstrate her gift with incredible and unerring accuracy but only when the bottled spirits (or in Auntie's case the unbottled ones) were not in evidence!

My eldest brother also had a modicum of talent and I am sure that had he worked at it and learnt the craft properly he might well have become a very proficient clairvoyant medium. (See e. of ch. - natural, etc. mediums.)

My uncle Bert drove heavy vehicles during the war and was the first person to drive a 70ft. lorry and trailer, nick-named a "Queen Mary". (Perhaps you have heard a person directing a driver through a narrow gap commenting that they could get the Queen Mary through there! In fact the actual saying referred not to the but a (the lorry) Queen Mary!)

Breaking down one very cold night in the New Forest he decided to try to find some where to stay. Unlike the cabs today there was not even a heater on board never mind a shower, TV, bed and so on! So alighting from the cab and looking about him he was surprised to see a light in the woods since of course in the war there was an enforced total blackout. Walking toward it, he made out a window and when closer still, he realised it must be a pub or an hotel.

Opening the door he went in and, just like in the movies, everyone turned and stared but spoke not a word! He walked to the desk and asked the attendant whether a room was available and he replied in the affirmative. Duly given a key and shown to his room, very tired, he turned in for the night. The next morning, to protests, he stated he did not have time for breakfast and on paying his bill and getting his receipt, he promptly left.

On arriving back at his lorry he found a couple of suspicious policemen poking around. Explaining he had broken down, they asked him where he had been all night and he told them. Thinking this very suspicious and accordingly shaking their heads in unison they pointed out that there was no building in the woods as indicated; there was only an old ruin!

My uncle said that was rubbish and asked the police to go with him. They did and to his amazement all that could be seen was indeed the ruin as they had said. He then remembered the receipt and, producing it, the coppers were gob-smacked! Closer inspection showed it to contain the name of the building that once stood there, the price charged for the room and the clear signature of the former owner! It was then noticed that it appeared dirty as if it had been the top sheet of a pad for a long time.

It was never satisfactorily solved, but Uncle Bert and the policemen too, no doubt, had many a treated pint when relating that story. He, Bert, always has to be coaxed to tell the story though and always becomes quite emotional when doing so. As a footnote, I would add that I have seen both the receipt, duly dated and signed by the dead owner and, some years later, camping in the New Forest, I also visited and saw what was left of those same foundations!

Over the years I have heard many times too of the experience of a great uncle who, apparently whilst driving his carriage at dusk saw ahead a shepherd, his dog and his sheep. As was the custom, he pulled to the side of the road to let them pass and they did...right through him, his horse and carriage! From then on he never travelled that road again at night without company.

(For the reason stated above, I do not want to pursue these "snap-shots" much further and from now on experiences written about will have a bearing on the text, rather than simply a chronicle of events. There is however, one more "photo" well worth relating).

A cousin of mine, Joan, when very young, was watching her mother mix the Christmas Pudding (even though they were very hard-up, she determined they would enjoy Christmas). She, in a matter of fact way said not to make a pudding for her as she was going to spend it with Jesus!

Hitherto Auntie Marge had always made a little one especially for Joan. So knowing she was going to the Sunday school party she dismissed her words out of hand. Then later, when Joan saw the one prepared for her, she scolded her mother saying she had already said she would not be there to eat it! Did she perhaps know something? Did she want someone to ask her what she meant?

It was extremely cold that winter, a cold that penetrated into the bed-sit that they rented, so much so that a blanket had been placed over the window in an effort to keep it out. A few nights after the "scolding" Joan, from her bed, told her mummy

24

that she was very cold. Uncle George was working nights and so she invited Joan into their bed. Try as she might however, she could not get her warm, so eventually, in the early hours, with Joan on her lap, she sat by the fire, the flames the only light in the room. This was kept in twenty-four hours a day for cooking and heating with free fuel supplied by Uncle Len, the coal merchant I wrote of earlier.

Suddenly, a very bright light penetrated the blanket, came down and rested a moment on Joan's cold, frail body, then retreated the way it had come, disappearing back through the blanket. It was at this moment I guess that little Joan made her transition. Tragically, only two short weeks later Uncle George, who worshipped his little girl, also died.

The subsequent inquest and post-mortem stated natural cause of death as a massive coronary. But the family always believed and accepted that a person could die from a broken heart. This narrative however does not end here!

Still considered too painful a subject to speak of, nobody had even spoken their names for some time. Some weeks later Auntie Millie (the crystal gazer) and Auntie Marge were walking along a street when, on rounding a corner, they both saw George and Joan, hand in hand walking towards them! This was too much for Auntie Marge who promptly fainted, whereupon father and daughter disappeared and have never appeared since. (See end of chapter - on ghosts!)

HELPFUL NOTES!

(On proofs!) Proof sometimes comes in the strangest of ways and often needs working out and or checking. Therefore do not just dismiss out of hand something you cannot place immediately. I heartily endorse investigation and challenge too; indeed, I would not want it any other way. Nevertheless, I appeal to one and all enquirers to retain an open mind, the prerequisite for obtaining good, solid evidential proof.

(Qualify what is received before discarding!) Interestingly, none of my immediate family could in any way be described as tall. Imagine my surprise then, and doubt too, when one night, at an open circle, a budding medium told me that a family member, a very tall lady, wearing a tall hat was poking me in the back with her stick. She was, he said, urging me to get on with my mediumship as I had so much to do! Thoroughly nonplussed and still doubting it was family as there were no tall people in ours, I returned home. On speaking about it to my mother though, it brought home another lesson! Listen, enquire, sift, etc. and only then conclude! For until that time nobody had even mentioned Great Grandma or tall family members; or for that matter, I guess, with due respect, had had any reason to!

(Natural, etc. mediums!) Very few people are natural-born psychics, in the same way that very few are born pianists, artists, singers and so on. Yet when explaining or demonstrating, so many people expect to be able to learn the whole thing in "six

easy lessons". Often, even intelligent persons never seem to understand that what seems so natural and easy for me is not just a question of imitation for them. A natural medium, born with the talent, still requires to constantly study, spend time, patience, agony and ecstasy in quantity! The "unnatural" (or trained) medium sometimes takes years to begin demonstrating. Even then the results can sometimes be quite disappointing for them and they, allowing their mediumship to fade, lose interest.

All skills have to be learned and understood even with a natural talent. One may possess the ability but until one has the knowledge, the pianist will probably never play more than "chop-sticks", as it were, the cabinet maker too will still only hammer nails into a lump of wood! Remember also you are "always the pupil, never the master", another lesson the reader should take to heart!

(On ghosts!) Entities (ghosts) often show up in the most unlikely places, at any time of the day or night and often when it is the last thing we expect. Interestingly as well, contrary to popular belief, when we work we mediums do not "call up the spirits", they come to us! True we "open" ourselves to them, but they contact us and if they do not want to participate in your séance you will sit in vain and, at the end of the day, receive nothing!

Many times too when one does a sitting a lot of contacts link, but not the one the sitter wants to speak to. There are a variety of reasons for this, the main one being because if an entity sees or feels the sitter becoming upset, or if the entity itself feels those same emotions, then that entity will most often withdraw, in much the same way as they would on Earth, thereby avoiding pain or sorrow to himself or herself or to others. Alternatively, they may not have learned how to "get through" but I will explain this more fully later.

By the way, have you ever stopped to consider that a person you see each day, say, for example, on your way to work, can only be seen by you? Logic tells us that the person is of the Earth-plane and that everyone on the street must be able to see him or her; but how do you know? Indeed, how can you tell? The fact is that you cannot, unless of course you are able to question everyone else on the street, who will at the very least think you are crazy, or, even worse, you may find that they are all ghosts!

Chapter 2
AWAKENINGS

Between the age of fourteen and sixteen I stayed out very late but it was not because I was running the streets - I was running scared! More or less for two years, give or take, I had been surrounded by (though at that time I neither knew what it was nor what terminology was used to describe it) very scary psychic phenomena. I am not actually a ritualistic animal by choice - indeed I frown a little on those that use ritual in their psychic and or mediumistic pursuits - but on returning home I always went through the same procedure.

Before opening the front door I would look through the letter-box. As such I was able to see down the passage and through the glass panel in the door to the kitchen-cum-living-room area. If someone was at home I would open the door and enter. However, if I saw no-body I would hide in the door-way of the metalwork factory opposite, waiting for anyone of my family arriving home. I would then saunter over just as if I had arrived at the same time!

No-one knew of the agony and fear I was suffering. The only person I turned to, since I was Chief Choirboy at the time, was our local church priest, who promptly dismissed, out of hand, the whole thing as a product of my imagination! He then proceeded to admonished me, stating that in my position I ought to know better and, furthermore, he hoped I was not spreading tales among the other lads in the choir! So much for help from the orthodox church and, I guess, to prove a point, at the end of that Sunday night service, just as promptly, I resigned from both the choir and orthodoxy!

Nothing had happened to anyone else in the family up until this point, or if it had no-one had said anything and I really began to have serious doubts that I might be less than one hundred per cent in the brain department! (I did not realise I was psychic and mediumistic until my Door Keeper revealed himself and various other helpers to me some time later.) Let's face it, up until my revelation, I had not, except from a couple of instances, even heard the words psychic and medium, let alone had thoughts of becoming one!

As a child I do not remember ever being aware of spirit playmates, although I am told that at about two and a half to three I would tell whoever would listen that I was really a young girl called Sheila. I would insist that I did not belong to my family, that I was only visiting and I lived in the country! I started school at three years of age and this was probably the reason for not continuing this "fantasy"! I deliberately place that word in quotes for now, possessing far more knowledge and understanding I feel that those pronouncements might well have been a soul-reflection of a former incarnation. (Interestingly too, throughout my life I have felt, on many occasions, that I somehow do not belong to my family.)

In my experience, I have found that spirit playmates most often attach themselves to an only child, or where there is a big age difference between the children in the family. In ours, from the eldest down, the next one appeared, as regular as clockwork, within two years! Always full of the neighbours' kids as well, it is therefore hardly surprising that if there was anyone about from spirit, they went unnoticed!

My mother really loved children and each Bank Holiday there was a fair at Blackheath. At such times it was not at all uncommon to see her trailing twenty or more kids for a day out, each one carrying their "compulsory" sandwiches and bottle of water!

My first recollection of phenomena occurring was when I was very young. I must have been about four when my younger brother Roy and I regularly played tag. So what, I hear you say! However, we played our game by jumping on the bed, then floating around the room, pushing off the walls to speed up or slow down, in order to catch or escape from one another! We kept this a secret as jumping on beds in our house was a definite no-no and would certainly, if caught, have resulted in a hiding! But perhaps too in our innocence we may well have assumed that all kids played the same game. It just could not have seemed that important I suppose for I do not recall ever telling anyone at school that I could fly! (Today of course with aircraft and flying being so common perhaps kids do and others simply think they mean in air and not Spirit planes!)

In the event it could not have gone on for very long because my brother Roy, one year and ten months younger than I only vaguely recalls it happening. I do not know why we actually stopped but it was probably as a result of Dad catching us and letting us off with a warning about the forbidden jumping on the beds thing! In point of fact, although totally unaware then, and for a long time afterwards too of what was happening, I know now, of course, that what we had were quite long bouts of levitation! (See end of chap. - on levitation and commitment)

In the days before most folk were unable to afford a washing machine there was The Bag-wash. Each customer of the laundry had a large sack on which, indelibly written, was a laundry mark. Filled with soiled sheets, tablecloths, underclothes, shirts, blouses and so on it was tied at the neck with string and taken to the laundry.

There the clothes, washed whilst still in the bag, were later returned, very damp, to the pick-up point, where it stayed, still in the faithful sack, awaiting collection by the customer. Some of these left it there a few days, after which time the laundry would smell musty. (It was easy to tell which mums did this by the way their kids smelt at school!)

But not my mum! She would literally have one of us waiting at the bag-wash shop for the van to arrive, when we would impatiently wait for our sack to be thrown down by the delivery man. Almost as a part of the same motion it was placed in the family pram and rushed homeward as if one's life depended on it!

Immediately set to dry it was afterwards ritually sorted out. Finally, according to an article's use and importance, each would be folded, mangled or ironed.

Every Thursday at lunch-time my mother would close the shop and go off to the local cinema. At the age of fourteen and a half or thereabouts, on returning from school, my chores were to open up the shop, get the chicken-mash cooked and feed the chickens. I also had to prepare tea for my younger brother and sister and, most of all, work my way through an enormous pile of mangling before Dad got in from work at about five forty-five.

(This job was handed down to each of us in turn but I seemed to be the last "mangler" for my younger brother and sister never got the job after me! An older brother Harry hated the job so much that he employed a very drastic way to never have to mangle again! He actually put his little finger in the rollers and wound it in thoroughly mangling it in a different sense! Unsurprisingly, to his dying day it remained crookedly out of shape!)

However, back to the bag-wash and the real reason for my writing about it!

On Monday mornings my mother, having stripped all the beds, would gather everything up and place the dirty sheets etc. in the bag-wash sack. Always filled to the brim quite quickly, I would ask if I could take it downstairs, before I went off to school. Agreeing she obviously thought I pushed it down but actually I sat astride it and told it to take me down! It would then gently lift and float down the stairs! Again I do not recall this being anything to wonder at except that it did not happen if anyone else was around and my brother could not do it! I do recall though being annoyed that the thing would not perform when, having told him about it, it would not work when he asked me to show him! (See end of chapter - on haunted premises, etc.)

The war in 1939 began and in no time at all pre-determined evacuation programmes were put into place. This meant that for the first time in their lives lots of kids, myself included, were going to be away from home and staying with complete strangers! Aged eight and a half, I, along with two of my sisters, my "flying" brother and hundreds of others, went by train to Hove, Sussex and that same evening we were deposited in a school hall. We stood around or sat on the floor, clinging to our suitcases and our gas masks in their cardboard boxes as if they were our most precious possessions, whereas in reality they were comforters, our only real link with those folks we had left behind.

Somewhat like cattle on display at a livestock show, labels prominently displayed on our coats, we awaited "selection". Absolute strangers walked among us, nodding sagely, whispering comments and making their choices. On enquiry we were told we were to be taken and put into their homes for "the duration", whatever that was! A few thought it meant that they were going to be put into prison and as the word spread, so did the tears and the people in charge had a hard time calming everyone down.

In spite of the billeting officers trying their best not to split up families, many a kid shed even more tears that evening because this or that couple only wanted one child, not brothers and or sisters as well! It was really a case of, in the main, whether your face fitted or not. The exception were the types who took as many kids as they could because they received money, per head, from the government. This was the lot of my sisters and brother who were placed with a very mean, illiterate couple living in slum conditions.

Half starved they were constantly reminded by their "hosts" that they should be very grateful that they were able to eat at all! Recited parrot fashion almost daily was more or less: "What with the meagre amount an' all we receive from the government, think yourselves very lucky that you get a meal of any kind each day." It actually became a sick joke between us after we returned from Hove. Little did I know then that worse was to come on a later evacuation, and this time a lot closer to home!

At Hove though I was very fortunate. Standing in our little group of four, I was selected, cut out from the herd by a couple named Marriot. But they were not interested in my brother and certainly (said the wife) not in my sisters! They lived very close to the school so within minutes I found myself being introduced to their two sons and another boy about the same age as myself. I do not even recall his name but I do vividly remember what a rotten kid he was; all the time throwing tantrums or crying for his mummy! I well remember, after only a few days, boasting proudly to each and every one of the Marriot's in turn that my brother was much better than this kid but to no avail! Lasting just three weeks he was never replaced by another child, in spite of my pleading my case for Roy.

Being very well off, my hosts had a maid, a young lady of about twenty years of age. She was really nice to us boys, and, I like to think, especially to me; but even she was not able to get through to misery-guts! I must have fallen in love with her too because I missed her for all of a day when she left to marry her soldier boyfriend! They replaced her with a much older staid but likeable woman who, understandably, did not gel with us as readily as did Dolly.

The house was opposite the dog racing stadium and this proved to be very convenient, especially for me living opposite. I imagine that when the hundreds of "evacs" descended on the town, someone must have gone "oops!" for it was realised that nobody had thought about schools to accommodate them! Thus it was speedily decided that since dog racing had been suspended for the duration, the stadium office accommodation was one of the places which, suiting the purpose, would serve until such time as things could be sorted out. Teachers too were at a premium, for of course many of them had volunteered and others had been called up to serve in the forces.

Schooling at the dog track started with my teacher telling me that she wanted me to be a "very special" monitor. I have always found it pretty easy to learn something that I find interesting and I could both read and write very well by the age of six (sadly a poor reflection on today's youngsters; perhaps they should start as I did at three years of age). So, for about three months, with a teacher looking in on me now and again, I had charge (and I kid you not!) of a class of over thirty kids, teaching them to read and write! I enjoyed it immensely but, unfortunately for my backside, I did not take to learning again when we eventually attended our new schools around the town.

Caught after several months of playing hooky, I duly reported to the headmaster's office. As punishment, I received a severe caning. In my defence, the only excuses I can offer are that I had never been to the seaside before! Boy, what a culture shock that was! Also, and much more important, I discovered that I preferred teaching to learning, something that has continued even up to this day. Up until that hiatus, and virtually always thereafter I really enjoyed my schooldays. Indeed enough to say that from then on I was never ever chastised again, at any school, by any teacher, so I must have learned a good lesson from the punishment I received.

Almost a year to the day we were back home again From then on time spent away from home was governed by the intensity of the bombing we were receiving at the hands of the Luftwaffe. During those periods I do not really recall anything specifically psychically outstanding occurring around me. True, things were moved to different places and some were lost but with a large family these sort of things happen and nothing was made of it. Certainly, at the time I was totally unaware that I was a contributing factor in these happenings!

I knew things about people though! When they were coming to visit for instance and when they had put something somewhere and then could not remember where it was. I could, and often did, to begin with, tell my folks where things were and who was coming to visit. But I quickly realised this did not sit too well with them! For example, I was accused of moving the things in the first place, of reading other peoples' mail or of having "flapping ears". So I quickly "retired" my new found abilities, staying, for the most part, shtum!

In all, I was evacuated three times but apart from the Marriot family at Hove, who not only welcomed me into their home, but also treated me very well, the two other periods were nothing short of horrendous! It is hardly surprising then that psychic things were not much in evidence, survival, much of the time, being the name of the game! I was at Durrington for almost two years and without fear of contradiction I state that this was the most miserable period of my whole life!

It was not that long after returning from Hove that the heavy blitz on London really got under way. Accordingly cases were packed again and my sister Pam, (who, with a badly scalded foot went home after about three months) Roy and I were sent to stay with our eldest sister, Olive. Mum, who had to return to London immediately, took us by non-stop train to Salisbury. On the way we were held up at

(I think) Basingstoke station which was crowded with soldiers. Within seconds bullets from an enemy aircraft were tearing through the carriages and although others sitting on either side of us were hit, we were unharmed! I had also, earlier in the war, been machine-gunned while playing in a park at Southwark, London. Kids were killed and injured around me but again I had not been harmed! Such escapes and incidents were the shape of things to come in later life!

Olive lived in a decrepit, wooden-built, badly maintained shack of a place situate in the village of Durrington, Wiltshire. Running with condensation too, whoever named it must have had a quirky sense of humour as it was called (would you believe) "Rainbow Bungalow". But there was certainly no rainbow nor did we go somewhere over it as the song says, but most certainly the "wicked witch" was in evidence!

Mum had no inkling of what was happening with Olive, who, after Pam's return home, would beat us for even the slightest discipline slip. And many times we would be hit with anything to hand from sticks to belts even when she was simply "off" and we had done nothing! She also made quite sure that we were never alone with Mum on the rare occasions she was able to visit. So it will come as no surprise when you read on that we were terrified of sister Olive!

We actually ran away once and lived rough for three days. Near to Amesbury, just a few short miles from Durrington, we were picked up by an army patrol from Bulford Camp. Believing we had travelled a long way, in reality we had only, by taking short cuts across fields, simply walked in circles. They took us back to their camp, where we were fed and told that we were going to be taken back to our home in London. Oh yeah? They returned us to our sister, who said she had been worried. Another oh yeah! She told us after the soldiers had gone that she had not even bothered to report us missing! Boy, did we take a pasting for that little jaunt!

(My mother only found out about these and other things some many years later and never really forgave my sister for what she had done to us. Equally, Roy and I, keeping these things from Mum for such a long time, plainly demonstrates what a hold Olive had over us)!

My brother-in-law, stationed with The Royal Airforce at Netherhaven came home more or less for one night each week. We were very pleased to see him as he was quite a nice man but other reasons also prevailed. For example, my sister was very careful to conceal our suffering from him so we ate well when he was at home. Also, using an old round, metal hip-bath, we enjoyed the luxury of a hot, top to toe wash-down in the scullery. The rest of the time we had to wash in all weathers under an outside tap! (If I have any fetish at all it is the thought of not being clean! I know I take after my mother's habits in this but I also believe it is a reflection on those terrible days).

We were forced to collect wood for the fire, often with snow on the ground two feet thick. The stream we had to cross, swollen for most of the Winter, meant that the bridge was usually under water. We used to have to take off our shoes and socks and wade across to the woods. She would accept no excuse from us if we returned empty handed. Equally she would pour upon us a tirade of hate and blows if the timber was wet, something that was virtually unavoidable during winter in Wiltshire! She might well have been the originator of (and this long before such a saying became common usage) the "catch 22" syndrome if I did not know better!

Food often consisted of just bread and margarine twice a day, with sometimes the luxury of a cup of milk. We could drink as much water as we wanted though, so long as we used only the garden tap, which was often frozen solid! We also had to tend the large garden in all weathers so it not surprising that I still abhor gardening to this day.

However, the foregoing treatment was small potatoes compared to the weekends. Forbidden to return before five in the afternoon, we had to be out of the house by about 8 a.m. on Saturdays and Sundays. Always a puzzle this until years later when it was disclosed that it was so that she could entertain her lovers, of which there were many.

It was on one of many such occasions, that Roy and I were cuddling one another in our "den" in an effort to keep out the cold. I had made this some time before, by wedging a piece of corrugated iron between two trees to form a roof. This kept off the rain and snow and provided the wind did not blow too hard it was fairly dry. When one is hungry and cold it is common knowledge that there is a tendency to fall asleep and I was about to do just that, when, in a state of waking sleep, I was moved to action!

A voice kept repeating in my ear that I should go down the lane, climb up the bank and look for the tree with the hole in it! It became so insistent that I was compelled to act. To my brother's protestations, we waded through the slush and snow and suddenly, looking up, I knew which tree it was. After clambering up the slippery bank I looked around the tree and discovered the knot-hole.

I have always been terrified of rats and mice but without thinking I immediately thrust my hand into the hole (something I would not easily do even today) and felt a furry thing! Within a flash I had withdrawn my hand faster than it had entered! The voice, laughing, told me not to be a sissy, it was only a sack! Not quite knowing why I felt so reassured, I reached in and pulled it out. On looking inside, we beheld, all in sixpenny bits, an enormous amount of money, more than we had ever seen at one time!

Telling nobody of our find, we used it to help fill our empty bellies for the next eighteen months or so! We never thought to move the money to another hiding place either! After all, whoever had put it there might have come back for it, yet nobody else disturbed or removed it in all that time.

I have pondered this over the years and, romantically perhaps, have come to the conclusion that it was probably stolen money. I like to think it was maybe the voice of the thief, who perhaps had died on active service and, returning to see if his cache was still there, was drawn to two hungry, cold kids, on whom he took pity.

Another incident at Durrington worth mentioning is that shortly after the tree episode, I heard another voice telling me to go into the parish church. A notice on the door stated that to enter the church children had to be accompanied by an adult. Roy and I, thinking that such a transgression might get back to Olive, were not too eager to venture inside. But the voice, insisting, prompted me to open the door and go in; we did, and were immediately confronted by the vicar! To my utter astonishment however, instead of bawling us out, he asked was I responding to his appeal for someone to pump the church organ? Nodding, throat already becoming as dry as sand-paper, I managed a yes. At the same time though, crossing my fingers behind my back, I also mentally apologised to God for fibbing in His house. It must have all worked (or was it because when asked how much, I said I wanted no pay) for I was immediately hired! Whatever, we did strike some sort of a deal though as he agreed that my brother could always accompany me and we were also allowed to enter the church at any time. Thankfully, in those days church doors were never locked and from then on the warm and cosy organ loft became our den.

I had not been able to take the eleven-plus due to periods of evacuation to different places; too young in one place, too old in another! So once more back home and going on twelve, I returned to Clifton Hill Senior School, New Cross. As I became bored with each lower class however, they simply moved me up. But even these lessons I knew inside and out, so I was moved yet again. Eventually, I was placed in the top class of the Senior School with kids fast approaching fourteen years of age who were about to leave.

Finally, excused all classes, two other kids and myself were put into a small room and, unsupervised, we spent our days reading, painting and making paper-maché puppets. That is where I first learned to draw Disney characters and did so for some years. But it was obvious that this could not go on until it was time to leave school.

Consequently, when I was nearly twelve years old, I was sent to Peckham Central School. This was the equivalent of a grammar school, except that one had the option of taking either technical or commercial subjects after the third year. As already stated, I am fortunate in enjoying and learning easily those things that I want to learn. I liked that school immensely and most of the staff too, so it was comparatively simple for me to catch up with my contemporaries.

At about twelve and a half or so V1's meant another evacuation trip, this time to Bolton, Lancashire. This lasted less than three months and I returned to Peckham Central. Due to the previous school taking a direct hit one night, the victim of a V1 missile, "P.C." was in another building. We actually had to move again a couple of times for the same reasons and the school became Coll's Rd Central. Incredibly, both these hits were at night, which was a blessing, as of course nobody was on the premises. After that last move I did not get moved around again, at least not until I was in bed at night! But more on this later!

War or no, each year the pupils of the school elected the prefects by secret ballot. Then, with the only condition being the Headmaster's right of veto, in yet another secret ballot, the prefects themselves elected the School Captain. Anyone over thirteen and a half could be nominated and seconded but up until that time there had never been anyone elected, even as prefect, below the age of fifteen. At the ripe old age of fourteen therefore a precedent was set when I became first a prefect and then the School Captain. Thankfully there was no embarrassing veto exercised and I retained my post via re-election each year until I left school at sixteen. I was also appointed Captain and Assistant Coach of the swimming team for the same period.

I was a Boy Scout from the age of eleven and at fifteen and a half, assistant to our Scout Master though as previously mentioned I was no longer in the church choir. Having also taken quite a few lessons in ballroom dancing, I could "cut a rug" with the best of them. And as any musician will tell you a bonus of singing or playing in a dance band means that, even without really trying, one attracts the ladies!

Miraculously perhaps, in spite of being bombed out of more than one school, evacuation and attending some eighteen different places of education between the ages of three and sixteen, I still managed to emerge with a modicum of intelligence and common-sense. Indeed in 1947, just before leaving Coll's Road, my parents were approached by the headmaster suggesting that I consider Teacher Training College. Due to the acute shortage of teachers, the course was at that time only two years and the consensus was that I would do very well in the profession.

I was also the only kid in the family who actually enjoyed serving in my parents shop and my father also offered me the chance to study as a chemist. (Even in those days though I was acutely aware that my siblings' were all jealous of one another and is something that has grown worse since my mother's transition. Quite strange this, since we had all had our full share of affection and accommodation from our parents. But I guess when a family is split up quite a bit as ours was during, and after the war too, cracks may well appear.) But for me and far more important at the time, singing with the band had whetted my appetite and I had a yen for show-biz! So I did not take up either option (or show-biz for that matter) but I have no regrets.

Later on my band-leader recommended me to the great Ted Heath and I auditioned for him but although I did well he wanted someone over twenty-one. Ray Ellington (of "Let The Good Times Roll" fame) who was also rehearsing with his trio told me that I would have been successful had I been of age. He went on to explain that contracts for a minor had to be signed by a parent or guardian and the "guv'nor" as Ted Heath was called, figured an adult presented less problems.

The reasons for including the foregoing, by the way, is not simply a flexing of my ego. I merely make the point that poltergeist phenomena can happen around anyone in puberty and early teens. It is not, as many "experts" would have us believe, simply the prerogative of mentally disturbed, introverted or insular adolescents, who seem, among other things, to spend far more time in the bathroom than perhaps they should!

So folk in my neighbourhood, even had they known, would have said I was the last person they would have thought would have had "funny" things happening to him! In fact, folks would have called and known me, if asked, a totally average, normal, well-balanced lad, interested in all the things youngsters get involved with. (And I knew of some that they definitely would not if they had had the choice!) Strangely though I also knew that though quite terrified at was happening psychically about and to me, I was, nevertheless, still most curious about what it was and why it should be happening to me...

HELPFUL NOTES

(On levitation and commitment.) *As an adult I have tried many, many times to levitate both alone and in circle, but have never quite achieved it. (True, I astral travel but that is in no way the same thing!) I would love to have blamed my later failures on a childhood whacking but I am afraid I cannot! Like the cult followers pictured on TV I would be kidding myself too if I blamed my father for my failure. These disillusioned souls, seemingly oblivious to the fact that they are kidding themselves, are persuaded by their leaders to "meditate", cross their legs and bounce up and down on mattresses. This they call "flying" and levitation!*

Kidding aside, know that this is absolute bunkum! Levitation is a physical phenomenon involving an enormous amount of dedication, patient sitting, power/energy and time set aside for Spirit, this last being something we never seem to have enough of these days.

Another reason could well be that today we are probably more lazy, less determined and under committed than the early Spiritualist pioneers. And of course we are also spoilt by all the modern gadgetry we have at hand today, which makes us a little lax in our Spiritual commitment!

In Victorian times for example one would frequently walk, irrespective of the state of the weather conditions, some miles to get to a circle. The most common reasons for walking were due to (a) either not having the fare for public transport or (b) because there was none! Afterwards they would simply trudge home again.

To-day Mr. and Mrs. Average will not even walk to the end of the road! They all too often on circle night also rush out to the car at the last minute, having watched their favourite soap or caught up on the latest news-cast, arriving right at start-time instead of being there well before-hand.

I have to conclude therefore, that in many cases the dedication and time required for development is sadly lacking in to-day's climate. Healing for instance is on the red end of the spectrum, the "physical" end. With respect to these folk, I state unequivocally that healing is a good deal easier to "perform" than the other physical talents. As such, it pretty-well always takes over and usually totally cur-

tails the development of any other physical mediumship that the healer in question may have. It is sad that some healers may well have the talent for producing phenomena such as transfiguration, direct voice (trumpet) or independent voice; materialisation and so on.

These are talents which, with more dedicated time and patience they might well have be able to develop alongside their healing. They could still minister to their patients without any problem, yet all too often, most times through lack of knowledge, they just allow such talents to be pushed aside.

One such was Harry Edwards although in his case it was not through lack of knowledge or, God bless him, for the dedication he always showed in his work. Brilliant as he was however, I know, having spoken and enjoyed his company, that he could have been an equally astounding physical séance medium and like many others he could have practised both! He knew it too but he also knew that Spirit never force their intentions upon us and he made his choices accordingly. Interestingly he produced some of the best photographs of ectoplasm and physical mediumship ever. He sat, contributing so much (obviously a power house) in the development of Jack Webber's mediumship.

(On haunted premises, etc.) When attending haunted premises, perhaps the most frustrating thing for the "hauntees" is getting the entity or poltergeist to repeat the phenomena that they say have previously occurred. The exorcist needs to eliminate all natural causes before entering into the "super" natural and a demonstrated phenomenon is of course the very best one could wish for!

However, many "ghosts" (poltergeists as well as entities of persons who have "died") are quite canny. Often they are very aware that the investigator is there to try to remove them or, at the very least, interfere with their goings on! Either way, in many instances where haunting occurs they are not at all happy (or ready) to give up and retreat so easily. Nor will they readily demonstrate what they can do, for fear of being (caught in the act) ensnared by the exorcist and shown the door! They somehow know (probably by picking up on their "victims" and or the exorcist's thoughts) that once it is established that something has occurred psychically, the exorcist will begin his real job of getting rid of any recurrence! After all, if an entity is present at other times why should it not be in on the conversation requesting that the exorcist attend upon the haunted premises? Logically then, on the day, those same entities will also be wary of the exorcist, particularly if they are enjoying themselves and the commotion they are causing!

To a large extent this lack of ability for entities to "turn it on" at the drop of a hat gives rise to so many people denying the existence of phenomenon per se! However, experience it; any kind of it, and you will never ever forget the experience, nor deny its existence again!

Chapter 3
FROM NIGHT TO LIGHT

A t about the time the dramatic phenomena (as opposed to friendly words in my ear, etc.) first began, unbeknown to me, some of my brothers and sisters had discovered a new game. By placing the letters of the alphabet in a circle on a table and setting a glass in the middle, they had immediately created a crude ouija board. Knowing no better they played with it in a very light-hearted way and this, together with my own psychic and mediumistic potential may well have been the catalyst for the phenomena which took hold. (See e. of ch. on ouija boards and planchettes.)

It was, as I remember, when I was nearly fifteen that the phenomena really stepped up a gear. Nobody seemed to notice the increase in things getting misplaced or moved around, even when it happened under their noses; nobody that is, except me! *I noticed all right as the thing mostly moved around was me!*

Various things would occur among which was me getting tipped out of bed! No! I was not always asleep when it happened! And yes I am certain that I did not just fall accidentally! If I did, how come a three feet wide iron bedstead and all the covers were totally inverted? It would happen virtually instantly, just as if someone had turned the handle on a giant spit! The result would be that I would be on the floor, face down! Beneath me were the blankets; on top of me there would be the mattress, then the iron bedstead! With the best will in the world there is no way that I could have fallen out of bed and ended thus!

When I was not being inverted the bed covers were pulled off of me in different ways. I was wide awake when this occurred! Sometimes, even though the covers were tucked in they were simply ripped back! Usually though, utterly petrified, even though I held on with all the strength I could muster, the covers slowly and surely were drawn off me, ending up at my feet! Whenever these things happened I inevitably screwed my eyes shut tight so I never saw the perpetrator. Whoever "they" or "it" were always won the tug-of-war but never replaced the covers.

I would be left thus, and, depending upon how warm or cold it was that night, they would stay on or off for varying periods of time. Perhaps more to the point and more truthfully I have to say, in reality, the time lapse depended more on how long it took for my courage to outweigh my discomfort!

Stood on end against the wall, behind the bedroom door was a small but fairly heavy billiards table, in itself quite innocuous. Nevertheless, anyone I think, would have to find it really scary when, having just got into bed this thing, in the words of the old song, "would fly through the air with the greatest of ease" and end up on top of me, not with a heavy bump as one might expect, but with more of a gentle, teasing caress! I would eventually put it back behind the door, the time taken regulated by the same "formula" as when I replaced the covers, i.e. courage = time + or

- the endurable level of discomfort!

The bedroom was well over twenty feet long and disproportionately very narrow. Easily accommodated, against one wall stood three single beds, spaced apart by a dressing table, tall-boy and a chest of drawers. My eldest brother was by now married and I shared the bedroom with two other brothers, Harry and Roy. Weird things had been going on for some time (it seemed like an eternity to me!) before I realised that it only happened when I was alone! Nothing ever occurred when either or both of them were in their beds before me, or when we went to bed at the same time!

Like the abused child I also invariably felt a little ashamed and that somehow I was to blame! This was always followed by an overwhelming compulsion versus fear argument with myself to return things to normal before being discovered! Of itself, to say the least, such behaviour must appear to be somewhat eccentric! After all, for a terrified anyone, never mind a young kid, having to first cover a distance of some twenty-odd feet to reach the light switch would surely, normally, result in the damn thing staying on the floor where it had been hastily shoved by me! By way of answer, I point to the reason for this somewhat unusual behaviour on the section about my revelation. It will be quite obvious that I was to endure this, at least as far as my family was concerned, totally alone!

My parents never worried about me being out at night. I did not run with a gang and I could always get up the next morning. (Still a night person, often not going to bed until three or four in the morning, I am invariably ready and able to rise again, feeling refreshed, at seven-thirty more or less.) So in order to be sure I would find people in and at least one brother in bed, I began to stay out later and later...

(It was on such a late night as I walked home that I conceived the letter-box ritual mentioned in Chapter Two. Wow! As I write, something has suddenly crossed my mind! It occurs to me that in all these years and even at the time, I had, and for that matter never have, until this moment, considered the following possible scenario! What if, when I lifted that flap, someone or something had stared right back at me through the letter-box? I dread to think, even now, what my reaction might have been!)

I saw my first ghost in the shop... (See e. of ch. - On ghosts.) Arriving home one night I went into my letter-box routine. Great! I saw through the glass panel in the kitchen door that Dad and Mum were in, so I unlocked the front door and went in. (I should state here that my father had a thing about slamming doors. This was especially true of the front door, for being an old property, slamming it brought articles tumbling down in the shop window!). So the rule was to turn and face it, then at the last minute push it gently shut. Turning to do so, out of the corner of my eye I saw a shadow move behind the L-shaped counter!

Unbelievably, I saw this take on the shape and apparel of a severely dressed woman. Clearly defined, her features displayed a most hateful expression. This was, I agree, perhaps made worse by the street-lamp light filtering in from outside which caused erratic light and shadow as it found its way through the shop window dressing. Notwithstanding, I knew what I was seeing! Fixing me with a look, her eyes making me feel that they wanted to bore a hole right through me, she began moving around the counter towards me!

I was rooted to the spot for all of two seconds and then, terrified, I hurtled down the passage, not bothering to use the two steps at the end and crashed into the kitchen! Ashen faced and reeling like a drunkard, I frightened the life out of both of my parents! At first they thought I was ill, or that I was in trouble and someone was chasing me! Boy, they certainly had the last bit right!

I told them what I had seen and what had happened! (Of course in the movies, even though they are scared out of their wits, and women especially, they always look in the dark, they never put on the lights!) But this was real-life stuff, so, true to life, brave Jack (my father) went up to the shop, put on every light and looked around staying all of ten seconds! On his return he stated: "There's nobody there, you must have imagined it!"

Insisting that I had seen her he told me to describe her, which I did, even down to the clothes she was wearing. With a strange expression on his face he looked at me, pausing as if searching for the right words; then shrugging he said: "Come on son, you imagined it, you must have done!" (see e. of ch. - About being persuaded by others)

(Brave Jack by the way "did not believe in ghosts" but after his experience on the stairs which I shall relate later he would never again change his clothes upstairs. He would insist, whatever the state of the weather, that it was too cold! He would not change in the room behind the shop either, referred to as the back room, always using only the kitchen or the scullery.)

In fact the back room had its own significant responses for when the secret ouija board sessions were started they were held in that room. From then on anyone, whether a couple or a single person slept there, they always had a restless night and felt very unwell for at least a day afterwards. Unfailingly, whether they were aware of its history or not, the outcome was always the same.

After quite a number of these "coincidences" Mum, often very inconvenienced, since most times we had a full house, would allow nobody to sleep in there overnight. At the time she was of course still totally unaware of my siblings activities! Accordingly, it can be argued that she was not, consciously anyway, influenced at all by the activities and or effects of the ouija board.

The next ghost I encountered was a man. He would frequently appear at my bed-side almost as soon as I switched off the light. He always appeared wearing a suit and an Anthony Eden type hat. He looked neither pleasant nor unpleasant; he never spoke, or if he did, I did not see his lips move nor hear his voice. Just the same he still scared the xxxx out of me!

Immediately *he* showed, I would duck under the covers and stay there until, eventually, through sheer tiredness, I would fall asleep! Coincidentally, whenever he appeared neither the tipping out of bed nor the moving of the bed-covers occurred. (See e. of ch. - Poltergeist vs. human activity.)

After these appearances began, things too numerous to mention here happened around me all of the time, day and night! When recalling them now I can laugh but at the time they were most frightening. Things like putting something in one pocket and yet, though I would never feel it move, in the proverbial blink of an eye, it would be put into another one!

And what about sitting on the toilet minding my own business, bothering nobody. So what you say? Well, I bet yours does not suddenly flush, *without the chain being pulled!* You can safely bet though that I would leap off that seat like lightning which itself is hardly world shattering! What is amazing is that there would be no sound of water re-filling the cistern, yet on pulling the chain, it would flush again! Then, as normal, the re-filling cycle commenced! *Any plumber will tell you that this cannot happen! It is impossible!* Oh Yeah?

I still said nothing, fretting the while that nobody would believe me. After all, things only occurred when I was alone! I often mentally screamed out why is this happening to me? Why, Why, Why? Not realising or knowing the answer, or the true situation, I also could not know that help was actually quite close at hand and would shortly let me know it in a very impressive way...

One day, home from school for something or other I was amusing myself in the kitchen area. At the sink in the scullery my mother was washing up some dishes. Suddenly, the chickens went berserk, cluck-clucking like mad and, on looking through the window, she saw a man in the back yard. There was no rear entrance to the property and the chicken-shed went right across the yard from wall to wall. So thinking it had to be an intruder, she shouted for me to come quick!

And there he was! My man! Complete with suit and hat, he was casually walking down the path towards the rear of the house! We heard his tread as he walked past the scullery door; then abruptly there was silence! Scared, we whispered to one another, among other things that he was, perhaps, standing outside. We half-heartedly (I am not sure who pushed whom) went into the kitchen-diner and looked through the window but saw no-one; he had simply disappeared!

It was then I told my mother that I had seen him before and related my experiences. She was very sympathetic and assured me that I had nothing to fear. This was the first time I had heard about the occurrences in Little Charlotte Street, Portsmouth, all those years ago. She did her best to reassure me by saying that whilst her family had been very alarmed by it all, nobody ever came to any sort of harm. And to be scared she continued was quite natural and normal but I had nothing to worry about!

In hind-sight, maybe I should have told my folks about my experiences as and when they occurred; at least I may not have suffered quite so much angst. I doubt though, with their very limited understanding, whether little more than misplaced sympathy would have been the result, actually achieving very little anyhow! Also (it seems very grand to state it) it was, I guess, with the benefit of hind-sight, a part of my destiny to go it alone. For now of course, having gained in knowledge, I know that some things have more purpose and intent than we are aware of at the time.

In the event, since my first "in the flesh" encounter with Tuan and my helpers I have had nothing but the best of attention, help and protection when needed from Spirit. Also the problems and experiences of my early years, hairy though they were at the time, have often stood me in good stead since. Since experience has to be experienced, I have found through the years, particularly when on "ghost chasing" calls, some of the things I have since encountered make much of my stuff look like a stroll in the park!

Pundits may still put forth the argument that poltergeist phenomena is due to one being in puberty. However, certainly anyway as far as actual *human* entities go the argument totally falls flat. My mother, of course, and the players of the ouija board most certainly were not in that stage of life! Conclusion and learning have clearly shown that entities of all ilk, appear, haunt, call it what you will to folk of all ages and calling.

Other bits of phenomena were served up but apart from mine and on the one occasion my mother's, it appeared that nobody else in the house was affected.

In fact, it later transpired that they too had been having strange things occur. These only came to light much later when things were openly affecting them as well. It was then that Mum and I, for the first time, spoke of the man in the garden. But until these phenomena became family business my siblings had never said anything about playing the "letters and glass" game.

The ouija board sessions were held in secret for they had been warned by "the spirit of the glass" of dire consequences if they told of them. This of course (uninitiated take note) clearly demonstrates malevolent or, at the very least, mischievous entities at work. Sessions had taken place when my parents were out playing in a darts match for our local, a regular occurrence. The others had conveniently decided to stay in, ostensibly to play monopoly while they "baby-sat" my younger brother. (Incidentally, in case the more discerning of you may have been counting, the kindergarten that my youngest sister attended was evacuated en bloc to a beautiful mansion in the country where she remained for the duration). Most nights too I was out either rehearsing or at gigs, singing with the band, which automatically excluded me anyway from their secret activities!

For your perusal and to demonstrate how the phenomena accelerated, I include just a few of the incidents which affected both members of the "ouija gang" and others in the family.

My brother Harry, at the time on night work, would come home at "lunch-time" with a couple of pals where a meal that my mother left ready each night awaited them. After a while, making feeble excuses to my mother, the two guys said that they thought it would be more convenient to eat in the factory canteen. Then a couple of nights later Harry said he would be joining them! Meals there were known to be very poor quality and expensive. Mum was a good cook and fed them for next to nothing, but as always, though hurt, without rancour or nasty comments, she quietly accepted their decision.

They all three later told that when they came in for their meal, no matter how many times or how securely they fastened the kitchen door, when no-one was look-ing it would open! All the time they watched it nothing happened (of course!) but whenever they turned away, even for an instant, it would open again! Most nights footsteps were heard walking down the passage; these always stopped at the door. Of course on opening it, as you have probably guessed, no-one was there! At times the temperature too, for no apparent reason, would also drop quite dramatically whether the door was open or closed!

An old dresser, fixed to the wall had, as was customary, the food plates and dishes stood upright and cups hanging on hooks from the shelves. Harry's first night alone passed without incident but on the second as he was eating his meal, the plates began rolling back and forth and the cups swung crazily on their hooks! Hence his decision to join his mates in the grotty canteen, his acknowledging that discretion really was the better part of valour!

Sister Sylvia was sleeping peacefully one night. Suddenly, violently shaken by someone, she awoke to find a lady bending over her who then slapped her across the face! She shot bolt upright, ready to retaliate, thinking it was Pam only to find that she was fast asleep beside her. She put on the light and awoke her.

Pam, annoyed at being awakened, grudgingly checked Sylvia's face and saw the "hand-print" on her right cheek. OK! Work it out for yourself dear reader! She slept on Sylvia's left against the wall so unless she was a contortionist, or had been out of bed and had somehow managed to climb back over her, *after* shaking her awake *and* slapping her, it had to be something else!

I was at Durrington the night the shop window was blown out so I missed this bit of excitement. German planes raided most nights during the blitz and the win-dow damage was caused by the blast of a land-mine exploding nearby. My family slept in the reinforced cellar each night and, on this one, footsteps were heard from above, coming down the passage. The cellar door was pushed open and a voice, heard by all, called out: Don't worry, you're quite safe!" Dad and my brother Jack, home on leave at the time, having heard the sounds of both the glass and the foot-steps were already out of bed! In record time they reached the top of the cellar steps only to find nobody there! Stranger still, they found the front door was still locked and bolted on the inside! On going outside, in front of the shop they saw that the smallish tree set in the pavement many years previously was still standing, but now the victim of almost total defoliation. Significantly though it was dressed in a different way for precariously hanging from its branches by a parachute was another land-mine!

The bomb squad subsequently defused and removed it but my folks and others too regularly quoted thereafter that "that tree, with a bit of 'elp from above, saved many lives 'round 'ere that night!" It also survived the war and a petition was sent to the council asking for a commemorative plaque. The council however, ignored the petition, pleas and protests and it was simply ripped out some years later and dumped when the council re-laid the pavements.

One night, when the phenomena was occurring quite regularly (yet still totally rejected by Dad) there was a thumping up and down the stairs! It was well past midnight with everyone except Harry, who was on night work, long settled for the night. My father, awakened and very angry, thinking that it was one of us throwing a tantrum, got up and stormed onto the landing. Shouting, and not very politely at that, he put on the light and saw that my bedroom door, something never done in our house, was closed!

He angrily bounded down the three stairs from the upper landing and tried to open it but it would not budge! He banged on the door shouting what was I playing at? My response was that it had shut of its own accord! At this, he put his shoulder to it and it gave sufficiently for him to put his head into the opening and switch on the light. The billiard table mentioned earlier had, it was seen, fallen over, it's position clearly indicating that it had been turned from the wall and wedged against the door!

On finally managing to get in, the thumping, later reasoned as being heavy footsteps, began again. Then Dad, in trying to discover what was causing it was pushed out of the way and unceremoniously dumped on his backside, by, he later admitted, something or someone he could not see!

And where was Roy some of the more perceptive readers may wonder? After all, he slept in the same room! True, but as might have been expected, he had slept through it all! But then, *he* would sleep through *any* noise; a very heavy air-raid and breaking glass was nothing! (Often too, for a bit of fun, I would question him while he slept. He would tell you, absolutely unaware that he was giving away his secrets, exactly where he had been that night and what he had got up to! I also wonder if, after he married, his wife discovered that little game too?)

During the relating of the foregoing incidents, my ghosts came up again. The consensus was that I had accurately described the previous owners, both of whom I could not have known in the flesh as they had "died" almost before I was born! Notorious for her hatred of children they were not allowed into the shop unaccompanied by an adult. It was common knowledge that all was not well in their mar-

44

riage and that they frequently noisily quarrelled. One of their on-going disagreements stemmed perhaps from his refusing to serve shop customers except by way of their prescriptions in his capacity as a dispensing chemist and even then he was never seen!

Apparently many customers wondered whether he actually existed as they had never heard his voice nor even caught a glimpse of him, working, as he always did, behind a screened off area. The next door neighbours also speculated, since lights at night seemed to indicate it, that they probably slept in different bedrooms as well.

At the time of his death she was quite elderly and very shortly afterwards she closed the shop and became completely reclusive. But she had never done her own shopping anyway! Foods, as and when required, were simply delivered by local shopkeepers and, doubtless, at the end, it was such behaviour that contributed to her undoing! It seems that she fell down the stairs and badly fractured her pelvis. Obviously unable to get up, it was said that if indeed she did call for help, for nobody owned to hearing her, her cries went unheeded.

Eventually, police broke into the premises and discovered the corpse in an advanced stage of decomposition. It therefore came as no surprise to anyone (who had whispered as much anyhow) that the coroner's finding was that, due to her accident and subsequent immobility, she had literally starved to death!

A couple of years after taking the shop my father, having previously only made a cursory inspection of the cellar said it appeared to contain "quite a lot of junk". So once the family had settled in, fearing mice and or rats might take up residence, he decided, helped by some of his football pals, to clear it out. Among the "junk" was an enormous quantity of very old fashioned apothecary bottles, pestles and stone mixing bowls. Dad not being aware of their intrinsic value, allowed we kids to use them as targets, hammers and plant pots respectively!

Far more serious though was that, to his utter astonishment, he also found diaries, letters and so on in boxes. These clearly revealed that the previous owner (my man) was a back-street abortionist! Blood stained tables and the like showed that he performed these primitive operations in that very same dirt-floor cellar, the only illumination, a fan-tail gaslight! (My father, on moving in had the gas cut off and electricity laid on.) One can only imagine the pain and agony some of those unfortunate women must have experienced. (Small wonder then that the emotion alone, impregnated as it must have been in the atmosphere and structure would, through the ouija board "game", stir up so much activity.) I reiterate! As previously stated; truth sometimes really is stranger than fiction!

In the early 1960's, I bought the shop and premises, as my father wanted to live in Guernsey. I had some spare cash at the time but it was hardly what might be termed an investment; indeed I mostly did it as a favour to Dad, though I also thought it might be fun as a side-line. Consequently, being, at the time, among other things, an estate agent I simply "double contracted" the deal, meaning that he bought it cheaply as the sitting tenant and I bought the contract from him.

Interestingly, on reading through the deeds I discovered that originally all the adjoining terrace properties had common-access rear entrances. However, many years before my father had even rented, the owners, by agreement, had closed these off, each one converting the extra space into flower beds, etc. Years later, simply by looking, one could not have known that a rear entrance had ever existed. But *my man* remembered, chicken sheds or no and exercised his prerogative in using it! Readers will have already guessed that he was, of course, the chemist, the husband and abortionist who had also, many times, stood by my bed (wondering perhaps who the heck *I* was?) By all accounts he had slept in the same room, his wife sleeping in the room where Sylvia was slapped! In the event, I have to conclude that he was not, after all, a protector of mine.

With due respects to my parents they had only really played shops so the first thing I did was to completely transform the premises. Working very hard I removed the wall between the back room and the shop to make one large room. I ripped out the antiquated display units affixed to the walls and the fireplace in the ("sickness") back room. With the new decorations and fittings it looked great and down the passage (the one that had seemed so long all those years ago), I next attacked the kitchen-diner and established a greetings card section.

I created separate entrances so as to secure the shop from the upstairs. I made my old bedroom into a very comfortable studio flat-let that I rented out. My sisters' old bedroom I kept for myself and the large front one became my stock-room. These I updated and increased enormously holding, within the first year, over four thousand different lines. By also going up market, my parents little back street, one-roomed shop, blossomed forth as the local "emporium"!

As a result of all this work and subsequent activity, I often stayed there till late at night, re-stocking shelves, doing alterations and the like. Sometimes I slept over so as to get an early start the next day. With fears of any kinds of ghostly phenomenon long gone this presented no problem though one night I did have a meeting but this time the boot was on the other foot!

It was very late and switching off the light in what I still called my sisters' room and, pleased with my day's work, I snuggled down in the same old bed. Suddenly, I saw a lady build up in a sort of fluorescent, greenish luminous light. But there was no way she was going to slap my face and as she bent towards and over me, I challenged her, ordering her away to her own place!

I always smile as I recall this incident; I have never seen a more surprised spectre in my life! She looked at me, veritably puzzled, with a sort of "Hey, I'm the one that is supposed to frighten you" expression. Then straightening up, she literally dissolved downwards through the floor! I had never before and have never seen since this sort of "lit up" entity, even when "ghost chasing" so I do not know what she was trying to prove or do, but whatever it was, it and she failed miserably!

Why do we confide sometimes in comparative, or even complete strangers? Perhaps it is simply because they *are* strangers! Often too, one finds that they will listen in a non-judgmental way and will certainly, not to one's face anyway, ridicule or embarrass one. Of course it is highly probable that they can also look and listen without becoming emotionally involved. Whatever the reasons, I am equally sure that sometimes we are guided to them for I certainly know that this happened to me! Sheer coincidence? I think not; for what follows was far too much of a mere "coincidence" for it to be other than as stated.

You see, as School Captain I more or less had the run of the school during my last year. I could easily duck a class on some pretext or other and on this particular day I found myself in the stationary store where a monitor was filling inkwells. There were no biros then so of necessity this task was undertaken each week! Other monitors had trays with holes in them containing replacement ink-wells to avoid any spillage. These, carried by them, were distributed throughout the school, as required, placed in desks with similar holes housing removable inkwells.

As the "skip" I would not normally talk to monitors (who of course held no prefect status) except in my capacity as their boss. Even then, if I needed an errand to be run or something to be moved, I simply crooked a finger at one of them and they came running! Such was my authority as Captain; it will be seen therefore, that I would hardly, out of hand, confide in one! One also never mixed with lower class-years anyway so there was no way he could be considered a friend, or even an acquaintance! A football fanatic too who played for the school? No way! My disinterest in that direction alone would have blocked any chance of a friendship blossoming! Yet I somehow knew that I felt confident in confiding in him!

So I hung around until the last of the delivery monitors had gone. Then, as casually as I could, knowing that if I was wrong I might become the laughing stock of the school, I asked him if he believed in ghosts and had he seen one? To my surprise he said quite seriously that he "'adn't, but his aunt 'ad seen loads of 'em" and then he asked, quite naturally, about mine! (I have often wondered if he too became a medium for up until then I had not said that *I* did, or that I was being haunted.)

Listening most attentively as I related some of my experiences he then mentioned that his aunt was a medium to which I responded, in my ignorance, a medium what? He went on to explain that she was a Spiritualist and held meetings with spirits in the dark, something I was not exactly happy about; after all I had had my fill of things in the dark! He said that he would tell her about me and let me know what she said. So, though frightened but still curious and anxious to get something sorted out, I asked him to go one better and to try to arrange a meeting with her to which he replied: "Cors-ar-will Skip!"

For a week or so nothing happened and I was not able to get him alone again. I did not see him during lesson periods of course and at other times he always played football! I became totally frustrated as I watched him apparently looking in my direction and laughing with his pals. I was also worried that my first feelings of confidence might be wrong and that he had, maybe, told his mates and was simply having a laugh on my account.

Anxiously, as I saw the days passing, the phenomena seeming to know that I had spoken to him and what was in store, for it rapidly accelerated, now barn-storming the family as well as myself! So I sent a message for him to report to the prefects' rest room. On enquiring as to what was happening, he told me that his aunt was away working. Then about a week later he sought me out! He said his aunt was back, that she would see me that afternoon and that he would go with me to her house after school.

On the doorstep he introduced me to her, a classic matronly lady who, though she looked somewhat like Margaret Rutherford, actually owned a loud voice like Peggy Mount's! Asked was he coming in with me, muttering some lame excuse, he declined and promptly left! I realised later that the thought of sitting in the dark with ghosts all around was probably too much for him to swallow as well. Nervously I entered. But though she spoke in rushes, like Claire Rayner, almost as if she was constantly short of breath, her sentences coming in short sharp "machine-gun" bursts, she soon put me at my ease.

Almost before I had sat down and begun to relate my story, she interrupted saying that her nephew had told her everything (breath): "There was no point in going over it again (breath)". It would prove nothing (breath). *(I had thought she was going to clear it all up for me!)* I tried again, but she cut right across my words saying I was not to worry (breath). I would soon have the answers (breath) and would be unafraid from then on (breath). *(I thought let's hope it is soon 'cos up to now I'm still terrified!)* She steamed on, telling me to get a copy of the "Psychic News" (breath): "The *what?*" Ignored! "Look for the list of Spiritualist Churches" and as I tried to interject: "Wher...?" "In and around the area (breath) - pick a church!" "Whic...?" but she was way ahead of me! Cuttingly, through her teeth: "*Any* church you fancy!" (breath). "Just go to a meeting!" I said "What kind of..." "Any!" (more of a combined sigh and breath here) At the church, she went on, all would be explained (breath) Then, continuing, she said that I was a natural and should think myself very fortunate too-o-o! (Lifting of bosom and deep intake of breath!)

With that the "interview" was over for in that moment, rising from her chair and before I could say another word, she politely, but firmly, propelled me towards the front door! Opening it, she bad me a speedy good-bye and swiftly closed it behind me, not even pausing for the, by now, proverbial breath!

Was she kidding? Fortunate? I did not even *really understand* what she had been talking about! Thus seeming no wiser or happier with my lot and totally bemused, I made my way home...

A few weeks passed with nothing untoward occurring. Similar to all kids I guess, I looked for the easy way out of my dilemma and I sort of thought "that auntie had done the business for me" after all. Consequently, with nothing happening, the advice I was given about the P.N. and the meeting I was urged to attend were all forgotten. Pushed into the back of my mind they might well have stayed there - except...

There was a shift in the type of phenomenon. I began hearing whispering in my ear, just as if someone was standing behind me but on looking around (of course) I saw no-one! At first the whispers were unintelligible, but then one voice stood apart from the rest, louder and told me to pay attention as I did when I was young. It did not seem as if it was the same voice and I felt acutely conscious that my fears were still with me. Yet it was nothing like the cold, clammy fear I had lately experienced! Rationalising this now, though unaware at the time, I must have concluded that since a voice had done me so much good in the past why be afraid of one now?

As I began to listen more instead of trying to blot it out, the voice kept repeating I was to go to a Spiritualist church as it was their way of helping me. So finally obtaining a P.N. I turned to the advertisements page. To my surprise, I read that there was a one in Boone St., Lewisham, not far from where I was to sing that night with the band! The timing was good too since I saw that I would be able to go straight on afterwards to my gig!

Just after the war, Spiritualist churches were always full, mostly with people hoping to get a message from a loved one lost in that conflict. But I was totally unaware of this and, arriving a little late, I crept in so as not to draw attention to myself or disturb anything. Imagine then how utterly gob-smacked I was when, on opening the door I saw between two and three hundred people! What is more, all of them seemed to be talking, albeit in fairly subdued tones, at one and the same time! I did not know quite what to expect, but I *did* know that I was not expecting *this!* Indeed it crossed my mind that I was in the wrong church.

After what my new found "friend" had told me about his aunt, her friends *and* the ghosts all sitting in a circle singing hymns what would you, as a kid, have expected? Indeed, as he had later explained to me, the reason he would not go into his aunt's house earlier was that he thought that it was going to be just that! Readers cannot blame me then in having had thoughts of wondering whether I should go and sit in the dark anyway! And if I did would I disgrace myself by showing my unbounded fear?

(For those of you that do not know, I had come upon an Open Circle. (See end of chapter - re: circles). At these, as is nearly always the case at meetings anyway, all the lights are on! The people are very down to earth, (no pun intended) simply hoping for a message and or some healing, as well as a bit of company and a good old chat. Anyone can attend open circles and if they are of a mind or feel inspired to demonstrate healing, clairvoyance, psychometry and so on they are most welcome to work.)

So this usually quite extrovert youngster, wishing he was invisible, slipped in (he thought) unnoticed and took a seat as near to the door as possible. Mysteriously, there were a few men and women stopping to talk in whispered tones to various people and then quietly moved on to others. (I now know of course that they were ministering to folk as above.) I nodded back in greeting to those who had turned and nodded to me. As soon as my rear end touched my chair however, a big lady in an equally big north country voice cried out:"Ee-oop lad! Me and mine 'ave been waiting for thee; wher'ast tha bin?"

She then shouldered her way through chairs and people alike. Standing over me, her generous frame easily "enveloping" me prevented anyone else from being able to see me! But she, obviously aware that many had turned to see what was happening just as loudly she boomed out: "Sorry to have disturbed yews, go ont back to wat yers wuz doint!"

Swallowing my hands in hers and closing her eyes, she stood quietly for a few seconds. Then (amazingly to me at the time) she began to speak in a voice that was totally different from the raucous one with which she had addressed me previously! Clipped but quietly resonant, with no trace of an accent, it was distinctly male! Unwavering and confident she (he) told me, in detail, all that had been happening to me. Continuing she said I would shortly experience a revelation, that the frightening phenomena would cease and I would never again be afraid of spirit activity. (I thought it, but lacked the courage to ask what on earth was a revelation?) This, I quickly recalled was what the aunt had told me earlier, and further, she went on, being a natural born medium, I would make a very strong, fearless and positive one! And that was that!

I do not know if she was actually aware of who had controlled her for she seemed surprised as, on opening her eyes she stroked her chin and mumbled something about the control being very strong. I certainly know that I was astounded and all I could do was dumbly nod in reply to her asking had I understood? For those of you who do not know, she went into trance and it was a spirit helper addressing me directly by using the vocal chords and voice box of the medium.

Back in her normal state (and normal voice) she asked me to believe what had been said and to take its content to heart. Of course, feeling very embarrassed and not really understanding, but not wishing to look stupid, I affirmed again that I both did, and would.

Utterly flabbergasted I was, nonetheless, equally curious. I wanted to know how had she known me and how had she known what had been going on at home? Even had she known that lad's aunt and had spoken previously to her, how did she know I would go to that church on that particular night?

A the end of the meeting a lady said that for those who wanted it tea would be available. Told that the medium wanted another word with me, I was shown into the kitchen area. Asking the woman there who she was, she responded by saying that I should count myself very lucky! She was a well-known north-country medium apparently who was only in the church that night by accident! (I know now of course that this was more than mere accident or coincidence).

Apparently, she had stopped on her way down to the coast to see her friend who always put her up overnight when she travelled South. This time though she was unexpected for she had arrived before her letter! The reason for her being there was that her friend had been asked to take the circle that night due to the usual leader's husband being ill. So "north country" had agreed to keep her company and said she would "do a bit" for her at the circle.

At this point the medium came in and told me that my guides (another new word) would explain all! I asked what were these guides she spoke of (after all the only guides I knew were off limits in the next field at scout camp!) and how would I know them? She beamed a toothy smile and replied: "Ee lad dowsent yer worree yersen none, yers-ull know 'em! Any road, if yers dowsent, them as 'eck'll know thee!"

With that someone else caught her attention and drew her aside, abruptly terminating our conversation. Totally nonplussed, I finished my tea, said goodnight and left, a little later than intended, for my gig. I completely forgot to thank her or even enquire as to her name. This I regret, for quite apart from the obvious manners thing, it was one of the few proofs I have had over the years from other mediums and certainly the most intriguing and evidential! So I would dearly liked to have given her a credit here!

Anyway, off I went to my gig feeling a bit light-headed, as though a weight had been lifted from my shoulders. I sang my heart out with the band and went home, still feeling good in having it confirmed that I was not round the twist after all! Arriving home, virtually tempting providence, I walked boldly up to the front door, and went in! I confess to breathing a sigh of relief however on seeing that somebody was already at home.

For about three months my everyday life was so normal I might even have confessed to my missing the crazy things that had gone on before! Yeah! And pigs might fly! But that medium had said it was going to stop and it had! So just as the other medium's message had previously, this new found "faith" soon diminished too. After all, who was I to argue or to start rocking any boats? Thus, in no time at all this latest message too foundered and faded away. Happy in my ignorance I simply thought that "it" (the revelation) had changed its mind! As such, content with my new found peace, I equally simply took the easy way out, letting sleeping dogs lie!

It could be said that this attitude was because I was so young and had other things on my mind. I of course appreciate that this appears to be a classic case of negativity but equally I own to never having been obsessed *with*, or *by*, my craft. Indeed, it may well have been this lack of obsession that kept me on an even keel when I was so young!

It has also taken getting on for fifty years for me to "go public" and to write it all down which, I guess of itself perhaps graphically demonstrates the point of non-obsession. And another thing; whenever I am asked how I became a psychic I usually tell them that I was haunted into it. I say this though, almost always, half-jokingly - and leave it at that! If genuine interest is shown however, and they really are interested, then I will spend more serious time and energy in explaining my mediumship and how it works. (See e. of ch. - The "etiquette" of spreading the "word.")

At sixteen I left school and began work virtually the next day at a firm where several of my family worked, my Dad's idea of a real job! I was apprenticed as a electrical engineering draughtsman, a grand title (as it turned out) in name only!

Still with nothing untoward concerning "ghosties and ghoulies" having happened for a long time I guess I felt it was over. I do not recall my dwelling upon the previous happenings, I think that I must have blocked it out, perhaps unconsciously determining that this was the way to stop it reoccurring. Also, as is the wont of youngsters, as new things come into your life, others (often thankfully too some-times) are left behind. For instance, lots of kids hate school but I loved it! Nonethe-less, school days too quickly faded away, placed in the back of my thoughts. But this was mostly because now, able to do so, my ambitions turned to thinking out ways and means of leaving J. Stone and Co. and getting into show-business!

On one particular night, not long after starting at J.S. and, as it transpired, the most important of my life (before or since) I returned home having had a very happy evening. Our band-leader had informed me that there was a chance of an audition with the great Ted Heath. If it came off and I was successful, it would be an incredible break, meaning that I would be a vocalist with one of the premier bands in the world and that could only lead to stardom!

Having climbed into bed and got myself cosily comfortable, I was going over the pros and cons of being a "star" when the bed began to tremble, making me immediately alert. The old anxiety began again as did a fear that the old problems had returned. Rapidly building from a tremble to a sideways vibration it turned into a violent shaking! I guess they wanted to make sure I was awake! Boy, I was that all right! Absolutely alert, *I definitely knew this was no dream!*

Then around my bed there was light; bright, dazzling light yet it did not hurt my eyes!The bed stopped shaking and the light rapidly toned down to a warm-white, candy-floss pink, a cosy sort of brightness. I was also acutely aware that, although I did not know why, I felt no threat; nor was I afraid. I did not know it then but that in itself is not surprising; our own helpers never intentionally frighten us. Invari-ably their effect is intrinsically calming to the mind and body. Just the same they may, indeed do sometimes, really startle one, especially when, unexpectedly, they appear in "solid state" (the materialised form) such as on this occasion!

(Wiser now however, I state that if one receives such an incredible blessing as

52

that which follows, though initially one may feel apprehensive, the over-riding emotion felt is awe-struck wonderment! It is more like being in the presence of a comforting "angelic" form than the "spectre-type-ghostly" apparition written of by spooky writers!)

From out of the light shapes took on outlines of people, but I was unable to see these clearly. But I do recall my wondering (the 'ol logic at work again?) how they managed not only to stand on nothing, their "feet" being level with the bedcovers, but also all around my bed when it was hard against the wall.

At the foot, a figure stepped forward from the light and though it was now behind him (this is one of the magic moments of Spirit encounters) he and his features were quite clear. Dressed in a beautiful white suit with gold trimming, he told me he was Indian and that his name was Tuan. His jacket, buttoned to the throat, reached down to his knees. He also wore a turban and had a heavy gold chain around his neck. This was set with a circle of precious stones, a magnificent array of opals, rubies garnets, sapphires and emeralds, in the centre of which was an enormous amethyst. In his turban he also wore a jewel, a large ruby. (See e. of ch. - Re. Tuan's jewels.)

Seeing that I was not afraid, he spoke again saying that he was my Guardian Angel. He would protect and guide me in a much more controlled manner in the future if I agreed. In return he would ensure that I would never again be intimidated or afraid of phenomena of any kind. Oh boy, even though he looked nothing like an angel, was I ever ready to agree to that!

At seeing my expression of surprise he smiled, obviously aware of my "angel" thought and exclaimed that guardian angels did not have, as artists insisted on portraying them, wings, harps, halos and robes! (See e. of ch. - On peripheral folk.) He went on to explain that GA's are human entities who have charge of a soul's pathway during its earthly incarnation and are of different nationalities and gender. On the other hand, *angels*, he declared, are not human, never have been and are of a *different* species! In anticipation of my next query he went on that, except on very rare occasions, they do not incarnate via a human foetus either!

Therefore, he continued, though hitherto variously called Guardian Angels or Guardian Spirits, he preferred the term "Door Keeper" and offered the following analogy. In the event, it is very difficult for one to visualise, partly due to those early artists, one's own exclusive angel, since they appear so stereo-typed in their pictures! It is far easier to imagine a more down to earth figure, a "bouncer" for example, a personage each of us can relate to in our own particular way.

Standing before the door of a private club (the soul's body for which he has charge) he allows members and friends (acceptable entities) to enter (into the aura or body as the case may be) and equally rigidly keeps out and or turns away all unwanted or uninvited people (unacceptable entities). As such, depending on the alertness and ability of the door-keeper, they will and do, guard the "door" virtually twenty-four hours a day.

So where was he when I needed him to protect *me*? He said he had of course been very aware of the happenings, but there was a reason and a time for all things. Re-affirming his position he stated categorically that all such as had previously occurred was ended, completely dispersed. In the future, he continued, I *could* and *should* totally depend upon his protection. (See e. of ch. - Tuan on d/k's)

Anticipating me again (Had he then been recently protecting me more?) he said that the gap between the previous phenomena ceasing and this event was the direct result of his actions. Deliberately occasioned by him, it was to calm my physical body and spiritual self (the soul) preparing me for this moment, or, as he put it, the right time. When asked why the hiatus had been so long he replied that had this experience followed directly on, I would have, quite naturally, thought that it was more of the same, simply a continuation of the previous happenings.

However, whilst making sure that no real harm befell me, they could not, until my karmic-time was right, interfere and take charge. Had they intervened at what would have been the wrong karmic time, I would still have had the karmic condition to work through at some time during this incarnation whereas now, it was past! As ever anticipating, he said incarnations were the earth journeys a soul makes using a physical body as a vehicle. My next query was what was the karmic time and condition?

Karma, he explained (and has explained again since) was the quality of actions, good and bad occurring throughout our incarnations. These are the lives we choose to live out (or not) on Earth and in Spirit. One may choose to reincarnate as one desires, (the action of freewill) the option being open for the soul to continue, should that be the decision, its spiritual progression solely in Spirit. However, if a soul declines to reincarnate then its progression is proportionately lengthened. Such choices are made for varying reasons. For example a soul may not like the earth's vibration or is committed to a spiritual task preventing an incarnation. A case in point d/k's who, having made the commitment, cannot simply decide half-way through their charge's incarnation to desert and re-incarnate themselves! (See e. of ch. - On karma, etc.)

The same karmic laws unequivocally, determine the future of all sentient beings. The Spiritual Progress of every soul-force-energy from the tiniest organism to humankind is a continuing one. Once the soul force has evolved to human spirit condition, that is, reached the individual state, there is no further, higher state except that of pure Spirit, that of being in At-One-Ment with the God head. Like all soul-force-energy, human souls too can never retrogress. A soul therefore is unable (indeed it is impossible) to go back to what it was previously in its evolutionary progression, for what is past cannot be recaptured and experienced (lived) again.

(Typing, I see the letters appear! But I cannot, even with re-writes or corrections on the way, live these moments again - they are forever gone! It is the way of things, Natural Law! As many have said before there *is no past present or future,* there is only the eternal now! Time is but a convenience for communicating around the world, otherwise we would all hold to the same clock, instead of having time-zones! Knowing that I cannot live in the past, I also know, logically, that the future is the only place where I can exist, the only direction open to me! And knowing too that I cannot *guarantee my future existence on this plane,* it still does not, and should not stop me from planning and having hopes for it!)

All soul-force-energy is interdependent one upon the other for its natural progression to the human state. Then when a human soul comes into being, it distinguishes itself by realising its real potential, that of being an individual. It can then move on in a more profound thinking manner towards its inevitable goal, the return to the God-head. The human soul, having evolved thus is also endowed with emotions, reasoning thought processes, inventiveness, the ability to use technology and so on which in turn makes it the most highly evolved of all the species. Thus, having the capacity for personal responsibility and also possessing freewill, it can continue its spiritual progress at its own pace. The true progression of every human soul is towards Light, Truth and Perfection for here is found the God-head, the intrinsic source of all life-force-energy.

As mentioned above, the goal is to be in At-One-Ment with the God-head and in this endeavour does the soul strive, both consciously and unconsciously. During its lives in the physical and Spirit dimensions the soul, learning, becomes more and more spiritually enlightened. Eventually, its karma conditions fulfilled and no longer feeling the need or desire to reincarnate again it will journey on.

Progressing on and "up" through the Spirit dimensions, seeking its way back to the God-head, it is drawn, as is the salmon to its breeding grounds, that it may contribute in the engendering of further energy-creativity. N.B. Ancient Hebrew has no numbers! Letters replace them and the language is revered as sacred, the only one accorded this reverence throughout the world! The words "love" and "at-one" add up to the same numbers total and both are found in sentences synonymously referring to God.

In time then the soul will leave behind its personality, it's given name, etc. but still retain its individuality. It may join with a group of souls set on a particular course of action, or it may find a niche elsewhere in the great scheme of things, the meanwhile continuing its spiritual progress. Then, eventually, the time will come when the need to make the supreme sacrifice will catalyse its spirituality. It will be absorbed into the One, the Wholeness of Being, ensuring in its small way, the continuance of the life-force-energy, the Alpha and Omega of life.

This explanation having concluded, Tuan then motioned to the others around the bed. These, he said, were helpers who felt a compatibility with me and as such would be desirous of us working closely together. But all I could see were silhouettes and saying as much he replied that this was a precautionary move on their part. He did not want me to get any definite ideas as to who they were; their identities would emerge in time. He then outlined what they would like to develop with me.

Since that first introduction I have learned much, much more from Tuan and my helpers than I have space for here; indeed I am still learning! They replied courteously when I asked about their origins but I was also aware that they did not put much store on this facet of their soul progression and as we became closer and closer attuned neither did I!

In a comparatively short time after introduction and or trance work I realised that *what* they were capable of was far more important. Thus harmony quickly took the place of polite question and answer sessions. To illustrate its unimportance two phrases, one well known; the other (Tuan's) says it all: "By their words shall ye know them" and "What you cannot believe from within you will never believe from without"!

("Floating helpers", mentioned at the end of this chapter, are also very helpful but my "personal" helpers, who, since my revelation, have consistently worked and travelled with me throughout my spiritual quest are, of course, very dear to me and I will now "introduce" them.)

When Yu Sin first controlled he spoke no English giving only his name. I have always known him as "Yu Singh" and confess to being perplexed that he, being Chinese, should have an Indian name! Until now I had never asked about this but as I typed Yu Sin I asked him to explain my easily made mistake.

He says that Yu Sin is pronounced with a "g" sound at the end and his name, phonetically, sounds like You Sing, easily mistaken for the Indian Singh of similar sound. Danny Lee, a Chinese friend and designer of the cover of this book, has since told me that it means Spirit of Light or Light Spirit, is spelt with or without a "g" but that it means the same. Yu Sin Dei Siw, his full name, spelled phonetically, is You-Sin(g) Day-ee-i She-oo but with me he has never used Dei Siw. He tells me this is a very ancient Chinese family name and, lost in antiquity, he always considered it to be unimportant!

A diagnostic healing helper, he learned both English and basic anatomy very quickly from an English doctor in spirit (a floating helper) who did not want to practise medicine any more. Apart from the very first time, when he mentioned only his name, he did not control again until he was able to communicate better. Thus, having learned the language, some three months later he proudly told the circle that he could now control my body correctly. (See e. of ch. On meeting one's helpers.) For some time I had had the honour of working with Harry Adey, a wonderful healer from Deptford, London. Yu Sin also thanked him and his helper, Golden Feather for teaching him many of the healing arts.

One of these arts was the ability to diagnose from a clean handkerchief, whether its owner was present or not. For twenty-four hours the patient kept it next to the body, then allowing nobody else to touch it; he or she placed it in an envelope. At the earliest opportunity Yu-Sin would control and taking out the handkerchief, he would "read" it, (using a form of psychometry) giving a complete diagnosis of the patient's health-state. Afterwards he would "magnetise" (in order to link personally - hence the quotes) the hanky and promise to visit the patient in sleep state.

Proving very popular, especially as the patient did not have to attend, in later years I had many handkerchiefs from people as far away as India and America primarily requesting a diagnosis and absent healing. (Today they just seem to want postal readings - a sign of the times maybe, but not one that indicates that the people of the world are necessarily healthier!)

Interestingly, I relate a little anecdote on this technique and too the importance of doing things right! A brother of my boss was very ill with cancer and he asked me to see what I could find out. On arriving at the brother's flat I asked for something to psychometrise. On looking in the wardrobe there was a handkerchief in a suit pocket. Ah-ha, I thought, a diagnosis from Yu Sin! (See e. of ch. On the alter-ego theory, etc.)

However, he would not control and in my eagerness to help I tried psychometrising the handkerchief myself. I picked up a hernia and back pain which my boss confirmed but said it was months ago and, I went on, I had no impression of cancer at all!

To my dismay his brother died within a couple of months from a carcinoma of the liver and lungs and my boss, cynically commenting on mediums said, how wrong could I be? Of course, after asking Yu Sin why I was not told of the cancer, he replied that in my eagerness I did not *listen to all that was said!* He told me that the handkerchief "had" no cancer (all that I was concerned with) only disclosing the conditions apparent at the time. By "switching him off" I had not heard him cautioning me that it had been in the suit for some months and *before* the cancer was evident in the body.

The moral of the story is (a) listen well and (b) never act the oracle or big-headed as I did, thinking you know all the answers! Check it out, re-check; then question! Then question the question until you are sure of what you are being told. Only then state what you are receiving and you will avoid causing unnecessary anxiety and pain to others, or at least lessen it somewhat.

Chi-ung (pronounced Chee-i-ung), full name is Chi-ung Wei Yung, is my clair-voyant, clairaudient and psychometry (clairsentience) helper. Like Yu-Sin he is Chinese; though in character and age they are as different as chalk and cheese, Mandarin and Cantonese respectively. He was actually quite snooty in the early years, the complete antithesis of Yu Sin, who is very frail and "as blind as a bat" except when looking into a body, while Chi-ung is much younger and has a very proud, upright bearing.

Generally I connect directly with the spirit personality but if he or she has a problem in transferring their evidence directly to me then he will endeavour to make the connection. And for all of his snootiness, in nearly fifty years of working together he has never become frustrated, edgy or the slightest bit put out when I have been unable to correctly interpret his information. He has mostly worked with me telepathically and when trancing me he always appears very severe. Lately though it seems that the "inscrutable Chinese character" trait has disappeared for now he frequently displays a dry sense of humour.

Those privileged to have known and/or watched my transfiguration helper work in trance through me in closed circles or in public meetings will always talk of the incredible evidence, both visual and the spoken word, that emerged at our seances. They would also undoubtedly recall, almost in the same breath, his dry sense of humour.

These seances, public and private, were controlled by a Native American Indian called Funny Eye. I was, of course, always in trance for this work and he, holding the body so magnificently, made it not only so much easier for entities to transfigure; more, he made it much easier for entities and me, too. He moved in and out of my body quickly and easily, moving the loved ones, etc. also in and out with equal aplomb.

He always liked a very lively and happy atmosphere and to this end he displayed a ready wit which, in turn, ensured a balance of levity, happy virbations and harmony. For example, if the people went silent on him, he would ask were they still there? On getting an affirmative, he would joke that he was just wondering, because he thought that they were supposed to be the dead ones! On other occasions if somebody dropped something and it made a loud noise he would often comment that he nearly jumped back into his skin!

He also encouraged people to talk among themselves *between* each transfiguration and this amplified the constant flow of physical power (energy levels) making, with his way of working anyway, for a better quality séance.

On an average evening the séance would begin with the opening prayer. Then Funny Eye would control (trance) me, after which various experiments would be undertaken. This involved other helpers controlling, mostly Chi-ung and Yu Sin, thus demonstrating how the changes would be effected and the age gap between them, ably showing that the one was much younger than the other. On occasions Zarlu would also come through to show how much bigger he was than any of them.

Yu Sin would also cause a lot of amusement and amazement too when he had a person grip his (my) hands very tightly and without *any detectable movement* they would be, on request, pulled apart by the person holding them. It was quite self-evident that one was at least an inch longer than the other! He could also do the same thing with his feet – but that was not all!

He would then invite two people to take a pulse on each wrist and instruct them to count, *aloud*, the pulse rate. First one would cease to register (the person declaring that there was none) and then the other would report likewise; then they would alternate! Finally he would change the speed of each with one slowing down and the other equally rising rapidly faster, again, followed by alternating. On command of one of the pulse-takers, the pulse(s) would instantly, at one and the same time, revert to a regular beat!

During the séance I would be in trance for about two and a half hours and between twenty-five and forty transfigurations would invariably take place, with ectoplasmic masks showing the recognisable features and their voices via my vocal chords as they were on earth. If they did not sound quite the same tone as when in the body, each was still recognised by what they said (evidence) and or by their dialect inflections.

Coming out of trance, I would be very dehydrated and would drink at least three pints of water straight off. However, within five minutes or so I was fully recovered and would be completely back to normal.

N.B. The reason for writing here in past tense is that after demonstrating this phenomenon for so many years Tuan said that I had done enough and my body had taken enough stress and punishment. Funny Eye too after a few more years of transfiguration work in my circles decided to move on. But he did not move on to another medium – he joined a group like "The Manna" and, interestingly, the last time he controlled to make his farewells he had quite a lot of difficulty holding the body. This is because his "vibration" is now more highly tuned. Therefore where previously holding the body was easy, now, until he learns to adjust again, it is actually painful to lower his vibration thus.

Originally called Running Deer his new name came about as a result of an accident. At twelve years of age whilst training to be a warrior, an arrow that had been shot into the air hit him slicing through his eyebrow and cheek. On the way it also took his right eye, immediately bringing his warrior ambitions to an abrupt close.

He was ordered to join the medicine man's entourage and, due to the shape and terrible scarring, was re-named Crooked Leg of Dog Face He actually became very proficient at the "moving tent" ritual, the main expression of which was for a completely empty wigwam to violently shake and rise into the air, showing that there was nobody, at least physical, within. This is a facet of North American Indian magic medicine now sadly almost lost in the sands of time and which today might well be compared to the phenomenon of telekinesis or Spirit engendered levitation and movement of objects.

On controlling me the first time and transfiguring fully he looked very intimidating, even ugly maybe, to the circle sitters. They thought at first that he might be an unwanted entity who had slipped in due to the fact that I was its leader and, in trance perhaps, had lost control. Within seconds however, he put them at their ease and, joking about his face, he went on that this was how he looked on Earth. He would not in future transfigure fully as it was too frightening for many of the public; he would also from then on use a much more acceptable name - Funny-Eye!

A little anecdote here! The most incredible group séance he ever took was at Eltham Church, an attractive building with a high ceiling and large stained glass windows. Due to the problem of blacking out the place we worked once a week gradually "eating up" the congregation. These took place in the Healing Sanctuary and comfortably held about twenty-five people. On one particular night about twenty filed in and a man asked could he tape the session. I knew it would be OK and replied accordingly.

They all settled and we began. Various entities transfigured and spoke then Funny Eye, commenting on the wonderful amount of love that was pouring forth from the group said that he was going to attempt something we had never done before. I reminded him that it was my body he was using so he should not do anything rash! He replied that I was not to worry and that I had also, when the new system of trance was worked out (when, even if in deep trance I, in my out-of-the-body position up near the ceiling, knew what was taking place) I had agreed that though I could observe, I was not to interfere.

Nicely put in my place he moved on and to my utter amazement not only was there a transfigured person but on either side of my body two other entities fully materialised. Even more amazing was afterwards for when the tape was replayed the three persons who had been killed together in a plane crash all spoke at the same time! I was also told that the assembled group were all Spiritualists and of the same family! Many times too, especially in Bristol, as we worked in transfiguration, globes of light could be seen floating about the room but never before or since have I had full materialisation: but then I never sat to develop it either.

Zarlu, who has a name which is too difficult to pronounce or phonetically write in English, simply changed his nation name from Zulu to Zarlu for my convenience. He is responsible for all the exorcism, obsession and possession work we are required to effect. Over the years we have attended some hairy, some strange, some sad and some downright funny hauntings together, some of which I will describe in Part Three.

He is still a very proud character and remains a Zulu warrior. If folk contact me because they are afraid or unhappy or feel in need of protection he will always respond. I tell people to think of me (link) and repeat and concentrate on his name. Surprisingly perhaps to some of my readers this has had a very real effect in many cases we have dealt with over the years. And many, many times I do not have to attend the haunted premises; he goes and exorcises the disturbed or disturbing entity and the haunted person reports back that the trouble has gone!

An example of this is the following:

Receiving a telephone call from Germany, a very worried mother told me that her four year old son was being visited by what she could only believe were (her words) evil spirits. They did not seem to faze him at all, he would merely awaken his mother each time excitedly telling her that they had come and sat on his bed to talk to him. His mother, on the other hand (for this had gone on for some time) was getting more and more tired and fed up at being disturbed nearly every night and her mother had told her to ring me as she had read that I was an exorcist.

At first, she said, disturbed from her own sleep, she had paid little attention, merely putting it down to an over-active dreamer. But as it increased in intensity, she began to question what his visitors looked like. Despite the fact that these were described by him in great detail, she recognised no-one until, on entering his room one morning she found him on the floor, wrapped in a blanket.

During the night she had heard no bump, no crying out, or noise of any kind. Assuming he had fallen out of the top tier of bunk-beds meant that he had fallen a considerable distance and, fearing the worst, she panicked thinking he was hurt. (I interjected asking why put him on the top bunk when nobody slept on the bottom one? How did I know that she said and I replied that I had linked in at the start of the conversation and this is what I was being told by my helpers!)

On being awakened however, he perfectly described his great-grandmother who had made her transition before he was born! Searching him for any damage and finding none, she asked why was he on the floor? Further questioning revealed that the lady (the great-grand-ma) had lifted him out of bed! On enquiring why, he said she had told him that she wanted to cuddle him but could not get up the ladder!

Still on the 'phone and very interested in the case, I then mentioned that, like myself, he was obviously very psychically gifted, a natural. By way of proof I also mentioned other personal details about him and her (that I will not relate here) which she confirmed.

Then, briefly explaining who he was and what he does, but not how he dresses I told her to say nothing to her son about Zarlu. He would, at my request, be visiting the scene very soon to check it out. He would then take any necessary steps to correct the entity intrusion and that this would allow the child to sleep undisturbed. I also mentioned that she should not be surprised if, in a few days her boy says he has talked with a big black man!

About ten days later, her mother rang again to say that a couple of days after speaking to me her boy awoke her saying that he had been awakened by, and talked to, a very big black man who told him he was to sleep at night and not to talk to people. He described Zarlu, telling her that he had feathers on his head, legs and arms and that he had a spear and shield. She thought he was confused and told him it must have been a Red Indian, like on the telly! No, he insisted; it was a big black man! However, and far more importantly, she reported that he had slept undisturbed every night since. Some months have passed and I have heard no more so I trust that no news is good news! (Update! Last night, invited to dinner at a friend's house, I mentioned this incident. Imagine my surprise when a lady in the company said I was speaking of her friend who now lived in Spain. Boy! Was I ever glad that I never "b.s" for those that do most always get caught out!)

Footnote! Though their numbers are drastically diminished from what they were during the Zulu wars, some of you may not be aware of what a proud nation the Zulu's are even today. Zarlu, formally a ranking warrior and hunter still goes to war (which is how he regards exorcism) totally committed, including carrying his assegai spear and his shield! Zulu's also wore such feathers when hunting or fighting in those places indicated by the child, something his mother did not know! She had actually identified with and visualised a Martin Luther King type of black man, indeed somebody dressed in a suit.

Particularly interesting in this case is the fact that normally children attract only child spirits who become their playmates and these only appear to them in their waking moments. Significantly his visitors were all adults. But more important is that once again proof of something outside of the "normal" happened here. Although I am used to such things after all these years, for me there is, just the same, still an adrenaline rush when proof, by way of a follow-up shows just what Spirit can achieve.

Another facet of Zarlu is his strength and many years ago demonstrated this during a séance in the house of one of the chiefs of Harwell Atomic Centre. At the time different controls were showing how the body could be manipulated and physically changed during trance states. Zarlu a big, muscular individual controlled and spoke of his prowess and strength making the point that it made people more confident of his exorcism abilities.

At this a rather cocky little Scotsman interrupted, saying that he did not look that strong to him and challenged him to prove it! Immediately Zarlu stood up and, almost in one movement, he reached down and grabbed the leg of the man's chair. He proceeded to lift him quite slowly, still on his chair, to shoulder-height and then, just as slowly, he lowered him down again, frightening the life out of him! Needless to say there was no further criticism from "debunker" Jock!

Just prior to Tuan bringing my revelation to an abrupt close that night he also told me that I was so naturally psychic I could develop any or all things within Natural Law. Some would take longer and require patience before I could demonstrate them, but the choice was mine. I was of course only a lad and, in reality, totally bemused by what was taking place. Even so, this naturally inquisitive kid still asked what was Natural Law? This simply brooked a response effectively implying that they could not stay much longer but that all of my questions would be answered in good time!

Had I been aware then just how awesome was the significance of what he was saying, I might well have chickened out right there! After all, all I wanted to do was go into show business! Affirming his protection yet again, he said that he was sorry but they had to go immediately! And they did, quick as a flash, proving that their "grapevine" worked beautifully for, within seconds, I heard my sisters coming up the stairs to go to bed. Bedroom doors were habitually never closed in our house which made it obvious that my sisters, nor anybody else for that matter, was meant to see anything of what took place that night!

HELPFUL NOTES!

(On ouija boards and planchettes) *I shall go into more detail on the workings of these later; but for now take heed! Whilst this is probably the easiest way to contact Spirit, one should, indeed must be cautioned. It is imperative that one familiarises oneself with the inherent dangers of not being able to close the door that was so easily opened! Unless one knows how to protect the session and sitters, not only our loved ones, but mischievous, very deceptive and sometimes even dangerous or malevolent entities can, just as readily, pass through this portal. It is always essential to ensure the exercise of proper control and operation in all "sittings", but more so when using such methods of communication. However, since there are other less stressful, more sure ways to operate, I advise all seekers and students never to employ this method of contact; the "thrill" rarely being worth the nastiness and problems which can ensue!*

(On ghosts.) *How do you know it is a ghost? Well, first and foremost you know it should not be there. Secondly, it does not seem to matter how dark it is you can see the features and clothes quite clearly. In my considerable and varied experience though, they only very rarely glow in an eerie light, the like of which I have only ever seen once. And believe it, they never ever wear the proverbial ball and chain or have their head tucked under their arm. (This last stems from the practice in the olden days of placing a beheaded person's head, simply because it was more practical, at the side of their body! Hitherto, placed as it was above the shoulders, often presented a problem. However, cradled thus in the crook of the arm, it prevented the poor unfortunate's head from rolling off of the stretcher - hence problem solved!)*

Entities do not cover themselves with a big white bed-sheet either, although it is quite understandable that such erroneous sightings are reported. However, in these phenomenon, which by the way is quite rare, what is usually seen is an entity wearing a robe, or appearing in a white, coloured, or dark mist, or even "light", all of which, in the moment of perception, can easily be mistaken for a common old sheet! The rarity stems from the fact that most entities are anxious to be recognised, so it is pointless to appear with a sheet over their head anyway, or, for that matter, as mist, of any colour!

I mention though (albeit stressing that this is not to sensationalise my words and discoveries) that dark mist appearances are often indicative of a poltergeist, a mischievous entity or even a malevolent one rather than those who are benevolent. Definition and clarification will depend of course on the exorcising medium's ability and experience to know and be able to ascertain from the depth of colour, shape, size and density which of these is the more likely.

Another thing, unless you know the difference, fooled into thinking that you have seen a ghost, you may actually have witnessed someone astral-travelling, or seen an emotional "play-back" (explained more fully later). Either of these mani-

festations can pass through, or be relative to, your space, which same may be done intentionally or unintentionally. Only experience can teach one to recognise the different "vibration" of such apparitions to actual spirit entities as such.

Neither can doppelgängers simply be dismissed out of hand and as such have their place here. There are many recorded and verified accounts of a person being in two places at the same time! Curiously however, in most cases "they" do not seem to function equally, "one" is nearly always ill, lying down or asleep whilst the other "one" is seen by others, really out and about, bent on work or pleasure.

(Do not be persuaded by others!) *Do not allow others to persuade you away from what you experience simply because they will not accept or even consider any other option, notion or belief than that which they already hold. It is also true to say that more often than not, many of these almost always also try to steer you away from the convictions you hold. This is more often than not simply because of one of the following or all of them! Fear, bigotry, religious commitment and or a ducking of the issue, which is usually for them the easier path to tread.*

(On poltergeists and human activity.) *The "movable bits" were poltergeist activity; he on the other hand was an actual human entity manifestation. Human entity energy is more highly evolved and stronger than that of the poltergeist energy. Youngsters energy, being of the more "raw" material kind than that of adults is easily employed by the poltergeist to make things move and to create loud bangs and noise. But a human entity also needs, as well as their own, our "living body" energy (used in conjunction to produce varying kinds and quality of ectoplasmic substances) to manifest. Therefore when he or she uses it, being more highly evolved spiritually, the poltergeist effect is drastically and effectively curtailed. This is because the poltergeist's energy alone (being unable to draw on any of its required "living body" energy) is, almost always, insufficient to effect phenomena, thus rendering it's mischievous activity virtually in-operable.*

(Re: circles.) *There should be, and in bona-fida churches always is, a medium in charge overseeing the proceedings at all circles, but more especially open ones. They should be totally capable of controlling the circle should anything untoward happen, e.g. somebody going into trance unexpectedly or perhaps an unwanted or unhelpful entity taking control of them. (I would mention here that both of these conditions can sometimes cause distress to the person being controlled.) The medium therefore must be able to encourage or discharge, should it become necessary, the entity controlling, thereby restoring things, and the controlled person, to normal. Here too I add that the medium in charge might well allow somebody who she knows is a trance medium to do so. However, these days, "random trance" is generally discouraged in open circles, mediums in charge feeling that such beginnings should be confined to closed and or home circles.*

Finally, never begin a circle, private sitting, healing session, meeting or what-

ever without asking first, through prayer and or meditation for protection for those present, against any and all undesirable, unwanted or unwelcome intrusive spirits, etc. It obviously follows that a prayer of thanks should also be said afterwards to close the session.

(The "etiquette" on spreading the "word.") *I know from within that it is not my spiritual brief, nor is it right to try to force my religious views upon anyone and I have no time for those, including other Spiritualists, who persist in doing so! For myself I hold to a firm rule, one that requires me never to discuss the subject with people unless they bring it up first. I think that there are more than enough of what I term bus and train evangelists in the world already. Found in every denomination, some are more forceful than others, with the leaders being Jehovah's Witnesses, the Baptists and the Mormons, but not necessarily in that order!*

Discussions with other sects generally proceed quite genially until the opposition is challenged to think or go beyond the basic concepts and parameters of their own belief. Almost invariably, it is then that they climb onto their high horse, becoming both offensive and defensive! Further probing exposes the reasons and it rapidly becomes clear that they are not able to expand the tenets beyond those propounded by their books and priests! Having learned and been persuaded by, in many cases, brain washing in varying degrees, they are simply not equipped to do so.

In any event their missionary brief almost always forbids them to step outside of the "establishment" parameters. The result is a classic herding of the flock by their laughing priests and elders! It is unfortunate that so many people, because their own religious and or philosophical knowledge is so limited, are generally so ill-equipped to deal with them. Notwithstanding, JW's and the like press home their obvious obsessive advantage, and openly show that they expect one to suffer their frequent and ultra persistent doorstep barrage! Equally, they seem to be blissfully unaware as they endeavour to ram their beliefs down another person's throat that they are doing little to advance their cause and at times are actually causing it to be irreparably damaged!

Consequently, I consider it improper and in many cases offensive too when mediums, at whatever level they may have achieved, force themselves onto a person in a public place. Telling them that they have a Red Indian or a Chinese or even their loved ones for them without, most times, even an introduction, never mind qualifying the statement with any evidential proof, is not only wrong, it also does them and their cause no credit! Mediumship should, indeed must be positive, controlled and dispensed accordingly so make a pact with yourself; try never to be a pain in the... well, you get my drift!

(Re: Tuan's jewels) *Whilst I obviously saw the jewels when Tuan first appeared to me I placed no actual significance on them, except perhaps that I was conscious of seeing the whole thing (him and the stones) in colour, as opposed to black and white!*

Since that first appearance Tuan has consistently advised and educated me in psychic and mediumship matters, either through his own teaching or by introducing me to other spiritual beings. He has also over the years explained the significance of the precious stones, but this is not the place for writing such explanations. However, in Part Three, these and others will be referred to again together with their historic, legendary and esoteric meanings.

(On peripheral folk!) *"Alternativist" is a term I use to describe those peripheral folk who claim that there is a Spirit world, angels an' all, and that Spirit can help us. But then they contradict that premise by declaring that they do not actually think we should commonly communicate with them and do not regard themselves as Spiritualists or even Spiritists! Yet many of these, writing and practising on the periphery are still making a fortune by the prestidigitation of their vocabulary! These even claim that individual angels abound and can and do simultaneously aid countless humans world-wide, from escaping death to finding one's parking space! But this is impossible as our logic tells us that, like entities of any kind, they cannot be in more than one place at a time! So beware of such peripherals!*

"Witnesses" also claim, and even more so in the western (Christian) world that angels appear as portrayed by artists; always white, in white robes and having wings! However, such portrayals are, at the very least debatable and cogitative, with many such appearances demanding closer scrutiny. After all, this wings and robes "diet" has been fed to us via art, literature, priests, statues in churches and, latterly, the media.

Early artists, simply because they lacked "spirit physiology" simply drew winged angels because they "came down" from Heaven in the sky! Reasoning that, like birds and insects, they would have to have wings to fly, they drew them thus, and hence, the image was born; with generations of artists following the same pattern, the legend has become self perpetuating. (Interestingly Jesus, the Virgin Mary and saints are considered angels, yet they are never pictured with wings!) Interestingly too, other visions in other religions claim their own "angels" and these look quite different to the Christian version!

Latterly, there are countless numbers searching the skies day and night for different "angels" (or are they perhaps one and the same?) who, they hope will arrive in space ships. So perhaps a new image (legend) is in the making!

In conclusion, knowing that our loved ones and other spirit entities can and do help us in times of danger or need, I equally cannot accept that any of these are "pure" angels. Accordingly, I offer this reason for their "appearance":

Many folk would be frightened by an apparition, even of their loved ones! So, since, when in spirit, we can appear in any form in proportion to our imaginative ability, sometimes it is perhaps better to appear as an angel, which will more likely only invoke awe and not fear, at least in the accepted sense! Clever of our loved ones, guides and helpers eh?

(Tuan on door-keepers.) *In confirming a door-keeper's strength Tuan has since affirmed that not all are as strong as might be desired and one should never assume that they are, in any way, omnipotent or even omniscient. One of the first lessons he ever taught me was to beware the door you open that you can close it again. Co-operation between their charges and themselves is essential to achieve optimum cohesiveness leading to success and powerful protection from unwanted or unhelpful entities.*

Another point that needs clarification. Individually, we have only one personal guide and these are rarely, if ever, related to us at all, family or soul-wise; the main attraction is of spiritual compatibility. D/k's are mostly male entities, the main reason, probably, stemming from much earlier times when men were the politicians, warriors, hunters, overlords, etc. Although culture-wise these nations were more nature conscious (spiritual if you will) women, in the main, were held back from the foregoing pursuits and their education consisted mainly of "womanly" chores and pastimes.

Yes, there are lady door keepers! These though are more rare and mainly align themselves with female charges. The reasons are as already stated i.e. in most earlier cultures only certain women in minimal numbers were occupied as vestal virgins and or priestesses. Mostly the rest were wives or courtesans and it was not considered proper to educate them, except in such things as embroidery, music art and so on. (Even up until Victorian times middle and upper class ladies were not even allowed to work in salaried jobs. Nurses too were mostly regarded as being on a par with prostitutes! Thank God for such people as Edith Cavall and Florence Nightingale!) Therefore if a woman excelled in, knew of, or even had a passing interested in "male" pursuits she was more the exception than the rule, two such being the English queens Boadica and Elizabeth I. However, Tuan says that if one does have a female d/k then she will be one to be reckoned with!

Men then, holding the reins of power meant that females had little or no say, at least publicly, in the affairs of law and state. (But be warned fellas! In the not too distant future, women will rule this planet and men will regret being born in the male gender!)

Spirit helpers, as opposed to door-keepers are just that; the door-keeper (g/a) alone is the only personal guide and sticks like glue to us. Door-keepers are entities who have chosen to accompany another soul throughout its earthly journey (and often both before and afterwards as well) helping it to fulfil its spiritual destiny. They should not, nay, must not be confused either with souls such as "The Manna Group" who are guides but not personal to individuals! These teach the world over and are explained later within these pages.

Unfortunately the soul (its charge), albeit aware of the d/k prior to incarnating, all to soon, caught up in earthly, material pursuits, discards, metaphorically speaking, this guiding friend. By not listening to the "voice within" the psychic ability and spiritual attunement of the incarnated soul, no longer aware of this guidance, goes its own way. So very few, by comparison, acknowledge the spiritual stepping stones offered by their d/k.

Natural Law decrees that they cannot impose their freewill upon another, so they have to stand back, allowing their charge to make its many (often avoidable) mistakes. The soul meanwhile, is blissfully unaware that the d/k's nudging is an integral part of the learning process. The d/k is, like even peripheral things, totally integrated into our karmic lessons and progress. Thus by "turning its back" the soul misplaces and or loses its psychic ability and spiritual attunement during its sojourn on earth, a tragedy in itself, never mind the waste of the d'k's time!

Why then are we not more aware of these? Well, we might take time to consider that most folk (in the western world at least) do not even consider, more than in passing that there is, or that there even might be, an existence other than this present physical one! It is quite likely too, since the advice offered is slanted more spiritually than materially, that many times they would not take it anyway! For those of you that are ahead of me, whoa! It is too simplistic to affirm that this alone automatically negates the whole process!

These friends, just the same still "stand guard" twenty-four hours a day and, since we are much closer to Spirit in sleep-state, they will often advise us more then than when awake. Also, in a somnolescent state most of us, unaware that they have fed us the solution to a problem that had been gnawing at us, self-effacing, think that on awakening, we alone have found the answer!

Not all d/k's are up to scratch either so they cannot always offer their charge complete protection, even failing sometimes in simple tasks. When disclosing a person's door-keeper during a reading I ask Tuan, himself very powerful, to score them on a 1 to 10. (I also qualify the reality of the entity by giving evidence from the d/k. After all, if he or she has been with that person since birth, etc. then they ought to be able to give evidence, thus proving and confirming their being and knowledge of their charge.) A 10 of course is great but all too often they only manage a 3/10 or 4/10 and sometimes not even that!

Students may find this surprising but the basic reason is most often simply a lack of psyche (soul) cohesion between the d/k and their charge, who is commonly unable to "hear" or "see" mediumistically. If recipients (sitters) show a genuine interest I will go into further detail, teaching them how to more easily effect this cohesion, whilst Tuan explains to their d/k how to better protect their charge.

Many door-keepers and helpers are Native American, Chinese, Indian, Arab and so on and I am often asked why. The second lesson I learned was to use logic; Tuan says: "Without logic it has no substance!" In applying logic, one very good reason for such manifestations forthcoming is that whilst they are more highly evolved than we, they nevertheless still retain their personality and are, quite rightly too, proud of their heritage. More importantly, their cultures when compared to contemporary civilisations at the time of their demise, (and in many cases still today) were so much closer to Nature and Spirit than are the western ones.

(On karma, etc.) *Many moons later I was in trance and The Manna Group, in reply to the question of how karma can be explained easily, used the following to explain reincarnation:*

"Taking the analogy of a ship (our journeying) for which the captain (the soul) is responsible, cargo (good and bad actions) is taken on board at and during each port of call (each incarnation). According to the dues "paid" some, or if one is very fortunate, (spiritually forward) all of the cargo is off-loaded in other ports (periods between incarnations). Most times though, only a change or adjustment of the cargo occurs, resulting in the need for further voyaging.

"As the ship continues (the next transition or incarnation for instance) further "ports of call" are scheduled. So, once having accepted and taken the cargo aboard, (the making of good and bad karma) we cannot simply by-pass, or off-load it where we please. Indeed even though it is out of sight, stowed away in the ship's hold, (the deep subconscious?) we cannot simply ignore it!

"We are obliged by natural law to take full responsibility for ourselves and the consequences of all our actions throughout both our incarnations and our Spirit interludes. So time (voyaging) must be spent in adjusting our karma, in both dimensions, paying off our debts and or earning credits. Therefore cargo cannot possibly leave of its own accord or simply be dumped by the captain pretending ignorance of its being aboard! But equally, since personal responsibility and freewill are, by definition, intrinsically obligatory, we can, in exercising one or both, also choose, or not, to reincarnate! There is no compulsion either way (one does not have to) but in deciding your path be advised that spiritual progress is made far more slowly in Spirit than it is upon the Earth-plane.

"In the event, we have to conclude that we cannot lay the blame or congratulations for the good and or bad karma ("cargoes") occurring along the way at anybody's door, except our own. And whilst many of us would declare that, given the choice, we would never have chosen our present incarnation, we tell you that it is precisely because we had the choice, that we did!"

Next, asked to define good and bad they continued:

"Good and bad have their root within the concepts of one's own initiative, code of morals, the laws of the country that one lives in and so on. However, personal responsibility stands alone, paramount!"

When another question was asked as to what yard-stick they might recommend for one's attitudes and behaviour, they answered with the following premise and as usual the advice was put in words "of one syllable."

"If I can honestly say that what I want to do, or am about to do, I would not mind having someone do to me and I am very sure that by doing it I am not consciously hurting or offending anyone that I know personally, then do it. However, if there is even the slightest doubt in my mind of any kind about doing it, then I should not be doing it anyway!"

How easy this is for anyone to understand and absorb! And how very wise to put in the words "Consciously...(down to)...anyone that I know of", thereby establishing that we cannot be directly answerable for, or to, all the peoples of the world!

Nobody can be personally responsible to all and sundry, so there is no value in insisting on, or trying to be, the conscience of the world! It is somewhat like regular exercise; one does ten press-ups to-day and increases the number each day. In two weeks you might well be able to press more than a hundred, which, if you continue, since you have to keep adding to the score, intrinsically result in being no more good than the original ten! Life and my helpers have taught me that the "intermittent exercise" of one's prerogatives has much more value and staying power!

(On "floating helpers.") *I also at times work with what my Spirit teachers term "floating helpers" (explained in Part Three). Many mediums seem to be unaware that there are such entities and indeed might well, if asked, deny their very existence, yet still hold to the ideal that we do not radically change when we make our transition! They will also say that Spirit is ever ready, willing and able to assist us! This surely implies that all talents are available so long as we ask for them and tune in accordingly. Mediums too perform one off tasks but do not admit to a one off assistant, yet I can assure you that this is as much as any a spiritual axiom!*

In the event I can assure the doubters among you that my door-keeper, if asked, will find a specialist schooled in that particular to assist me. It may be something very special like the painting on the cover of this book, or equally yet a mundane bit of DIY brick-laying! So for those of you who still doubt my words consider for a moment! The held view is that Spirit is always there for us, so logically it demonstrates that the brick-layer, if I need him is available. It is simply a question of asking one's d/k to assist your tuning-in as one did originally with one's healer or clairvoyant, etc. and trusting (it goes beyond belief or faith) that the result will be forthcoming.

(On meeting one's helpers.) *I always ensure that helpers, should they have any, quickly overcome any frailty they had in earthly conditions. There is no need to control an earthly body that is healthy and then to complain of and "have" for example, a withered arm! In transfiguration an entity controlling may disclose a previous condition; these may also be picked up by clairvoyants during demonstrations but they have no place once a helper begins working through a medium.*

Why then, you may ask, is Yu-Sin blind when he controls me? He is not, and was not unsighted when upon the earth either. But since there is usually somebody to assist him he does not need to see He simply uses only those senses that are necessary to the job in hand; thus it is an economy measure. He simply saves the energy used to negotiate his way around for his patients. As such when in contact with patients he actually has developed, if you will, X-ray "eyesight" when controlling me. Consequently he is able to (and does) look into their bodies to see and diagnose the conditions.

His frailty too is a bit of a ploy! In his culture the "ancient ones" were venerated and when he made his last transition he was very old. Acting so frail, inoffensive and loveable too, he also looks (and is) quite harmless, thereby instilling confidence and trust (as indeed any medical person should) in worried patients!

Zarlu on the other hand can walk the length of a fully furnished room in total darkness and not touch or bump into anything on the way! His attributes and sensibilities are therefore adjusted to his work as an exorcist! In the event this ably demonstrates and describes two contrasting examples of techniques used by helpers, i.e. tools for the job!

(On the alter-ego theory, etc.) *Recently, when discussing spirit helpers and guides, a medium asked me whether I accepted the theory of alter-ego put forward by some. Drawing from my own experience I have to say that I do not, indeed cannot, hold to this idea. I have had proof many times that helpers and guides are entities independently existing outside of myself and I quote three examples here.*

First the above incident (the little boy in Germany) indicates that it was not me travelling in the astral form. Indeed if I was, I must have powers beyond those of which I am aware since I have never gone in disguise or costume before!

Secondly, during my many years demonstrating transfiguration all over the UK and other countries there is no way that I could produce, to order, getting on for fifty different alter-egos each evening at each different venue! During these seances too, the spirit friends and loved ones of the recipients consistently gave unshakeable evidence to them and also looked, and most times talked in their own voice, or, at the very least, used the same inflections and accents as on Earth. Surely, it would be admitted, even by the most sceptical, that, even by stretching the imagination to the limit, it would be impossible to present such evidence simply by the exercising of an alter-ego!

Thirdly, many years ago I had an ego-flush, telling someone not to worry I would simply tell Yu-Sin to control me (Remember my boss's brother?) and diagnose what was wrong with him. Try as I might (the word is ask not demand and ye shall receive) I could not enter the control (trance) state and in the end I gave up. The following weekend I visited my brother, who had received some psychic training. For openers he asked had I had any difficulty going into trance recently? I affirmed, and, smiling, he said that Yu-Sin had been giving healing to his wife at the time and was complaining that I was trying to draw him away and that he could not be in two places at once!

Chapter 4
BEWARE THE DOOR YOU OPEN THAT YOU CAN CLOSE IT AGAIN!

After the introductory aural sessions the voices quickly became clearer. Interestingly, this direction (clairaudience) was chosen by my helpers for two reasons. The first was that I had heard voices as a kid so it was simply a case of tuning me in again. The second was that Spirit knew I would accept voices more readily as real and not imagined if they were external as opposed to internal. Today the position is somewhat reversed, for now, more often than not, like many other mediums (though often they would not admit it publicly) I hear my *own* voice in my head. This is written about in Part Three in the section on forming and running circles.

Tuan over-saw all the instruction I received in those early days (and still does for that matter) working like a good movie director; in control of proceedings but allowing his actors to perform naturally. I soon obtained a tape recorder and it was not long before, on the nights I was not singing, I began going early to bed. Having switched the machine to record, I would settle down and in no time at all, slip into trance. It was incredible listening the next day or whatever as to what was said and how I sounded.

This deep trance state did not last very long however, because my nose got in the way! I wanted to know what happened and what was said while I was _in_ trance, not just listen to it afterwards! Making Tuan aware of my thoughts (pointless this, for he knew my every psychic thought anyway) explaining that I had no control in, nor knowledge of, the proceedings at the time and that this worried me. This was met with a great deal of approval from him and my helpers resulting in the development of the method that has been used ever since.

Consequently, whenever I am out of my body and a helper is controlling it, I am able to position myself above looking down on the general scene. I am also aware of what is taking place though I still often miss some things that are said. But at least I am there for most of the session, which in turn means that I can afterwards relate to sitters more easily. More importantly, I can be totally honest, blaming nothing I am not too happy about entirely on Spirit.

This again is something that some mediums are apt to do - "don't blame me dear, I have no control over it, it's Spirit you know! Nor do I know what is said anyway!" Another misnomer! Very few mediums can state honestly that they have never known anything about what has been said or what has happened when they were in trance. And if they tell you different (physical mediums being probably the one exception) they are kidding you and or themselves or worse, they are downright lying! (See end of chapter on mediums and trance, etc.)

Led by Tuan, yet another of the early lessons taught was to learn to control your controls (work *with* them) and then they will not control *(use)* you! They had led me to this point purely for the purpose of showing me that (a) mediums can go into deep trance and then claim that they are not responsible for anything that occurs, (in effect, the shirking of personal responsibility) and (b) one can achieve the same results with much lighter trance states, provided that the mind is sufficiently and receptively malleable. I learned many lessons in this way as to the modus operandi of the psyche (the soul and or spirit mind)!

Interestingly, I profess to being quite a good mimic and I have found that if I can hear a voice in my head then I can usually, after a little work, do a fair to good impression of various show-biz types as well as friends and acquaintances. Yet, strangely, although I hear my helpers' voices clearly I cannot get their voices even nearly right! When trying to imitate these the inflection and or the tone is wrong. In some cases, the voice is not even close to the recordings I have of them speaking through me! Yet another of life's little mysteries, I guess!

I count myself very lucky, nay privileged, to have such an absolute soul to guide me. Not only have I received instruction from Tuan and the helpers but it was he who interceded in my behalf with the Manna Group. He has so consistently and conscientiously protected me 100% throughout these long years that I have never, since that first enlightening meeting, doubted him or his incredible abilities. Despite what had happened previously, I immediately had no fear nor lack of confidence in him and this enabled me in the early days to safely "sit" alone.

At one end of the scale he has taken me on the most wonderful excursions into the realms of spirit to teach me or have me taught by loftier, more highly evolved souls. At the other we have also journeyed into the lower vibrations when we have worked, together with Zarlu, on some pretty hairy hauntings, the like of which I have known other exorcists to shun, not wanting to get involved. For instance over many years in the Devon area, presidents and their committees, afraid and or unequipped to take up the challenge always referred hauntees to me, even though they never booked me to serve their church.

In waking moments I have sufficient to do and sleeping, unless it proves to be more useful than the obvious is, for me, a waste of time I have therefore received much of my esoteric and metaphysical education during sleep, a deal I worked out with Tuan many ye rs ago. In this way I can and have, many times, been introduced to other helpers and guides and received instruction and or the answers to problems on behalf of others and myself.

In the waking state too, this modus operandi (no time wasting) has often occurred in what at first glance may appear to be the strangest of places, such as in the bath and even whilst sitting on the loo! Of course we have to be willing to open up the mind for they never intrude upon our privacy. But on such occasions when performing our natural functions we are generally alone. So with little or nothing to think about do you not agree that this can be an opportune time for our Spirit friends to impress upon us their thoughts? And if you agree, why is it then, other than that it may not have occurred to you personally, really so surprising that such co-operation can be achieved?

The "privy" after all was once far more communal with no partitioning between those partaking! On certain occasions a watchman was actually paid to guard the door! This was when councillors, etc. sat alongside their masters holding confidential discussions and or offering advice. Here too much of the decision making regarding the law, parliament, the monarchy and the state, not to mention plotting, was undertaken. Hence the title Privy Councillor, a name, incidentally still in use to-day! Now my earlier words can be seen in true context! That it is not at all strange when in today's more solitary accommodations with our minds just drifting, thinking usually about nothing important, our teachers, etc. steal up on us to introduce themselves or educate us.

Here too, sadly, the novice student and "ordinary" folk are, all too often, unaware that when a pleasant "memory or face" passes through their mind it is not their own imagination! It is actually a Spirit's impression, lovingly sent telepathically and hoping that it might be received, understood and accepted.

When one is asleep (and most people are not even aware that this is possible) one leaves the body, usually hovering near the bed, (an "out of body" experience). Thirsting for knowledge I would go with Tuan *and still do*, "sitting" in the company of enlightened souls such as The Manna Group.

Listening to these great minds, they will answer questions and discuss how to achieve the goals they set me and others throughout the world. How to sit, how to trance, to see, feel and hear. How all psychic persons, once they have the knowledge, are able to employ natural law and become mediums. They warn though of being careful in its use, for whilst it should only be used for good, equally by "inversion" it can be used for ill!

For example, by using magnetic healing (energy force) certain people are able to cure someone of an illness. Equally, since natural law says all things have an equal and an opposite, it logically follows that they could, by "inverting" that same force, cause a person to become ill. Further, if their "magnetic force" is strong enough, they could if they wished, even kill in certain circumstances.

Crowley, the self-confessed black arts practitioner claimed that he killed people in his time and indeed certain of his adversaries and acquaintances too did die in strange circumstances! And remember, and be cautioned, for it is easy to scoff or dismiss out of hand that which we do not understand and most times, do not even wish to think about either!

OK, ponder this! How many of us can put our hand on our heart and say we have never thought ill of someone and then when something has happened to them, have never said serves them right?

Because we do not know how something works or why something happens it does not necessarily follow that we are not in some way responsible for it working or happening! Most of us, intrinsically, do not know how many of the gadgets work that we use each day in our homes or workplace. With it plugged in we simply operate the switch, the power flows, and it functions! However, that very simple operation of connecting and switching on makes us automatically responsible for it. Not true? OK, if *that is your attitude* I would suggest that you do not get into your car, start it and drive off, for you could quickly regret it!

It is a bit like the lady patient who, when told by Yu Sin to breathe more deeply in order to conserve oxygen asked, is it really that important? Smiling, he told her that in order to test the importance of it she should try not breathing for half an hour or even a few minutes!

Equally, I have no clue as to how this computer operates yet I am responsible, in typing them, for the words which "magically" appear on the screen. Then if I switch on the printer and click to print I will again be responsible for those same words appearing on paper! It is of course the Law of Cause and Effect at work.

Whilst I was encouraged in the beginning to sit alone, I do not recommend this to novice students. I am, not to place too fine a point on it in my last incarnation, a very old soul and I was reminded by Tuan that I knew him before our meeting in this incarnation. "All is known within - there is nothing new under the sun" and to *know* goes beyond mere faith. I had therefore, immediately after my revelation, ultimate unwavering trust in Tuan's knowledge and strength.

I caution all budding mediums to be conscious of this chapter heading. I also urge you to read carefully the chapter on haunting, obsession and possession. So, in endorsing the first sentence in the preceding para. I state that (and certainly at the beginning) it is preferable to sit in a development circle under the guidance of a well trained, experienced medium. You might ask how will I know the quality of this medium? Well, this is also explained in Part Three.

At seventeen I was a member of Florence Wells' circle in Chislehurst, Kent and we were at that time sitting for the development of her physical phenomena. A very strong character, she exercised a great deal of logic in her psychic and mediumistic work and stood no nonsense either from Spirit or her members.

Many persons have claimed to have "started me off" but it was she, herself already an established medium and an extremely good clairvoyant and speaker who propelled me onto the public platform. Drinking the compulsory cup of tea one night after circle she casually mentioned that she had inadvertently double booked the coming weekend. Great, said I, thinking that she had two bookings for the Sunday. Patiently explaining that double-booking meant that she had inadvertently booked two demonstrations on the same evening, she quickly moved on, saying that she had a stand-in, so not to worry. On asking who it was she said: "You!"

To my stuttered:"But I've never worked in public..." she promptly said that everything and everyone had a beginning time and an ending time. *My* public demonstrating clairvoyance start-time was now she went on and if I really wanted to do the work I should just put my trust in my helpers and it would be OK. After all, I stood up and sang in front of an audience so what was the problem? I replied that I had a big band behind me to which she retorted, grinning: "And you will have a big one behind you there as well!"

Of course I went and since I was nervous the President, knowing that I did not feel right talking very novice philosophy to a group of people who were much older than I, kindly did the address (the sermon) for me.

(Subsequently, Tuan asserted that since the address was inspirational and the helper delivering the information through me would, no doubt, be much older and wiser than the congregation anyway, he as usual neatly putting the whole thing into perspective. As it transpired, what with the R.A.F. and so on it was a number of years before I actually did do both the address and clairvoyance).

On his introducing me the President told the folk to give me a lot of love as this was the *very first time I had stood on a platform to demonstrate!* True his words were well intentioned, but it was about the worst thing he could have said and it was then that I wished (about the only time in my long career, I might add) that more time had been taken up by the hymn singing! I also wished for a moment that I had the twenty five or so musicians behind me! However, on standing up I mentally asked Tuan and my helpers to see me through and to please make it really good if this was what we really wanted.

The first thing I got? A red Indian (now referred to as Native Americans) called Red Cloud! Oh no, I thought! In circle Florence had always said do not give off Chinese, Red Indians, nuns and so on unless you can back up what you have given by proving their association with the recipient. I should have known better than to fret for it actually set the tone for the rest of my demonstration. A helper of one of the healers, my description of him was apparently spot on; his nose bent to one side, due to the peculiar shape, and a vivid scar on the right shoulder!

More importantly, when questioned by me, he was not, like they used to say in the old "B" Hollywood movies, "one o' them thay-arr pesky Red-skins." He immediately and clearly furnished me with lots of information about the healer, his home and his family. Other evidences followed to other recipients in rapid succession.

Interestingly, after the meeting the healer asked me to accompany him to another room and there, in the healing sanctuary, was a photograph of a painting of Red Cloud, his healing helper. The original had been painted by the late psychic artist Frank Leah who had apologised for *not getting the nose right,* saying he just felt that it wanted to be crooked! It also clearly showed the scar on the shoulder and, needless to say, the healer was delighted to have had such a wonderful confirmation from his helper.

Needless to say too my reaction on the night was that I felt totally knocked-out by it all and on the way home in a sort of daze, I realised, I guess, that I had arrived! (See e. of ch. on positive evidence.)

HELPFUL NOTES!

(On mediums and trance, etc.) *Although not recognised by me at the time, I now know, through countless conversations with Tuan since, that he was very aware of my inherent sense of personal responsibility. Not consciously aware of it then, I had nevertheless, Spirit-wise, quickly become acutely so. Consequently, once understood and accepted, I have always regarded it as being of paramount importance in my mediumistic pursuits. I would add that though it has not always been as successful, I do at least try to carry this over into my daily life as well.*

I am afraid that many mediums consciously or not, do hide behind the "deep-trance state". In this way they can refute any self admonishment for what was said during it, thereby abdicating their own responsibility! ! This is not any kind of sour grapes either - this is intended as an instruction to budding mediums to know that one can trance, as in a hypnotic state and still be very aware and "conscious" of the proceedings!

I have many times discussed trance states with all types of both trance and inspirational mediums at all levels of knowledge. They assure me that much of their opinion on this gels with mine, they too being convinced, like me, that one can be completely in trance and yet, as it were, conscious. It is sad that even some of those who are aware of this will still play out the "I know nothing scene" just so they can remain slightly mysterious. Knowing full well what had occurred, they "come back" uttering such inane remarks as "Was it OK?" or "What happened?"

Genuine deep trance is perhaps more the operating prerogative of physical mediums. Even then, some will still move in and out as it suits the occasion, helpers and, of course, themselves. That said, even when demonstrating transfiguration during those years I was "aware" a great deal of the time. It is, believe me, quite an experience to watch Funny Eye mould an ectoplasmic mask behind my hands in just a few seconds and fit it, like a latex one, over my face. So there are also advantages to being aware of what is going on and none, I think, in missing all of the fun!

I reiterate! Please take to heart the knowledge that mediumistic trance is very closely related to hypnosis and this is explained more fully in Part Three on circles and the running of them.

(On positive evidence.) *Endeavour always to deliver positive evidence by definitely stating it and if it is not accepted, try harder! Whilst one sometimes might have to ask a question, make it a point not to develop this very bad habit. Too many mediums already elicit information through the questioning of recipients, proving nothing except perhaps unconscious fraud. Sadly, these (quite unsuspectingly most times, since they are badly trained) are deceiving both themselves and many of their recipients.*

For example, over the years I have heard many mediums "give off" Red Indians, Chinese, Spanish dancers, nuns, Gypsies and so on as if they were going out of fashion! But as Florence had said, many times they do not follow it up with proof! Surely, if such entities are indicated by a medium as being helpers of recipients, then logic tells us that the helper should, nay must, at the very least, know something about them!

If in fact mediums do speak of such entities it is incumbent upon them to hold the link more strongly, to delve further, and to pass on to recipients things that the helper knows about them. It does not necessarily have to be world shattering either as oftentimes the smallest detail can make for the biggest proof! Indeed, in such cases, should it be the recipient's first contact, evidence is even more important!

Sometimes helpers, in the beginning, like some of our loved ones, unable to "energise" sufficiently, find communication difficult. In such circumstances, if only mediums would just reach out for that extra bit, then the evidence can, most times, be received through their own helpers. Calling for and gaining some extra assistance from the contact, these will "ghost-write" (no pun intended) the script, as it were and deliver it telepathically through the medium directly. Often too, if all else fails the d/k, in far closer contact with the medium than any other helper or entity and is of course the medium's best communicant and will intervene and assist accordingly.

The importance of delivering positive clairvoyance cannot be overstated. Florence held the view, and I have to agree, that many mediums sometimes utilise "imaginary helpers" in the same way that a lifeline might be thrown to them if they were drowning. It is simply that the medium is either not on form or is not of a standard required to work fully publicly. It is then that they will often resort to and not always consciously either, padding of one sort or another!

I reiterate! Whatever talent you may possess, when demonstrating whether it is in your own circle, in a one to one sitting, or in public, make it a rule, nay a habit, right from the word go. Never, unless it becomes absolutely necessary, ask questions of recipients. Know it! Questions of any kind, especially those like asking if a person's mother or whoever is in spirit, will quickly lead you down the path of negative mediumship. Always endeavour to make statements or comments and give off helpers only if they can prove themselves. You will find that your own helpers will respect your wishes and develop the same habits, only passing on to you direct, positive evidences!

My Auntie Millie used to, most times, give the punter a stock reading e.g. putting questions to a person which can only have a yes or no answer; either way she had the upper hand! Carrying through in this vein, switching the answers around to suit the situation, she ensured that the person, unless they knew better, though duped, left satisfied.

Mind you, I have always taped my readings for recipients and always supply brand new tapes, opening them in front of the sitter. (In those days though they mostly did not have this facility; even wire recorders and dictaphones were substandard and quite rare, so the remembered word or notes was all that they could rely upon). Mind you, I get through such a lot in an hour and a half that they could not remember it all anyway! I also tell folk what they ought to know and not as Aunt Millie did, which was: "Simply tell them what they want to hear luv and they go away happy!"

Chapter 5
DISAPPOINTMENTS ARE OFTEN WINGS THAT BEAR
THE SOUL SKYWARD

On leaving school at the age of sixteen, having declined both offers of a career in teaching and pharmacology I still hankered after show-biz. My dad though insisted that I must have a proper job! His quick solution resulted in me being indentured as an electrical engineering apprentice with J. Stone and Co., Deptford! One condition was that I had to obtain my City and Guilds Certificate so on one day each week I attended college. That was good - at least it meant I did not get dirty or deaf on that day - but the rest was not! I rapidly discovered with disgust that the grand title written on my indenture papers and the firm's promises stood for nothing!

At my interview I was told that I would have to get practical experience in the factory for six months, after which I would move to the drawing office for experience there. So, although I hated factory work, I knuckled down to the task. But from the word go, I was stuck at a bench, always with the promise that "in a couple of months" I would be transferred to the drawing office. However, enough is enough I thought and just before my eighteenth birthday, being no nearer to a drawing board than when I started with the firm, I told the Charge-hand that I would probably be leaving soon. I had enough of empty promises and the factory I continued, to last me a lifetime. This brooked immediate response, with him jumping up and down like a yo-yo yelling that he would (I quote him exactly by the way) "'av yer-rupp before one of the 'igh-ups to be prepriminded! You was indentured and that's that!" I just turned my back on him and pretended to get on with my work. Within a few minutes with, on one side, "little Hitler" (the foreman) and on the other "Runt" (the charge-hand), so called due to his diminutive stature, I was marched off!

With great ceremony and set grimaces to match, I was ushered into an office and confronted by a person with the longest and most pointed nose I had ever seen! Not invited to sit down the "'igh up" straight out told me that they could "do just as they liked with me!" In no uncertain terms he spoke of my indentured apprenticeship and said that so long as I was being trained for the job they could dictate accordingly as to what work I did! I began to protest but was cut of in mid sentence and the finger-wagging turned into a tirade of abuse. Among this was that the law stated that I was bound to them and whether I liked it or not, my indentures could not be broken by me!

Deliberately "executively" leaning back in his chair, the 'igh up continued in the same vein smugly adding that even conscription could not interfere with apprentices. Surely then, like many others, I should at least be grateful to the firm for that! He paused, a sardonic smile fixed upon his rat-like features. Then speaking through his all but clenched teeth he sneeringly said that the choice was mine. He paused again, then, spelling out his words, he told me that before I said any more, I should perhaps consider the consequences of the company suing my parents!

About a week later I was talking to one of the band about my predicament. He told me that he was a union man, a shop steward and that they were wrong to threaten me. He then said that he would get in touch with another "brother" at J. Stone, who would fight my case for me. I told him to forget it; I really did not want the aggravation it could bring my parents or myself. Well, he continued, there was another way out of indentures; all I had to do was join up and there was nothing they could do, legal or otherwise! Replying that I was excused from national service he said that was nothing to do with it; all I had to was *volunteer!*

So on my eighteenth birthday (1949) I joined the Royal Air Force on a five year term. Here too, after encountering more than a few more little "Hitlers" on the way, I could not wait to get out in 1954. When originally I took the entrance and suitability exams, I achieved top marks and was offered training in any trade I wished to choose. I wanted to be a photographer but the advisers told me that it was not among the top trades; they thought I ought to be in engineering! Boy, were they ever wrong about that!

After basic training bull s*** at Cardington, which (and this may surprise some of you) I took to like the proverbial duck to water, I went to Wellsbourne Mountford near Shakespeare's Stratford. There I took my photo course and passed out with 79%, just one point short of making corporal immediately. However, with the lowest possible pass mark being only 40% I was of course well pleased with myself! Later though I discovered that nobody got the magic 80%! There *never had been* nor *ever would be* a corporal made up right away! This was simply a ploy to encourage one to study and work harder. I subsequently discovered it was just another of the many "jerk-arounds" (A Service Jerk Around or "Asja") frequently experienced, usually by service bullies who, in every case, outranked the bullied!

In training we were told that the RAF only had some eight hundred photographers and this meant that if a section had more than three bods it was considered large. Imagine then my surprise when, posted to RAF Benson, I quickly learned that this was the largest photo section in the service, boasting more than a hundred personnel, male and female!

During my time there and indeed throughout the five years I ran circles and also attended others wherever and whenever I was able. I did quite a lot of trance work, spiritual and magnetic healing, clairvoyance, etc. the while, through my helpers, keeping up my search for thing's psychic, mediumistic, spiritual and philosophical.

It was within the first few weeks at Benson that I experimented with, among other things, an ouija board brought back by one of the lads after a weekend leave. Along with others during "stand-downs" (waiting for aircraft to return from sorties or overcast days when air photography was impossible) once we had moved beyond the "you're pushing it; oh no I'm not; oh yes you are" syndrome, we had some remarkable and evidential results.

One afternoon however, quite suddenly, the words "stop now" came right in the middle of a message but we ignored it! Almost immediately the glass jerked away from under our fingers and, spinning very fast across the table, it took off and rose vertically, rising up above our heads. It then flew across the room and smashed against a wall some fifteen feet away! Certainly no-one (in the body at any rate) was pushing it when *that* happened! Everyone, including me, was open mouthed, utterly stunned! But of course after getting over the shock, nobody openly admitted to believing that it had happened through supernormal means. Nonetheless, I was never able to get any takers to "play" after that...

Subsequently the board, with the owner's consent, was destroyed by me. Unfortunately, that incident also virtually put paid to any other psychic sessions taking place in the photo-section or in the billet. Nevertheless, a couple of other lads and I still visited circles and churches locally.

The photographic centre stood on the site of an old two-story farmhouse. Originally, with shorter take-off aircraft using the runway this presented no problems. However, due to the war a fighting airfield became necessary; thus by extending the runway a potential hazard was created. The house was now right in the flight path with the tarmac runway overlaying the former vegetable garden!

Compulsorily purchased, the old folk were moved to their new home and the building was unceremoniously flattened. In its place, almost immediately, hurriedly and haphazardly thrown together, were erected a conglomeration of wooden huts with felt roofs. As there was no other accommodation available on the station for the influx of extra air-crews these were put together to provide temporary accommodation.

Very soon after the war Benson became the station for the Royal Family, later called "The Queen's Flight" which title, at first, for obvious reasons, caused some amusement! There were several special aeroplanes and crews on twenty-four hour call. Consequently, in almost no time at all, some of the best quarters in the RAF were erected for airmen, officers and married personnel. This in turn made the huts (or "The Hovel" as it quickly came to be known) totally redundant and they were abandoned. It appears by all accounts that not long after with hardly any repair at all to the virtually derelict huts, the photo processing section was set up, under the lofty title of No.1 Photo Processing Wing, RAF!

Each night two lads were on fire-picket duty and in order to ensure proper cover, each one was required to patrol alone. In this rabbit warren of a place, lit only at intervals by very subdued lights this presented a fairly daunting prospect. Quite apart from the eerie atmosphere it was also common knowledge that almost everybody heard the doors to the dark-rooms being opened and closed. Regularly too, in those rooms, voices were heard whispering, though one could never distinguish what was said; footsteps and voices were also clearly heard in the passage-ways. (The official reason for the noises were put down to rats! This caused many a wig to comment that they must have been bloody clever for not only could they open and shut doors but they also spoke English and walked with loud human foot-steps!)

Unannounced, the Senior Warrant Officer, a heavy drinker, would pop in on his way back from the local pub. If you were caught going about your tasks in pairs, depending on how much he had drunk that night, he would bawl you out, or worse, put you on a charge.

I never discovered who haunted the place for in those days I did not undertake exorcism. In the event, we would have been denied permission to go in there at night in case it was an excuse to produce "rabbits" (illegal private work). Quite apart from this though there would have been no-one brave enough to have joined me in a séance! The entities could have been previous haunters of the farmhouse or air-crew who had died during the war, though it could have been others so it remained speculative. For instance, Mosquitoes, the photo squadron aircraft were principally constructed in plywood. When they crashed, and there were quite a few even in the comparatively short time I was at Benson, crews hardly ever survived.

Pilots were almost always impatient, anxious to see what photos the automatic cameras had taken when aloft. So immediately after de-briefing they would inevitably call at the section to view or await the prints. Therefore, it may well have been one, or even more of the deceased Mosquito crews wandering the section perhaps looking for theirs!

Almost everyone was scared to be there alone at night but the powers that be would never admit to anything ghostly. Just the same they finally agreed it was wiser to double up the number of airmen on a shift. Their reason was (they said) that it was too big a fire risk and too rambling a building for just two pickets to cover. Being wooden and containing many inflammable materials even we "idiots" could see that! They therefore doubled the number of pickets ensuring its security being properly patrolled. Believe me, when that was decided, a sigh of relief, even from the machos, went through the section. (see e of ch. on darkrooms and red light.)

Nobody seemed to want us to know exactly when the previous building had last been occupied or exactly when air-crews had first quartered the huts. We knew however that they were certainly occupied right through the war years. So, as they say, the plot thickened for it might well have been any of the wartime crew members, some of our pilots, or indeed none of them causing the disturbances! It is also possible, even probable that we were using the ouija board carelessly. Ignorant of just what we might stir up, we almost certainly sent out a "signal" that we were holding "open house" to the spirit world. Surprisingly, too, we never actually got any direct evidence of air-crews, it was always philosophical or personal contacts.

At the time it did not bother me unduly that the haunters were not discovered or cleared. But soon after the ouija board sessions, politely rebuked by my helpers, I quickly learned to rectify my error, that of ensuring, as best I could, the protection of séances. In mitigation however, the while admitting that these may have stirred things up somewhat, I would also add that the photo section had held its haunted reputation for a long time before I came upon the scene!

Much of the work we did in the photo section was utterly boring and repetitive. True the pictures were all of different areas but most work was done on continuous processing machines. This meant that in the dark we loaded the spool of film, usually more than a hundred yards long, in one end. We then waited in the dark for it to emerge at the other end, as the dried, finished film (the negatives), re-rolled automatically, onto another spool. The printing machines did the same thing except that we worked in red light. We also had to quality control the exposure, using an automatic meter as we went along but the prints too emerged in one continuous roll. The new bod would have the job of operating the guillotine to separate each print. Oh! Continuous processing was so exciting, well, at least it was first time you were in charge of a machine!

I was fortunate though for I had found, besides my psychic work, that I was able, with the co-operation of the station commander, to write, direct and perform in a fair number of revues.

Much to my chagrin however, the section officer in charge was one Flt. Lt. Metcalfe who quickly became the biggest pain in my relatively short career! At our first meeting he asked if I played football. Just his asking and the glint in his eye should have made me realise that he would turn out to be another bloody football fanatic! I replied in the negative and added that I really saw no point to the game. I was immediately aware that the withering look he gave me was a warning. I knew then that I would have to tread carefully with this one or I would easily end up on a hiding to nothing.

Much more of a reason for his hating me (and he did too!) though was the fact that I had the full backing of the Station Commander who himself was quite stage struck. Unfortunately due to his being the highest ranking officer at Benson (the top bod, the big nebbie!) he was unable to take part in the entertainment. Metclafe's hate for me stemmed not only from the foregoing, but also because almost all of the personnel in the photo section were in my shows! In all honesty this did rather disrupt his organisation and work schedules, so I was really as much a pain to his rear end as he was to mine.

The reason for this was that the cinema was in use each night which meant that rehearsals had to take place during the afternoons and when a show date loomed near this meant *every day*. This resulted in even less of a skeleton staff than at other rehearsal times so utter chaos reigned in the section, with Metcalfe metaphorically tearing out what little hair he had left!

He knew you see, but could not prove it, that when he refused (and he always did) to release my show people for the afternoon, I simply went over his head when the boss, bless 'im, always came up trumps. Never mentioning that I had said anything he would simply ring Herr Metcalfe, "informing" him that a rehearsal was necessary and all personnel involved were to attend same.

Once, so commanded, there was no way out for poor ol' Metcalfe. On the other hand, of course, when there was a football match to be played there was never a problem. More especially if he was in the team they all got off, even though most players were key members of the section! A modicum of give and take was all that was necessary but in the service, especially if you outrank the other party, it is invariably a case of *you* give and *I* take!

I had been at Benson for about eighteen months when I was posted abroad to RAF Habbaniya, Iraq. Once there, along with everyone else, I lived the absolute life of Riley on this truly fantastic station. Innumerable facilities included an ice cream factory; a bakery, a hospital, churches and schools.There were numerous swimming pools, dozens of tennis courts and football pitches (of course), a golf course, about twenty Naafi's and stores and some fifty mess halls, etc. With thirty-nine miles of tarmac roads in the off-duty areas alone we even had a village market with shops and stalls!

Just like a small town it was situate fifty miles from Baghdad and bounded a huge lake, complete with boats of all shapes and sizes. The station garden areas were irrigated twice a day and with beautiful flowers, plants and trees lovingly attended it was a veritable oasis. Truly beautifully kept, one was hard put to realise that the desert was so near. Taxis were permanently based there, operating twenty-four hours a day. Very necessary for if official and works areas were counted in, the tarmac roads would probably be in excess of seventy miles. Employing some ten thousand civilian Iraqis, they worked for, including married quarters and the WAAFs, just over a thousand personnel. Sadly though, since there were less than a hundred WAAFs, these were strictly officers and senior NCO's bunce!

It was an education to travel by car some fifty miles along a dirt track road to Baghdad. In this town rich and poor contrasts were painfully evident, with mud huts and hovels standing between beautiful hotels, apartment and office blocks and clubs. I actually did a few gigs in a night club with some of the lads who had formed a harmonica group when I played a large mouth organ called a vamper.

It is not common knowledge that in Iraq the temperature drops so dramatically from the daytime high that at night one often needs a greatcoat. So, only being able to afford one taxi, albeit a luxury one, seven of us, including the driver travelled, or rocked and jolted more correctly, to and from Baghdad. In the early hours of the morning though, with the windows closed to keep the heat in and the dust out, one wished to be in a totally different place. So after only a few nights of this hell, we gave up on the cabaret gigs.

Including the sergeant, our section numbered four and since we only worked half-days, it was more like a holiday camp atmosphere. Being so short on bodies and having so much fun too, circles and the like took a compulsory break! I was still learning in my sleep but physically I was more interested in trying to get up to the Canal Zone in Egypt. The Forces Broadcasting Service operated from Fayid and I was hoping that I might be accepted onto the staff.

My chance came I thought when, promoted to the dizzy heights of corporal, which meant one too many in our section, I was transferred to RAF Deversoir, Canal Zone, Egypt. This was a large unit too but manned only by male personnel. But even though we pigged it out in tents I settled in, happy to be in the company of a lot of guys I knew from Benson.

The Suez crisis was brewing and we were unable to leave camp, so, unfortunately, I never got to see the Pyramids, the Sphinx or the Valley of the Kings. The situation worsened and we had trouble with the Arabs. They were forced by their government to strike and with the reasons being solely political it was known that they would not return. Consequently, a regiment of African soldiers was shipped in and they took over all of the menial jobs that had hitherto been handled by the Arabs.

Not long after their arrival I was summoned to attend the senior medical officer's consulting room. He told me he wanted me to check on someone. Perplexed, I followed him along the corridor and into a twin-bedded room. A black person lay in one of the two beds in the room whilst the other was unoccupied. There was also a corporal medical orderly who nodded to me by way of acknowledgement.

The MO proceeded to tell me that the guy in the other bed had died. However, the post mortem had revealed no reason or cause of death and certainly none that would justify such a rapid demise. And now, he continued, it appeared that the other one was going the same way. I looked at the MO. as much as to say so why am I here? By way of answer to my unasked question he told me this seemed more my bag than his! I looked at him, harder this time and he said that the man claimed that he had been spelled (sung to death) to die. It had apparently been laid by a soldier and "witch doctor" who had very strong powers. The only possible cause he said might have been psychological fear but psychological or not he continued, we do not want another death if it can be avoided; so, over to you!

Asking me if I needed anything I was tempted to reply only a miracle, but I just shook my head by way of reply. He abruptly left but the corporal stayed and he must have read my thoughts! I was still wondering how this guy knew me when he spoke saying it was *he* who had persuaded the Medical Officer to ask for me. Small world! He had seen me doing trance healing in England and had convinced this officer that it could do no harm to try and it might even do a lot of good.

To cut a long story short I went into trance and apparently one of the soldier's uncles, long dead, with Tuan's permission, took control. Speaking through me with the patient in his native tongue, using family (tribal) secret signs and gestures, he stated that the curse had no real or genuine effective power. He said that being a true medicine man, his magic was much stronger, demonstrated by the fact that his spirit was able to take possession of my body (his words speaking through me). He assured his nephew that the soldier was not truly magic, he just knew a few things so his powers, by comparison to himself, were weak. Anyway, he continued, he was about to be arrested so he must now get well in order to testify at his trial.

Then Zarlu took control and, speaking to the medic, he explained what the uncle had said. For the patient this was "big magic" personified. The corporal, feeling very gratified with his intervention, rang for the MO.

On arrival, he was gob-smacked! For here was his patient sitting up smiling and chatting with us; yet only an hour or so before he had been at death's door! And from a death-bed situation in the morning he was discharged, completely fit, that same evening! That was probably my first (and perhaps my most important) "public" transfiguration seance.

The "witch-doctor's" locker, searched a few days later revealed all sorts of goodies. He had cigarettes, sweets, jewellery, numerous watches, knives and other weapons. He was arrested, charged with threatening behaviour, extortion and stealing. Tried and convicted he was sent back to Africa where he was imprisoned for ten years. So much for his brand of magic!

I made overtures to the Forces Broadcasting Service and was lucky enough to do a few bits and pieces in my spare time But as the old saying goes, nothing comes easily and I virtually remained on the sidelines! Interestingly, Anton Rogers, the now famous actor was doing his National Service then and was one of the presenters. Among other things he read the news and was also Uncle Christopher to the child listeners. He would wish them happy birthday and tell them where their presents were hidden. (Actually I still have an odd ode I wrote about him, his partner in crime, Michael Whinnera and the rather stupid army sergeant who was in charge of their tent-line at Fayid.)

Our photo section C.O. was posted to another station and the new man took his place. I just could not believe it! Bloody Metcalfe! He had heard about my radio excursions and immediately on returning from one of these I was told to report to him pronto! He tore into me in no uncertain terms saying that I should do well to remember that *he* was my CO, not some little radio poof! He ranted on stressing that as such he would never allow me to work at FBS. or to produce shows again. Protesting it was in my own off-duty time, he, sneered, hissing malevolently that there was no such thing in the RAF! (Another example of "Asja".) He took pains to remind me that this was not Benson so there were no powerful friends to help me here. And, he continued, he would make certain that I would not be given the opportunity to make any new ones!

He obviously knew that I was aware that when a person became a regular broadcaster, irrespective of rank, he had a pass to every officers' mess in the zone! So he was going to make absolutely sure, for this reason alone, that I never worked for FBS. again! As a result my "about to be born" career with the FBS Canal Zone was terminated before, as it were, it even had a chance to become really embryonic!

From then on he not only had the knife into me; he took great delight in twisting it! Due to the emerging crisis we were later put on a rota of twenty-four, eighteen, twelve and six hour periods of guard duty day after day for several weeks. A totally pointless exercise this, since we had no ammunition for the guns we carried! ("Asja" personified.) Then when the RAF Regiment took over M. put me on every rota he could find. I got all the duties going, from duty corporal to fire picket - you name it, I got it! If ever there was a fatherless son *he* must have been the original! He even sent me on loan two thousand miles down the zone to Kabrit when the FBS. tried, once again, to enlist my services. Though bitterly disappointed, in a way Metcalfe also "struck out" here too!

For the three months I was there I did absolutely no work! Nobody needed me and could not understand why I was sent there in the first place; they did not even have a photo section! So having buried the FBS as a non starter, I knuckled down to the exhausting task of enjoying what for me was one long holiday. In the event, I swam in the sea almost all day, every day and in the process nearly perfected my spear fishing. The sea was only about fifty yards from my hut so even with a lazy stroll to the beach I could be there in a couple of minutes!

As luck would have it, I was still in Kabrit the night the film store at Deversoir burned to the ground. Everything was lost and had I been in Deversoir and knowing how Metcalfe had it in for me, I might well have been on the fire picket *that* night! I dread to think where or what I might have been today, for I am sure he would have laid the blame at my door in some way or another and I would probably have ended up in the glass-house for some years.

At Deversoir the film store building had no windows and always, apart from the office, had only the minimum of red lighting. Here were stored thousands and thousands of reels of celluloid new and used film kept in cans and stacked upon rows and rows of wooden racks, a veritable arsonist's dream. The new unexposed film rolls ran to many thousands of feet and the negative rolls, used regularly, were surveys of many areas of Africa, Libya, and of course Egypt these last considered very important indeed. They were also constantly updated with new films being stored with the existing ones.

The i/c duty picket, the main witness, swore that what he said was the truth. The investigating service police could not break his story down or get him to change it in any way either. As he knew I was interested in such things, it was not long before he was prepared to relate, in private, the incident to me.

(Just about everyone knew of the shadowy figure who moved up and down the aisles. He or more correctly it, was never identified because as it never appeared in solid form, no-one could make out its features).

On that night approaching break-time, he was about to pour tea from the flask supplied by the cook-house when he heard a noise. Thinking it was someone breaking early, on looking up, he dropped the flask, utterly petrified. The "figure" who normally only haunted the red areas was in the office! It came towards him and in a weird (his word) voice told him to get everyone out of the building immediately as there was going to be a fire. Then as quickly as it had appeared it vanished!

He recovered himself and screamed out a warning. Incredibly, as soon as the last person was out, the whole place erupted in flames. Composed basically of very dry wood and celluloid, an inferno ensued totally gutting the film-store, destroying the thousands of reels of completed, stored and filed film negatives and the unexposed film too! Within ten minutes only a heap of twisted corrugated iron and ashes indicated where, only a short while earlier, a huge building had stood.

Not allowed cigarettes or matches on fire picket duty and searched prior to entering the place, the cause or blame could not be laid at their door. Besides, the centre of the fire was said to have begun in a locked section to which the pickets had no access. The official verdict was that the blaze was caused by spontaneous combustion in one or more cans in that locked area.

My guess is that the lads concerned will always remember and tell how during one night they were saved from death by a ghost. I also know that they will continue to tell it long, long after they have forgotten the official version! Whatever the cause of the fire, there is no doubt that had the pickets received no timely warning, they all, most definitely, would have perished that night. (See e. of ch. on "evil" spirits.)

One day in Kabrit, I was told to pack my gear and return to Deversoir. On arrival I was summoned yet again (I thought for the moment that I had been tumbled and he knew about my "holiday") and was told I was being sent on a six-weeks course in Cyprus. Metcalfe knew that on returning from Cyprus, I would only have three days back at the section before going home to Blighty to be demobbed! There were many reasons for my not wanting to continue a career in HM forces, but this type of spiteful and irresponsible decision making (another "Asja") was by far the larger part of those.

I knew there would be no point to my objecting and anyway by now he was rambling on about all corporals having to do the course. Then he said that it would do me a lot of good and added the snide that it might even improve my acting and singing! He seemed surprised when I made no attempt to dissuade him but of course he was unaware that my brother, also in the RAF, was stationed at Nicosia where I was to be sent! Course or no course, with six weeks to go I should worry about being sent to Cyprus? Was he kidding - Cyprus after the Canal Zone? With its terrific night life, real billets instead of tents to sleep in? *And* after the slops we had dished up in the Canal Zone good food too? It would almost be like going on leave until I flew back to England for my previously mentioned demob!

Like in the early days of square-bashing, I actually took to this course and came second of forty guys, a few points behind the first placed one, a full (twenty-two year man) career service cop! I had in fact enjoyed it without really trying! I also had a whale of a time with my buddies, my brother, the cabarets and night life. I came away well chuffed, especially as I knew that I had achieved a higher pass mark than any of the other corporals in the photo section back at Deversoir, including Metcalfe's pet "brown-noses".

Even before I had time to unpack, I had to report to you know who! "Well?" He said in his nasal, slightly falsetto voice. Telling him I had passed B1+, the now very familiar, sneering face asked was that the best that I could do? I took enormous delight in pointing out that I had received a higher pass mark than anyone else in the section and had actually achieved second place on the course! Present also was the senior W/O who confirmed this and watching Metcalfe's face going redder and angrier as he turned back to me the old saying, "If looks could kill..." passed through my mind.

After being summarily dismissed I about turned to march out! As I had expected, I of course received no form of acknowledgement or congratulations. At my back he bawled out that I had to get a new uniform (a sort of stand-by punishment since each airman had to pay for his own gear). I did a sort of double-take and before I could open my mouth, he, half-laughing and half-sneering, confirmed that it was not up for discussion.

As usual though, he had not reckoned with my being able to think on my feet. There was *always* someone who had been ordered to get a new one and on leaving his office I rapidly cast about. My enquiries quickly produced a body which in no time at all meant I had struck a deal and a plot was hatched.

We went into action just before I was due to board the aircraft! Excusing myself, using the old "Gyppy tummy" excuse, I made my way to the toilet block where my co-conspirator was already hiding. We changed uniforms while another bod kept watch and then, quick as a flash, I ran across the tarmac. Back in my old one I shot up the step-ladder of the aircraft. At the top I turned, whistled to all and sundry and, as I got their attention, I yelled his name loud and clear. Getting his attention, I obscenely yelled expletives that questioned his parentage and with equal ones warned him never to cross my path in Civvy-street. Finally, giving a very rude two-fingered salute to my tormentor, I laughed really loudly. This was very artificial I might add so that he could clearly hear me. I then stepped into the plane and the doorway was immediately closed. Within a few seconds the aircraft began to taxi out to the runway...

I finished up at Wyton, near Cambridge where I stayed for about ten days or so before the finalising of my papers. It was bitterly cold there in 1954, with ice and snow covering everything and after my experiences in Wiltshire as a kid the only snow I can stomach is either on film or Christmas cards! Another good reason why I now live in Spain!

One night a guy I had become friendly with suggested that we go into Cambridge for a drink. He had a car and agreeing it was a good idea (although a horse drawn sledge would probably have been a better idea with the roads the way they were) off we slid! He had to drive slowly because of the icy conditions; but then, we had nothing to hurry for anyway.

On the main road into town we saw a tail-light some way ahead. Due to the snow making the night a lot lighter than normal, we quickly perceived a motorcyclist. It continued ahead of us for a short while then suddenly, almost as if it had travelled backwards, we were right on top of it! My pal braked to avoid a collision, but due (of course) to the skin of ice on the road he was unable to stop. To our combined dismay and horror we ran into the rear of the 'bike, feeling every bit of the impact and hearing the sound of tearing metal! The tail-light, motor bike and rider had disappeared as we slid to a standstill; we, and saying as much, thought that by now he was under the car.

Fearing the worst, we got out of the car and looked under it, behind it, around it and even on the verges and in the ditches on either side of the road. But although we searched thoroughly, we found not hide nor hair as the saying goes; absolutely zilch! I told him what I thought it was, but, obviously in shock it was lost on him and so I received no reply. Not quite knowing what to do, we noted the exact spot and continued into Cambridge where we reported fully the incident to the police.

For about three days the driver held his breath! Then, visited by the police, we were told that no accident had been reported, that nobody had been treated at the local hospital, nor had anyone been reported missing! Then smilingly, obviously wigging us, they asked if we were sure this had happened *on the way* to the pub and not on the way *from it!* Finally (as indeed we had also previously done more than once) the police officers inspected his car but could see nor find even a scuff-mark on it! When they had gone my friend wryly looked at me saying he had heard me that night and thought, though said nothing, ever since about what I had said. But he continued, up until he had seen it with his own eyes (how often have I heard that said?) he had never believed in ghosts...

Yet I would bet, if he is still in this world, that he often tells of our experience over a pint and most times probably, nobody believes him! Well, if anyone reading this has heard an ex-airman tell that story but did not believe it, I confirm herewith what happened on the road to Cambridge that cold, snowy, icy night...

HELPFUL NOTES!

(On darkrooms and red light) *In those days film-processing rooms were kept in total darkness, except when the processing machines were cleaned or serviced.*

This was a safety rule in case an exposed film had been inadvertently left out of it's can. On the other hand, photo-printing rooms were always in red light and the red end, or more correctly the infra-red end of the psychic spectrum is the "physical" end and this attracts such phenomena. It follows therefore that if the light source is red and or the place is always in darkness, it may well attract phenomenon of a physical kind. These often manifest as voices, noisy bumps and doors and other objects being moved. It also encourages spirit people to appear, either in ethereal (apparition see-through) form or even in a full or partial, materialised state.

(On "evil" spirits.) It is a very rare experience to come across what is generally called an evil entity bent on harming the persons being haunted. In all my years of work in exorcism I have never come across a truly evil entity. Maybe I have been close a few times to the real definition, but the word is often misused in my opinion. In fact the worst scenario I have encountered could at the worst only be termed malevolent in the sense that it bore some grudge against its own kind.

Let me go on with this idea of word misuse for a moment. Appearing more and more in everyday language, I think it is overworked as an adjective, the connotations applied often outweighing the grammatical sense of the word. Indeed one finds it very often used, for example, conversationally by Mr. and Mrs. Average in the throws of a divorce, about their spouse! This surely demonstrates how this word is uttered in a haphazard, that is, throwaway, or random way. In speaking on spirit entities therefore, I defer to more specific use of such words as uneasy, unhelpful, unwanted, undesirable and even perhaps malevolent; but evil?

More usually the so-called evil spirits are simply mischievous, cheeky, angry and or noisy; or indeed all of these, often having some axe to grind concerning ownership of the haunted premises. Sometimes too they are not aware of their discarnate condition and do not realise they are upsetting anyone. Others that are aware often only want (or need) to be noticed and or acknowledged.

Spirit people therefore express their annoyance (or happiness) in various ways but this does not make them necessarily good or evil! Others yet try to warn someone about something that is going to happen (as above) or try to tell them something or to show them where a particular thing is hidden. So we must not, indeed cannot lump all these variables into one heap. Neither should we put them under one heading and I for one cannot, in all honesty, use that word for Spirit. This is because in the vernacular the terminology of it is used too familiarly, thus denying to it its dictionary definition.

Chapter 6
ON THE TAPESTRY OF LIFE EVEN ONE'S TRIVIAL ACTS AND WORDS INTO THE WARP MUST GO!

At Deversoir, due to the looming Suez crisis, we were not allowed to go beyond the camp perimeter, except on official duties. This came as no surprise really since relations with the Arabs in the Canal Zone worsened daily. In consequence I had accumulated three months leave so, once back in Civvy Street, I enjoyed a long, relaxing holiday. That over, I immediately began looking for work.

The National Maritime Museum is situated in Greenwich, London, and it was here, as a photographer, that I began my post service employment. The whole place is crammed full with the most interesting maritime artefacts and paintings. The present building, constructed many years ago, extends on either side of the historically interesting Queen's House.

A main road now separates this and the museum from the majestic and beautiful old buildings that now house the Royal Naval College. Standing virtually Thames-side, on the south bank, the whole area is steeped in history and is where the original grand palace of Placentia stood. Ornate gates at the river's edge open onto the steps and the tie-up point for the royal barge which, in years gone by, was rowed on the Thames, transporting the monarch and his chosen courtiers, etc., on both official business and pleasure trips.

Many historical characters have also lived there or graced it with their presence. To name but a few, Henry VIII and his daughters Anne and Elizabeth rank among the many royals who were actually born there. It holds many dark and royal secrets, too, and is where King Charles entertained Nell Gwynne, the "secret" staircase she used still bearing her name to this day.

Likewise, many of the houses in close proximity to the river that today are split into flatlet properties, not to mention the old pubs and inns, can, as well, boast to their housing and entertaining and turning a blind eye to the goings-on of many an historic mariner of note, including, among others, Lord Nelson. Later, killed at Trafalgar, his body was preserved in brandy, brought back to lie in state in the Painted Hall at Greenwich Naval College and subsequently rowed up river for burial in the State barge of King Charles. Today, also preserved, that too can still be seen, along with his famous ship "Victory", at Portsmouth Dockyard.

Adjoining the buildings on the northside is Greenwich Park, originally forming the gardens and hunting grounds. It is still a royal park, a Crown property and belongs to the estate of Her Majesty Queen Elizabeth II. Kept today in an enclosed paddock are a herd of deer with a breed-line going back many, many years and whose ancestors once roamed all over the park. The herd is coddled and cared for most carefully, for, interestingly, Crown property rights automatically become void if the lineage ever fails to produce a continuum of prodigy.

The Queen's House itself suffered the indignity of being sacked and plundered by Oliver Cromwell during the Roundhead and Cavalier conflict. Much later a part of the palace too was used as a hospital for the wounded from the Battle of Trafalgar. Ceded since and reconstructed on the old site is the world famous Seamans' Hospital. When digging the new larger foundations area skeletons found by the workers were at first thought to be those of plague victims. In fact they were French and English sailors buried side by side after dying from wounds received at Trafalgar. It was simply an expedient way of dis-posing of the bodies quickly.

For many years too, moored up in the Thames just off shore at Greenwich was the infamous "Dreadnought" a cruelly run prison ship. Archaeologists also made public their findings on examining some of the remains. Clearly displaying shackle-irons damage, their conclusions were that prisoners from the ship were also buried on that same hospital site.

Later again (prior museum) the buildings were converted into a hard-life, very heavy-handed disciplined "training school for bad lads" (intentional quotes, see below re Chaplin) who, whether they wanted it or not, were destined for a long spell in the Royal Navy. A mock-up of a ship together with full rigging stood in the grounds.

Old photographs held in the museum archives clearly show very young boys in the rigging, as much as sixty feet above the ground. Worse, reports of the activities of the time confirm a common punishment! Boys were often made to stand at attention for very long periods on those lofty cross-spars and some paid the final account, actually falling to their "accidental" deaths!

At a very tender age, Charlie Chaplin's elder brother Sidney served at sea in exactly this manner, whilst Charlie was sent to the work-house, considered too young for the alternative. These however, were not bad boys; neither was it considered a punishment in any way. It was more, like the previously mentioned burials, a matter of expediency, simply the easiest way of dealing with cases such as theirs. Their mother, a very eccentric and depressive woman (to put it politely) was never able to work and was considered, even in those days, unfit to care for them. Since at that time nobody ever adopted poor kids, it was thought by the powers that be that the alternative was a better solution than starvation.

Considering the history of the place, it naturally follows that there were tales of apparitions and ghostly footsteps, etc. These were especially noted by the security guards; but then, it was these who mostly walked the corridors, often alone, throughout the night! Yet during working hours I was often alone in remote, dingy places, photographing something or other.

Outside of work-time too, I would very often be quite alone in the locked darkroom. This was habit, simply a normal precautionary measure against anyone inadvertently opening the door and ruining one's work. And you will recall what I said earlier about photo sections, a darkroom is dark, very dark *far more so than the blackest of nights!* However, for myself, I confess to neither feeling, sensing, or seeing anything of a psychic nature whatsoever in the photo section or anywhere else!

As a working medium, one might think that in such an atmosphere I *must have* encountered some sort of phenomenon but several things stood in the way of any investigation. The first and foremost was that I needed the job and everyone joining the Civil Service is, to begin with, on probation. Another was that the Executive Officer, an ardent Baptist, had heard early on about my interests and these did not sit well with him. Consequently he made it quite clear that though I could do as I wished outside, within the precincts of the museum or college *he* was the authority. Further if he heard that I even spoke openly about my mediumship, I could expect to be immediately dismissed. (So much for the tolerance of one religion for another!) However, as a natural medium, I am somewhat like a shop insofar as I can open and close my door at will, so that was that - no problem! (See e. of ch. on entity interference and "wavelengths" of mediums.)

The museum job was only a means to an end financially for I still hankered after a career in show business and to this end I attended a few auditions but without success. Of course, we all know that with hindsight it is usually easy to see the reasons for our failings and it was not long before I realised mine. The thing was one *had* to be hungry and determined to succeed in that business (read Michael Caine's autobiography and you will see my point) but I was never really either. In reality, therefore, I did not stand a chance!

I was never rich, but money was never a problem either, for as well as having no dependants, I always had a decent job. In fact I left the museum and became the first person to start taking photographs of houses for estate agents. But it took me no time at all to realise that they had a much better standard of living than I. Conclusion? Of course if you cannot beat 'em, join 'em and I rapidly became a very poorly paid trainee negotiator in a busy office in Norbury.

I was no monkey however, so I knew that I could not survive on peanuts! Obviously in order to earn good money and promotion, one has to learn fast and be seen to be proficient. In eight short months I did just that and as a result I was made manager, much to the chagrin of the other members of staff, of the new office the company opened in Mitcham, Surrey.

I quickly went from strength to strength and within two years, a wiz-kid at selling houses, I moved on and became a snag man. My job brief was to take control of a run down office and build it rapidly into a paying one, when it would be sold on. This paid extremely well but instead of investing in property, which with hindsight is what I should have done, my cash went out just as quickly. I worked very long and hard for it so I felt I deserved to enjoy my off duty times. But in reality such is the thinking of fools of any age and gender!

After eleven years, with no holidays, but earning very well, the speculators in refurbished property were becoming more and more greedy. Shabby property was simply "tarted up" with the cracks simply "papered over" then sold by giving bribes to building society surveyors to pass the property for mortgage. In this my staff and I were expected to con young and old alike out of their hard earned cash.

I was no saint and did not mind the falsifying of the books by my bosses for other greedy estate agents to take over an office but to con young married couples and first time buyers was not my bag. So I set up in the estate business myself in a very exclusive way, selling just two properties a week. In this, as sole agent (the only way I worked) I was able to take the cream of both properties and buyers and by only having just two to concentrate upon each week, I achieved the sales usually within that time.

I had sold my "first-buyer house" and bought a big semi with seven double bedrooms. This I speedily converted into three flats in which I lived and rented accordingly. Later still I bought my father's shop and premises. With the rents I was receiving and the improvements I made, the takings in the shop sky-rocketing, and still selling on average two up-market quality properties a week, I did very well indeed. My mediumship too easily slotted in although of course in those days it was a labour of love for one often earned even less than the proverbial peanuts!

Even so, I still ducked in, out and around show business, doing something here, something else there. Mostly I worked back-stage, but I also appeared before the footlights too doing various bits and bobs, none of which, I hasten to add, are exactly worthy of mention here. I think I also knew, though at the time I was not ready to admit it, that my long term destiny lay in mediumship. As such I quickly realised and *knew* that demonstrating publicly would be as close as I was going to get to show-business!

N.B. In spite of what other mediums may tell you I *know* that if your helpers *are* controlling you, ("they made me work, you know dear") your best will not be forthcoming! It is a reciprocal arrangement. We should work *with* not *use* one another.. I must therefore stress that that my door-keeper and helpers had made it clear that although they would like it, in the event the choice either way was mine so there was no pressure from that direction. And always since it has been that non encroachment, freedom of decision way too!

During an early flirtation with show-biz, (I was doing a couple of cabaret spots in a run down west-end night club) as I recall about 1955, I went one evening to another small church in Lewisham called The Sanctuary. Had I not known better, I would have thought I had stumbled upon a film set! The lighting, dramatically sombre, complemented the all-around dirge-type music. The speakers obviously concealed, no doubt for extra effect, paid off, for coming as it did from "nowhere" it added a somewhat extra dimension to the atmosphere.

Soon, just as dramatically, through the drapes appeared a facsimile of Isadora Duncan (except that this one was well into her seventies) attired in flowing muslin. The equally eccentric looking and aged congregation quieted. On enquiring of the skinny old girl next to me as to what was supposed to happen, she "hushed" me, saying, as my eyebrows involuntarily raised, that the medium required absolute silence while "conjuring up the spirits" (her words not mine).

Tempted to comment that the music, which, although much brighter, was now also very loud and surely more than compensated for my whispered question, my discretion nevertheless prevailed. Suddenly "Isadora" flopped down onto a chair and the music was cut off in its prime! Nudged in the ribs by a bony elbow, the lady next to me whispered out of the corner of her mouth that the medium was now in a trance and it was all right to talk, but only in a whisper.

At this point I confess to thinking about leaving this obviously fraudulent or artificial and amateur attempt at talking to Spirit. Fearing however, my going might cause me trouble with the believers and simultaneously finding my natural curiosity aroused, I thought better of it, deciding to see it through!

The entranced medium said she wanted to speak to the young person. Here we go I thought, for since everyone was at least forty-odd years older than I, it had to be me! As instructed by bony elbows I whispered in the affirmative. A further dig in the ribs was accompanied by her telling me to speak up so not wishing to go home with bruised ribs, I did. The medium's helper then told me that I wanted to steer my own ship and tread the boards, but the boards would be different to the ones I wanted to tread.

She is way off beam, I thought! She is simply picking up my late services connection and thinks I am going to join the navy but what she is *really seeing* (thought big-head) is stardom for me, arising from my blossoming show-biz career! Boy! Was I ever wrong on that one; but how right she was! (Se e. of ch. on prejudging.)

I managed to get a few more gigs, doing cabaret and even pantomime, but I still got nowhere. They say it is *whom*, not *what* you know! Yet I knew then (and still know now) many people in the business. In consequence, on many occasions during my life I have rubbed shoulders with the best of them and spent many enjoyable hours in their company. However, I have never traded on, nor encroached upon our friendship. I have never looked for a leg up, or even a favour, possibly another reason for only ever being on the periphery of show business.

I have also written (and had published) over the years a number of songs, which same languish in some dark forgotten dungeon somewhere below the publisher's offices. Like a mediaeval, fair virginal maiden awaiting the proverbial white knight to rescue her, my songs too wait longingly, not for a white knight, but for a passing minstrel (pun intended) to release them!

In 1979 I flew to Los Angeles, having been asked to write the music for a film; but this "big break" too came to nothing. I ran into an almighty strike, where virtually all sections of the industry, including trainers and animals, picketed the various studios over some video wrangle or other. It was quite a sight to see trainers walking up and down the streets with lions, tigers, chimps and many other animals on leads. Even stranger still were the placards carried on the backs of the animals demanding their individual animal pay increases and better working conditions!

Although nothing to do with me directly, this dispute resulted in the Musicians Union being far more sensitive than usual. Due to the strike my credentials were scrutinised a little more closely than they might otherwise have been. So my application was vetoed and I was unable to work at all in Hollywood; another brilliant promising career ended before it had hardly begun!

I did work in another way however, demonstrating clairvoyance on several occasions in a Spiritualist Church in Los Angeles. With Zarlu's help to the fore, I also carried through a successful exorcism on a lady who was possessed by a not very helpful entity. Thanked by the president of the church on the following Sunday, I then demonstrated clairvoyance for about an hour and a half.

In Spain, too, I have been very involved in the theatre, but far more often with amateurs than professionals. Producing, directing, stage-managing and writing various things, I wrote an original story, a fantasy tale called "The Magic Tree" and presented it as an English pantomime. I also composed all of the songs, including music and lyrics. I have also stage-managed quite a few charity shows, both professional and amateur, at the famous Benidorm Palace, which boasts the largest stage in Europe.

Interestingly, I had thought I would take a short rest from my mediumship about the middle of December 1996. As I have said before, God and Spirit really do move in strange ways. For late in December, right out of the blue, I was asked to appear in a German production filmed in and around Benidorm. It is a sort of black comedy, a film called "Go For Gold" and was released in May '97. So I can now claim to having a cast list credit on a full length feature film as well but more, I can also add the experience to my list of unusual happenings in my life.

It was also really interesting to see how things have moved on since I was last on a film set. For example, the film was on a very low budget so it was a real advantage to have instant video play-back. A video camera is attached to the film camera and when a take is done, having the same line of sight, it copies exactly what is filmed. It can then be viewed immediately on a video screen to see if it is OK or not, thereby saving time, daylight and film.

So to end this little narrative, I did get my rest as Spirit put the 'phone in limbo for two weeks. Nobody called, at least not for a reading anyway! I also received far more money from the film job than I would have done for my psychic work. So I was more than compensated, ending up with a sort of extra Christmas box from Spirit and more money in the bank than I expected to have!

Such things as the foregoing film bit apart, some things are *not* meant to be. Realising, knowing and accepting that is half the battle of working through our incarnations. Just the same, I am still stage-struck even today and still sing my share of songs in some of the many bars in and around Benidorm. Whilst knowing if the opportunity came along I would still flirt with show-biz, I also knew for certain *years ago* that, much as I would have loved it, I was never going to be a star or even professionally in the business, *per se*! Nevertheless, I've still had my moments! But that's life! Or as the Spanish say - ¡Es la vida! (See end of chapter on TV shows, etc.)

Nevertheless I have still had my share of "fame" within the psychic realm (something I am still enjoying even today), having clocked to date in excess of fifty years of serving Spiritualism, both privately and publicly. I also had more than thirty years of rostrum work all over the UK and eight other countries. I admit to revelling and bathing in the glory of more than my share of column inches, too (who among us does not enjoy praise?) in both the popular and the psychic press and I thank those concerned for acknowledging my work.

At my peak too, for what it is worth (though do not misunderstand me, the accolade was very pleasing) many church presidents and the like rated me as being among the top ten all-round mediums in Britain. Interestingly too, for many years there were only three mediums in the UK demonstrating transfiguration to public audiences: Queenie Nixon, George McAllister and myself. And, unless anyone else has done it since (in which case I hereby apologise for not knowing) I am also the only medium to have demonstrated clairvoyance at the famous Speakers' corner in Hyde Park, London for a marathon three hours!

I also recall being in the offices of "Psychic News" one day speaking to Roy Stemman who was, at the time, a staff reporter there. (He now owns, edits and publishes the very popular world-wide magazine, "Reincarnation International" and is a several- times published author.) He introduced me to Maurice Barbanell (the medium for "Silver Birch") and late editor of PN. He mentioned that he had heard that I was the young medium who could *do it all!* Knowing how barbed "Barbie" could be, I was unsure of his motive on that comment! In deference to him therefore, I like to think of it as a compliment, albeit maybe, somewhat backhanded! So in replying I said well, not really, but I will keep on trying and learning, to which he replied: "Well, you couldn't do, or say, better than that!"

In the early sixties, for various reasons, one of which was a divorce, I sold my house in Thornton Heath, near Croydon in Surrey. By taking on an even heftier mortgage than before, I subsequently purchased the previously mentioned large, seven double-bedroom semi-detached property situate in Beckenham, Kent. I intended the rents received from the flats to help towards other expenses I expected to incur when eventually, as was my ambition, I would one day set up and open my own teaching centre somewhere.

It was in Beckenham in about January 1967 that the Manna Group (see Part III) first manifested through me. Hitherto they had always instructed me in sleep state but on this night, trancing me, they spoke at length about their work and of what they hoped to achieve with their united thought-force-energy. This was the first of many rewarding and very philosophical face to face sessions with them.

(Interestingly, an incident occurred just recently when these wonderful souls shone forth. Up until I went to the ISF congress in 1996 the Manna had always only addressed those they termed soul-members of the group. In a quiet moment in my room one day they stated that the time had come to expand. They wished to widen their horizons and explained that their main reason was that we were not getting to enough people.

Subsequently, I held a private group in my room and one lady was told that she was a member of the Manna Group, something of which she had been told some twenty-five years previously. Afterwards she spoke of how all those years ago a very famous male medium had said that she was a member of a very special soul group and one day she would know their identity. True, Spirit was a long time coming forward, but far more in evidence was Spirit's subtle move, *for she was the only one unknown to me* among the four persons they had asked me to invite!)

From then on, each week, they controlled me in an after circle-time period. They would give advice, lecture on any suggested topic, both philosophical and otherwise and answer questions of all kinds. It was during one such session that they also stated that I was to get married soon and that my wife would be a circle member. At the time several members had to be absent for a while and there were only six of us left sitting.

A few weeks before receiving this cryptic message I had brought a budding healer I knew into the circle. Treated no differently from anyone else and giving her absolutely no personal encouragement nor reasons to think otherwise, it became painfully obvious, not to put to fine a point on it, that she was determined to get my attention. In deference to her I said nothing to the others but although I made it very clear to "J" telling her point blank that I was not the slightest bit interested, she persisted!

Since they could not have failed to notice, the other members, naturally, enjoyed the game, doing nothing to help with their innuendo and cheeky comments! The trouble was that they put two and two together and made six! So of course there was much speculation, much of which went unsaid I might add, and "J" seemed very pleased with herself! However, I still felt nothing more than friendship for her so my reaction to the message, since I had been making sure that we were never alone, was somewhat apprehensive! But as you read on, it will be seen that I did not even know my future spouse then! So relating an anecdote here, I think is not only relevant, but also worthy of the space.

About three weeks after the Manna Group message, on our circle night "J" brought a half-dozen roses. She had originally wanted the two half a dozen bunches that were left, but apparently there was little to choose between who arrived first, her or another customer. So the vendor suggested that, to be fair, he should let them have one bunch each. This was agreed and they paid and went their separate ways.

She kept laying it on a bit thick about the love in the circle and that it must have been meant because there was one for each of us in the circle that night. I then mentioned that we had an extra person that evening and thought it would be better just to put the flowers in a vase and say nothing. I went to fetch one from the kitchen and returning, I put the six flowers in it, so I can confirm that there were only six! But I run ahead of myself...

In the last few days of May 1967 I visited my brother Jack (the one who could have been a good medium) to give some healing to my sister-in-law. During the session he asked if I would visit a friend of theirs who had suffered for some time with phlebitis. I readily agreed and on arrival at the flat Patricia answered the door. Introductions were rapidly dispensed with and during the time I was there hardly a word passed between us. Yu Sin controlled and we had one of those magical healing sessions; the swelling around the knees went down under his hands and the friend had no further trouble for the rest of her life!

We must have made an impression upon one another though because during the next two weeks, after just *three half-hour chats* in my car, we married and I reckon that has to be some kind of a record! After all, not many folk, without even going out on a date and spending a total of only one and a half hours together, get married! And further, that they were still going strong after twenty-five years! N.B. That last sentence is in the past tense, for once again I am solo!!

It was therefore with more than a little satisfaction that in early June (the night of the flowers) Patricia, having been upstairs getting ready, was presented to them. Somewhat smugly, I admit, I then went on to say that, having obtained a licence, we were quietly married a few days previously at the local Registry Office, Bromley, Kent.

Three things happened; they were all gob-smacked and "J" left the circle that night. Far more exciting though was the third for during the physical part of our circle, one of the medium's helpers, a child called Jimmy, controlled. He joked, saying that he knew there was a new lady coming which of itself of course is not particularly significant. But then he went on, saying that he had pinched one of the other lady's flowers, so now there really was one for each of us! Nobody had mentioned the flowers prior to this, nor I think, in the matter of Patricia's entrance had they even noticed them, so there was the usual comments of not understanding. "J" somewhat grudgingly explained about bringing the roses!

After the circle we discovered not six but seven roses, the seventh, looking out of place to the rest, hanging half-out of the vase! (I have always hoped that the lady who found she only had five did not blame the flower man for selling her short!) (See e. of ch. on considering apports.)

A footnote here is also interesting. We had both been divorced for some six years before we met and five years earlier Patricia had had a reading with Joe Benjamin. A very good friend of mine, he told her that she would marry a medical man in a white coat. A bus conductress at the time, after the message she had scrutinised her passengers far more closely, looking for a guy who might be a doctor. In her enthusiasm she had not of course realised that most of these possessed cars and did not use public transport anyway!

His message was virtually forgotten by the time we met and having bought the shop premises (mentioned earlier) some three years previously, I had though not *owned* it when she had received the message! I had mentioned the shop and that I was an estate agent but in assuming that it was my office, she did not realise it was of course the drug-stores, the one my parents had previously rented.

Whenever I was there, to protect my clothes, I wore a white coat both in the shop and the stock rooms! Also, like the other healers working with me, I wore one during public healing sessions! Sadly, having made his transition and no longer demonstrating (although knowing him he is probably working through another medium somewhere) I think that Joe, God bless him, as was so often the case, was right on the ball what with his medical link, i.e. the shop and my healing work. Patricia, on the other hand, like so many recipients did not make any connection for quite a long time with the message and me even after we met (even though I wore a white coat to do the healing on her friend.) (See end of chapter on qualifying messages received)

Still gnawing at me was the desire and need to open a centre of the kind I had for so long envisaged for I had been acutely aware that for many years in Spiritualism there existed a hiatus; even worse, in most areas, a yawning chasm! There were then very few, if any, *actual*, totally non-denominational *teaching centres* that concentrated *solely* on the development of psychic, mediumistic, healing and spiritual knowledge!

Of course, throughout the UK there had been Spiritualist church affiliations and or memberships for many decades and, to a lesser extent, there still are even to-day. To be expected, these took their lead and instructions from such societies as The S.N.U.,The G.W.C. Sp. Assoc. and The S.A.G.B. Unfortunately, their founders however were heavily biased towards one or another of the Christian orthodox credos. In so doing whilst they automatically established the churches, they ignored the fact that Spiritualism is a truly non-denominational religion, embracing all shades of belief. This meant the appearance of the cross and other Christian religionist accoutrements on the platforms. More importantly however, it also meant the automatic exclusion of many who might otherwise have become involved! Thus their churches were built on sand... but more on this in Part Two.

So it happened that on one circle night The Manna Group asked that we delay no longer and open the centre in our home. They also suggested the name and by August 1967, with Patricia's help, I had, up and running, a pretty successful teaching centre by transforming (with a floating helper's assistance, it has to be said) our lounge. By building a rostrum, lectern and installing chairs, not to mention flowers, etc. into an attractive sanctuary, we found that we could seat forty or so. Somewhat surprised but delighted also, we were, from the word go, full to capacity most nights.

Kindred psychic and spiritual souls and others of all shades of opinion and beliefs were welcomed. We had demonstrations by mental and physical mediums, tarot card readers, palmists and astrologers; psychologists, doctors, magicians and mentalists; agnostics, sceptics, the curious and the out and out anti-brigade too! All were invited to ride their favourite hobby-horse and to demonstrate or speak on their chosen theme if they so desired.

Given an open platform, every speaker was paid their fee before the meeting began. I would tell them, and particularly in the case of demonstrators, not to feel obliged that they had to deliver the goods! Told that if they felt there was nothing there or they felt off, for whatever reason, it was better to say so and to close their session. Politely told that none of us are indispensable and anyway if such a thing occurred and it was found necessary, we could always have a follow-on discussion or whatever.

However, they were assured that should they not concede their lack of ability at the time, then problems could arise. The audience would rapidly become aware of the speaker's dilemma and would not be fooled or hoodwinked! They would quickly become bored and someone would challenge their words long before questions were invited! This advice was always received as it was given, kindly and in good faith and I am happy to report that rarely were the speakers at a loss, the meetings generally fairly buzzed along!

Indeed, almost always, catching the atmosphere generated, the speakers stirred up enormous interest and in-depth discussion, which of course was the whole point of the exercise. Bred from the knowing of my own innate desire to seek and receive knowledge, I strenuously cultivated these attitudes. It was therefore gratifying to see both speakers and audience gorging upon one another's ideas and thoughts, each in their differing ways, leading as it did to others and their own self-awareness.

I confess too to being delighted that the plan was working in that minds were being stimulated into new ideas, new thoughts and thinking. But most pleasing of all were the expressions of appreciation by everyone alike in knowing that they could say, without fear, favour, rancour or embarrassment exactly what they thought and felt.

With some regrets we closed the centre in December 1968 when the Manna told the circle, my wife and myself that our next step, should we wish to take it, was for us to move to Paignton in Devon. Regretfully, we had to close the circle too but each was charged with the responsibility of carrying on their own search. Addressing them all, the spirit equivalent of myself, the circle leader, Hussan, speaking through me, placed on record that they too were now equipped, should they so desire, to run their own circles, either individually or in concert. Be acutely aware too, he urged of Spirits' blessings and the need to spread the teachings that they had received.

Up until I had married again I had never much worried or bothered too much about money. But this changed when Patricia became pregnant and at the same time the council decided on a rapid compulsory purchase and slum clearance scheme. Within four months or so they had bulldozed some five thousand houses around our parade of shops. Then the J. Stone & Co. factory let me down for a second time! Employing some three thousand staff, many of whom were my customers, they also closed. It looked a little like the recce-photos I had seen of Hiroshima with everything, in all directions, as far as the eye could see, flattened around the shopping parade!

Under normal circumstances this would have been a total disaster but it was not anything like as bad as it might have been. The fact was that I had earned a great deal of money in commissions in my last estate office job and my ex-boss, to his credit, honoured to the last penny all the terms of our agreement. So I was still receiving, some three years or so later, after tax, over two hundred and fifty pounds a month! This was bunce to me; I did not need it so it went straight into building societies and various bank accounts, providing me with sufficient "rainy day money" for months to come.

With no customers and no hope of them for some years, the only option open to me was to close the shop and sue the council for "Right to Purchase". (This took more than three years of hassle and I received the cheque almost four years later in Paignton. The money I eventually received though was disgustingly paltry in comparison to the intrinsic value of the property!) I put my ex-shop staff, glad of a keeping a job, on a couple of stalls in the local market and that, together with the odd sale of property and the rents from my flats kept body and soul together without having to touch my savings.

I completed the purchase of a guest-house on the twenty-third of December 1968 when, together with my wife and our three months old daughter, Dawn, we moved to Paignton. The next evening, Christmas Eve, I was telephoned, when a young man begged me to call on him as he and his companions were scared out of their wits. Not expecting to be away very long and considered a mission of mercy, I went immediately expecting to carry out a fairly tame exorcism. But this particular entity was most obnoxious and obstinate which required my staying at the house all night. I will not relate it here in full, but will, in passing, mention that curtains were destroyed, furniture was thrown about and broken and beds were tipped up. Once again it was phenomena triggered by "playing" with an ouija board!

So there I was ensconced in a large guest house with a very much larger mortgage together with a wife and a baby daughter just a few months old! This required different attitudes and perspectives regarding finances for I needed to earn money, and quickly! In fact the guest house was very successful, but since we had only bought it as a means to an end, we sold it after two seasons.

(Early in 1969, a concerted effort was made by certain sections of the church membership to vote me into the presidency of the local church. I began to think that this was why we had moved there but something always seemed to get in the way. Eventually, mainly due to the church politics, I realised this "club" too was not for me and I declined to take it further.)

I had always wanted to get into the hair health and beauty trade, with particular emphasis on healing, so we bought a four-bedroom house and opened it as a healing centre. Already a practising clinical hypnotherapist, a qualified acupuncturist, an osteopathic manipulator and masseur, I trained Patricia as a masseuse. She also became the leading Avon rep. in the south west of England and a trained beautician. We both trained as nail sculpture artists and I established the "Fingertips" logo but did not register it as a trademark. Other nail studios, liking the catchy name, took it on and it can now be seen all over UK!

Eventually, it was necessary to extend the premises and so, with "floating helpers" working overtime, I drew up the plans, employed contractors and supervised all of the construction. I also personally installed all the plumbing and electrics resulting in "Serenity House" ending up as a ten room property!

About two years later, during a weekend, a couple of workmen and I installed the hairdressing salon. Out went the sauna suite and while a couple of guys knocked out walls and made good, I once again installed the necessary extensive plumbing and electrics. It was ready by the Monday morning and officially opened with the traditional champagne flowing!

Although I never qualified as a hairdresser, when I added the hair salon in the seventies, simply because I wanted to learn, I took a course on hair colouring and permanent waving and actually hold diplomas in both. (From then on until we separated in 1992 I always did Patricia's perms and hair colour, often changing the colour from week to week!)

We worked for some ten hours a day including me doing the books and Patricia washing some sixty plus towels each night. We also had sun-beds and most folk could only come outside of normal working hours. It was this continued effort spanning about nineteen years and not simply luck, as many folk think when one makes a bit of money, that resulted in our being able to semi-retire to Spain in 1987.

(In Spain, too, though nothing like as hard or long, I carried on working, renovating each house we bought, selling at a good profit. I also earned extra money playing keyboards for two years in the Torrevieja area. With very few musicians there one was the proverbial big fish. But I do not play that well, having taught myself. So for the contra reason, that really good musicians are small fry in Benidorm, there is no way that I would ever play in this area in public.)

Besides this busy schedule each weekday in Paignton, almost always at weekends I was demonstrating somewhere the length and breadth of the country; between times often carrying out exorcisms in South Devon and other areas. There was therefore no time anyway to have been of use as the church president, my on-going psychic quest, my serving of churches and business leaving very little time for anything else.

I mentioned before that spirit friends sometimes nudge their mediums in the right direction. The main reason for this is that the door-keeper is (most of the time) more aware of the next step his charge should be taking, and this long before he or she even dreams about it, let alone considers or takes it!

I have said too that mediums do not become wealthy, in the accepted sense, from their work and I now know why we left Beckenham. Spending a large part of my nest egg in setting up and running the "Oasis of Psychic, Mediumistic, Healing and Spiritual Development" meant that we would never have earned sufficient to enable our migration to Spain to take place, let alone be successful. So in moving to Paignton, stuck with having to make ends meet, it made me take a different view to the altruistic one I had previously held, i.e. that money was not that important.

So for those of you taking that view and thinking of mediumship as your main earner, read carefully these words. You should not do so, for altruism alone will not fill your belly, clothe you or put a roof over your head. You must have an alterna-tive form of income, a second string to your mediumstic bow. Also you will in time have to accept and realise that in the real world, the man-made materialistic one, you cannot buy anything without money.

So although it is true to say that things for me, from the psychic and mediumistic standpoint have been very rewarding, in my experience, simply depending on mediumship as income will not see the *pennies* rolling in, never mind the pounds! It also places a burden on one's talents, often requiring a medium to work far longer than they should. This too may well be one of the main reasons why so many of them burn out or even make their transition at an early age.

As it transpired, I also know now that Spirit never intended that I should be president of Paignton church; we had moved there for a totally different reason! Since being in Spain, during the considering and preparing of this manuscript, together with the value of hindsight, I have come to realise that Manna, my door-keeper and helpers moved me to Paignton simply as a stepping-stone. It was initi-ated so that we would be able to have sufficient money to move to Spain in 1987, where I went into retreat, mediumistically speaking, in order to gain even more knowledge.

Since "opening up" again I no longer have the time to appear in, or to stage manage shows but I still pop out to venues in around Benidorm, albeit less fre-quently, to sing a few songs. Each week for an hour I have my own local radio show which is unscripted, and, thankfully, uncensored too! As resident psychic, I demonstrate clairvoyance over a 'phone link and also give talks on a different as-pects of psychic and mediumstic matters and answer questions on spiritual phi-losophy and such.

I also demonstrate clairvoyance publicly, hold seminars, run two circles and still undertake daily, my private sittings work. (though I never work in the daytime mediumistically when I have evening work to do.) I also have a column each week in two newspapers here on the Costa Blanca and Costa Del Sol and in between I write for "Psychic World", "Psychic News" and "Reincarnation International". Other than that I do nothing really!

I ceased my public work around 1982, when, in the New Forest, on my way to Gosport Spiritualist Church, I wrote off a new car, which same incidentally, my wife had never seen! I telephoned the secretary at Gosport to tell her what had happened and, offering my apologies I told her that there was no way, short of walking, that I would be able to make the week-end date. In any event I told her, I was a bit down and just wanted to get back home to be with my wife and daughter.

Then, sadly and typical of some church officers, she was off and running! Not how are you? Nothing said about injuries I may or may not have had. (I had none as it happened.) No, it was all about what was she supposed to do with well over a hundred people (I had stipulated on booking a *maximum* of one hundred) coming from all over and who had booked for the transfiguration? Did I realise the inconvenience this would cause and how was she going to get in touch with them, etc.? I began to tell her thanks for asking how I was, when she interjected that this was terribly bad of me letting them down at the last minute like this. (Sorry, I deliberately wrote off a car just so that I could let you all down!) Continuing next came the veiled threat that she was not sure whether the committee would want to book me again.

At about this point, my mental "Dr. Jeckyl" had taken the medicine and"Mr. Hyde" was about to speak, but the good doctor prevailed. As she ranted on I quietly, yet purposefully, replaced the receiver, totally disgusted with her attitude. After all she was a person representing her church as one of its elected officers! As I turned and walked away from the kiosk, a thought emerged, then kept returning. It was that if Spiritualists' learning and tolerance had only reached thus far, it just wasn't worth the travel or the worry any more. I shall comment further on "attitudes" of church officers later on, when I write about payments to mediums, etc.

Unable to get home that night, I managed to put up in an old inn and during the night I spoke with Tuan who understood my disappointment and disgust. He advised me to suspend my public work until the time was right to return. Interestingly too, many times in the past people had commented, by way of compliment, that I seemed to be twenty years ahead of my time in the way I presented my meetings and in particular, the addresses I gave. Strangely, the same sort of thing had been said by the presidents of the churches at the last three weekends I had worked prior to the accident. These were, respectively, Laurie Sayers of Portsmouth, Bob Cherry of Enfield then later Paignton and the Leicester Pres. who's name I cannot recall. (The irony of it is that it was also getting on for twenty years before I *restarted* public work!)

In passing, I would add that to get back to my home in Paignton, even though it was only a mere hundred miles or so, I spent a whole day zigzagging up and down the country on various buses and trains, so I could never have made it to Gosport in time anyway! I don't know whether the routes and so on have improved over the years, but in those days it was virtually impossible to travel *across* the country by public transport; routes only traversed North to South and visa-versa.

Though no longer publicly demonstrating, I still did groups and private work up until I left UK. I was also involved quite frequently in a goodly number of haunted premises, dealing with unwanted entities (or "ghost chasing" as it now called) all over South Devon and other areas of England. As already mentioned church officers and their mediums, stating that they did not possess sufficiently strong powers, recommended me, who, they said, most certainly did! This, since I was no longer officially one of them, was actually quite complimentary. It proves, I think, that whatever their reasons they still had enough confidence in me to tell folk to call me. This leads me to conclude that I must have made some impression upon some of them after all.

The Spanish too have their share of haunted premises and recently I have attended on quite a few of these with very successful results. I can report therefore that over those "lost years" I have, although being out of the lime-light publicly, still carried on my work with a creditable number of exorcisms, private and group activities *and* continually pursued my search for spiritual knowledge with those loftier soul-mind forces who are accessible to all sincere seekers.

Footnote! Being required to do the final revision on this book prior to publication I am delighted to be able to report that in November '97, I re-established the Oasis of Psychic, Mediumistic, Healing and Spiritual Development. We seat about thirty persons in all and to date it is thriving well. If you are holidaying or visiting Spain you will be most welcome to call. (See front of book for address and telephone number.)

HELPFUL NOTES!

(On entity interference and "wavelengths" of mediums.) *In the event Tuan is very powerful and automatically prevents any intrusion by unwanted entity interference in my daily chores. He, my helpers and myself also enjoy ultimate respect for each other, so such intrusion would not occur anyway. We, each of us, keep to our own place until it is desirable and or necessary for us to con-join in our spiritual work.*

Another point worth mentioning is that mediums do not all, automatically, tune in to the same wavelength as the entities who might be around. This is because, personalities being what they are, it is impossible to be compatible with everyone on this or any other plane. I have, on occasions, had to follow up when a medium has been to a haunted premises and has, (a) not been able to link or (b) has been scared out of their wits! Equally, people have sat with me and I have not been able to link with their loved one yet with another medium they have had excellent results and the converse here is also true. So, although I have no doubt that most places are active in some way, it may well lie dormant inasmuch as nobody has opened up the door for it to manifest. Until a contact is made by a person, voluntarily or not, or a séance *is held there, it may stay that way as was the case for me at The National Maritime Museum in Greenwich, London.*

(On prejudging.) *Remember, it takes all sorts! So yes, make challenges, ask questions, sift the evidences given of course, but do not pre-judge as I did. I reiterate! How right she was! The boards I trod were not on glittering stages but platforms, mostly in Spiritualist churches, all over the country, which same I had been already doing and continued to do for the next twenty-five years or so.*

(On TV shows, etc.) *Years ago I was asked several times to demonstrate my talents on TV both with the David Frost Show and on Southwest TV but I never did, simply because they would not let me to work my way, nor allow me any control at all. In deference to Spirit, I may have missed out on my moment or two of TV glory but it really is not that important. What matters more is that I respected and stood on their guidance far more than that of an unenlightened, very sceptical and very juvenile researcher (why are they always so young?) who would invariably say that I had to do it their way. Hence no go, well not for me or my helpers anyway! And I have to say that if other mediums were just as positive, endeavouring to lead rather than be led, we would soon be accepted more readily, and on our terms, by the public and media alike.*

(On considering apports.) *In considering apports (apports and asports are mentioned and explained elsewhere within these pages) it is obvious that apart from those affirmed as being "manufactured" by Spirit, in the main they must come from another place on earth! This then leads us to suppose that they are either "begged, stolen or borrowed" which possibly is the reason for some asports, including some that arrive earlier as apports and then disappear again just as suddenly as they originally appeared!*

(On qualifying messages received) *Joe Benjamin never said it would be a doctor that Patricia would meet! This is just an example of receiving a message and then building on the words spoken at the time. These are often amplified, given a grander or lesser perspective, good or bad respectively. Then assimilated by the recipient they believe and say that that is what they were told! Sadly, human nature being what it is, this is something which is all too familiar with people, including sitters, and another good reason for mediums to tape their readings.*

109

Chapter 7
MAN KNOWS NOTHING WHICH HE HAS NOT ABSOLUTELY EXPERIENCED

Since my "wake-up call" here in Spain I have done readings for most European nationals. The Costas are intrinsically cosmopolitan, adequately demonstrated by the fifty-eight houses in our little urbanisation which alone boasts nine nationalities. Most of these speak English but until comparatively recently the Spanish seemed not to realise that it might be important for them too. English though, now a compulsory subject in every school is resulting in most shops and bars, etc. boasting at least one English speaking native, though often it is the youngest member of staff!

Virtually from the day I stepped off the ferry at Santander I began learning the lingo and now speak it, conversationally at least, quite well. Unbelievably though, many English folk, some of whom have lived in Spain for more than twenty years have just never thought it necessary! But it has proved a boon to me for recently here, mainly via the media, there has been an enormous upsurge of interest in psychic matters. Many adult Spaniards only speak their own language, so, being able to converse in theirs, I can give readings and public meetings for them too.

Also in Spain, as opposed to England for example, it is much more common and a very social thing to visit bars, where people, like me, drink only soft drinks or coffee without being frowned upon by the owner. So although many people frequent them, they are by no means all drinkers in the accepted sense. Also, since there are no village halls as such, demonstrations of clairvoyance have to be held in a functions room attached to the bar, or even in the bar itself!

Thus, when visiting mediums demonstrate it is quite amusing to see their astonishment as they see folk go back and forth to the bar to top up on their spirits, while they are talking to the other kind! Such behaviour, even by us foreigners, is considered quite normal here in Spain and, in its way rather personifies the intrinsic laid back attitudes that abound.

With reference to my *twenty years ahead of my time* comments in the previous chapter, almost without realising it, I began wearing my "public hat" again. It became evident that my helpers had been politely but firmly nudging my thoughts in this direction for some time. I confess that looking back I realise just how much I missed my real work and had really been itching to re-start. However, initially I simply dismissed all thoughts of it, convincing myself that it was just a case of removing the thorn in my side by getting down to writing this book.

This thought had drifted in and out of my thoughts many times since arriving in Spain but I just never seemed to have the time. Then the impression, stuck in a groove, just would not go away so, better late than never, I decided that I ought to take the appropriate action. The truth was, of course, that time was not the issue here; it was good old fashioned *self discipline* that was required. Like many teachers I guess, we often forget to practise what we preach, probably more for convenience than for any other reason. For instance, in the old days, when a circle member said they had no time for this or that, I would tell them that there was a simple solution. *Make time!* Arise earlier in the morning for example, or go to bed a bit later.

At the risk of repeating myself I have to say again that my helpers do not control me! We work together, although sometimes I think they perhaps sneak up on me. Impressing upon me certain things, such as the self-discipline mentioned above, they endeavour to point me in a particular direction. This is effected sometimes without me actually being aware of it. Spirit can, if it is found to be necessary in the wider scope of things, block and or impress one's intuition as required. The appropriate action is taken when, for example, unwanted entities need to be held at bay, or impressions for one's good need to be effected. But this is not encroaching upon the freewill, it is merely giving protection and direction to one's progress.

Simply believing that such and such is *my* idea I go merrily on my way. Oh yeah; who am I kidding? Any good medium will understand that this, in real terms, is a joke, or perhaps, more correctly, an in-joke! For instance, my "wake-up call" might have appeared to have come about by what seems like a coincidence but I *know better.* I have often quoted Tuan's words on this who says: "Coincidence is when God (Spirit) takes a hand but prefers to stay anonymous!" Nevertheless, since under normal circumstances Spirit cannot impose upon our freewill, the choice of pursuing a certain impression or not is of course still our own to make and act upon or not, as the case may be.

Friends I had known here in Spain for a number of years had never disclosed their interest or belief in psychic phenomena of any kind, a common thing among LAD (life after death) believers, fearing ridicule or worse from those with whom they come into contact.

One morning I was in a small bar drinking a cup of coffee. Although I was minding my own business, I could not fail to hear the conversation of the group of people at the next table. A lady was saying that another one, who had popped off to the loo (as it turned out later for a cry) wanted very much to get in touch with her husband, recently passed over, as she was missing him terribly.

A comment was made as to whether or not one should dabble in the unknown and this led to a general discussion. Imagine my surprise when someone else said that *my* friends were great believers and nobody could say that their feet were not firmly on the ground. Then his wife joked that they were probably more stable than most folk, including her husband and herself! She added, for good measure I guess, that the lady could do a lot worse than to speak to them for if they could not help they possibly knew someone who could.

At this juncture, totally out of character, I, who normally hate "flag-wavers", could not help putting in my two pennyworth and, disclosing that I was psychic and a medium of many years standing, I said that perhaps, although I did not know the lady, I might be able to help. I said I would also mention her to our mutual friends when perhaps a sitting might be arranged. Then, before the lady in question had returned to the company, I left, leaving them with my name and telephone number.

Until then, discussions on and sojourns into the "other world" had, for a long time been between my door-keeper, the teaching guides, my helpers and myself. I was on a sort of sabbatical, although perhaps retreat would be a better word but soon I was about to go into "attack mode" and be thrust into the vanguard again.. (See end of chapter, on being aware, etc.)

Shortly after me talking in the bar and before I had time to speak to the interested friends, I was invited to a party. I had stage-managed a show at Benidorm Palace and the presenters had invited everyone involved as a way of saying thank you.

A German lady introduced herself and after a short time, out of the blue, she talked of her visit to a clairvoyant whom she had said feared for her daughter's safety. (*So why tell me?* Well, dear reader, if you have been paying attention, you will quickly recognise it as a little shove, a signal from the good 'ol boys (my helpers) who wanted me to get back to work, and quickly.)

The "clairvoyant" (intentional quotes) had warned her that her daughter could be taken into white slavery! I asked her where this was and, upon her naming the village, I knew who she was speaking about. I did not however disclose the fact there and then that I considered her to be no more than a charlatan who cleverly used the old stock reading con so dear to my Aunt Millie. Without realising it at the time, she had disclosed to her what she thought might happen to her daughter, etc. Cunningly, her worst fears were simply "confirmed" by the "clairvoyant" who "saw it all in the cards, me dear"!

This was too much of a challenge for my crew, and, realising this was another nudge, I told her that whatever she had received, rest assured it most definitely was *not* clairvoyance! Upon her enquiring then what *was* clairvoyance, I tuned in. Her grandfather linked saying that he had committed suicide in a bird cage! Unable to look after them or himself any longer he had sealed his aviary and gassed both the birds and himself.

With him was her father who told her that he was aware that she could not get back to Germany in time for his own funeral. He also said that she was to stop feeling guilty about this or anything else that had been said by her siblings and mother; she was to put her mind at rest and look forward not back. He then spoke about her daughter saying that she was in no danger whatsoever! She would shortly leave the digs she was in as her friends, the ones who were supposed to be arranging for her kidnapping, were returning to the UK. She however would stay in Spain, move into *her* house *but not be with her* so there was no need to worry.

Utterly flabbergasted, she said she could hardly believe what I, a stranger had told her and had she known me, she would have thought I knew these facts. I responded by reminding her that I had also asked nothing to which she retorted then what was the trick? It is not a trick I protested, it is simply genuine clairvoyance! I added too that unlike her "false prophet" I did not have to use tricks. She went on to confirm that what was said about her grandfather and father was absolutely true. She *had* fretted, feeling guilty about her father's funeral. She was a bit nonplussed about her daughter moving into her house, yet not being with her though. However, shrugging it off she said she had to think that was also correct.

It transpired that, although seeming strange at the time, Spirit was right on the button! Owning *two* houses her tenants, on a long-term unbreakable contract, suddenly did a moonlight flit. (Just prior to this her daughter was asked to move from her friends' place as they were returning to England.) Convenient for all concerned and being so accurately evidential too, it all slotted in quite nicely.

As a direct result of this short message, obviously very impressed and somewhat intrigued, she arranged for me to take a group sitting. My helpers, throwing me in at the deep end, as indeed they had at the very beginning of my career, set before me a mixed bag comprising German, Dutch, Spanish, Italian Norwegian and English sitters, the English ones being the friends aforementioned, one of whom, thank God, turned out to be a natural "powerhouse".

The evening was a complete success with a well blended mix of evidence and humour but more importantly for me, coming back after so long, was the feedback. Apparently the consensus was that a most uplifting, evidential and enjoyable evening was had by all. Like music, mediumship can bridge language barriers, as long as you are not afraid to tell it as you see it!

(More than this it also displays yet again just how closely in touch we really are with our doorkeepers and also, though to a lesser extent, our helpers, even though we are not consciously thinking about them for months on end. Like the analogy in the introduction, for me this proves that they stay faithful to *us* when it appears that we would or even *have* abandoned *them*.)

This group also impressed my English friends and they arranged another one. Here the sitters were all English, one of whom was the lady who had unwittingly, by a visit to the loo kick-started my public mediumship again. So I make no apology in declaring that this too was a cracking night with blessed and satisfied sitters, never mind the delighted medium!

During May 1994, I saw an advertisement for a new group who were meeting some way down the coast and I was told by Tuan to ring the number. Asking the lady who answered if they required mediums to demonstrate and telling her that I would be willing to help them get on their feet, she booked me for the evening of the 17th. June. Replacing the 'phone, it crossed my mind that there might even be someone at the meeting who remembered me from the old days. But then I remembered that in Spiritualism, as in many other walks of life the old adage "The King is dead, long live the King" is, to coin a phrase, very much the *rule to the exception!*

Thinking about the venue over the next few weeks, a mixture of thoughts and conjecture trailed through my mind. Foremost among these was how long it had been since I had stood before a congregation and conducted a public demonstration. Following this came images of old friends, acquaintances, churches and halls...

Then quite suddenly I began musing on just how long I had been in Spiritualism – something I had not thought about before. Then quickly leading on came the realisation that there are by now possibly, even *probably*, far more of my "fans" in Spirit than there are in the body. Further, those still on the earth-plane who might recall my demonstrations would be, like me, much older too. And having started so young, when it seemed that *everyone* was older than me, many of them would now be in their late eighties or even early nineties and almost certainly not likely to be living on the Costa Blanca.

The date arrived and driving to the venue some weeks later, I confess to being nervous, something I had never felt before, either going to a new church, or, for that matter, appearing in cabaret or on the stage. Strange in one respect because new, and even repeat dates always present the same things for mediums. We always, as it were, go on "blind" unlike the rehearsed cabaret act or stage role.

I should *not* have been nervous of course but the thought had crossed my mind that it might be a difficult evening, working with some twenty or so people who probably knew one another quite well. It was also many years since I had demonstrated publicly and I did wonder if I still had it. I do not know why I was fretting, since it was really like a reprise of my first time all those years ago when I had said: "If this is what you want me to do, etc."

Given directions to a leisure centre it was no surprise to find that it was simply a glorified pub. Entering the premises and expecting a small group I identified myself. The lady in charge beamed at me, telling me that there was a full house, with some seventy plus in attendance. I worried no more; any performer, of whatever ilk, will tell you it is easier and preferable to work to a full house! Thanks to that and my helpers too, within a few minutes, just like the old days, the clairvoyance was generously flowing. As if I had never been away, that there had never been a hiatus, a gap of all those years of standing before a crowd. Just as always Spirit did not let me down and many, many evidential proofs were given and happily acknowledged.

Even now after all the years of work and experiences, I never cease to be amazed at what Spirit are capable of arranging or doing. (This too is a lesson students should take on board. Never, ever, allow yourself to become either obsessed with, or blasé about, your talents!) Remember, for over six years I had virtually been in the psychic wilderness, with almost nobody declaring even a *remote* interest in such things as LAD. Then suddenly, in just a few months, without my even broaching the subject, I stumbled across an absolute plethora of them.

I *know* that if you *really* want something, provided it is justifiable within the context of your soul progression, when push comes to shove, you can depend on your spirit helpers' shoulders being first at the wheel. So I was not really more than very pleasantly surprised at this turn-around. And for those who might simply write it off as sheer coincidence? Believe me it was not and if you think that then you are not thinking at all! You are taking the easy way of having an un-thought-through *over simplification* of a well planned series of events. *Trust them!* Try it, and in no time at all *you will know it too.*

I mention here that I make no secret of the fact that I have had three marriages. Unlike other mediums' efforts I have read since finishing this book though, I cannot and do not lay blame at my ex's doors alone! There are *three* sides to every story - the other person's, mine and the truth! Further, autobiographies notwithstanding, I feel that any book about Spirit should never contain the proverbial washing of one's dirty linen in public. Neither, by the way, should it contain page after page of "Ain't I great when I demonstrate!" In reiterating then, I confirm that I did not set out to write an autobiography, so either way, in the event, my personal life has no relevance within these pages.

My intention has been to try to write an informative book which, I sincerely hope, will be of some practical use to aspiring mediums and progressive psychics. By imparting and sharing what I have learned on my journeys through these and other incarnations, I hope it will encourage students to continually search, as I do, for true knowledge.

Therefore with this intent uppermost, my endeavour throughout has been to err, biographically speaking, on the side of astringency. As such I am trying throughout to mention only incidents concerning the psychic side of my life. And even those experiences represent but *few* of the things that have occurred during *over* fifty years of my studying these matters and of practising my mediumship.

Much the same as many others, I have experienced facets of life that have been both happy and unhappy, rewarding and unrewarding, painful and joyful. I have even seen life in the raw too! But this is no way written by way of a complaint; indeed it has provided me with experience that I can and do, quite often, by demonstration and or explanation, pass on to others. So in fact I count myself lucky and more, very fortunate to have done things in my life that many will only begin to dream about but will probably never have the opportunity to experience.

Far more incredible though is that I have also been very fortunate, nay blessed in being allowed and able to witness the most fantastic array and demonstration of psychic phenomena by other mediums I have had the honour to sit with. Further, I have, on many occasions been the medium, Spirit's instrument, blessed with the power to demonstrate some of it too!

An enormous amount of phenomena I have seen defies explanation, worthy only of the definition, magical or miraculous! Indeed, had I recorded even *some of my personal magical ones here,* (for instance, when broadcasting live here in Spain and having had no rain for months I declared that I would make it rain within twenty-four hours and it and I did!) I could not blame the majority of my readers for not believing a word. Had I done so, I would have expected nothing less than most of them virtually dismissing the whole book, out of hand, as pure fantasy. But as I have already said previously, we all know the old adage about the truth and fiction... And without boasting, for it is said from knowing, not just believing, I do not have to (and never do) b.s. in public, private, or in my writing!

From now on I will make every endeavour to write only psychic or personal incidents that relate to and or have a direct bearing on the subject in hand i.e., to tie in with the instructions and or advice I hope to impart. I must also stress again that the greater part of the psychic knowledge I have gained is the direct result of Spiritual communication and communion with a mini-multitude of discarnate intelligences and minds. I have indeed been blessed in this and consider myself most fortunate to have associated with such highly evolved spiritually God-Soul-Source powered enlightened entities.

The road has been long and winding as the old saying goes (and continues to be so) and I make no bones about it. It is a long haul, with the varied twists and turns that the intrepid enquirer has to make in search of the mystery of Light and Truth. Often, as I quenched my psychic thirst at the various watering holes along the way, I *thought a particular thing to be fact.* However, once *revealed* and thought through, it turned out to be only *supposition* on my part. Another early lesson I took to heart was yet another of Tuan's many philosophical sayings: "Assumption is not fact!"

The Universe and all things in it, both in and out of the body, are in a state of constant change. But for those of you who genuinely and sincerely desire and strive for Truth, fear not, your struggle will not be in vain. Do not despair of ever finding it, for the Truth is out there.

It is however precisely because of this constant change that the student *must* beware. Do not become fixed or dogmatic in your ways, for, as Tuan says:"As surely as something is right today it could be wrong tomorrow." This happens oftentimes when, with the dawning of a new day, we gain a different perspective, hence one of the reasons for continual study. Be prepared therefore for a Truth to be *made* true. Never forget that assumption really cannot be fact *(truth)* until you *know* it yourself, from *within,* to be so and thus will you be secure in your thinking during your search for knowledge. Note:- Chamber's dictionary definition of truth is:- agreement with reality. Then again, we must pose the question and indeed search for the answer to what in reality *is* reality?

Finally, we see in Spiritualism just how free our religious thinking can be, for unlike the purely orthodox ones, we are able to exercise our thinking and freewill without restrictions from priests and hierarchy. Indeed, to experience all things and with certainty finally arrive at a definite conclusion we have to try them.Things' psychic are no exception either; you *have* to investigate for *yourself*, when you will reach certain conclusions,which same for me, after many years of investigation are the only logical ones.

Unlike orthodoxy with its priests and books nobody can make you accept communication with disembodied souls through blind belief, by persuasion alone! You need to investigate and experience these things for yourself and in so doing you will reach your own conclusions not through a priest but through *conviction*. Or, to put it another way, the words of "The Manna Group" speaking through me in one of the developing circles I supervised some years ago are as follows:-

"In order to experience experience, we have to experience experience! It follows therefore that experience can, indeed will, only be achieved by the experiencing of experiences, for only through the experiencing can we truly become experienced. It is only then, when experience has been earned by the experiencing, that experience (knowledge) can be passed on by the experienced to the inexperienced.

"Foolish pride often prompts man to pass off inexperience as experience and thus, making his own pronouncements, he opines them as experience. But such as these should beware for they will assuredly be brought down by the experienced! For man knows nothing which he has not absolutely experienced."

So it is with these thoughts I leave Part One in the hope you have enjoyed it, or at least that I have whetted your appetite enough for you to want to read Part Two. Indeed if that is the case, I have partly accomplished the task that the guides and helpers asked me so many times over the years to undertake. If you feel as I do that there is light at the end of the proverbial tunnel, then you have at least had a glimpse of what is experienced by intrepid psychic and mediumistic travellers. This will, I trust, make you more confident in your *own* on-going journey however hard and difficult that may or may not be.

In Parts Two and Three I will try to show you the way through the veil. It is my expressed hope that you too will find the joy, the peace and the hope for the future that I am certain lies ahead for all mankind. Unless we share and take on board the consistently held optimism proffered by those blessed Spiritual Soul-Force-Energies, we cannot hope to enter into, nor begin to understand, the great mystery of life and what we erroneously call death.

HELPFUL NOTES!

(On being aware, etc.) *I hear some of you commenting that as a medium I should perhaps have known that these friends were interested. Well, apart from the fact that I am a natural medium and do not walk around "open" all of the time there is another reason which basically is yet again down to the way Spirit helpers work with me.*

For example, since arriving in Spain in 1987, I had, now and again, simply read the tarot cards for friends and so on until 1993. Question and answers were made through the pendulum if a diagnosis was needed for someone, or something had been mislaid or lost. But I had done nothing like private sittings in the accepted spiritualist sense of contacting Spirit. Except on rare occasions therefore, such as when I knew that the sitter wanted more than just some guidance, I did not "tune in" for that kind of work. Cards, being all that interested them was, therefore, the only avenue I pursued.

You will I hope recall that earlier within these pages I stated that I never speak about the subject unless the other person broaches it. My "psychic brief" has always been constant, that is, not to "open the shop" at every tiff and turn and never to waste the talent for an ego trip or its own sake. So hopefully you now will more readily understand and accept my answer in the preceding paragraph.

Quite apart from these reasons there was not exactly a plethora of folk beating a path to my door, clamouring for my talents! In fact I had begun to believe that Spain was a psychic and spiritual desert and that my work publicly was at an end. However, as is often with our own thoughts, I was, of course, wrong!

PART TWO
In consideration of!

Those who give out understandingly, *teach.*
Those who receive with comprehension, *learn.*
Therefore if a man or woman *can* communicate with
others he or she *can* instruct, *but not by words alone.*

✳ ✳ ✳ ✳ ✳ ✳

A good lesson I use as a motto:

Recognise its usefulness!

Absorb its value!

Use it wisely!

Chapter 1
IN MY FATHER'S HOUSE...

Let me begin by stating that I am most definitely not a professional theologian! But then I have never coveted the idea or desired to be one, for most display acutely slanted attitudes and a covert lack of honesty. Some might label me a theologaster but if I have a label at all then the nearest I guess would be a theocrat! I have a profound interest in all that we term God and try mightily to reach out and grasp the essence of Him, Her, or It! But in truth I, like so many others, can only theorise.

In consequence over some five decades I have learned of and adopted segments from many religions, all of which have something of value in them. However, although this has come about through deep and considered contemplation I still do not feel, nor claim to be, in any way, an authority on religion per se. But this does not disqualify me out of hand from setting down thoughts on the often cut and thrust conglomeration of ideas, ideology and resulting cultural proclivities that prevail throughout the world. Equally, I would strenuously defend the right of others to do likewise.

History clearly demonstrates for centuries past no real freedom of thought was allowed in religions by the hierarchies. Today though somewhat more relaxed various established rules still prevail and, to some extent, "flocks" are still kept in order. In such faiths one has little or no freedom of expression and small chance of escaping the sinner syndrome! To openly state any kind of contra viewpoint in those circumstances would automatically bring down upon one's head condemnation and in some cases, such as in Islam, even a threat to one's life.

Notwithstanding, from scholars of theology, down through to the professed atheist I am certain that virtually all individuals, right across the board, will have an idea or opinion as to what they think God is, might or might not be, or even ought to be! For reasons best known to themselves however, many of them will not (and some cannot) openly express or even discuss that idea or opinion.

Ask anyone do they believe in God and if so what is their interpretation of Him, Her or It? In reply many will first variously respond, yes, no, I am not sure, or even I do not know. But often somewhat huffily they will almost inevitably reply to part two saying that it is a very personal question and, the same as their politics, it is a matter between them and their conscience. Obviously this really means two things (a) that they have probably *never* voted and (b) neither have they really considered the God concept anyway, leaving it to the religionists, a word I use quite deliberately.

Chamber's dictionary definition: *Religionist:* One attached to a religion; a bigot; one professionally engaged in religion. The many meanings of *Religion* are also interesting. Belief in, recognition of, or an awakened sense of a higher unseen controlling power or powers, with the emotion and morality connected therewith. Others: any system of such belief or worship; monastic life; a Protestant. A *religious person* is, among other things *R.C. strict, very exact.* Protestants are not mentioned, so if taken literally, it defines Catholics as religious but without a religion and the Protestants as the reverse! Meanwhile *Faith* is defined amongst others as:- trust or confidence; belief in the statement of another; belief in the truth of a revealed religion; any system of religious belief, especially the religion one considers true.

Taken literally again we find further contradictions, for now it appears that *anyone*, and not just the Catholics alone, provided they have faith can be considered religious! By this premise, provided that one believes that ones religion has been revealed or has confidence or believes the statement of others, well, that is OK. too. But it is not...

(In recent years various and varied religious cults have been established only to end in tragedy. Unfortunately, only those who are imbued with sufficient cultist brainwashing accept that theirs are deserving of recognition. However, as "revealed religion" it is plain to see that such as these must be scrutinised and controlled more closely. The result then might well be that many of the instigators would never gain sufficient converts to make the exercise worthwhile!)

The foregoing definitions from the quoted source are *not* out of context and though seeming to be somewhat tongue in cheek I draw a parallel here for both orthodox and some other religions are just that! Almost without exception these are simply strong financial institutions, run on corporation lines. The clergy, depending on rank, hold the equivalent appointments of managers, executives, directors and so on, paying, in reality, little more than lip service to their God. Employed by the church they control banks, property, pension funds and many other profitable enterprises.

Accordingly, almost immediately after ordination, the more "politically" ambitious among them soon become aware that up there (and they do not mean Heaven) the living is easy and very comfortable indeed! As such, many "career" priests set about clawing their way up. The purely vocational ones simply remain in their parishes working only at their pastoral duties and calling. Their real validity, plain to see, is that they make good and effective buffers for their bosses.

A famous cynical quotation in orthodoxy, though I know not its originator said: "If you want to be a good priest, do not think about, or even consider the thought of trying to become a bishop!" Thus, left to their own devices, so long as they toe the official line without a hint of protest, the vocationalists are virtually ignored by peers and hierarchy alike.

Using money, mainly squeezed out of the poorer peoples of the world, the well-fed priest-hoods continue on, glibly promising their devotees Heaven's reward. Owing their very existence to their followers, these live like parasites off those lesser unfortunates' backs! With such an on-going harvest the church can laugh all the way to the bank. But the cracks cannot be papered over forever and the status quo, the "laughing priests" syndrome, maintained for centuries, *will* change, and quite dramatically as well.

By definition, education of the masses inevitably leads to, and brings with it, its own consequences. Horizons too are becoming closer and closer and just as inevitably changes will arise challenging the present situation. If these go unheeded, ignored by the "establishment" the first casualties will be those very same religions. Built, using fear of church-made vengeful Gods against adherents, education shifts beliefs and changes opinions. Consequently, many religious castles, built only on sand, will crumble to dust.

For those of you who do not yet see, I ask that you look to and digest the plethora of evidence that abounds. So *look*, for like something in full view, yet not seen, it stares us in the face and clearly seen are the weapons used. Pompously and pre-emptively proclaiming their narrow-minded attitudes as the only way, they expound these in God's name as if they have total endorsement, implying that the book or priest, or both, are infallible

Consequently in many instances, religion down the centuries has become a *burdensome*, not a *pleasurable* pursuit. Yet most, sheep-like, have complied, following the leaders, accepting the doctrines propounded. Perhaps even aware that tenets have been altered to suit the hierarchy, rather than risk the alternatives, "flocks" still conform, deferring to priest and book alike. These continue to blindy suck up like sponges the perverse, suffocating totalitarian indoctrination that is daily distilled by their priests, elders and propagandists. Yet it is this very same blind faith, this metaphorical iron fist, instilling various religious fervour throughout the world that has resulted in humankind being continually at loggerheads with itself.

Endorsed by differing hierarchies, all too often *encouraging* rather than *discouraging* believers to declare war on others, most faiths have at one time or another both persecuted and or annihilated other faiths (the unbelievers) in the name of *their* God! Indeed, even as I write, to the shame of us all, such conflicts rage on and almost all in the name of religion. Often religion *should* read bigotry, closely followed by man's inhumanity to man! (On reflection, the religionist definition (a bigot) previously quoted is not, after all, quite as outrageous as it at first appeared.)

Take a hard long look at theology and theologians in *all* persuasions. It is at their doors that we should lay blame for this state of affairs! It is well known to those who will listen that most present day *official* Christian theologians, for example, squirming on their paymasters' hook, merely toe the official line to keep their positions and bellies full! I make no apology for stating that they only believe little of what they say either publicly or in print; their expressed definitions and opinions being simply a matter of expediency and pay cheques.

In spite of such pressures or probably in many cases *because* of them, other thinking humans, with freer access to education, are enabled to think for themselves. This has resulted in, almost without exception, every main-stream religion everywhere, losing ground. Artificial truths, expounded by religious pundits are now slowly being eroded by apostastic thinkers and these form the vanguard of a relentless human tide challenging the (at last emerging) fragile status-quo.

Examples of this fragility, self evident, abound. In God we trust, except the pontiff, who uses a bullet-proof car! The move to ordain women; the birth control rebels and other challenges to Christendom. Catholic priests discarding celibacy and wishing to have personal relationships or to be married. Other instances are the Reformed Jewish church; the marrying out of one's faith; doctors and scientists concluding more and more that the soul exists and the return to the worship of Nature. The think-for-themselves folk of today, no longer wishing to toe the ortho-dox line, are acutely aware that when push comes to shove *persuasion* will not, nay *cannot*, match conviction.

Since the beginning of time man has always worshipped a God, or Gods holding it or them variously to be anthropomorphic, omnipitent, omniscient and or capable of metamorphosis. In effect though it matters little as to name, definition *or* de-scription. Whether expressed adoration and reverence is via the ceremonial dance, blood sacrifice, song, prayer or other ritualistic practices matters even less. The fact remains that throughout history the certainty of the God idea has always ex-isted consistently with, and *coexisted* with, the human race. The earliest caveman's drawings, the hieroglyphs, the Veda scriptures and other ancient languages, etc. are daily producing more and more evidence for this.

Noted archaeologists and such have long discovered through these that man has always believed in a Spirit World and an after life. These invariably and intrinsi-cally in various ways demonstrate a link of Nature worship. If these are right and cross references clearly demonstrate that they are, then other hitherto contentious arguments are also confirmed; that Spirit communion and manifestations have been experienced and practised for thousands of years together with a belief *in* and per-ception *of* reincarnation too! Further that these have been held as sacred truths (until comparatively recently) by virtually *all* cultures throughout time.

These writings tell of mankind ever seeking for the hidden force behind the trees, the mountains and valleys; in the thunder and in the roar of the sea; in the murmur of the brook and in the rustle of the leaf, indeed in *every* thing. He tries to touch it but it constantly escapes his grasp; then as he tries to find a name for it, it becomes the unutterable. With the majority of humankind, unable to see beyond the veil, it cannot detach the finite from the infinite, often mistaking the one for the other. In consequence, we find him worshipping first tangible objects, as in fetish-ism, then adoring the *semi-intangible*, and finally reaching out to the most myste-rious of all, the *intangible*.

Today, in the western hemisphere many are tending to take a closer look at what is happening to our world. Aware of the value of experiences in this life they are, consciously or not, pursuing Nature, the basis of many ancient and eastern beliefs.

Called simply "The Greens" these environmentalists are almost religious in their fervour in demonstrating that a better world is within reach. Many, attracted to Buddhism and other eastern ancient religions and mentally oriented martial arts display their inherent needs, i.e. to be in at-one-with-Nature and, therefore God, the intrinsic purpose and ideal of such disciplines.

Some of the civilised religions based on Nature are as follows:-
     The Norse, consecrating Valour.
     The Greek,   "   Beauty.
     The Roman,   "   Justice.

Many people throughout the world also follow, unbroken or changed by time, the same ancient rituals and ideals that have been part of their religious and social structure for thousands of years. These too recognise the importance of Nature *and* the communion with discarnate spirits. Their practices, laws and forthright worship, without qualification, have about them a sincerity that leaves the more accepted "civilised" Christians, Muslims, Hebrews and the like trailing far behind in piety, honesty and altruistic religious pursuits.

The Masai Tribe of Kenya still perform a ritual (it is in fact, a séance) which they regard as quite natural. When, for example, the elders are unable to agree on a case before them, they ask those who have gone before, their revered "dead", to appear to them. Then those elders actually materialise, both counselling and dispensing penalties or pardons accordingly!

Religions also frequently have something in common, though they may be miles and even centuries apart. Roman priests and others in the then known world would examine the entrails of an animal to foretell future events; still today the Mentawi people, located on the smallest island of the Indonesian Archipelago have the same ritual! The wailing prayer-form of the natives of West Papua, New Guinea asking the spirit of the tree to forgive them for cutting it down is found unchanged, apart from language, in other religions too. These include the Shinto (Japan), the Native North and South American Indians, the Aborigines (Australia), the Bushmen (Africa), and many others.

Other examples abound such as the Mayan and Egyptian pyramids and the hieroglyphs, so similar in construction, shape and meaning. Markings on the ground that can only be seen from the air and cave drawings with strange figures very alike are also to be found in different cultures (countries) thousands of miles apart. In most cultures people will nod in agreement and shake their heads to say no. Even stranger, investigations show that there seems to be no evidence that these races ever crossed paths in the past, so why, when and indeed, *how* did the common ties come about? Do these perhaps contain some cosmic answers as yet undiscovered, or are they already discovered but not yet revealed to mankind? (See e. of ch. on name calling.)

Some eastern religions are much more intellectual, being based on science and imagination:-

Osirianism, characterised by Aspiration.
Brahamism,   "   Spirituality.
Buddhism,   "   Emancipation.

Yet others are Moral religions, based on Authority and Reflection:-

The Doctrine of Confucius, cultivating Reverence.
     "   Mohomet,   "   Faith.
     "   Zoroaster,   "   Purity.

All ancient Eastern religions have a common thread, a diapason; that the salvation of the soul is through one's own works, i.e. that salvation (spiritual progression) must be "purchased". The sacred books of The Tripitika of the Buddhist, the Paranas of Siva and Vishnu, the Veda of the Brahmins, the Mohammedan Koran and the Zend-Avesta of the Parsees all propound the same message, but these revered books all present rather a dull uniformity of thinking.

Today, with most people being able to read, this kind of thinking can no longer keep the masses in check. Indeed, in many cases one is not now required to blindly adhere to these beliefs, except by the more perverse religionists, who continue to hang on to their outmoded and, in some instances, possibly even dangerous concepts of worship. (And the same is true, to a large extent of Islam and Christianity.)

In medieval times book-worship was normal but nowadays, because the ability to read is within the reach of almost everyone, it is virtually non existent. Hence, people are more able to challenge and reason out the pseudo-mysteries portrayed therein. However, it is easy to understand how books achieved this sacred status and came to be worshipped as such.

At one time only a very minimal number of persons understood the scratches made by another and both of these would be looked upon in awe by the majority of persons. It would have made little difference whether such marks were made with a stick, a chisel or stone on stone; with dye on an animal hide, or by drawings and so on in caves. Even when the art of writing *had* become more common, to copy a book or *even* a page was still a long, costly and tedious process, so that books remained the prerogative, in the main, of the wealthy and or educated. (N.B. The average person is still pretty well awe-struck by Egyptologists who look at hieroglyphics, simply reading them like a book and the same is true when unsighted folk are seen reading Braille).

Thus, as with the king's invisible suit in the fable, early readers read into the (especially religious) written word the desired and required interpretation, unable to declare openly a single doubt as to the authenticity of the text. So they claimed it as the truth and nothing but... and with the majority abysmally lacking in education and reading anyway, they could hardly have known or argued differently.

Actually it was quite the reverse, for the masses began holding books in high veneration. It was not long before they were, figuratively speaking, hooked, only one short step away from being reeled in. Thus resulted the conviction that virtually all books had been written by *God Himself!* Taking full advantage of this priesthoods of *all* persuasions were quick to capitalise, encouraging such beliefs to the very extreme!

Sadly old habits, especially bad ones, die hard! So still today, priest-hoods apart, many will declare and believe that the Bible, re-interpreted by numerous scholars over the centuries, is as ever, *literally the word of God.* Many editions have been slanted, re-written to suit the times and even the whim of kings and emperors! Published thus, with the best will in the world surely we must conclude that much of what might have originally been recorded is, at the very least, suspect.

The entry of the Dead Sea Scrolls and a more knowledgeable understanding of earlier languages is daily providing new argument. And if these recently discovered scrolls are proven to be as forthcoming as the researchers are indicating, a *totally new* version of the Bible may well have to be the result! If this happens the earlier versions, regarded as containing little original text and not the "true" word will probably be judged as having no intrinsic foundation or value. So, save for library copies, they may well be consigned to the rubbish tips.

Historical records clearly demonstrate that for thousands of years religious leaders in all cultures have always held sway over the masses, achieved through pressure of ritual ceremony, confusion and persuasion. With their superior education, priests have always threatened lesser mortals with punishment by one or more of the various and many Gods. Later the more "modern" Christian, Islamic and other monotheistic religious hierarchies, needing, purely for their own ends, to have total control, also adopted this proven format. (Though undoubtedly more subtle today, in many ways such pressures are still in place and on-going and functioning as per.)

The Roman Empire, partly through the conversion of Caesar Constantine, but also through political engendering, effectively replaced a failing military empire with a religious one. With the clerics' common language of the time being Latin and Greek, this was fairly easily and smoothly accomplished.

As such, Christianity took off and rapidly, mainly through political manoeuvring, it accumulated much material wealth. It soon changed tactics however and in the main has fed off the poor and uneducated ever since. To coin a phrase; many widow's mites proved mightier than one rich man's fortune! Such gathering of these soon outstripped the wildest dreams of the hierarchy, producing far more wealth and power than it could ever have wheedled out of a few fat cats, governments or royalty. And it was not long either before kings, queens, Caesars and governments *too* bowed to this priest-power, almost invariably thinking twice before chancing their arm in invoking the church's displeasure.

Narrow-minded Christianity also became the norm in England some four hundred years after being brought there by those first "fishers" of men. Christianity was well established and consummately accepted, at least openly, by virtually all of the populace. In their constant endeavour to establish and perpetuate an even more awesome clerical dynasty, the priests discarded their sackcloth and sandals and took to wearing costly, beautifully embroidered robes. This quickly imposed a feeling of even stronger church authority among the people, making the priests more "holy".

In the formative centuries of the faith many practitioners of the Spiritual gifts, e.g. clairvoyance, clairaudience, healing, speaking in tongues were simple, ordinary folk. Farm workers, labourers and many others practised their gifts in and out of the church too. In post crucifixion early Christianity these were encouraged as was, incidentally, a belief in reincarnation.

The priests found to their chagrin however that the new uniform a medium did not make! Since they could not replicate the gifts they simply took the easier way out. So around 400 A.D. the demonstration of mediumship was officially terminated and not only in the churches! Anywhere and everywhere per se - period; to practise any of the spiritual gifts was forbidden, the hierarchy declaring it henceforth to be the work of the devil. (See end of chapter on the Christian "cover-up" and the Bible on the practise of gifts of the Spirit.)

To compensate and to turn the peoples' minds from the banned practices (Christmas is a prime example) they borrowed many pagan customs. This was partly for convenience and partly to keep their flock happy. Cleverly disguised under a banner of convenience these were integrated into their own religious festivals and rites. Any deviation or digression from "priest law" was, henceforth, summarily dealt with. Yet those who offended these laws were simply worshipping Nature, doing the same things that they had previously done in the Christian church. But since the priests were unable to demonstrate these things, it was like rubbing salt into their wounds and that was definitely *not* the way to find any pity, let alone grace, in their eyes.

So, even a slight transgression, invariably adjudged akin to practising the black arts, invoked almost always expedient measures. Among these were torture, imprisonment without release, or speedy trials without representation, quickly followed by beatings and or death. As a result, there is little wonder that the "flocks", overtly anyway, obediently toed the line. Secretly, however, many still operated by way of an underground movement.

Many tenets were also re-vamped, an example of which was to be in At-One-Ment with God. Simply by removing the hyphens this became atonement for ones sins against God, obviously man-made! Now, no longer the loving father hitherto preached, He was a frightening omnipotent figure of a man with a long white beard somewhere up in the sky! Worse, this new God would *wreak His vengeance on any and all who did not obey totally and, without question, a priest's slightest whim.*

Surely then, anyone who thinks beyond the narrow confines of orthodoxy has to question the tenet that God created man in His own image for this seems to have been merely the means to an end! It is easy to visualise that this may well have been invented, or at the very least, *inverted*. After all, by simply inventing *God in the image of man* and then reversing it, it was, in an uneducated and superstitious society, comparatively easy to implant such a doctrine! Then after establishing this lofty, vengeful God image, it would have been just as easy to create, in the same way, a Heaven and Hell!

It is also painfully obvious to those who would see that such doctored mischievousness could only have been effected at source. With so few able to read, even in the so-called civilised world, it was easy to make *any* adjustments. And, unlikely as such, had these been challenged, the "bosses" would probably have claimed them as clerical errors! Those words today have a different meaning, but the "cleric" connotation may well point to the beginning, in earlier times, as to display perhaps something of a self-evident indictment of the priest-hoods.

Consequently, the big man up in the sky is simply discarded by my spirit teachers, all thinking persons and me as totally unbelievable and illogical to boot! In any case, surely nobody can really believe that everyone's good and evil deeds are written down by Him in a big book. Further, the notion that on the day of one's "death" (judgement day) God reads it all out to one is, of itself, sheer balderdash! To begin with, inconveniently hundreds of thousands of "Christians" die each day and even God would not be able to get through them all at once; and anyway, it negates (God-given) freewill and personal responsibility. But enough already, for equally, the very concept is fatuous and therefore unworthy of discussion or argument! (See e. of ch. on beating the system!)

One can only look on in wonder though at the audacity and strength of these ecclesiastical prestidigitators who, from those early times until now have flagrantly and narrow mindedly managed to perpetuate their own pseudo piety! Yet still holding many to their cause their cohorts continue to follow in a blind, sublimated and faithful manner. Almost *unbelievably too*, there are others who, straying from the "norm" will join other unorthodox type groups, often then becoming far more blinded than hitherto!

Good and evil have been, and still are foolishly banded about, basically only as words with undefined definitions. In considering the difference between the two, therefore, it is too simplistic to label it just black and white for the measure and workability of it has to fall within one's *own* parameters. This concludes that it is solely judged by the *individual's* barometer of conception of it. After all, if good and evil *was* absolutely definitive it would automatically stand in place with no need for anyone to decide what they are one way or the other!

Ordinary people, governments, religious pundits and the money-men all employ their varied descriptions but each have something in common which is that both are used according to the prevailing need at the time. In particular, between lovers friends or foes engaged in argument or persuasion the words are without any differentiation used as required by way of description alone.

In all monotheistic religions, irrespective of creed or culture, hierarchies have fully prosecuted the "Good and Evil Syndrome". They ensure that adherents are fully aware and understand the implications of an unforgiving, omnipotent and wrathful God. The contention is ever that his intent is to take taking retributive action in respect of *any* digression from His path. This, in real terms, means digression not from *His*, but *their* path which is self-evident, for when folk confess their transgressions the forgiveness is by the *priest alone*, albeit in the name of God. Though rarer today, a mere mortal (for even Popes and Ayatollahs, etc. are only priests) is still able to prosecute an excommunication. If only God can forgive, how are we to believe that such unfortunates are "denied entry into the Kingdom of Heaven" by a mere priest?

I submit therefore, that this enforced concept of Good and Evil by priest-hoods is not acceptable as a satisfactory solution to the question of its definition, yet it is one to which, even now, millions of people, in many different religions, submissively obey. I am certain that the following opinion is one I share with many, many other thinking folk. It is that in reality, many of the adherents, and this includes the whole shebang, merely pay lip-service to their church, and for *that* matter, to their God too. I am of the opinion that most do not really believe that if they commit the odd sin, big or small, they will be judged accordingly otherwise we would have a world of automaton do-gooders!

I contend that the true feeling is that if the pundits *are* right most will still take the chance and cross that bridge as and when. Indeed, should they really have to face the big person up in the sky then they maybe hope that, in mitigation, He, She or It will listen to their pleas. They optimistically hope that "big person" will let them in, agreeing (and who among us does not think it?) that there are many who are a lot worse.

An example of this applied good and evil is graphically illustrated by the behaviour of certain early Christian missionaries. Observing that the natives followed the practice of animals, mounting from the rear when they had sexual intercourse, they told them this was wrong, being ungodly. The missionaries, usually living alone, only had day servants for company. More than one of these took the initiative to teach the natives the proper, "Godly" way of intercourse, effected by using young, easily persuaded native girls to engage in it face to face. From that time, called the "missionary" position it soon passed into the sexual manuals and is still today referred to as such.

Inevitably, it was not long before the mixed blood children began to appear. In consequence, it became the rule that missionaries were "expected to be married" by the time their mission began and equally, also to take their spouses with them!

Can we really accept or believe that they were doing, as many would undoubtedly have laid claim, God's good works? I submit that their motives more probably hung more on satisfying their own sexual hunger and gratification than in the more implausible "noble" reasons suggested at the time. Is it really so hard to believe that there was *no lust involved*, with perhaps just a smattering of "evil" thrown in there somewhere? They could easily have used the plethora of books that abounded. In fact, during the Edwardian and Victorian eras, records show it to be the most pornographic literature period in modern times and also the most active period of the early missionaries! Coincidence? Nah!

(Even in the more broad minded thinking that abounds presently, it is easy to see the outcry that would follow if teachers demonstrated sex education this way!)

Religion and politics have always had dogmatists, "persuaders" to combat its competitors and or opponents. Christianity is no exception and examples abound among which are the Spanish Conquistadors, obsessively driven in total commitment to converting every territory and peoples they conquered to the Catholic religion and crown. Though of course this is well documented for those who do not know, I describe, by a thumb-nail sketch, one such invasion.

The Incas and other indigenous nations had been already established there for thousands of years. Notwithstanding, a force of only some two hundred very well armed individuals "re-discovered" the territory and claimed these as newly found lands for the cause. Alas, comparatively speaking, within a few short years they had annihilated an entire culture and many of the people too. Decimation from some seventy million souls to less than forty millions was due almost entirely to merciless slaughtering and diseases.

The population was dramatically reduced through "civilised" diseases brought and spread by their Christian deliverers! To name but a few, tuberculosis, smallpox and a range of venereal diseases easily spread as the Indians had no congenital immune resistance to these. Previously unknown too was the common cold and more especially influenza, to which they were particularly vulnerable.

It began initially though by tricking the ruler into a social visit and then taking him for ransom. He had arrived with 5,000 troops but at a pre-arranged signal they were all, except the two hundred or so who escaped, slaughtered in an hour and a half! This in turn caused the rest of the army of 45,000 to capitulate; thus was the empire doomed. (If that sounds incredible some explanation may be necessary.)

Hitherto the natives had mostly expanded their empire by "capturing" their enemies' *temples* and afterwards they absorbed the others' beliefs into their own culture. Against this enemy *they* had only copper and wooden weapons whilst the Spaniards had steel swords, muskets, cannon and other fearsome things for they had never seen *white* men, nor *steel* armour, nor *horses*. (Imagine the fear instilled by these half-man, half-animal creatures alone!)

A ransom of some six tons of gold was handed over, as well as many more tons of silver. The spoils were, as was usual, distributed, first to the Spanish King then, according to rank and file. But the arrival of reinforcements meant that the new guys would get nothing unless more gold and silver were produced but there was none left.

Shortly after the ruler was told that if he became a Christian he would be released but he refused. Tried as a *Spanish* subject, he was found guilty (of course) of treason both against his (Spanish) king and God. Condemned to death by burning alive it meant that, in his religion, his soul would be destroyed. The "compassionate" Spanish though said that if he accepted the Christian faith, they would not burn him, they would only *garrotte him* instead. Agreeing, the priest read him the words for Christian conversion and in a matter of minutes he became both a Christian and a garrotted ex-member of the Catholic church! They then burned his body anyway - so much for respect.

More examples! The early Christians who faced lions in the arena in Rome; the Witch finder General in England; the Spanish Inquisition. The persecution of Puritans resulting in the Pilgrim Fathers' sailing from Plymouth to America the Witch hunts in America, and in Salem in particular.

Even in today's world horrific persecution and persuasion like the recent dreadful holocaust and the killing fields of Cambodia still continue in various ways. (Many folk are still unaware that the Nazi S.S. with the death-heads on the lapels of the uniform and the dagger in the belt was part of the symbolism and ritual of cultist black magic.)

The Chinese, who aggressively over-ran Tibet and who since, in spite of denials, have ground this gentle race into complete submission. Their Buddhist godking, the fourteenth *Dalai Lama* is actually a term in Mongolian meaning Broad Ocean and is never used by Tibetans. His Tibetan name is Gyalpo Rimpoche (meaning Precious King) and he has, since the invasion, been in forced exile. Sadly, those toothless protectors of freedom, the UN, have simply, as in so many other instances throughout the world, for whatever reasons, chosen to ignore their plight.

Communism vs. Capitalism, the Irish Catholic and Protestant struggle, the Islamic, Jewish and Christian Jerusalem "contest", the Indian Hindu and Sikh "war" and suicide sect pacts etc. are others actioned by zealots. In the name of their God and or their political beliefs they continue to perpetrate and perpetuate such things. Islam even goes as far as issuing a death sentence on those who dare to challenge the "true faith." What is more, if a killer succeeds against a transgressor so named, they will be rewarded with money in this life and a place in their "Heaven" in the next! (A case of having their "angel" cake and eating it perhaps?)

The foregoing are just a few of the examples (See e. of ch. on other examples of oppression.) of what a tragic and disastrous world we "civilised" people are continuing to make of this wonderful planet that was entrusted to us. Called simply progress I submit that if there *is* a big God up in the sky after all, we will have much to answer for when we stand before Him. The queue will be never ending for *all of us* are guilty in some measure!

Alternatively if we have no God to blame or appeal to when we make our transition, finding that it is all down to the collective individual, it will be a bit too late to say: "Sorry, my mistake!" Either way, now is the time, before it is too late, when we ought to take some personal responsibility for what we are doing and for what *we* are *allowing* to happen.

Psychologists tell us that everything we do is motivated by selfishness, even the good things like enjoying the pleasure of giving or doing! I do not totally accept this for it appears to be rather glib as an all embracing premise, but this is not the place to argue it through. But of *this* I am certain; if all people honed up their *positive* psychic (never mind mediumistic) abilities, our world, in toto, would be a happier, safer and healthier planet.

Inevitably the time must and will come when foolish minds put aside their differences and conjoin their better facets, when world government will be the norm and war, hunger, poverty and the like will be no more. I sincerely believe that evolutionary cause and effect will play a big part in bringing about these changes as people become more and more integrated. Look about you for it can be seen that the "rules of the game" are already changing.

He who is brave enough to think for himself, has eyes to see and heart to understand, *knows* in truth that the "old" is passing away. In its place the "new" is certainly and surely permeating all grades of humanity. The knowledge of Spirit Truth and Light quietly and gradually is making ground and sooner or later, surfacing, it will open every eye. It will proffer an order of society which forms, then reforms, diversifying and transcending all that has gone before and I pray that those who come after me will have the courage and fortitude to embrace all that this will undoubtedly offer.

The liberation of the human mind, the right to possess and exercise the prerogative of the Divine-human faculties of intellect and perception through the Soul infinitely transcends the vested interest of any dogma or creed. So what is needed now is a truly *Spiritual* rostrum.

The aforementioned hard core constrictionists, hiding behind their bastions of outmoded doctrines need bringing down to earth with a bump. Their castles, built even perhaps *deliberately* on shifting foundations of sand, thus allowing them to change their rules at their whim, need tearing down. By doing so, untainted Spiritual truth and Light will be set free from the shackles of jealous priests, of all persuasions, steeped as they are in the prejudices of their paper-thin sincerity.

The Truth of Spirit and its communion is a positive knowledge and is the tool that can refine and re-shape the present rough, fierce life and way of mankind. The chief agent utilised in the discovery of the secrets of Natural Law is the Astral (Spirit) light and this is open to all, not just a handful of bigoted priest-hoods! Thinking people of the world no longer want or need to just rest on blind faith, something that has for centuries been thrust down their throats (I have said already that belief presupposes that something may not be true!) and these are demanding to *know* and to be given and or allowed to receive and acknowledge genuine God founded Spiritual Truths.

In referring to the tearing down requirement (above) I also state that it must include a building up for Universal Spirituality cannot exist by simply pulling other institutions down! We have to build one that is intrinsically broad in concept and capable of shaking off the follies of past religions, yet retaining their fertile seeds of truth. A religion that will *ensure* a Spiritual future throughout the whole spectrum of these truths, yet allowing that *all* may think and worship without fear or pressure of any kind from others, no matter what *they* believe. By such attitudes and thinking such a religion will *naturally* become the vanguard of future world Spirituality. And equally only through on-going optimism will Humankind stand any chance of evolving into a true brotherhood.

In achieving this we can begin by recognising and mobilising a trinity of Spirit, Soul and Matter, each one a functionary in itself, yet within one law, governing the Whole. And since centralisation appears to be the absolute tendency of all conditions, why should there not also be a harmonious action of these three? The harnessing of this trinity *universally* would replace the yoke of dogma, creed and intolerance forever for such endeavour must surely bring about a combined universal power resulting in man being kind to man.

It follows therefore that what is needed today is a religion without intolerance of any kind for it can only be the direct way forward. The chains of this or that religion for too long have bound mankind in many an opposite corner of belief. Stuck with their particular "book of truth", each sect, most often encouraged by their priests, still stands today, hurling abuse across the great abyss of non-communication.

Religion should be like music, international and interchangeable where one can, irrespective of nationality or language, communicate thoughts, words and deeds without penalty of any kind. A Gnostic type of religion where one may take on board all those things that seem acceptable at the time. Equally, one ought to be able, as one spiritually progresses, to cast aside, at will, whatever one desires, without fear or rancour. A religion where Personal Responsibility, the Law of Cause and Effect, Psychism and Humanitarianism is accepted for what it is. A religion that recognises that the "Christ" (not to be confused with Christianity's definition of Jesus) Spirit is in all peoples of the world. A religion where one is not answerable to a priest who can, with a wave of the hand, forgive you for sins that can be committed and forgiven over and over again! Nor one where that same priest-hood can have you banished for ever from the religion to which you belong!

Maybe we are wrong to make God such a personal thing, whereby we think somehow it is wrong to discuss openly with no holds barred, that which passes between *our* God and ourselves. Perhaps subconsciously, or even consciously, we consider our faith to be a mite fragile, afraid to place it under others' scrutiny, fearing that it too only has a foundation of sand. In considering such options, we may prefer to take the view that some faith is better than none. As such *any* open discussion is purposely avoided in case cracks or fragility of belief become painfully evident.

Could the reason for this be our childhood and school years when, in praying, we were never required to speak aloud our original thoughts or desires? We were never invited to openly express our opinions on what we thought about God, or what God was and so forth yet we were required often to read or recite aloud to the class. Certainly in the many schools I attended I know I was never asked to talk freely about God, prayer or even read the Bible aloud. The only prayers uttered were those mumbled, parrot fashion each morning, and these too rapidly dispensed with so that the head could get assembly over as quickly as possible. At home also, especially in Winter, they were just as speedily said in order to gain the comfort of a warm bed!

I am also of the opinion that we should allow children to grow up and enter into the religion *they* want. In many cases parents themselves rarely attend church and are not, for that matter, particularly religious. Yet almost invariably they automatically trot along to have their children baptised into the faith they were born into usually because they simply thought it was the right thing to do! But I submit it is yet another aspect of the "laughing priests" syndrome.

Example! More often than not, when couples wish to marry, unless they can produce the evidence of their baptism in that faith, the priest will refuse to perform the service. But quite apart from the misgivings about such "enforced" baptism dogma, we also respected our daughter's inborn right to exercise *her* own choice of faith. As an adult therefore whenever (or even if ever) she might feel the need to choose a religion or credo, whatever path that may be will have my unwavering endorsement.

The true secret of successful religion is to be in At-One-Ment with God and Spirit both. Prayer helps but do try to have a clear conception of what it entails for if it is just repetitive words, no matter how poetic and beautiful the prose, it will avail you nothing. If we give some serious thought to what we are asking, we should quickly see that by a conscientious effort of will we can actually effect many of these things ourselves *without* the need for prayer. Indeed, the reflection and effort put into the thinking is, in itself, efficient (and often sufficient) prayer to bring about our desires.

Real, true prayer is not then simply a collection of joined together words, but a certain loving receptiveness, a child-like attitude reaching out to, and asking of, the Father of All Being. The constant promise has always been "Ask and ye shall receive" and was known long before the Christian Master's ministry. So first, form a conception of what we long for and desire. Then aspiring to the highest and best of our ability let it become a living reality, a real thing in the Universal Life Principle. Then, asking, endeavour to reach out to the living energy, the God-head for with loving thoughts, a *breathing-out* of the Soul into the all-surrounding Spirit of Life takes place and is reflected back as an *in-breathing* of Spiritual energy-force. This is the economy of all occult things; reaction; simply: "As you sow, so shall you reap." I caution you to remember too that "no" or "not yet" is still an answer!

Some fifty years ago, though still wet behind the ears, like so many of my contemporaries since, I rejected the concept of a personal, omnipotent, anthropomorphic God as being yet another of orthodoxy's methods of controlling their sheeplike followers.

It is true that this planet cannot survive without the Sun. However, it would be incorrect to deduce from my opening words when I pray that I also subscribe to the worship of same. Though often beginning: "Dear Father; God; Thou whom art the Source of all supply and the Soul of all Energy..." this simply sums up, for *me* at least, what God is and does! Thus it effectively demonstrates the power of the Spirit-energy-force existing in all things both animate and inanimate. One might say this points to an Animism persuasion but I deny that too as I am constantly in a learning mode so I will not allow myself to be tied to any single belief or object.

My learning is that thoughts are things and that God is in all things. Further, that the process of thought goes on, loaded continuously and unceasingly onto the astral dimensions and the Self-existing Whole supported by zero point nought energy (0.0 energy) - in a word, cosmism. After all, there is nothing one perceives that did not begin as a thought, which process in itself is also a thought. After transition too memory and thoughts remain as a mind-force long after the physical body has turned to dust which ably demonstrates the power of same. So thoughts, irrespective, big or small, always requiring the expenditure of the Spirit-energy-force, must be intrinsically the source of those thoughts.

(If the following seems somewhat presumptuous it is not my intention; I merely wish to indicate, in the easiest way I can, just what God means to me.) Thus the use of Spirit-energy-force, together with all that I hold to be good is, for me, the nearest I can get to a definition of God. But in reality such explanations are only speculative, not definitive for if one is a "sieve" and always prepared to learn, one automatically finds one's parameters too must change. These must give way as new thoughts, new lessons, new ideas and, for that matter, ideals, take the place of those presently held in esteem.

One thing is certain; we cannot buck immutable law! Everyone has to be born to come into this world and everyone has to make their transition to leave it, a law that is, in itself, quite a leveller! A man in a nudist camp cannot be judged as to his poverty, wealth, profession or rank in life merely from his state of undress. In the same way nobody can bring into this world anything but a naked body nor leave it any other way! Why then is it that all to often we are judged by our contemporaries and peers merely by our clothes, wealth and station in life?

In spite of this (or because of it) Spirit stands supreme, an on-going process that cannot simply be shelved. A great chief once said that when we die, to be remembered as a good person was all we were entitled to expect of life! So endeavour to try to leave behind some memory, some example or other good thing for others to follow while equally being acutely aware that none of us have a "God-given right" to force upon others our *own* beliefs. Humankind has been blessed with a mind that is able to reason and an ability to exercise a free-will through it! So thank your God in a constant endeavour to use it wisely.

In vain do men talk of happiness, they who never subdued an impulse in obedience to a principle. He who never sacrificed a present to a future good, or a personal to a general one, cannot know true happiness. He can only speak of it as blind men do of colours. *True religion* teaches and all *true* men and women *know* that the perfecting of humankind can only come about by the ever-increasing predominance of the Soul over the body.

What then is the Soul; is it the mind perhaps? If so, then where in the body is the mind located? It is certainly (as yet) not an identifiable or visible organ in either the body or brain, and if such things as *invisible* organs exist, they cannot be seen anyway! A very famous medium has, apparently, declared that the soul is to be found in a cavity behind the heart! Well, though laying no claim to any qualifications here, I do have a fairly broad knowledge of anatomy and as far as I am aware no such cavity even exists, never mind the soul being so contained.

I will state however, unequivocally, that should it be discovered and identified as a physical part of the body, it will make the finder an overnight sensation and successful for life. Indeed it will be common knowledge the world over in less than twenty-four hours! However, if in fact it proves to be *physical* then it cannot survive its transition and as such, dying with the physical body, it completely negates the argument of the soul's immortality.

Looking to the dictionary again, surprise, surprise, it too has no clear definition! Some twenty-four of these are listed, varying from memory to ego, to a spirit, to direction of the will. So, is it then, after all, a part of the brain and if so why is it not mentioned, listed among those definitions?

Much greater scholars than I have put forth views as to what the soul is but so far have never produced a satisfactory comprehensively agreed definition! Maybe it is indefinable, but I think not; it is more likely that we mortals are not yet ready to receive such wisdom! Therefore I have very little chance of defining it too and can only put forth such crumbs of knowledge as I have acquired. Nevertheless, this in no way prohibits my commenting or expounding upon what and how I feel.

Poets and the like may perhaps be forgiven for speaking of the soul in a romantic way. Orthodoxy on the other hand, must be taken to task in lacking an explanation of the soul. Theirs has only ever been on a very superficial level suggesting that they also appear to have no laid down methods or writings on its actual definition. It is left to the priests at ground level who mostly express only in platitudes and clichés to grieving relatives as to what happened and where their loved ones have gone. And since their hierarchy also appears to have no will, determination nor policy to investigate its progress after the change we call death such inadequate explanations will continue.

Grasp the nettle - understand that the growth of the Soul whilst here on Earth is one of the weightiest questions of all human life. Strive to brush away the clouds of doubt and fear and once free and awake you shall gain the Light along The Paths of the Hidden Way, for the purest light is obscured by no cloud. Do not bog yourself down in trying to be definitive by merely using words, for such definitions will always find argument and ever without conclusion. Move on to loftier thoughts and the realms of Spirit Truth, leaving mundane thoughts and actions to those who delight in harbouring and wallowing in them.

Above all things learn to control anger, jealousy, hateful thoughts or actions. Use sympathy in a practical way, asking what you can do to help the unfortunate person rather than just paying lip-service. Many times one observes people expressing sorrow to someone about the loss of their friend or relative, yet often they do not even know *the person they are speaking to, let alone the loved one.*

It is also good to learn that a pitched battle is better than a continued skirmish and definitely preferable to a full-scale war! Remember, every time you get angry or speak impetuously, you weaken your own nerve force, causing unnecessary stormy conditions within your *own* aura, but more importantly, of your *soul* too. Sometimes as well, you add to the misery and undermining of another's nerve force, who often, without cause or reason, has to bear the brunt of your outburst.

How often does a parent get angry with a child when chastisement, probably, in one form or another follows? Examination of the facts would show, in many cases, that it was the parent who felt off-colour or angry and the child, whilst not totally innocent, nevertheless did not deserve the degree of anger expressed. The parent (not necessarily knowingly) simply found fault to work off their *own* anger or frustration, using the child as a mental punch-bag and sometimes, tragically, even as a physical one.

Therefore, in silence, learn to know yourself; conquer the storms that lie within *you* and in so doing find yourself feeling better and better within as each new day dawns. In this way will your Soul stand forth, revealing itself and its secrets through the unseen guidance of those who have gone before, those enlightened souls, anxious and ever willing to assist you and others in your search for the Truth and Light.

In concluding this chapter it must, I think, also be remembered that there are very many creeds, sects, and religious beliefs in the world. This alone should make us stand back and ponder seriously the proposition that whilst we *all* think we are right and that *our* particular belief is the *only* true one, by the same premise we could all be wrong and the real truth is yet to be shown to us Earthlings!

Consequently, I know that the search must go on, with questions constantly asked and, like the sieve, I will continue to sift that which I discover. I shall try always to keep a truly open mind, safe in the knowledge of *knowing* that a greater force is at work and one that cannot simply be contained by dogma, artificial truths, or highfalutin ideas. Neither will it, nor *can it* go away just by simply closing our minds to it all.

The truth is out there - "Seek and Ye shall find!"

The following is a poem that came into my possession many years ago by way of an apport. For me, the words sum up what the God-Force (Spirit) is. It also presents an easily understood definition of the connection and interaction we have with the Infinite God and Spirit. The poem is very, very old, the author long ago lost in time. It is seen throughout the world in many different and varied situations and has also been translated into many languages.

GOD

Oh thou eternal One! Whose presence bright
All space doth occupy, all motion guide;
Unchanged through time's all devastating flight
Thou only God! There is no God beside!
Being above all beings! Mighty One!
Whom none can comprehend and none explore,
Who fill'st existence with Thyself alone;
Embracing all, - supporting, - ruling o'er,
Being whom we call God - and know no more!

Thou from primeval nothingness didst call
First chaos, then existence; - Lord, on Thee
Eternity had it's foundation; - all
Sprung forth from Thee; - of light, joy, harmony,
Sole origin; - all life, all beauty Thine.
Thy word created all, and doth create;
Thy splendour fills all space with rays divine,
Thou art, and wert, and shalt be! Glorious! Great!
Light-giving, life-sustaining Potentate.

In its sublime research, philosophy
May measure out the ocean deep - may count
The sands or the Sun's rays - but God, for Thee
There is no weight nor measure; none can mount
Up to Thy mysteries. Reason's brightest spark,
Though kindled by Thy light, in vain would try
To trace Thy counsels, infinite and dark;
And thought is lost, ere thought can soar so high,
Even like past moments in eternity.

Thy chains the unmeasured universe surround;
Upheld by Thee, by Thee inspired with breath!
Thou the beginning with the end hast bound,
And beautifully mingled life with death!

143

As sparks mount upward from the fiery blaze,
So suns are born, so worlds spring forth from Thee
And as spangles in the sunny rays
Shine round the silver snow, the pageantry
Of Heaven's bright army glitters in Thy praise.

A million torches lighted by Thy hand
Wander unwearied through the blue abyss;
They own Thy power, accomplish Thy command,
All gay with life, all eloquent with bliss.
What shall we call them? Piles of crystal light -
A glorious company of golden streams -
Lamps of celestial ether burning bright -
Suns lighting systems with their joyous beams?
But Thou to these art as the noon to night.

Yes! As a drop of water in the sea,
All this magnificence in Thee is lost;
What are ten thousand worlds compared to Thee;
And what am I then? Heaven's unnumbered host,
Though multiplied by myriads, and arrayed
In all the glory of sublimest thought,
Is but an atom in the balance weighed
Against Thy greatness, is a cipher brought
Against infinity! What am I then? Nought.

Nought! But the effluence of Thy light divine,
Pervading worlds, hath reached my bosom, too;
Yes! In my spirit doth Thy spirit shine
As shines the sunbeam in a drop of dew.
Nought! But I live, and on hope's pinions fly
Eager towards Thy presence; for in Thee
I live, and breathe, and dwell; aspiring high
Even to the throne of Thy divinity.
I am, O God! And surely Thou must be!

Thou art! Directing, guiding all, Thou art!
Direct my understanding then to Thee;
Control my Spirit, guide my wandering heart.
Though but an atom 'midst immensity,
Still I am something, fashioned by Thy hand!
I hold a middle rank 'twixt Heaven and Earth,
On the last verge of mortal being stand,
Close to realms where angels have their birth,
Just on the boundaries of the spirit-land!

The chain of being is complete in me;
In me is matter's last gradation lost;
And the next step is spirit - Deity!
I can command the lightning, and am dust!
A monarch, and a slave; a worm, a god!
Whence came I here, and how? so marvellously
Constructed and conceived? Unknown! This clod
Lives surely through some higher energy;
For from itself alone it could not be!

Creator, yes! Thy wisdom and Thy word
Created me! Thou source of life and good!
Thou spirit of my spirit and my Lord!
Thy light, Thy love, in their bright plentitude
Filled me with an immortal soul, to spring
Over the abyss of death, and bade it wear
The garments of eternal day, and wing
It's heavenly flight beyond this little sphere,
Even to it's source - to Thee - it's author there.
O thoughts ineffable! O visions blessed!
Though worthless our conception all of Thee.
Yet shall Thy shadowed image fill our breast
And waft it's homage to Thy Deity.
God! Thus alone my lowly thoughts can soar;
Thus seek Thy presence - being wise and good!
'Midst Thy vast works, admire, obey, adore;
And when the tongue is eloquent no more,
The soul shall speak in tears of gratitude.

HELPFUL NOTES!

(On name calling and missionaries.) *When the name of atheist, heretic, heathen, pagan, savage, infidel and the like is hurled at a person it is most often for no reason other than that the religious opinions and beliefs held by others simply differ from those of the one hurling the abuse and accusations! So it is well to remember that such abuse and accusations are often prompted either by one's own lack of true faith and belief in the brotherhood of man, or both!*

When the missionaries originally invaded "heathen territory" their primary function and brief was to gather the unbelievers under their particular umbrella of religious persuasion. As such, they would, of necessity, be obliged to condemn the native beliefs out of hand, stating that they were devil worshippers and would go to hell if they did not change their ways forthwith!

This though, for the "heathens" presented somewhat of a dilemma. It appeared that both credendum, seemingly, had the same goal. Each believed that when one died one was admitted to the Spirit World, simply Heaven by another name! Therefore whether they chose their normal cultural practices and rituals as taught by their own priests, shaman, or magi, or went the alternate Christian route, they still ended their journey in the same way. Thus if the result was the same what then was gained or achieved by their changing?

Such changes however only appeared to be the same, for as the doctrinal creases were ironed out the differences were clearly seen and argument speedily gained apace! For example, Nature and the spirits in all things and the Earth Mother who regarded all people as her children were dismissed out of hand! There was, the missionaries stressed, but one omnipotent white God and his only child, also white, was called Jesus!

However, the main objection causing resistance to the missionary's path was that he expounded the idea that they would not automatically be reunited with their loved ones or be able to hunt, fish or whatever in his Heaven! It was this then and not, as might be thought, merely the pressure of the native priests, etc. though naturally these would turn such things to their own advantage. They would tell that their Spirit World had sustained their tribes for far more years than the missionaries propounded (Heaven) one! More, that they were all children of the Earth Mother and that the missionary's rules were far too strict!

The net result was, in many cases, one of better the devil they knew, etc. So who could blame them for expediting the situation and following their own shaman advice with, in many cases, the unfortunate missionary simply becoming dinner?

More unfortunate however, as history reveals, was that when armed reinforcements arrived, they mostly took (who among those were the real heathens I ask?) savage revenge. Then, once subdued, they were quickly seduced by gifts to the chiefs, including rifles, to which ploys many succumbed. (A crafty move this for all the ammunition given was that contained in the guns at the time. So, once the bullets were fired these, at best, could only serve as clubs or hammers!) Thus, deferring to the white mans way, the missions sprung up everywhere and the rest, as they say, is history! But one cannot help speculating and wondering what would have happened had this not occurred or even had the reverse taken place perhaps?

(On the Christian "cover-up" and the Bible on the practise of gifts of the Spirit.) *The Church of England, in the thirties, commissioned an independent enquiry into Spiritualism and healing quite expecting a negative report. However, much to their surprise and, it has to be said, their total embarrassment too, the report was actually very favourable, so much so that the church authorities refused to make it public. A copy was leaked to the editor of "Psychic News" and was accordingly published. To my certain knowledge, officially, that report is still under wraps.*

Yet we find in the Bible the following:- "Heal the sick" - Luke X, 9. "Work miracles" - I Cor. XII, 10. "Your sons and daughters shall prophesy" - Acts II, 17. "Shall see visions" - Acts II, 17. "Discerning of spirits" - Acts I; COR. XI, 10. "Casting out devils" - Mark VXI, 17. "Shall speak with new tongues" - Mark VXI, 17. "Shall dream dreams" - Acts II, 17. "Raise the dead" - Matt. X, 8. and there are many more.

These were the teachings and commands of Jesus, the messiah (the message bringer or Christ-Spirit) and were set to become the basis of Christianity to be "observed to the end of the world." Yet the Jehovah Witnesses, Baptists, etc., always on the attack against Spiritualism, simply ignore such quotes, referring only to those that suit their own biased and narrow doctrine!

The Cardinals too, when electing a new pope sit in conclave, meditating, waiting for the "Spirit to move them" so that they may cast their vote in accordance with the will of God. A part of the Church of England service for the promotion of a bishop has something similar as well. Seven other bishops form a circle around him and invoke the "Spirit of the Holy Ghost". Both of these cases, on the face of it, demonstrate what happens in a properly run, controlled Spiritualist séance or circle, i.e. communion with disembodied spirits. Yet this is frowned upon, indeed banned among the orthodoxy as a code of practice! One has to conclude therefore, that it is, to quote the old adage "Don't do as I do, do as I say"!

(On beating the system!) *Anything that was deemed by the orthodox church to be witchcraft had, by definition, to be kept secret by its followers. In consequence, quite ignorant of their "witchcraft" leanings, the authorities innocently employed many of its practitioners in the construction of its churches. Christianity, by the Renaissance period (when Gothic architecture was in full flow) was already a powerful and wealthy religious establishment and undertook much of this construction. The very familiar gargoyles high up on old churches as water exit-spouts and so on can still be seen today.*

Their employers' main concern was to complete the building as soon as possible so that the church might be put to use. It was because of this that the much maligned group of, in the main, Nature (White and not and Black Magic) worshippers were able to get their own back. Some of the architects, sculptors and masons also worshipped in the old ways, so many of these too played their part in the deception. Foisting the gargoyles onto their Christian bosses, they said that they were artistic and instilled the idea that, being so ugly, they would frighten off evil spirits. The church authorities took this up and have perpetuated yet another lie ever since, one more to nail!

(On other examples of oppression.) *The Native American Indians worship Nature. In earlier times a hunter asked the buffalo's spirit for its forgiveness and blessing. This ensured its, and his too, fast transport to the happy hunting grounds. The spirits also told the buffalo that Indians depended on them for food and warmth so, aware that they only killed for those reasons, such animals accepted the hunter's prayers.*

In considering this a rather romantic belief, even a cop-out from the killing of animals I contend it to be far more spiritual than that of the so-called sportsmen who never even bothered to get off a train to hunt! Buffalo were shot this way for "sport" and with the trains moving on, the carcasses were left to rot and the wounded animals to die in agony where they fell. (Native American folk lore tells that before the coming of the white eyes a man could walk on the backs of the buffalo from horizon to horizon and never once touch the ground!) Factual accounts of the day prove that the "sportsmen" and their like killed hundreds of thousands and the herds have never really recovered from that carnage.

It is of hard perhaps for many to imagine, even today, the culture shock experienced at the desecration of Indian belief, their offended faith, dismay and confusion on seeing such irresponsible wanton destruction and waste. Remember too the thousands of Indians, many of whom were women, children and the old ones. Striking only when the able-bodied men were off hunting or fighting elsewhere they knew that those in camp were quite unable to offer any resistance yet the "gallant cavalry" slaughtered them just as readily as the aforementioned buffalo.

History recorded the treachery of the politicians and their like. Bent on bringing about the total eradication of the Indian nations, they almost succeeded! Tired of war and starved out of their lands chiefs went to Washington for discussions on the future of their people and were conned once again. Told the reservations abounded with game and water was plentiful, they returned from the capital. Unwittingly, they led their people onto virtual wastelands that supported no game and very little water. Protests and treaties ignored, dissent or uprising immediately and brutally put down, they quickly became a forgotten people. Government papers now available blatantly show a lasting blot on America's conscience and history. The intention was "to let them die out naturally (from starvation for instance) so nobody need take, or feel any blame for their deaths." (Interestingly, Sitting Bull, perhaps the most famous of the chiefs sat in on many such pow-wows but never ever subscribed to, or signed, a treaty with the whites!)

The Bushmen of South Africa, regarded as vermin by the farmers, were also slaughtered in huge numbers (and are almost extinct today) by bounty hunters. Native law said that land could not be owned by anyone and any tribes could roam and hunt them. Thus they saw no difference between farm animals and the wild ones they had hunted for centuries, and before there was such things as farms or farmers!

All animals, birds and all things were part of Nature and, like the land, belonged to the Gods and the Spirits within them. Just so long as they knew the "boss" for their different pursuits, of hunting, fishing, playing, etc. they were allowed to function when and where they pleased. Many times when hunting the God would not allow a kill or whatever. Whether the hunter was not perhaps as good a shot as he thought he was made no difference; it was the will of the God. So how could a mere mortal claim outright that the land and the animals, etc. were his alone? (Similarly, the Aborigines in Australia were slaughtered for the same reasons as the Bushmen and are today also far smaller in numbers!)

The slave traders deliberately taking young, healthy African tribesmen and women meant that only the old, infirm and children were left. Almost always these died of starvation or disease given to them by those same traders for not content with their evil trade alone, they also raped and pillaged. Whole tribes, estimated at some four hundred thousand plus, were wiped off the face of the earth by these "civilised" murderers but it did not stop there.

These "good and faithful upright white folks" felt no qualms, taking unmitigated advantage of those poor unfortunates. After being bought in the slave market, tribe members and or family were frequently split up. Then, for convenience and to demonstrate their wealth, owners gave slaves their name, thereby destroying even their heritage! With the last vestige of identity torn from these tormented souls, many never again saw or heard from kith and kin.

They were not allowed to get above their station either so all slaves were forbidden to learn to read or write. The punishment was death or at the very least, a severe flogging, which often killed them anyway. Young men from "good families" were also given, with full parental consent, young slaves on which to sow their wild oats. If offspring resulted, most times they were quickly sold on, or often even smothered at birth! Should we wonder then that they regard white folk, in the main, as "trash" and still today hold an inbred grudge against the whites?

The rainforests indigenous Indians in South America are, even now, being slaughtered by mercenaries, when the ground is cleared for producing cattle for beefburgers. Pushed deeper and deeper into the jungles, their hunting grounds and food supply is ending in the inevitable result - starvation! Their shaman, as the forests diminish daily, despair too, knowing that if mankind does not come to its senses very soon precious healing plants, herbs and trees, rapidly disappearing, will be lost forever. Meanwhile "civilised" land-grabbers and unconcerned governments, bending simply to greed, continue to ignore what to the "ignorant and uncivilised" Indian is so painfully obvious.

This forest land is not suited to rapid or continual grass production and the animals rapidly eat out the areas. But they are simply moved onto the next felled part of the rain forest to do the same thing! It is common knowledge that the world's weather is being turned upside down, removing at a stroke thousands of years of evolution, though worse perhaps is the total disregard for ones fellow man, or do we still have no respect in western society for mere "savages?"

Another ecological paradise is systematically being destroyed. Inhabited by almost a million "savages" speaking some two hundred and sixty languages, West Papua New Guinea had long been coveted by Indonesia. For twenty-five thousand years the natives have worshipped, protected and lived in harmony with Mother

149

Earth. *This beautiful and fertile land, their birthright, with its rich natural resources such as copper, gold, timber and oil, to name but a few, were things that did not interest them. But Indonesian politicians and military quickly perceived the potential for easy pickings!*

So in 1963, the indigenous natives there were given a "free" vote to decide whether or not to become an independent state under Indonesia's "umbrella of protection." Knowing little or nothing about ballot voting but suspecting something was amiss, the elders and chiefs resisted. Very quickly the Indonesian military rounded up 1,025 of these from various tribes. They then persuaded them to vote for independence - by dropping those who did not agree to their death from helicopters! In the resulting uprising by the natives, using only bows and arrows they fought against helicopters and machine guns and 100,000 natives died.

In that same year, 1963, it became the twenty-sixth province of Indonesia and six short years later the UN. Assembly agreed to Indonesia's annexing of West Papua. A picture that differs from historical norms is seen here, i.e. that two very different religions and cultures apparently overtly co-operated together. (Indonesia is basically Hindu, while the western world is virtually Christian, yet over the centuries, each has poured scorn upon the other's beliefs! What a waste and a pity that it was not put to better use!) Obviously to anyone who has half a brain can see that it was nothing to do with a coming together of each others religious beliefs. Covertly co-ordinated, it was prosecuted solely by the "powers that be" for political convenience, material expediency and nothing more!

Head hunting, a part of their worship and culture is now banned and from the comfort of our armchairs, we may shudder and think it only right and proper too. But we might also consider the native's viewpoint on nuclear warfare. When this was explained to them they also shuddered and thought it abominable and quite unwarriorlike.

Very few died in their head hunting "wars" anyway for these were more a question of hurling insults and out-guessing the enemy's strategy than actual close combat. They always became very poor shots if a war started but the reasons are easily explained. If a head was inadvertently taken, a volunteer would whisper into its ear, telling its spirit to return to its own proper place. This inevitably failed and then the taker automatically had to assume the dead man's responsibilities and this meant moving into his village and taking care of his spouse and children!

Since '69, funded by the World Bank and backing from America, over seven hundred thousand Indonesians have settled. This has eased the burden on overcrowded Indonesia but these now account for almost half of the population of West Papua. Large tracts of jungle have been cleared for houses and farmland. Pushed further inland the natives too have, like the Brazilian Indians, lost both their sago trees and hunting grounds, their food source.

With a ban on nudity, their normal "dress" and schools being set up where, by law, only Indonesian is spoken, children are now taught that their own culture is dead. Told they must now become Indonesian such tactics are classic demonstrations of indoctrination, mind-bending and brain-washing.

Anthropologists state that the irrigation and cultivating systems in the valley areas rate among the most sophisticated in the world. For many centuries the natives have paid homage to the land, believing that everything on it and in it has a soul, especially the forest. Now a road is being pushed through these areas, killing yet more trees.

Large numbers of native children rounded up to work as forced labour gangs in the timber industry, paid only in tobacco quickly became addicted to smoking. Native men have now mostly replaced them "harvesting" the trees. The bark is stripped and they carry the trunks to the river's edge. Oh yes, they get paid - they receive just one dollar a tree and the timber company receives, on average, five hundred!

With little or none of their customs practised any more, their beliefs and culture steam-rolled, their spirit and will is being and, in many cases, already has, been irretrievably broken. A resistance group still functions but their weapons are still only bows and arrows...

Chapter 2
SCENARIO A LA MEDIUMSHIP

I wrote previously of the discontent among the Arabs in 1953 and as such we were only permitted to leave camp on official duties. Unfortunately, because of this, I was unable to visit the Pyramids or the Valleys of the Kings and Queens. However, I do not state this simply in passing for here too is found that other great archaeological masterpiece, the Great Sphinx, itself an enigma both as to its age and purpose. But more importantly I think are two words carved into it, which, for the sheer brevity alone, makes it possibly the most profound sentence of all time namely Know Thyself! And hard on its heels is the statement that it is probably the most difficult lesson one has to learn in life too!

(Incidently, scientists have discovered that the Sphinx's deterioration in the last few years is more than in all of the previous thousands of ones. Standing not only as a grand tribute to its builders it also classically demonstrates things going badly awry on this planet of ours. So perhaps it is also time that we began to "Know thy planet too!")

Neither height nor depth can measure the possibilities of the human soul. Spiritual philosophy teaches that the development of a person's Spiritual, Psychic and mediumship talents to their own certain, true knowledge, settles for them, four questions of momentous import. (a) That individuals have a conscious existence beyond the grave. (b) That physical disease and infirmities no longer exist being left at "death" with the earthly body. That individuals, continue to exist mentally and morally in exactly the same way as when they leave this earthly life. That they retain until such time as it becomes no longer of value to the individual their identity, memory and character. (c) That this future existence is one of mental and spiritual progressive un-foldment and is open to all human intelligence. (d) That the initial process of death in no way essentially transforms the mental constitution or the moral character of those who experience it! But equally that progress will lead inevitably and eventually to a higher spiritual level of thought when both character and mental constitution will have transformed into a higher sphere of enlightenment.

So mankind should be aware of and realise that he has a spiritual as well as a corporeal nature. In other words, the real man and woman is Spirit. This is an organised form, a mind or energy-force, composed of spiritual matter, which does not, indeed cannot, die. This enables him or her, once they are "dead" to reflect their own, or any other image they may wish to (mentally) construct. This may be for the benefit of recognition or to convey something to another mind-force, whether the recipient is in the spirit or corporeal form.

Being found to survive the change called physical death, it may therefore reasonably be supposed he will also survive all future vicissitudes. Defined thus, that is that energy cannot be destroyed, only altered, it follows that mankind is immortal in the purest sense. Once the seeker of truth recognises, absorbs and thence *knows* this, he or she begins the real journey towards Truth and Light. Passing from just *belief* he or she now enjoys the new found freedom of possessing *positive knowledge*.

He or she now *knows* that the Vital Spirit in the flesh and blood performs the office of the Soul. In other words our souls direct our destiny, endeavouring, with the help of our door keepers, to point us in the right direction according to that destiny. So make *your* endeavour the search for the inner temple of knowledge within, for what you cannot believe from within you shall never believe from without. This guiding process, this consciousness, is in us all; indeed it is an integral and intrinsic part of our make up.

For example there are certain things which one cannot bring oneself to do or say. For the purpose of argument here it matters not what these are and in the event they may differ, even if only slightly, from person to person and from race to race. Called simply Moral Obligation, (the conscience) this has been adopted and adapted by humankind as a way of life. It is undoubtedly the foundation, the spring-board from which all man-made laws, irrespective of culture base, have leapt, becoming established throughout the whole planet.

Such responsibility though, passing as it has from the individual to the state has also, to some extent, produced a *psychic void*, a negative effect. Unwittingly, as time moved on, it is obvious that man gradually no longer bothered to think, question or search for answers himself. After all, he had the law and his faith (often one and the same, i.e. the church) to guide and make decisions for him! This allowed, somewhat tragically for man, the psychic part of his nature to slip into decline; indeed into almost total oblivion.

Unless the psychic mind works both in conjunction and in total accord with the physical one, this consciousness *will not,* indeed *cannot,* be utilised to its best advantage. In consequence much of the guiding process is therefore mislaid and, in very many people, through non-usage, even lost. Over the centuries, seeking for recognition and acknowledgement of their achievements by their peers, humankind has more and more looked without and less and less within!

Though more evident in wealthier western societies, the Third World countries are also rapidly catching up economically. Commendable as this may be sadly, at the same time, they are becoming infected with the same psychic loss. In short this means that today more and more people are moving further away from Nature and her laws. Unchecked, this virtually leads to a dulling or even losing completely, the ability to tune in to the infinite, wherein is revealed the knowledge (the Truth) that there is nothing new under the Sun.

Others though are fighting back, a sort of revivalist rearguard movement who are gradually gaining both in ground and numbers. These are to be found espousing that Spiritual Truth declares and affirms that all humankind are born psychic and that these abilities can (and will, if true desire is there) be developed to the benefit of all things in Nature, thus restoring the balance.

However, a problem also occurs with some of these. This happens when the conscious and voluntary power, already actually possessed by the vast mass of psychics, is used unconsciously or even involuntarily. This kind of psychic practice is often of a very poor standard, with the psychic and even recipients (often unaware) struggling with the lower forces in conflict with their own intuitive dissemination. It can also leave all participants tired and sometimes depressed, feeling much like a tired old steam engine fighting its way up a steep incline.

The reason is that it does not embrace nor is it subjected to the purer and healthy growth that should occur through the progression from psychic(ship) to *mediumship*. Using merely psychic ability will not, indeed cannot, manifest the highest and the grandest demonstration or exhibition of Spirit Power and its Truths. These can only come through genuine Spirit communication and communion; true mediumship will therefore always demonstrate and outstrip the performance of the sole use of one's personal intuitive psychic abilities.

T.V. programmes and literature presently abound with information on psychic philosophy and phenomena, much of it discoursing on mediumship. The media often state that there are natural-born mediums (like myself) and also developed mediums. This last is a misnomer! Never has there been, nor is there even today (a very mis-used word this) a developed medium! One is constantly developing, or at least should be! Like other professions and trades there are new things emerging every day, so it is wise to keep abreast of one's craft. It is imperative therefore that mediums, natural or trained, stay constantly and consistently in the learning mode, adopting as an ever present lesson the maxim that one is "always the pupil - never the master!"

Often when people see me working so casually they think one learns mediumship in six easy lessons. Not true! To become adept at anything one must first learn *how* and mediumship is no exception. Having an open, enquiring mind is the basis from which all learning begins. It also requires total involvement and the maximising of one's patience and desire to achieve results. I have to say that however one might try there is no true valid short cut. Mediumship especially, even with us naturals, cannot escape either! We cannot choose not to go there or there! We have to follow through or else later realise we have lost something quite unique and valuable.

In essence, each day, irrespective of the length of our experience, we should make the effort to set aside a little quiet time, even five to ten minutes is often sufficient! The developing circle should never be given the cold shoulder either. One should always, irrespective of one's attainment, try to sit in one somewhere for I state without fear of contradiction that we can all learn and or pass on to others something of value.

Whilst both of these ideas may be considered as good they should be more than this! Consider them as being a very necessary part of one's continuing development. The reason is simple; it keeps us more closely in touch not only with our guides and helpers but with other like souls too; if you like, it keeps the "door", as it were, ajar. And remember, provided one is sincere, there is never a wasted moment in communion with Spirit; hence the need to always be conscious of the learning mode.

Spiritual Laws and Man-made Laws though often found in opposite corners are, nonetheless, intrinsically linked. Men usually desire four things in life, viz.: Love, Wealth, Fame and Power. Most other things are generally considered to be purely for amusement or something to be forgotten. The educated, wealthy, successful and or sophisticated person therefore frequently finds it difficult to come to terms with the idea that an uneducated, totally unsophisticated person often displays brilliant psychic and or mediumistic abilities. They find it frustrating too when they themselves, with their "superior cards" cannot even get into the game! It is not though a requirement to be well read, particularly with trance work, to hold the necessary credentials. In the event, it is the communicating spirit helpers and guides who hold all the aces! One does not have to be an educated person, an ardent church-goer or even a seen to be do-gooder either.

A medium, and for that matter *anyone*, can be Spiritually progressed and yet, perhaps due to their Karma, surroundings, upbringing, their level of education and or a variety of other reasons appear to the "pious" to be too down to earth; indeed not being sufficiently religious to carry a Spiritual label. But, as already stated within these pages, one does not have to don robes or demonstrate a pseudo piety to be able to do God's work! Indeed, I am privileged to have had the opportunity to sit with some very ordinary persons who have been the most extraordinary of mediums. These have ably given, without preamble, in or out of trance, brilliant material advice and, for that matter, wonderful spiritual advice and philosophy quite beyond their normal intellect too.

There is what I term the "piano-learning syndrome" which I think should be explained. Although anyone, if they are of a mind, can learn to play the piano, learn to paint or sing, or for that matter learn to do anything they wish, common-sense and reason tells us that we cannot, of course, all become concert pianists, world famous artists, brilliant cabinet makers or whatever. Logically, there *must* be and *are* varying degrees of ability and this is no less a case with psychics and mediums. It has to be said however, that irrespective of the ability, until one has the knowledge, the potential cabinet maker might well, figuratively speaking, only be able to knock nails into wood while the future concert pianist consistently stumbles through "Chopsticks" on the piano!

As with people in other fields, not only are there varying degrees of mediumship, there are also specialists, e.g. psychic detectives, who help the police and other private investigators and psychic artists who draw spirit persons. There are psychics who mainly attract child spirits; there are dowsers and psychometrists. There are those too who have prophecy, healing powers, physical mediumship, etc. And these too can be broken down *yet again* into levels of ability which result in excellent, good, not so good, bad and, sometimes, very bad demonstrations of mediumship.

Unlike other professions, many people are of the opinion that our powers are gifts and therefore we mediums should not receive remuneration for our efforts. These same people however, would willingly pay out huge sums for a ticket to see their favourite Tenor, Pop-star, footballer, classical Pianist or whatever. Whilst agreeing that these artistes also have a gift, they then attempt to both qualify and justify their expensive ticket declaring that these artistes have, sometimes undertaken years of practice and hard work to achieve their status. Many mediums, myself included, have *also* spent many years honing *our* gifts and, like some of those other gifted individuals, we *continue to do so* each and every day.

It can be said that *any talent* one has of whatever ilk is a gift but it still requires practice and hard work to perfect. Surely then the old adage "the worker is worthy of his hire" applies equally here, does it not? If this is accepted as reasonable then my response to these criticasters has to be the same as my attitude to things psychic. Think *logically*, open your mind and do not be biased in any way.

The concept of non-payment is, after all, way past its "sell-by" date anyway, having been conceived in Victorian times. Further, there is no gift, even though I concede that they are all God given, that gives one the ability to do without food, clothes or shelter for one's dependants and one's self! I would add too that even those mediums who *are* well paid *never* get rich and like many others in public life, they invariably do an awful lot of charitable work with no reward financially.

I will suspend further discussion on the subject of monetary reward, but in passing, I do know that many people, not only mediums, are coming to, or have come to, the conclusion that mediumship is a respectable profession and deserves rewarding financially. The day is long overdue when mediums, if they so desire, should be able to choose to work professionally without the penalty of having to wear sackcloth and sandals! (See e. of ch. on mediumship and payment)

There are times too when people try to cajole us into "performing" in order to spice up their party or whatever, when we are "begged" (and are frequently expected to oblige as well) by "normal" people to read the cards, hands, teacups, sand, rune stones, flowers or operate an ouija board or whatever, mostly because they think that this is the sort of thing we normally do. I have a lot of respect for these types of demonstrations and actually still practice some of them! However, they are only valid and will only receive worthy comment if the demonstrators *know* their craft. (Having the knowledge of the workings of these, I cannot therefore, like many of my contemporaries, dismiss them out of hand, as invalid for

Spirits' use for this is often where one's potential mediumship begins).

Even if we *were* prepared to demonstrate, we would be considered a real party-pooper if we said that there would be no more drinking or smoking and that we would have to form a circle and also open (and close) in prayer. Yet all too often these same folks are a little put out, even when you tell them that what you do is *not* a party trick. I will point out that they would not expect *their* husbands or wives to demonstrate *their* particular work at a party. So unless one feels absolutely comfortable doing it, one should decline and not simply satisfy a whim.

If other guests did perform though imagine the scene as a car mechanic glibly explains to the hostess that it is just a bit of harmless fun, when she, on returning to her lounge, finds him stripping down a greasy motor-car engine with no regard at all for her carpet! Then take the scene a little further. Imagine all the other guests joining in, demonstrating *their* trades and or professions! *Of course it is ridiculous!* But due to such "harmless bits of fun" at a party, it gives rise to a reason for our profession not being taken seriously by many people. In their ignorance because they do not understand, nor care to do so for that matter, they simply take the easy way out, regarding the whole thing as a trick or whatever. (But there are other reasons for this lack of interest and serious attention to mediums such as are related below).

So why are mediums not up there in the limelight? I am afraid it is due mainly to out-outmoded thinking and the casual approach of the organised Spiritualist authorities. They have, since the rise of modern Spiritualism in Victorian times, persistently clung to Christian Orthodoxy, with its crosses, Bibles, Jesus statues, religious pictures, hymns; indeed almost all the trimmings associated with the stylised Church of England, the while claiming to embrace all religions and persuasions.

The reasons for this stand out like the proverbial sore thumb! The early writers on psychic matters whether clergy, scientists or lay persons were virtually all from Christian stock. Whether practising or not it is pretty well a certainty that they were baptised as such! Horizons then were also still very far apart for unlike today one could not just hop a jet and in a few hours be on the other side of the world. So this meant that there was also nothing like the interchange, integration and social intercourse between cultures that exists today.

In comparison to the population at large, even in the late Victorian times, there were but a few extraordinary people and only a handful of intrepid adventurers, missionaries, explorers and sailors who ever left our shores! Even had they had the necessary finances, I doubt that, like today, many of the ordinary folk would have had the urge to back-pack around the world just for fun and little else.

Consequently, in the main, it was probably somewhat this lack of awareness of others cultures, religions and so on, that made these writers unwittingly, but naturally too, so slanted in their Spiritualist material towards the Christian concepts of religion at the time. Also converts were more easily brought into Spiritualism by writing about a Christian Spirit world that had houses and streets and countryside complete with trees and animals, etc. much the same as on Earth. However, the clincher was that this paradise was, by far, more beautiful with more colour and friendlier people. In short the writers presented for them a different concept from the previous image of St. Peter finger-wagging at the Golden Gate and to a cloud-like heaven. They simply replaced it with a more readily understandable "physical" one.

For centuries, having been led by the nose by priests, this new and struggling faith, anxious to get off the ground, needed to show people how easy it was to understand. The writers then, since there is safety in numbers, seem to have simply written what they thought would appeal to the average person in the street! We may conclude too, perhaps, that the writers, in danger of being labelled apostates or even heretics, would naturally err on the side of caution anyway, penning only that which was more likely to be simply regarded as eccentricity by those in power.

For students I "pen" some idea of the kinds of things that were said then and that some still propound. The spirit land has eternal sunshine so there is no rain; therefore there is no need of gutters and down-pipes on houses, etc. There is also no need for toilets or dustbins since spirit people eat different foods to when they were on the earth-plane. Therefore, being spiritual food, there are no waste products. Those who have gone on before us wait eternally for each and every one of us, including our animals, to "pass over" (what a quaint phrase) to their side! (Nobody wrote on what happens when others join the waiting masses.) For instance does someone save their place, and if they do, will they not be admonished for queue jumping? Such things as written and spoken of by so many, in reality, can only be regarded as sentimentalist at one end of the scale and totally illogical at the other.

Whatever, it is obvious to the discerning mind that these Spirit teachings were more than gently massaged. They were slanted and slotted into an acceptable form by these early day writers for the reasons stated, but they are by no means the only ones. One outstanding reason is that orthodoxy, having led the masses by the nose for centuries, stood forth audaciously and pompously proclaiming that Christianity was the only civilised religion in the world, all others being heathen or barbaric or both! It was somewhat inevitable therefore to find Modern Spiritualism, initially, hitching its own wagon to the same star.

Even today there are many mediums and churches, who, by now, really ought to know better. Still publicly praying and preaching however, solely in the name of Jesus and Christianity they, in the same breath, claim Native Americans, Chinese, Arabs and such as their guides and helpers! Do they prattle on, blissfully unaware of their helpers more extensive spiritual and religious knowledge? Do they really care enough (or even at all) what Spirit thinks? Or maybe they know something that I am unaware of; that spirit missionaries have converted all of the spirit dimensions to Christianity!

This is of course untrue and I make no apology for the intended facetiousness! I actually feel that such mediums are simply being selfish, expecting Spirit to toe *their* religious line. I have to think that they understand that the Spirit dimensions encompass all creeds, respecting them all as one universal cosmos - or have they learned so little? If they are so aware and I believe they truly are, then surely they must also be acutely aware that their prayers should be "open-ended" and not constricted by religious bias one way or the other?

(By way of example of what I have written above, I place before you the somewhat amusing scenario. I have often related this in public over the years to explain why, at such a young age, I found it necessary to discard such writings as aforementioned. This in turn led to the prime reason for placing my trust in Spirit to teach me of Spirit. However, since many of these things are still propounded by the less enlightened, I am equally saddened that yet again I feel the need to relate it here.)

Imagine then thousands and thousands of queues of people stretching away into the far distance. Shoulder to shoulder they wait in tidy lines on a gigantic parade ground. Every so often the odd "body" (the spirit kind of course!) breaks ranks. Having asked someone to save their place for them, they nip down to the café for a bit of non-waste-type refreshment.

A first-aid tent is provided for those who faint from the heat of the ongoing, eternal sun! There is also a "lost children tent" set up for the kids who, becoming bored and having strayed, subsequently get lost and here they anxiously wait for someone to collect them. And so on and so on... The mind boggles does it not? And some would say that animals also have their own "queues" (with Noah perhaps as the shepherd?) with similar facilities!

Ask most Jews, Muslims, Buddhists and so on who are interested in developing mediumship to look inside the average Spiritualist church. Without doubt they would, in all probability, baulk at the symbolism portrayed and be utterly dismayed too in discovering that they are expected to worship in a Christianised manner! It is well to remember that any one of these could well be a potential medium who, through such hidebound attitudes, is lost forever both to our cause and cost too.

Presently too, where both parents, often for economic reasons, *have to work*, they not only want to be together as a family at week-ends, but also often *need* to be together. This is not only for "togetherness" but also in order to effect the chores they are not able to complete during their busy weekdays. Why then, with a few exceptions, do churches still follow orthodoxy and insist on having their main services on a Sunday?

With the repeal of the Vagrancy Act in 1951, a bill was passed through parliament making Spiritualism, besides the Church of England, the only other state-recognised religion in the UK! As such, a wonderful opportunity to capitalise was presented to Spiritualism - but did they shout it from the rooftops? No! Mainly through muddled thinking and lack of planning for the future, instead of making the most of this once in a lifetime publicity vehicle, it just came and went.

In consequence, over the years, they have never thrown off the mantle (or, as I believe the bridle?) of Christianity in toto, replacing it, as originally proposed, with a purely non-denominational Spiritualist one. Indeed, many church committees pedantically continue to endorse this Christianised format, albeit in a somewhat more pseudo fashion, yet adhering to the same old worn out symbolism. I have to add too that this is not only found in Christian Spiritualist churches either. It is also prominent in *all* Spiritualist organisations, including the S.N.U. and others!

Conversely, the orthodox church has begun to see the light in understanding the necessity to revamp the antiquated, out-moded direction they have taken for so many years. Slowly but surely, since the birth of modern Spiritualism, they have realised that there is a vast pool of humanity interested in more than the platitudinous and often covert religious practices that had, for so long, been an integral part of their inexorable institutions. Finally realising that Spiritualism is *not*, after all, the work of the devil has resulted in a substantial number of orthodox ministers and churches hi-jacking much of *our* practices. For example they now run healing groups with the laying on of hands and meditation circles. The exorcising of so called devils, hitherto always a secretive, whispered part of their credo, is also today more and more practised quite openly.

But our Spiritualist bodies, still hiding their heads in the sand, continue to feebly offer the excuse that what the orthodox church is doing is not Spiritualism! To such a statement I retort, nor, in the main, are those who profess to be *Spiritualists!* And this is amplified by their insistence on dropping the word religion for movement. Well, I will go along with movement so long as it means taking a metaphorical laxative to clear out all the waste products and debris from what they call Spiritualism today. Beware you "Spiritualists" for by any other name orthodoxy *is* practising psychic talents and mediumship and as such, we are becoming the *mount* and not, as we always should have been, the *rider.*

Another reason for Spiritualism lacking the lime-light is that the churches have always, basically because they are cheaper, employed mediums of a mediocre standard. Something else that is not always quite true is their claim that they cannot pay much because their funds are very low. The fact is that presidents and committees simply want to pay as little as possible in order to show what clever bursars they are! If money really is a problem, in order to run more efficiently, they should actually be applying their talents in other directions than mere penny-pinching!

For example, they should make every endeavour to convince their congregations that the church needs bigger collections, etc. in order to run more efficiently. It is also true that even after all these years they still have not grasped one of the fundamentals of business which is if you pay peanuts, you get monkeys! Equally, if you do not move with the times, you get left behind! I know from my own experience there is a wealth of interest throughout the world. I know too, for the same reasons, well-publicised meetings, plus good quality mediums = always, full churches.

(As an example only and not from any egoistic point of view, last year (1997) I did a small tour in the west country, the churches and myself agreeing to spilt the fees. It was delightful to work; every venue a full house and some with standing room only! I do a full two hours straight, with no break, demonstrating clairvoyance and answering questions previously (anonymously) written by the congregation. At one, with ninety-odd persons present, a recorder of events told me that I had answered more than twenty questions and given almost thirty messages as well. Believe it, it can be done and over a period of ten days and six venues, I made enough to cover my return fare (Spain to UK) and hostess' costs and venues and produced for the churches, after expenses, an average of sixty-five pounds each meeting!)

In view of the attitudes aforementioned however, the church officers will rely mostly on mediums who work for a bit of pin-money, earning what are termed "expenses" only. These demonstrators are often drawn directly from their membership and I have no quarrel with that, provided that they *know their craft*. But I have said on many occasions over the years and in churches too and without reservation that which is written here. Many times the lady who gets down on her knees to clean the church (almost always voluntarily) is more worthy of the fee than many of the mediums who demonstrate from the platform!

Notwithstanding, in their defence, many of these mediums are pushed onto the rostrum much too early and in consequence are placed in an untenable position. This is because (a) they work for nothing or they come cheap. (b) Due to the fact that they have little or no experience of the public platform they are a little over-awed by the public, unable to cope with the limelight. More importantly, should they *seem* to be in touch on that *first* time, two platitudes here come to mind; the proof of the pudding, etc. and one swallow a summer does not make!

However, the blame should not fall per se onto the shoulders of the church officers or, for that matter, the mediums alone. Often haphazard results are due to novices being told by their circle leader that they are ready and through not explaining fully that one must be committed to a continual search, they leave their circle training behind. But only having "developed" to a level where they can perhaps more or less passably perform in public, they are convinced that they have arrived.

Having thus managed to get through one or two public meetings, they, quite erroneously, take the attitude that further instruction is not necessary! Through both a lack of understanding and, it has to be said, an expanding of the ego, they believe that they are fully "developed" and further, that their search for further knowledge and training is over. But another problem often arises here too; that of amplifying their new found "knowledge". First they quit their present development circle, then, though untrained for the task, they begin running one of their own. Even worse though, all too often out of their depth, they undertake the tutelage at seminars and workshops!

The interest in supernormal matters is moving forward apace, especially among the young folk, thank God. These today, in my experience more than ever before, are showing an avid no-nonsense interest that reaches far and away above and beyond mere ouija board experimentation. It is therefore incumbent upon we old-ies to be acutely aware that we must always feel obliged to instruct them as cor-rectly and as fully as we can to our own levels of Spirit-learned knowledge. Further we are equally obliged to do so without, in any way, adding padding of any kind! What is more, once our own level is reached and absorbed by them, we are even more obligated to move them on to others who possess greater spiritual knowledge than ourselves.

When I first became interested, people like the late Gordon Higginson, others and myself were the exception to the rule, in that we started platform work at so young an age. (I would remind readers that Gordon took his first public meeting at the age of twelve)! At that time there were some dozen or so boy and girl mediums working around the UK. Perhaps, if the war had not intervened, I might well have also started before attaining the ripe old age of seventeen! (See e. of ch. on child mediums.)

However, like Gordon, I did not develop my speaking until some years later. Like him I too would not be persuaded to deliver an address before congregations until this easily flowed, without pause. I also needed to know that the words spo-ken were truly inspirationally flowing from Spirit and worthy of them. Again I make no apology in stating that much of the addresses I have heard delivered over the years, allegedly from "spirit guides" are somewhat trite, simply composed of platitudes, clichés and hackneyed phrases that were already old hat in Martin Luther's time!

Therefore, stay within the confines of your circle learning and practising. Record the words and afterwards take time to listen and to constructively criticise them until you are confident that they are not merely a repetition of things you have already heard from others. Spirit loves a thinker and whether your congregation agrees or not with what you say, originality of thought makes them think. My aim therefore is that the address may contribute in helping the recipients become think-ers too.

In 1948, indeed up until I was in my late thirties, everywhere I worked in UK I found that most of the congregations were older than me. Other mediums may not have noticed this so much as I, because many of our "veterans" working today did not begin demonstrating publicly or even coming into Spiritualism until they were in their forties! (Perhaps some of these, Tekla Khan and the late Doris Stokes and Jessie Nason to name but a few and others too might remember me giving them advice so long ago!)

I recall one such meeting! Demonstrating at Croydon Sp. Church during Harold Vigurs time (and that is a few years ago) I was asked to chat to a "a chap fairly new to, but very interested in Spiritualism." Wilfred Watts (some twelve years older than I) might remember that occasion. Yet today, and I mean no disrespect, quite the reverse, he, having contributed so much to the Spiritualist cause, appears to have been around for ever.

Envy, like jealousy, malice hate and anger are wasted emotions so I mean it in the nicest possible way when I say I "envy" the opportunities offered today to young mediums. Way back then there was no social security back-up or long-term dole payments to support developing mediums. Today many of the younger ones take full advantage of these things, drawing such subsidies while becoming established. I do not worry nor care that their remuneration is a part of the black economy; that is their business; their conscience! It is other contingencies that I find somewhat alarming.

One such stumbling block lies in the propensity of their being able, at the drop of a hat, to "tour the world" demonstrating their talent. However, in many cases, they are totally unequipped emotionally, or in their mediumship either, to take on the extra responsibilities often thrust upon them. Their mediumship, philosophy and general spiritual knowledge is, all too often, totally inadequate for the tasks undertaken. Often their knowledge is book read which is OK so long as they "sieve" and do not simply quote parrot-fashion. Consequently, many are found wanting, bogged down by their own limitations. They then find themselves having to spread their teaching, speaking and answering of questions and even their demonstrations too, in some cases, much too thinly. This leaves them and their delivery wanting with their answers left, at best sketchy or worse, simply airy-fairy.

Nowadays various, and sometimes even dubious stars of stage, screen and TV will often burst onto the public scene. They will and do influence today's youngsters far more than in earlier times when there was less media. Young mediums thrust into the limelight will sometimes also take this stance in the belief that they too, as it were, are stars! But whilst this may be fine for budding musicians after having just one "top-twenty hit" it is *not* for inexperienced mediums. In the belief that they are able to perform whenever and wherever, they feel that further regular "music lessons" (development) are no longer necessary. As such, they will, all too often, as their minuscule "true knowledge bubble" bursts, come down with a bump.

Nowadays too they themselves are expected, indeed *required* in many cases to tutor seminars and workshops, etc. as well as their actual demonstrations. Consequently I caution them to take on board the necessity (not as it appears, simply if they feel like it) of constantly continuing their learning. The moral is clear (and church leaders take note) - if this "cancer" is not cut out, it being considered more expedient as a money spinner by churches and mediums alike, then it will spread. Eventually, unchecked, it will expeditiously kill the "body" without a second thought.

It goes without saying that in Spiritualist churches there has always existed the need for a continuing flow of funds. On booking though, secretaries rarely mention that more will be expected from the medium than that which is being booked at the time. These extras are usually brought up soon after arrival, when (in my case until they know better) pressure is brought to bear, usually by one or more of the church officers pleading poverty. Sometimes too, though thankfully far more rarely, even one's hostess will expect a reading as part of *their* bunce.

I worked in a somewhat exclusive area of mediumship though so I had more ammunition to resist such pressures. For example, in the 1950's to 80's I had a good business as well as my mediumship so for my transfiguration service I would take only twelve pounds expenses. With a hundred or more each paying at least a pound the churches I served were, as a Cockney would say, on a nice little earner!

Even today, no longer demonstrating physical mediumship publicly, I still always resist the pseudo glamour of taking extra groups or a great number of private sittings just to make a bit of extra cash. The church takes at least a half of what one earns from these extra curricular activities and anyway as I usually draw a full house, again in the vernacular, it can be said that they get more than their money's worth out of me!

I reiterate! There is no such thing as a developed medium! Yet over the years I have heard many say that they developed years ago! Me? Sit in circle? Why? I don't need to! I left all that behind as soon as I developed! Sadly, such comments are very common. If only these people knew (and they *should* know) how untrue and misleading such things are to those whom they profess to teach, they would realise the futility of their words. Leading from the front (as indeed they should) they would do well to learn and take to heart the lesson that: "A little learning is a dangerous thing; drink deep, or taste not the Pierian spring!"

The foregoing reminds me of a time when, aged about twelve or thereabouts I offered up "a little learning" to my dad. You will no doubt recall my lack of interest in football but I had heard the kids in school praising one J. R. Smith, who apparently was a football wizard! Due to play at Millwall on the Saturday and hearing that my father was, as usual, going to the match, I casually asked was he going to "The Den" on Saturday? His answer was of course in the affirmative so then, throwing in my "knowledge" I asked if he was going especially to watch the great J.R? He retorted, no, he was not, he was going to watch two teams. So my potential "Brownie points" were never won that day! Therefore remember as they say: "You can kid some of the people some of the time..."

Recently here in Spain too I was present a one such "kidology" incident, or was it unconscious fraud? I attended an advertised "Lecture on Mediumship, followed by a demonstration of Clairvoyance." The meeting, a public ticketed affair, was held in a room over a bar. The medium, during her discourse, graphically demonstrated exactly the kind of thing I tried on Dad all those years ago. Patently obvious to the psychics and mediums around the room, including myself, was her badly flawed knowledge of both spiritual philosophy and the workings of mediumship. Her inexperience at being able to flannel a crowd too (a speciality of my Aunt Millie) even showed that she was on the proverbial hiding to nothing.

Sadly, even what the lady *had* learned had slipped through her fingers as easily as would a hand-full of water. In all, a futile exercise and a complete waste of both time and a truly precious commodity. Her clairvoyance lacked credulity with the "evidence" (intentional quotation marks) mediocre and her messages banal in the extreme. The delivery, intermixed with much questioning of the recipients, was hardly the way to convince the sceptics in her audience. Even worse, those who knew nothing of the subject left that room with a completely wrong impression of what mediumship is and with little or no idea as to how it works.

Afterwards we were introduced and, impressed by Yu Sin, I said that she would, quite unexpectedly, have to return to England for a gynaecological operation. She did not quite tell me that I was talking rubbish, but boasting that she was a hundred per cent fit throughout, she said that I had my vibes mixed, as she was in tune with her Guide twenty-four hours a day. (In further chat I realised that she actually meant her helper and had mis-used the "g" word (as do many) wrongly here). It was *I* who must be mixed up she continued; I was obviously getting a message for someone else there for she had decided to settle permanently in Spain. Mentally reading the bubble over her head, (the one artists put speech into in comic books) it read: "So there!" I smiled politely and said how pleased I was for her.

Some time after this conversation a friend living further up the coast phoned to tell me that the lady had returned unexpectedly to England for an emergency (Yep, you guessed it!) gynaecological operation! (Some weeks later incidentally, I was told by another lady who came to me for a reading that after I left the venue she said that I had only spoken out to frighten her because I was afraid of the competition. To both my sitter and myself however, it simply proved just what a silly girl she was and how little development and progression she had actually grasped.)

Unconscious fraud by various mediums has been around for a long time and is committed in different ways. They fluff, flannel and generally skirt around what they are receiving because they have lost their way and or their contact but will not admit this, even to themselves! Another problem is to "give off" something that you knew was for you but it goes unqualified. Often this is because the actual intended recipient is a little reticent in taking the link. Then, before he or she has a chance to open their mouth the regular message grabber (and there is at least one at every meeting) yells out that they can take it! This gives rise to two things; (a) the given message is without qualification and (b) it leaves the real participants, from both sides of the veil, gasping in dismay! It also assists greatly in helping the hic-cupping medium, unable to complete their link, out of a possibly embarrassing predicament.

Over the years I have watched in dismay just how easily the wrong message goes to the wrong recipient. In demonstrating this failing, I give what we call Link Clairvoyance. Beginning by linking with five or six persons simultaneously, I give four or five evidential facts; names, places, relatives or whatever. At this stage, I explain that they are all somewhat "linked" for each is able to take every name, etc. that I have mentioned up to that point. But it is at *that* point that I separate them!

The evidence takes a sudden turn as I proceed to give each recipient a piece of evidence that *they alone* can acknowledge. Confirming that the others cannot, I explain that up until the separation point any of the five or six could be the recipient. I go on to say that if I did not know differently or I had become confused with my links, the wrong person could well have received a part, or even *all* of the evidence in error.

Sometimes I demonstrate "blind" clairvoyance and with my back to the audience or by sitting in another room I relay the evidence. Here in Spain also, when broadcasting, I give clairvoyance over the telephone, when obviously I cannot see the faces of recipients. Facial expression or gesture of recipients, if the medium is unaware that they are using them, can also produce another type of unconscious fraud, completely eliminated when the techniques mentioned are employed. Sceptics also find such modus operandi intriguing at the least and more often than not, it whets their appetite to find out more.

On occasions I will also invite a novice medium to come up onto the rostrum and work with me. Their demonstration might be pre-arranged by me, perhaps working with one of my own students. At other times I might simply call someone up spontaneously from the audience to try out their own clairvoyant faculty. Then (and this is something I have always done with my students in circle) I link into *their* vibration and as I do, it does two things. It gives them extra power and, should they get stuck, I can, by seeing, feeling or hearing the same things as them, help them over their hiccup. It is quite surprising how much an absolute novice can sometimes deliver this way. I never cease to be amused as they, the audience and novice are equally amazed, for after all, it is nothing more than the operation of a *natural* process.

In private readings too I make a point of not looking at my sitter. I explain before I start how the face can give away so much to the discerning person and by definition most mediums are, to an extent anyway, exactly that! I usually sit initially with my eyes closed and even when I do open them I will purposely not look into the face of my sitter. I also do postal and proxy readings together with diagnosis when obviously I could not see facial expressions anyway.

One other is intriguing, somewhat bibliographical in that...well, for example at Sutton Spiritualist Ch. years ago... Telling a lady that her husband was linking and that she had photo of him in her bag, she replied yes and no and reaching for the bag I said not to! I went on and delivered the evidence and then said the husband wanted to prove he was there! Asking a man at the back of the church to fetch any book from the library he obliged when I told the lady to pick a page and line; she did, and I asked that it be read out. The gentleman read: "I really rang the bell tonight!" She confirmed that her husband was a fireman in the body and I went on telling her to look in her bag. Realising she had picked up the wrong one on leaving home, she gasped as she brought out a photo of her husband as a young man in fireman's uniform, complete with helmet!

I also prefer to do without the padding in church services. I enjoy starting with a rousing hymn followed by the opening prayer and then I like to go straight into the reading, address and clairvoyance: Again, this may not be necessarily in that order either, since I work as the Spirit moves me! When the time has run out, I close the service with another hymn of good cheer and a prayer. (See e. of ch. on padding and power waning.)

Many churches really enjoy this "free from all the trappings" type of service my helpers and I have employed for so many years; indeed, those officers who are forward thinking have often said as much. They privately bemoan to me how they would like to see many more mediums able and willing to do the same thing! I understand that when approached by officials of a church a medium will often make all sorts of excuses not to deviate from the norm. Off the record the belief is that many mediums are *incapable* of continually working for up to two hours without a break. In consequence they need the padding of several hymns and so on to prop up their work. Without it, church officers have told me, such demonstrations would be, more often than not, prematurely terminated!

Mediumship is not just a fortune-telling or "wrapped up message" (yet another favourite phrase) phenomenon. It is a worthwhile, philosophical way to the real truth of Spirit communication and communion. I sometimes give my clairvoyance first, then the reading and address. On other occasions I have also had a mixture of reading, address and clairvoyance simultaneously and or other combinations.

Working as the Spirit moves me, rather than in the more restricted way of having to wait, metaphorically speaking, for the next bus to come along, is I feel, a far the better way to work. The recipients and many church officers obviously prefer it and certainly I know that Spirit does! More importantly, this ability to switch around as one works brings more forcibly to the fore not only that survival is a fact but also the reality that it not only *can*, but *should* be constantly and clearly demonstrated by many more mediums! (See end of chapter, on looking more deeply into the pool of knowledge.)

From the foregoing it will be seen that in demonstrating this truth *competently*, thereby *proving* survival, it demonstrates that not only is it *possible* but far more, *desirable* as well. Thus it is that the foremost obligation of a medium is to demonstrate through *proof* and *not* by telling someone how to run their life. Notwithstanding, they must still maintain their responsibility to both their recipients and to the entities who contact. Hence, if a message of a personal nature is given, it should be qualified through evidential proof that it is coming from the communicating entity and not from the medium.

However, so many times the source is not the mediumship that is employed but the medium's psychic power alone that is in use. So here I offer students yet another cautionary note. *All* mediums, myself included, obviously have our own attitudes about life and how it should be lived. It is precisely because we do that sometimes we do not recognise the obvious. So be sure to the best of your ability and knowledge of Spirit that the "life-line-way-to-live-your-life" message you give is not tainted or even flavoured by your *own* thoughts and ideals. (See end of chapter, on spirit levels of advice!)

It is also self-evident that mediums must remember that they have a responsibility to themselves as well. Therefore they should, nay must, always endeavour that such mistakes mentioned in the foregoing paragraphs are avoided and better, do not occur. If there is any doubt that they are relaying their clairvoyance to the correct recipient, etc. then they must clarify the position. In order to do this they should ask the entity to try to give them some piece(s) of evidence that only the actual recipient would know and understand and therefore will accept as proof. This in itself also backs up what might have already been given both as evidential proof and advice on a problem. Finally on this point, as I work, I constantly seek from the entity communicating to give me information that the recipient is not thinking about and if all mediums employed this detective attitude it would quickly sort the wheat from the chaff.

Irrespective of all that I have written, the prime mover is to *know* one's craft as well as just learning it. Demonstrating true mediumship, whether one is natural or trained has to be as the Spirit moves one. So if you are at a meeting and feel, for whatever reason, that you cannot work, then have the courage to say so. On more than one occasion I have done just that! It is better to face the truth and retire from the demonstration gracefully, in spite of disappointing the recipients, rather than probably ending in an even far worse scenario by trying to flannel your way through.

Adhering to the old maxim "To thine own self be true" is much the preferred course to the alternative of fluffing and flanneling through your demonstration. It is undoubtedly an insult to one's own mentality never mind others' to undermine in any way these jewels, these precious gifts, talents that are bestowed upon us by the God-Energy-Force. Whilst agreeing that we have freedom of action and thought (freewill) there is, nonetheless, something that is much more important and to the point. It is an insult to both our seen and unseen friends to even entertain the idea of deception in *any* way, shape or form, never mind to then practise it.

FOOTNOTE!

Purely as an exercise, I am taking the liberty of offering up this hypothesis, i.e. that there is perhaps, a link between psychic powers and electricity. Science and medicine have already proved that we run on electricity; indeed most species could not function at all unless they kept their "batteries" topped up. So psychic ability levels may stem from the fact that people are born with a greater or lesser resistance to electricity.

Apparently I have a high resistance! Some years ago I received a very bad electric shock resulting in burns down to the bones of my fingers. I walked to the hospital and, returning some days later for a change of dressings, I discovered that the medical staff, on duty on my first visit, were amazed to see me not only arriving on "shank's pony" but also that I had survived a shock that would have killed many another person.

There are many recorded cases of persons being struck by lightning, resulting in little or no injury while others have died from a relatively small shock received in the home! Some people who have had out of body experiences often find that they cannot wear a watch afterwards because it tends to malfunction. Also when a person goes into cardiac arrest electricity used to stimulate the heart with sufficient current passing through the body can re-start the heart-beat, bringing someone "back from the dead." Other observers have discovered that when the body cells die very rapidly an energy surge (from an in-built electric source?) often passes through the body at the moment of death.

In America, investigators of the paranormal, using equipment at the highest level of sophistication have discovered, when investigating haunted premises, that there is a much stronger magnetic field present in those areas where phenomenon have occurred most frequently. They deliberately have no prior knowledge as to the "hot spots" and obviously the inanimate equipment cannot know either! Prepared equipment wise, they deliberately go in "blind" as to where and what type of phenomena has occurred at the premises and how frequently.

Other investigators, using only approved, tested and sealed equipment frequently record voices that have no earthly source. These are not audible whilst the recordings are being made and are only heard when the tape is played back! The liner Queen Mary, now in use as an hotel and tourist attraction, produced for researchers two very lucid recordings, classic examples of their kind.

Yet another researcher, in trying to communicate with his daughter, set his video recorder in front of a lighted, but blank T.V. screen. On playback however he got nothing but in spite of those failures, he kept on trying. Then someone said why not check it out frame by frame? When he did there they were; faces on the screen, one of which was his daughter, but in a pose not discovered in any family or friends' earthly (when she was in the body) shots!

Evidence is now pouring forth both in Electronic Voice Phenomena and Instrumental Trans-communication when voices and messages are coming through cassette tapes, computers, fax machines and even telephones! Sitting here at the P.C. I start to wonder how long before, instead of mediums writing on psychic matters typing and working inspirationally, Spirit inspirers will begin actually operating the keyboards directly, as in psychokinesis?

The foregoing I think, illustrates the importance that electricity might play, not only in the functioning of organisms, but in psychic happenings too and whilst scientists obviously cannot go around haphazardly giving people electric shocks, I am certain that it would be easy to find a way to investigate the idea. Who knows, the outcome could prove to be quite electrifying!

HELPFUL NOTES!

(On mediumship and payment). *Budding mediums! I urge you not to take a fee, apart perhaps from expenses, until you are sure of your own and your helpers' proficiency. In short, until you can deliver the goods never, ever, try to fool any of the people any of the time! Remember the "old stagers" in the audience. These, though they may never have demonstrated mediumship in their lives, have nevertheless, possibly, even probably, long forgotten much more than you have learned.*

What it comes down to is harmony and if you are completely in tune with your d/ k helpers and guides you will know both whether and when you are ready. Until then keep striving toward your goal and eventually you really will bridge the gap. With practice you will be able to link in as and when you desire, moving into the other dimensions at will.

Oh, by the way, when doing private readings always ensure that you have change for whatever denomination is offered. If not it is fairly certain that your recipient will tell you to keep the change. Then later, when relating the incident to others they will often say what were they supposed to do? The obvious implication here is, I hope, clear to readers and students alike!

(On child mediums.) *These were actually around long before Gordon and Co. For example, Eva Lees, in a well documented interview after her father's transition in 1931 (the year I was born) spoke about him and his work. She said Robert James Lees was, at the age of fourteen, already a brilliant trance medium, with an equally brilliant control working through him. At that tender age he was invited to the palace and Queen Victoria was so impressed that she told him that he was to be her personal medium.*

His control however had other ideas and, speaking through him, said that they did not want that. The control then went on to say that there was a young lad at Balmoral whose name was John Brown and he would be the one to serve the queen, which is how the relationship between Brown and Her Majesty came about! Brown was duly brought to court in 1864 and his brief was to be in constant personal attendance upon her Majesty on all occasions and the rest (once again) as they say, is history! Lees incidentally, was also the author of several books, among which was *Through the Mists*, still regarded today by many as a book well worth reading.

(On padding and power waning) *The only valid reason for stopping is that the medium gets tired, or the time allotted to the meeting has passed, or even that the bums on the seats get achy and or tired! One should remember though that mediums usually work in very differing ways and in all sorts of spheres and levels of communication. So I stress that the foregoing "only valid reason" sentence is not intended to be disparaging in any way.*

The intention is to bring to students' notice certain facts. (1) That once the door is open and one is tuned-in the flow is continuous, for Spirit is on-going and thus never tires. (2) That even if the medium's helper suffered a shock of some kind and, for whatever reason, was not able to carry on, there is always another spirit worker, ready, willing and able to fill the void. (3) That, notwithstanding, if only the one medium is operating on this side of the door the buck stops with him or her!

It is therefore imperative to know one's own capabilities and durability. To be aware well in advance of one's "tiredness-curve" approaching, so that one may gracefully draw the session to a close. Equally, if a medium finds that they are not in tune with the person(s) they are working with then they should also curtail the session. If not, should the medium insist on carrying on, the result might well be that what started out as a remarkable event degenerates into just the opposite! This stands for all types of mediumship, without the need for qualification, across the board!

It is therefore of paramount importance to know and to discipline oneself as to the time and sensibilities one can safely allow and feel, respectively, for private sittings, public demos and groups, etc. Be very aware also of one's individual recuperation time needed between sitters; indeed consider also the number of sitters you are able to cope with in a day, a week or whatever. But heed this warning! If you spread your talents too thinly, the results will often be transparent!

(On looking more deeply into the pool of knowledge.) *The thing that makes most people look deeper into Spiritualism's philosophy is, almost invariably, the proof that survival after the change called death is a fact and not just belief. Some will disagree with that, but like it or not, mostly enquirers are motivated by personal loss. Initially they need to be convinced beyond all doubt that communication with those who have made their transition is not only desirable but also possible and provable.*

Therefore, it is only when one knows that such communion is a certain fact that the desire to progress might, or even can be born. It is only when one is convinced of survival (and not until then) that one might or should wish to progress further. Without fear of contradiction, I state that there are far too many peripheral people dipping into and or simply playing with, mediumistic and even psychic matters without heed or precautions of any kind. (Often exorcists like myself have to pick up the pieces and rescue them. All too often afterwards though, friends, family and even they themselves will blame Spiritualism and not their dabbling, for the resulting problems.)

I reiterate; such peripheral meddling, dabbling and downright foolishness do not a medium make! The greater knowledge of, and communication with, more lofty souls cannot be reached, for example, by becoming a meditation teacher, a reiki master, or for that matter, a reflexologist or masseuse! Yet many of these pretend mediumship (often kidding themselves too) when all they have, far too often, is a modicum of low-level psychic ability! Anyone, if they have the money, can learn those professions!

However, to attain to mediumship requires patience, the will to succeed, and constantly learning how to recognise absorb and use one's inherent lost or mislaid psychic abilities. It is then that with the right kinds of tutors that they can move on to the various mediumship levels. But remember always that each today is only the beginning of your quest toward those whom you would learn from and follow. But remember too that these can, and will, if your desire is strong enough, lift your soul to exciting and exalted levels of Spiritual consciousness.

(On spirit levels of advice!) *It is well to be aware of another apparently obvious thing with our loved ones communicating. They can only advise us about a particular thing according to their level of knowledge of that on which they are commenting or advising. For example, when a sitter asks me if their mum or dad or whatever advises them to get divorced, or to sue somebody, I invariably reply that their answer will depend to a large extent as to the entities feelings not only for the sitter but the spouse and children, etc. involved.*

An unbiased response therefore should be sought from the medium's d/k acting as an intermediary and requesting help from a QC or as applicable, who will be in a better, more purely professional, rather than an emotional position to adjudicate and advise them on the situation in hand. Logically, under normal circumstances, that is what one would probably do anyway. Sadly though, in the meeting place, or on a one to one sitting, so many mediums give the impression that all spirit communicators are oracles and total opposites of the legendary three monkeys.

Chapter 3
THE PATHWAY TO PSYCHIC AND MEDIUMISTIC DEVELOPMENT

The most significant display of a miracle is perhaps the least taken note of in everyday life; it is the fact that there are no two people or other species exactly alike! It follows then, that since we *are* all different, the "paths" we travel must similarly be many and varied.

However, there are still common denominators! One of these is that order to exist on this planet, all species, one way or another, have to be born and have to die. Likewise, whilst on earth they must also occupy some form of physical body. Standing alone, this fact irrefutably establishes the inescapable probability that all living energy life forms might well issue from the same source. Equally the probable inevitability is that these, when the change of "death" takes place, return to the source of all energy, whatever that may be.

Another common denominator is the brain for since the formation of this planet and the first organisms, each has also, in one form or another, needed one to exist and function. Of these the very fragile, soft, wet human brain, weighing around three pounds and consisting of some thousand million cells could very easily be held in the palm of the hand. (Actually, if it was laid flat it would cover the area of a pillow-case.) Evolution though decided, thankfully, that to carry it around in the hand would be too inconvenient and that pillow-case flat heads would look quite strange! It also must have decided that our heads were big enough and that required it to become all wrinkled up inside the skull!

Nothing like the biggest among species, it is, nonetheless, the most advanced and intricate of them all, capable of effecting many millions of operations simultaneously. Through the ears and eyes alone it is able to discern and differentiate some 200,000 sounds and sights, changing and re-evaluating these virtually within the blink of an eye. Yet most of the time we are not even conscious of the changes taking place!

Within it lays all human thought, all experiences of what we call life and is considered by many academics, scientists and intellectuals, not to mention ordinary folk, to be the most powerful force on earth! All humankind's accomplishments, good or bad, by definition, had to begin as a thought and through the brain have flowed the loftiest and the basest of these. It has been employed to invent and discover everything from weapons of ultimate horror and destruction to life-saving machinery and surgery.

Every painting, scribble and art-form since the earliest cave drawings right up to the present are the results of generated thoughts, i.e. use of the brain. The stretched skin drum and the bamboo and reed pipe found in early cultures had to be, originally, initiated by thought, so that their primitive music could pour forth. It is safe to say that such original thoughts and ideas have indisputably led to the continuous thought processes of musicians, artists and designers resulting in the beautiful symphonic sounds, sights, inventions and discoveries around us today.

Thoughts old and new have always been the means by which changes are wrought in the world. These though have not been (and are not now) always good by any means but their effects are clearly demonstrated throughout the world and latterly in outer space too! Be it politics, religion or law, a simple handy tool, or a world shattering discovery, thoughts continuously pour forth, making their mark.

We may therefore conclude that *nothing* is forthcoming without thought for any and all actions or words are, of course, impossible to utter or effect *without* thought and the use of the brain. So perhaps we should also remember that even on those occasions when we accuse someone of doing or saying something without thought we are, technically speaking, in error for, as such, it is an impossibility!

Steadfastly going on its way the influence of the brain has always been and continues to be so. Both subtle and prominent, it displays itself in many ways and undoubtedly influences every society and culture on this planet. Equally and just as surely, whether obvious or not, the exercising of it profoundly illustrates a well-held contention; that it has always been, and still is, the most regularly used and hard-worked of all things here on Earth!

Therefore, when considering the brain relative to mediumship, the raw student can be forgiven for feeling somewhat overwhelmed and bemused in wondering *just how one initially sets about seeking out the psychic path?* Well, the first step in the quest is to take as a yardstick and accept that (for the purpose of argument at least) there is nothing new under the sun, that all is known within.

It is impossible however to learn mental illumination and knowledge of psychic and mediumistic matters in the same way as one learns the alphabet or multiplication tables. It does not come in the same way that one can study the various external sciences either. Much of this illumination and knowledge is already within the concealed depths of our inner selves and, to a large extent it is the searching for, discovery, recognition and acceptance of this concept that opens up the channels of communication more quickly and easily.

Indeed, having taught many, I state that the biggest stumbling block of all is the initial inability to accept that thoughts can be other than from their own minds. Worse, and these will get nowhere fast until they concede, is the outright refusal to accept that this can happen! Usually this occurs at the beginning of study for up until that point it had never occurred to them to define the source. They had always, without question or pause, believed that all their thoughts were their own, generated by *their* brain alone.

Why are we then so loathe to accept that thoughts received by us may be from a source other than our own minds? Well, from an early age being taught by example is one obvious reason. Our parents, teachers and our contemporaries constantly tell us to use our brains, to think about what we are doing, etc. so we are automatically persuaded into thinking that our conscious reasoning and the thoughts we receive are solely of our own making.

This school of thought is far more comfortable anyway; it is so much easier to grasp and understand than any alternative. Therefore, in the main, wishing to be in step with those around us, we never consider taking on board any other option, or indeed that there might perhaps even be one! So faced with, and accepting these parameters, one can more easily appreciate perhaps the greater difficulty and effort required to begin the endeavour of looking within. Nonetheless, once sincerely begun, the journey quickly becomes fascinating and truly rewarding to the intrepid seeker of Truth and Light.

Yet another reason lies in the fact that we are creatures of habit, gregariously preferring to run with the herd, taking the easier course. After all, for many people to posit such a thing as someone, in or out of the body, feeding our thought process is too outrageous to even consider. The peer-conditioned mental reasoning of the average person will find the whole thing a mite too cumbersome and intrusive in their everyday life. Yet if we stop for a moment and think this is exactly what is happening all of the time!

Through the media, books, teachers and so on we absorb information (thoughts) continuously and often we are not even aware that we have learned something new. *Most*, if not *all* of these are from an *external* source but because they are the norm we simply do not recognise them as such. How much harder then to accept the notion that one may well have switched on the T.V. for instance but not because it was one's own thought? That it might well have been a neighbour who, thinking of putting on theirs, inadvertently sent the message telepathically and it was you, and perhaps even others, who received it simultaneously? Even harder still that an entity wanting to watch their favourite soap opera made one switch it on? (I would add that although I of course write this with tongue in cheek it is not actually beyond the bounds of possibility!)

Far too many folk will *not even* consider the idea of psychic power (energy). Trotting out the old chestnut, they state that we should not dabble in the unknown. My response to this mode of thinking, apart from the fact that it is just an excuse for not wanting to bother, is that nothing *unknown* becomes *known* until it is investigated. For example, medical science has made and continues to make enormous progress, both in diagnosing diseases and curing them and in many instances this has been due to investigators being able to dissect cadavers, thereby discovering the workings of the *living* body.

However, because of religious prejudice, cadavers in the nineteenth century were very hard to come by legally. In consequence, they quite often, to quote in the thieves' vernacular, "fell off the back of a lorry" (Or should that be a hearse?) It was during this time that an infamous duo, namely Burke and Hare, were tried and convicted of stealing bodies from graves. Commonly known as body-snatching, medical pioneers of the time truly considered it a necessary evil. Notwithstanding, as history tells us, the pair were still found guilty and punished.

There has always been a mystical taboo on the cutting up of dead bodies. Many people, through religious persuasion believe in a *literal* resurrection. Thus they fear it is impossible for their loved one to be saved in a cut-up state! So, almost always, even today, relatives, etc. refuse permission for a corpse to be used for medical research and many too think that organs should not be donated either.

To point to such ideas still hanging on, I, recently at a public meeting, answered a question for a lady who was against her daughter's wish to donate her eyes. She claimed that when she reincarnated she would definitely be blind (I think that such a kind gesture would ensure her of maximum 20-20 vision myself!) Asking her mum did she prefer cremation or burial she emphatically came out in favour of the former, to which I said so how will the person reincarnate from a pile of ashes? And she was worried about an eye or two? She confessed that this simple fact had not occurred to her! Thus satisfied by simple logic, spontaneously turning to her daughter, she publicly gave her blessing.

In many cases these and other taboos still hold today! By law, relatives, as next-of-kin, literally own the body of their deceased and have, within the law, authority to decide on its disposal. So frequently they categorically refuse to allow that which the deceased had requested, e.g. that vital organs be used for transplants or that the body be used as a cadaver.

Many a relative too is not at all happy when, by law, certain corpses have to have a post-mortem and will put up the strongest protest against having a loved one cut about. It stands to reason that mankind would be the worse off if everyone took this eye-blinkered view! Medical and other knowledge would be no further forward than it was in the Dark Ages! Surely *all* learning requires some probing and often in the dark too in its search for knowledge and the hope for answers.

There are also those who think that people like me, by donating their body to medical science, are not decent, and or must be more than a bit crazy, or even have an irreligious attitude to God! These, while mumbling about decent burials, will though, almost *indecently*, quickly cart off the body they have charge of before anyone can even think of reaching for a scalpel.

Even with the more enlightened attitudes prevailing today, many people still misunderstand what the intrinsic meaning of the resurrection is. Various creeds believe that at judgement day (Armageddon) all the right and proper saved souls will rise up from their coffins, their bodies made whole again. Their argument against the alternatives (cadavers, etc.) is that there would be little or nothing left to rise up. Of course they conveniently forget those people who have been blown to bits by explosion or whatever, or make the excuse that (a) they will nevertheless be made whole and lie in the arms of the Lord or (b) that they will not be resurrected as, probably, they were not pious enough to be saved by God in the first place.

The thought occurs that those who have lost just a leg prior to their passing will perhaps be given a crutch when they arise, or maybe even an artificial leg to be going on with until the new one emerges. If not, they could well be hopping mad (pun intended) even though they have been resurrected after Armageddon!

In passing, it is worthy of mention I think, that if a JW tries to get their foot in my door and I say that I am a medium right away, they cannot get off of my doorstep fast enough! I still like the challenge of a good debate though, so if I have the time, I will discuss their limited parameters with them. Speaking with an elder just recently at a neighbour's house he commented that she would be resurrected and so would her dog, but that the trees in her garden would not. I responded by saying that I thought he could depend upon there being one heck of a lot of disappointed dogs in the new life and, if given the choice, they probably would not bother! Also, I continued, in spite of all those bodies being made *whole* on the "r" day, the priests still recite parrot-fashion the ashes to ashes, dust to dust bit over a grave. Surely this suggests that in their religious fervour they appear to want their cake and to eat it! He declined to reply!

Resurrection is *not* the physical body emerging or rising up from the coffin! This is another misnomer the "laughing priests" have never bothered to clarify over the centuries. The resurrection spoken of by the ancients is a Spiritual one, not a physical happening and souls do not have to wait until Armageddon to be saved for, in the event, the soul does not die with the body. At the moment of what we term death, the soul leaves the body and moves into another dimension, (the Astral) that which might be termed a mind-force sphere. No longer obliged to reside in a body, which is, after all, only its physical vehicle while on Earth it is now unencumbered, totally free to progress and journey according to own particular, its spiritual destiny.

(It was not so long ago incidentally that Canon Law forbade cremation or internment for at least three days after death. That same Canon Law defines the soul as the spiritual part of us, intangible *and* indestructible and though we cannot touch or hold it as we might other solid objects, it nevertheless states and declares it to be a real thing. If it is all of these then why was the reason given for the three day period that the soul would not have had sufficient time to leave the body?)

N.B. there is an old Masai legend that tells of a pact between a hyena and a hunter. The hunter agreed not to kill it in return for Nature's secrets. He did not keep his word however, killing the hyena, resulting in the loss of the secrets. So Nature, the custodian of these then had to find a way to keep all things in balance and harmony.

Similarly today, the actions of humankind draw a parallel to the hunter as he betrays Nature's trust, killing without any considered thought many natural resources so precious to our planet. But Nature still holds many secrets so we must read the clues she proffers before it is too late. If not and we finally tip the scales too far in one direction or another she will, inevitably, as she sets about rectifying the balance, exact a terrible toll.

I also sincerely believe that all is not lost, that the move is afoot; that in the not too distant future, politicians and the like will finally awaken from their self-satisfied greed and pomposity and will come down from their ivory towers. Conceivably this will lead to the real resurrection, that of altruism. Lofty ideals will be put into their rightful perspective and will from then on solely benefit our God-given planet and *all* of its inhabitants. I place my trust in those lofty souls who will eventually inspire humankind to take the necessary avoiding action and that it will be much sooner than the doom and gloom merchants would have us believe.

N.B. Recently in a séance, questions such as these were answered by the Manna Group. So in concluding this area of thought I use their words here. "The Armageddon and resurrection doctrine has been, and still is, preached and prophesied by 'priests and prophets' with predicted dates coming and going. But even though they have a common thread running throughout their prophesies they do not merit any accolades, for that thread is only that they have all been wrong and they have never predicted anything good."

Much more was said but space does not permit their actual full discourse. However, they concluded by stating that future souls are already preparing, learning and honing their talents and in a comparatively short time, when compared to earth's history, there will be far more mediums on earth than there are labourers! (Would that I could be *here* to see that day dawn but I will still observe it with optimum interest from Spirit!)

Finally, Natural Law has until now always prevailed and Mother Nature's declining and defying every prophesy to date shows that she has handed us a way out up until now; it really is something we should heed. This is not because the world will end overnight; it is because it is gradually being dissected by humankind's neglectful ignorance. So, unless we learn very soon and begin the healing process, she will, one way or another, bit by bit, slowly die.

Finding the pathway to psychic development is not easy; but then is anything if it is really worthwhile and or rewarding? Like many things, it requires an enormous amount of time, energy, patience, will-power and motivation to go the distance. At the beginning of their search many students, not knowing where to begin, will turn, simply through habit, to orthodoxy, because when looking for religious questions and answers they have, almost without exception, always done so. Thus initially, influenced by the more familiar, comfortable feelings this provides, they stride forward! However, (but not quite so surprisingly to the more astute free thinkers) due to its narrow philosophies and theological prosecution they quickly find themselves in a bind, stuck in a groove of that very same quagmire of familiarity, etc.

Eventually breaking away, they might then research other reading matter, attend lectures, watch programmes on TV. and so on for as yet they are still unaware that there are other ways. Eating their way through reams of paper, often toiling into the small hours, after a while they will readily admit that they have taken on an enormously arduous task. Yet unwittingly they are really only toying with the search, looking without, when they should be looking within. So, having hardly begun their journey, they quickly begin to lose their way and interest; and soon, all too often, they surrender to the frustrations that beset them.

"Learn, Oh man, to know thyself and walk with the knowledge of the Spirit within thee" is the chant of the Grand Lama. These words though are not exclusive to Buddhism and should not be regarded as such. Such phrases have been known to man almost, as it were, before there was man. These have been expounded by many, many Christs (the Messiahs, those messengers of Spirit) in one form or another since time immemorial and have been and are part and parcel of virtually all ancient and modern religions throughout the planet.

The secret Psychic Pathway, for so long spoken of in hallowed whispers and shrouded in mystery is really no secret at all! This is just another smoke-screen put up by those who wish to keep the masses in the "them and us" idiom.

Knowing and accepting that life and death are one is the first step but here one should also take something else on board. Any physicist will state that, like all things, we are basically a form of energy, a mass of minute particles charged with electricity, basically atoms electrons and neutrons. Depending on the speed at which they interact with each other, they shape, form and respond to one another, finding an accord with, for instance, gravity as well as other natural laws.

Science tells us that nothing is solid and according to the laws of physics each "solid mass" acts and reacts with every other such mass. So if we all knew how to "bend" these laws we could, if desired, pass through a wall or some other equally "solid" matter. However, whilst this may appeal to the salacious peeping Tom, it does of course present all sorts of other complications! Any thinking person will quickly note that though we may *pass* through a wall, we ourselves are not *invisible*; neither can we *see* through it. We could therefore, not knowing what was on the other side of it, be in for a rude awakening if we just take a chance!

These laws though, like most other things in this world are in a state of constant change. Science, by definition, moves very slowly. But there is an enormous stirring in the quantum physics area of research with some physicists claiming that they have discovered something that moves faster than light. In spite of their theories on space travel in this regard I and many other mediums can assure them that in other dimensions this has always been; Spirit movement and action for example, personify speed!

Ask the average person and he or she will tell you that there are three dimensions, namely height breadth and width yet there are others, such as the astral spheres. Another is time and today, on the verge of penetrating space even deeper, the discovery and unlocking of this secret is rapidly becoming of paramount import. Thus, particularly now they are beginning to understand it more, finds space scientists stretching their minds, searching for, and endeavouring to put into practice, the correct theory of time travel.

The dictionary definition of the *astral* is: belonging to a mitotic aster; of the astral body it reads: an astral counterpart of the physical body. If one accepts the dictionary definition of the astral, defining, as it clearly does its having shape, it must therefore have dimension, thus establishing it as tangible! The conclusion must surely follow then that the astral, along with many other dimensions, too complex for me to go into here, are also just as real and, what is more may be measured.

To analogise the astral for instance, it is like moving from one place to another. This we do naturally, whether it be to another firm, town, house, or even another room. We do not look to take the surroundings with us each time we move; indeed we do not even consider it, knowing that it would be totally impracticable to try. In the physical state when we move to something or somewhere else, everything is new and different again in our life. Challenges will no doubt present themselves and, in all probability, there will also be a desire and or need to explore all the possibilities and experiences that may arise.

Of course for those who, as a result of their move, suffer deprivation, hardship and so on the desires may well take a different turn. In this instance the person may simply feel resigned to the situation so the challenges, ignored, simply fade away. Actually, they may even give up on life entirely but inevitably, there will be others who will grasp the nettle, facing the challenges head on.

So it is with the change we call death for although what was (the physical body) is now considered dead, the intellect of the individual has, by vacating the body, simply removed. But the soul-force is still very much alive in this other dimension. As likely as not he or she will also be just as excited or dismayed in this environment as they were when they removed to some new place on Earth. Because for various reasons it will never run again, we leave, either with sadness or gladness, a worn out vehicle in the car-breaker's yard to be disposed of. In the same way so do we leave our physical body to be consigned accordingly by others to the cemetery or crematorium.

Even if it were possible to do so, we would not want this physical body in our new space. After all, it would still have all of its physical diseases and pain, etc. and, for whatever reason, it will have run its earthly course. So, not only would it be totally impractical to attempt to lug it around the astral spheres but it would also have ceased to be of valid use anyway! This is because, just by thinking about it, we can re-create the image, for whatever reason, e.g. recognition, of how we looked anyway, so why bother to even consider the idea? For that matter, depending upon what might be termed our "imaginative ability" we can also, should we desire, "produce" anything else!

The majority of us will find this new-found-again freedom exhilarating, a freedom to be able to move at will, without encumbrance of any kind. Although there may be for a time, through perhaps leaving loved ones behind, *emotional aches*, all the physical ones will be gone. Such things as wheel-chairs, crutches, sightless eyes, deafness and artificial limbs, so prevalent on the Earth-plane, will be conspicuous by their absence.

It is also true that there will be those who may well be angered, disappointed or feel they have been cheated by being precipitated into a sphere for which they were not ready! Much like prisoners-of-war, criminals in prison, the hospitalised and or disabled persons, it is easily seen how they can feel this way; certainly until such time as they find their feet anyway. Eventually though, like these, *all* have to, and *will*, adjust, one way or another, to their new environment.

Bearing in mind that we are all *basically* energy, by using our mind-force only we can, even while in the physical body, move into and through this other dimension. In the main we are hide-bound by our own inadequacies and this is all that prevents us from literally doing so. Among these are narrow minded-ness, the lacking of knowledge of Spirit, of de-materialisation and the belief in the total limitations of the physical body.

Consequently, most of us never "tune in" and many of those who do will do so only mentally, never voluntarily venturing out of their body. Others, like myself, have striven to go further and will leave the body, travelling the astral. We are also able, if we wish, to stay near to the body while in trance state. Interesting too are the well attested cases of adepts and yogins who, virtually in seconds, are able to dematerialise and re-materialise many miles away. What is even more surprising, especially to those to whom it happened, is that they have done the same thing with them too! But when all is said and done to tune in at all is a starting point and I will always heartily encourage those who, all things being equal, (see Part Three on circles and sitters) wish to progress thus.

A simple exercise to demonstrate mind-force movement (not to be confused with trance or the astral of course) is to imagine yourself in a different place from where you are at this moment. Make it a place that you know; another room, house, bed, or whatever. Simply close your eyes; now mentally "see" it and unless you qualify as the most unimaginative person alive you will, mentally, be in that other place immediately.

However, something that will probably *not* have struck you is that your "travelling" was not impeded in any way by walls and other obstacles. The reason was that you did not even consider going through walls or doors or anything else! You simply went to the place you set your mind upon; you did not stop to think yourself through the actual *physical* motions.

This exercise should give the student some idea as to the speed and unlimited movement of Spirit. It is obviously seen too why and how a person in spirit having no such physical encumbrances, can move extremely rapidly and easily through space and solids as we know them. Equally then, one can immediately see that such encumbrances are only in place because we do not know how to rearrange those darned old minuscule electrically charged particles! It is lack of knowledge alone that prevents one from *literally and physically* doing the same thing whilst in the physical body, as do the aforesaid adepts, yogins and those they choose to honour thus.

When asleep we are often said to be "dead to the world" and in that state we might as well be "dead" for we actually own nothing. We have no control over anything physical and are a part of the "solidity" of our surroundings solely because we still possess our earthly body. Dreams, some contend, are the result of our inner desires, fears, obligations and so on whilst others claim that they are pointers and the meaning of them can be interpreted. (My studies thus far have not covered sufficiently the dream syndrome. As such I am therefore unable to give neither a valid nor worthy opinion as to the authenticity of such theories and decline therefore to comment further).

I do know however that in the sleep-state we *all* leave our bodies and are then on the astral. But most of us only hover near the bed, afraid or lacking the knowledge or encouragement from other entities to wander farther than the end of the bed. Yet we are still able to "see" and "talk" with those in Spirit and many of us, though unaware of it, do! The uninitiated will still say that we were dreaming but those of us who are aware *know* different. Sadly, they are unaware that they have been blessed in being able to experience communication with those loved ones from another dimension.

I have certainly learned, and continue to do so, a wealth of psychic, mediumistic and philosophical knowledge. Equally important and deserving of mention is that I am even more certain that this learning is not the residue of a series of fantasy dreams! It is the result of Tuan's, my helpers' and my own conscious efforts and desire to learn and interchange thoughts whereby I gain in knowledge with and from those loftier souls. It has, since that very first introduction (my revelation) always been so, and these have graciously and lovingly given of themselves that I may learn and pass on that learning.

I know that much of the knowledge and philosophy I dispense within these pages will be challenged; indeed I would not have it any other way, being myself such a critical sieve. Nevertheless, the fact remains that I have, more times than I care to count, gone to sleep, meditated or slipped into a light trance asking for the answer to something or other. Upon awakening I find, almost invariably, that I know the answer.

On these occasions I have been on, and still frequently do go on, trips with one of my helpers when I meet with these other minds. A mind transference (the only way I can describe it) of knowledge takes place, telepathic-like, often without a word being spoken! What is more a whole sheaf of "paper-work" can be virtually transmitted instantaneously. By way of explanation of the inspirational address, this is what actually occurs when a medium gives one without having prepared beforehand (such as a priest does with *his* sermon) what is to be said.

On other occasions I am totally unaware as to the way that I gained this or that answer, or indeed with whom I had spoken but I have no problem with this. Neither should a student for, on reflection, he or she will quickly realise that they too have often absorbed information without consciously knowing, or even considering from whence it came.

It is therefore with no surprise that at other times I find that knowledge has stolen up on me. On such an occasion I find that, though previously asked, when I did not know the answer to a particular question, I find myself replying, answering it to everyone's (including my own) satisfaction. The gap between the first and second time of that question being asked is also never constant with sometimes days, weeks and even months having elapsed before it is repeated. Even after all these years, I still find it somewhat strange to find myself answering, without hesitation in any way, something that I thought I did not know!

Explanation of *how* this occurs is less important here than *why* it does. The why is simply to accept the merit of asking and *knowing* that the asking will bring its own reward for such teachings are readily imparted to one if the *desire for the knowledge* is strong enough. If that strength of purpose and desire is not forthcoming then knowledge will pass you by. So always endeavour (God loves the trier!) to link your own soul-force to those more lofty soul-forces. Place yourself in the care of both *your* God and door-keeper to guide you and protect you on your journeying. By way of example the following words of such lofty souls should be of value and taken to heart.

"In vain do men talk of happiness, they who never subdued an impulse in obedience to a principle. He who never sacrificed a present to a future good, or a personal to a general one cannot know true happiness, nor find the pathway. He will stumble as blind men do in unfamiliar territory and speak of it as they would when describing colours. True religion teaches and all true persons know that the perfecting of humankind can only come about by the ever-increasing predominance of the Soul over the body. But remember, this does not necessarily mean that one has to be 'of the world but not in it!' You are here to learn.

"The attitudes of some religious orders whereby silence, celibacy, withdrawal from all earthly things, etc. is demanded and enforced as a part of that order's doctrine are out of step with the real world. History alone proves that isolating a few individuals within such bastions of authoritarian religious fervour, have never by such attitudes and aims succeeded in real terms. Many also join such accommodations *not* through a calling but only *to escape from society at large!* As such, by comparison, their converts have always been but few in number! Equally, mainly through such constrictions, they have never had, nor can they ever have in the future, any real or lasting impact upon, nor assist towards, the perfecting of our earth-plane as a whole. *Remember too, dear friends, that religion can only be true when it benefits all humankind!*"

The development of the Soul while here on Earth is one of the weightiest questions humans have to face and experience. Yet many folk, in real terms, do not even think of the soul, or of the effect it has upon them, never mind its development! For those of you that *do* have feelings of *any* kind of *soul awareness* I urge that you strive to brush away any and all clouds of doubt and fear. Once free of these you shall awake and gain the insight to the lighting up of the pathway, secure in the knowledge that clouds of any kind cannot possibly obscure pure Light and Truth.

Here one discovers the altruistic Trinity of Spirit, Soul and Matter, each one a functionary in itself yet with one law governing the whole. Centralisation seems to be the absolute tendency of all condition. If one sees this as true then one must agree that the harmonious action of these three, united, *must* bring forth a *universal* power. Through this man is able to pass through the veil at will and find true knowledge, eventually becoming an illumined soul.

(As previously mentioned within these pages the man in the street was forbidden to communicate or demonstrate the God-given Spiritual gifts. As such, the masses could no longer be taught such a trinity. Accordingly, considered as being more easily and readily assimilated by the masses, the Father, Son and Holy Ghost was substituted for the previous trinity teachings. So yet another alteration to the scriptures was effected by the all powerful and oppressive early orthodox church hierarchy.)

Throughout history and latterly in modern times too, elevated souls have reincarnated among us in very differing forms and are in no way only the sack-cloth and sandals variety. Such people have made their mark in many different ways as leaders, inventors, educators, philosophers, progressive surgeons and even industrialists. All have influenced and or made their mark upon the world in varying ways, influencing and making a difference to both the thinkers among us and the rest too! They mainly tend to have the edge via their ultra-magnetic personalities and will have little to do either with fey religious and or narrow-minded bias, of whatever ilk.

The learning game is of course much more than simply sitting in classrooms listening to lectures or whatever. Ask just about any kid what subject they are not keen on at school; indeed ask any adult the same sort of thing about their school days. Though not a betting man, I would still lay odds that you will find such answers as (a) they did not feel comfortable with the teacher (b) did not like him or her (c) did not gel with the person teaching that subject or (d) probably a combination of a, b and c!

Logically therefore, it is necessary to seek out the teacher you like and trust if you really desire to learn a particular thing. It is better for instance that a teacher tells you (i) not to put your hand into a fire because it will hurt rather than (ii) to tell you to see what happens if you do. Whilst perhaps (ii) makes you learn faster it is also usually more painful, particularly when the only option is the *try it* method. Of course (i) is generally more comfortable and in any event one can always be more trusting to those that do not deliberately cause us pain, harm, or discomfort.

From the foregoing it follows that although the motivation of each student stems from a desire to learn combined with a willing eagerness to explore and investigate, it is of course equally important, nay necessary, that one learns via a teacher whom one likes and trusts. Teachers who have no petty jealousy and who move you on when they can no longer help your education will go a long way in perpetuating the stimulation of a student's motivation. They will also ease the frustrations that are bound to occur from time to time. Therefore, being able to trust the teacher, one may not only discuss anything but also it ensures the maintaining of open, challenging minds on both sides.

I have said that like attracts like (a Natural Law) and whilst we are at school our teachers, by definition, being thrust upon us, means that we have no choice or say about our liking them or not. In our psychic studies however, we *do* have that choice. Through Natural Law, if we "open" ourselves (our channels) correctly, we will draw unto us like minds, minds of the same or slightly higher intellectual standing. As we achieve our "grades" though, so correspondingly, we will need to move intellectually higher.

The beauty and harmony of such soul-actions pouring forth will ensure that as soon as they have reached their peak they will introduce and move us on to another higher grade teacher, thus assisting us further in our quest for even more knowledge. The transition is made quite readily, without rancour or any other display of anxiety or show of temperament on the part of the relinquishing tutor, thus ensuring the continuance of our learning process. Since no resistance or impediment of any kind occurs, there is an automatic rise in one's spiritual intellect. Thus, metaphorically ascending higher and higher up the spiritual ladder, one is taught by more and more highly qualified teachers.

I have already made it clear that teachers are found on both sides of the veil and are not always on the Earth-plane. It is obvious that there can be advantages of different kinds in having a teacher from either plane. However, for want of a better term, having passed beyond what we will call "the lower levels of communication" our spirit teachers (guides), our doorkeeper and helpers, able to receive instruction from loftier Spirit-planes, simply kill two birds with one stone. A medium thus instructed is, on a recipient's behalf, better attuned and therefore able to pass on clearer and more evidential links from their loved ones. For themselves too they (and for those who will listen) *can* and *should* receive more and more advanced philosophical thoughts and teachings, which in turn they can pass on to others less attuned or receptive to Spirit.

Figuratively speaking, many psychics (unable to move forward into true mediumship) are like the learner driver who carries L-plates ad infinitum. No matter how many tests are taken, something invariably occurs to disqualify their passing! Their repeated failures may stem from a lack of concentration, insufficient knowledge, not quite having the knack, the wrong instructors and variously other individual or multiple reasons. In the end, usually by choice or circumstance, many of these give up the lessons, never to drive again. Others though, inexperienced and or not sufficiently tutored, take a chance and remove their L-plates. Hoping that they will get away with it they become taxi-drivers (like my Aunt Millie, end of the pier quality "professional" clairvoyants). Yet others will continue their learning process with the same poor standard of instructor and a shaky faith in their ability to eventually win through one way or another.

The analogy I think is obvious! Psychics, with such short comings cannot successfully move on to mediumship until such time as they have gained sufficient knowledge. If they do their shortcomings will be patently obvious to those who know the difference. The moral is therefore that one should not, must not, discard the "L" plates until such time as one is certain that one's abilities have become knowledge!

The explanation for such negative actions become clear to the true seeker of knowledge the moment they feel that nothing more is to be gained by staying with their present tutor. The alternatives are also clear and are (a) look for another teacher, (b) give up the study, (c) erroneously believe you know it all, or, and most important of all (d) the teacher advises you to move on to greater things.

Sometimes students, for various reasons, have to suspend their development until later in their lives when they have more time. For example this might be when their children are "off-hand" or when they are more settled in life. Others are *late starters*, who, quite suddenly, *feel a need* to search.

There are also those who go through their lives with intermittent flashes of what they might term feelings about things (intuition) that are different from their normal thinking patterns. This is actually undeveloped psychic ability; had they become more interested or felt a greater need to develop *theirs*, then they might well have become practitioners in their own right, moving onto their own particular spiritual pathway.

The unseen world is open to every person who becomes attuned to the natural harmonies of Divine law. In order to find this the seeker of true knowledge must press doggedly on and above all be sincere in their search. Once found, it will be like discovering a new continent and once visited, they will want to return again and again. They will want to learn the "language" and absorb its atmosphere; to mingle and hold communion with its people. The desire to understand its ways will act as the predominant catalyst! They will wonder at this truly incredible experience, amazed that such things were at their fingertips for so long without their becoming involved in it. Then will quickly dawn upon them the realisation that the principle reason was their own lack of will and determination and knowing.

Nevertheless, because Natural Law and karma walk hand in hand and always prevails, the timing has to be right! There has always existed a beginning and an ending time for all things. Often though these starts and finishes are not always apparent and are only perceived with the benefit of hindsight. Nevertheless, until that time occurs, whatever your desire, you will not reach your goal for what is, is! (See e. of ch. on What is, is!)

I have to say here that I think, rather than sitting alone, the wisest course is to attend a good circle, or at the very least, to sit with a reliable relative or friend. You will remember, no doubt, that *I* sat alone, yet here am I advising students not to do this. In the event, I only "sat" this way at the very beginning and, on Tuan's advice, I joined a circle as soon as I could. In mitigation, I add that if you ever experience the sort of revelation that I had (mentioned in an earlier chapter) then you too would not be afraid of sitting alone - indeed you should not need this book either!

It is well to remember that all things animate and inanimate are subject to gravity. As such, everything is constantly moving at an enormous speed (yet appearing to be always stationary) with the rotation of the earth in space. There is no conception of movement simply because there is no evidence of it from the senses! Although seemingly to be at rest, this non-concept of action or movement, like all other objective sense-perceptions, is directly the reverse of the real truth and "crossing over" into the Spirit World is no exception.

Consequently, if you do sit alone be advised, for one can easily pass through the veil onto the Astral yet be unaware that they have actually done so! How? Well, for example, without the discipline of control (that is just letting oneself wander aimlessly through the meditation session) the chances of moving onto the astral by accident, rather than by design, are greatly enhanced. It can be quite a fearful experience until control of it is learned, when it becomes absolutely pleasurable.

Unfortunately however, due to a lack of knowledge and control, this sort of psychic accident is, in reality, more common than one might suppose. In truth, such displays are a breakdown in true communication with Spirit. Although it appears that experimentation by the students is the fault here, tutors should always, early on, caution them and repeat such cautions until it is considered unnecessary. If they are not correctly advised it will, in many cases, irrespective of where the fault lies, result in students abandoning their search.

It is therefore imperative to ask that you be protected throughout your session and that any experiments carried out be completely controlled by both yourself and your door-keeper. In this way you will quickly recognise the good-feel-state of co-operation with him or her, which, in turn, will give *you* more confidence to move on to a more profound search. After all, door-keepers are desirous of assisting us in every way or why bother to be there in the first place? Like attracts like; so as you learn they too gain in knowledge and power.

Provided then that you search honestly and diligently they will quickly learn (or already know) how to protect you against unwanted entities or entrancements, etc. Therefore you must strive to work *with* (and never do your own thing) these very important entities or their protective powers may be stretched to the limit. Without this togetherness, one might well result in a session being very frustrating, disappointing and sometimes may even be harmful.

Ensure too that unwanted interruptions are not your lot, e.g. door or telephone bells, unexpected callers, the cat jumping up on your lap, indeed any intrusion that could possibly upset your session. Without attention to these precautions you could at the very least be disturbed at a very inopportune moment, or worse, in that moment of distraction, as mentioned above, possibly attract an undesirable entity who could perhaps, depending on the strength of your door-keeper, cause you some discomfort, or even harm! However, as you progress you and your helpers will become stronger, able to withstand, without disturbance, for example, a dog suddenly barking, or such other unexpected occurrences.

Here perhaps I should mention that I find when meditating for communion with Spirit alone, lying down comfortably on the floor, bed or whatever is more conducive to the production of better results. But meditation as generally taught is simply to relax and to find the inner self and it could be said that the aim is only one of egoity. So whilst it is good perhaps for what it is intended, it is nevertheless, essentially, solely for the benefit of oneself! Whilst all meditation can be rewarding, relaxing and enjoyable, as is mediumship, here the similarity ends. (see e. of ch. on east/west cultures.)

The so-called "speaking with one's higher self" is yet another New Age thing that must be explained. Poor levels of instruction and leadership lead (and continue so to do) to confusing the *inner* with the *higher* self. Many self titled "masters" have only read what others have written and quickly move on to promoting their own workshops and seminars as an "authority" on the subject advertised. But there is never anything really new at these, or, for that matter written by the "newagists" - apart from the punters that is who attend such things, and of course those who buy the countless books, eating up this pulp fiction.

In point of fact, the Higher Self is not one working *alone* at all! It is our d/k communicating with us endeavouring to help us on our earthly journey and towards our spiritual destiny. (I also explain later how our d/k's use, via telepathic methods, simply for convenience, this method of communication when we "hear" our own voice within our heads.)

Consequently our *own thoughts, imaginings and resulting consequences* are fed and resolved via the *inner self* using only our own brain capacity albeit, when meditating, in a more relaxed and clear thinking manner. It is very much like what I said earlier about prayer and how we can think our way through a problem when it is as if a prayer has been answered.

Communication and communion with oneself therefore is not *mediumship*, though it can sharpen one's intuition and psychic stance and perception. Mainly though, if one stays within those limited parameters it merely serves only oneself. It presents a comfortable way to feel cushioned from the outside world. In reality however, speaking solely *with oneself, for oneself alone,* demonstrates a profound massaging of one's own ego.

It can be seen then that communion with Spirit is very different to the meditation usually taught and does not, indeed cannot, as students are so often erroneously told, *automatically* lead to mediumship per se. It is merely points one towards *self-awareness* and is and always has been only targeted at and towards the gaining of this. It must be said however that I have yet to find anyone who has actually either taken or attended a workshop who can lucidly define what they mean by self-awareness. It can be though, provided one is aware of its limitations, a stepping stone for becoming interested in, and the first basic steps towards, the beginning of mediumship.

On the other hand the aim of the student of mediumship will be, (or should be) in co-operation and co-ordination with their d/k, in a constant endeavour to aspire to a higher level of mentality and communion with more highly spiritually evolved *discarnate* souls in other dimensions. As opposed to self, this tends automatically to promote a desire to share and demonstrate one's knowledge with any who are in need of, after what we call "death", proof of a continued existence of the soul in spirit form. I reiterate! The best way forward then, whether novice, intermediary or advanced student is to get yourself into a strong and sincere circle led by a good medium.

So if one should join a circle under the leadership of a good medium how does one get to know about these? Well, for starters, you could do a lot worse than to visit your local Spiritualist Church or centre (and there must be one near you) attending various meetings. *Always* arrive early so that you can, in a quiet meditative state relax, asking your God for the direction you desire. In such places and situations you will undoubtedly meet others of your kind who as might, as well as you, be complete novices or in various stages of development, the intrinsic reasons for them being there.

After the meeting most churches provide some refreshment, when one may buy a cup of tea, coffee, etc. Stay on, listen to others' chat and points of view and proffer your own, without fear of ridicule or rebuff. I know that if your desire and will to learn is strong enough then you may rest assured that before long the first of your many teachers will be guided to you. Your door-keeper and helpers will, almost certainly without your knowledge at this stage, have already been working behind the scenes on your behalf to arrange this. (I once asked Tuan how to find my guru and he said that if my desire was strong enough, I needed to look no further than the end of my nose!)

Remember my earlier words! *Know* that you will attract like-minds! Accept and understand that people will be eager to offer help and advice in developing whatever talent you may have. You will quickly find your niche and hopefully will not become a sponge. Be as the sieves mentioned earlier, sifting *all* that you hear and discuss! Challenge yes, but always in a fraternal, pleasant way, never getting angry or pedantic, remembering that "a quiet answer turneth away wrath." Also remember not to comment simply for the satisfying of your or anyone else's ego. Never hold to an opinion on something you know nothing about; such opinions have no meaningful validity. If anyone in the group should proffer one such, it should be qualified, bounced around and only be for the purpose of exciting the discussion taking place.

Do not ever adopt a gregarious attitude just for convenience sake or, for that matter, any other excuse. Make sure too that you do not fall into the trap of bending to peer pressure just because it seems the easier course to adopt or because you are, even momentarily, overawed. Work through the information you receive, keeping an open, enquiring, probing mind. Even at the risk of becoming a pain discuss all the relevant points fully until you receive answers that you feel are satisfactory not only from without but from within. But do not be unduly worried if, in the event, those answers are not forthcoming for provided your *desire for knowledge is great enough*, you may rest assured that it will come, one way or another.

There is an old proverb, told in many different ways and, in relating my version here, I make no apology. Any plagiary is unintentional but, in keeping, I sincerely thank the author for the idea anyway. The writer's name, long ago lost in the sands of time, is simply referred to as the familiar anon!

A man was in the habit of taking a grist to the mill. The grist would be put into one end of the sack with a large stone placed in the other end. This enabled the weight to be balanced across the back of the pack-animal. One day, his son, forgetting the stone, put too much grist in the sack.

Not wanting to go to the trouble of taking some out again, he took a chance and threw the sack across the animal's back, whereupon the grist automatically found its own level and balanced perfectly, being evenly divided. When he saw what had happened he called exultantly to his father, saying: "Papa, look here! See what I've done! We don't need a stone at all!"

His father replied, "Stop this foolishness! If that is the best way to carry a grist, don't you s'pose I or my father or his father before him would have found it out? There is only one way to carry a grist you idle boy. Take it down immediately and re-do-it properly!"

Like unto that man is he who will persist in believing that nothing alters, persisting too in believing a lie, merely because it is an old one, or convenient for his purpose. (Such a quote could easily have come from "the laughing priests" of any persuasion, don't you think?)

So do not just take some else's word on face value alone - search for the Truth and question each question until *you* are satisfied! The message of the parable seems clear enough but there is something more here not quite as easily seen. It is the *ability* versus the *knowledge* thing I wrote on earlier rearing, by example, it's head once again.

190

In other words, if you have the ability to be a great violinist, do not give up because all you produce as you draw the bow across the instrument is a torturous cat-a-wail! Find a good teacher if you want to turn your ability into knowledge. Do not just stand there agape; search for *any* and *all* knowledge for it is yours to discover by right; though having the will and motivation to succeed is an absolute necessity. It is then that you will learn to utilise your abilities to the full.

SUMMARY

The possibilities of the human soul are immeasurable. Spiritual philosophy teaches that by developing our Spiritual minds we come to the certain true knowledge that "death" is not the end; we only make a transition to another dimension. Once the seeker of truth recognises, absorbs and thence *knows* that life does not end at what is called death, they will move on from simple belief to *knowing* that they now possess *positive* rather than negative knowledge.

Remember that the Vital Spirit in the flesh and blood is the "concert hall", with the soul as "the arranger", orchestrating our destiny. But to avoid the strings, woodwinds and so on creating disharmony and or being out of tempo one with another, the "music score" needs a "conductor" and this is the d/k, the guiding process available to us all. Integral and intrinsic parts of our make up, the psychic mind (in co-operation with the d/k) and the physical consciousness *must work in conjunction* in order to utilise our *full* spiritual potential, thereby correctly fulfilling our destiny during our present incarnation. Hence, the best conductor we can employ is our d/k.

Sadly though, all too often he or she is thrust, mainly through ignorance, aside. Because the education authorities are subject to the whims of state religion they are obliged to toe the line. But, in doing so they simply pay lip service and as such truly spiritual things are never taught or discussed in depth in the classroom. In the event, most of us, in fact, throughout the whole planet, in a masochistic fashion tear ourselves apart conducting the cacophony we call living. Thus it is that we, in the main, contribute and assist, albeit through ignorance of Spirit, in all of the chaos that occurs daily throughout this, our world.

The message of Spirit is clear to those who hath an ear! Humankind in toto must strive to achieve and embrace this essential, engendered of Spirit love and harmony on Earth in order to restore and preserve what once was. We can *still* have, even *now*, if we care enough, a beautiful, happy, well fed, more healthful and safe world. So make *your* endeavour to resist the headlong, lemming-like pursuit so obvious in others.

Driven by negative energies such as greed, hate, envy, jealousy, anger, uncaring attitudes, religious and or (often hand in hand) political persecution, etc. these rush headlong on to their *own individual* Armageddon. The result here, irrespective of whether it is intentional or not is that those who indulge thus are, by such emotions, contributing to the gradual, wilful destruction of this God-given planet.

If you are one of the seekers or one of them it matters little for we are all, in some way, contributors until we (and I implore you to do so) take "one step forward" and vow to become a volunteer in this struggle. Forget such irrational things as Heaven and hell too for these are uttered by those who know no better. Such things are man-made for, as Tuan says: "It is in anticipation that most people find their Heaven and hell!"

Throughout our incarnation many of us have been content to take the easy path, allowing the priests (the original law-makers) to think *for* us. As such, for centuries, we have been using this to insulate ourselves from the real world. Because it was easier, we have allowed ourselves to be "guided" (intentional quotes) by these ecclesiastical and political prestidigitators. It is this that has caused us to mislay and or turn our backs upon our God-given Spiritual inheritance.

Consequently true mediumship has also suffered and today, in many cases, it is of an appallingly low standard. The result is that many mediums, through lack of knowledge and often blissfully unaware, struggle with the lower mind-forces, and are equally ignorant as to why they are often so tired and or irritable and depressed.

Know that to become adept at something one must first learn how and mediumship is no exception! An open, enquiring mind is the basic requirement to acquiring learning and knowledge. Prayer and a lot of patience to achieve results is also required, even by we "natural" mediums. But if one is sincere, retaining an ongoing desire for knowledge, not one moment is wasted in communion with Spirit and it is certain that once on the pathway to *your* development, with doubts and fears long since gone, the direction you need to take will become crystal clear.

As a natural I have been fortunate to have had from a very early age (and perhaps, before this incarnation too) my psychic and conscious minds *always* working in conjunction. But it was not until I was going on sixteen that I truly became aware and understood this conjunction. Since then I have enjoyed the guides and helpers working through and with me.

The beneficial "organisms" involved and enjoyed here are, simply speaking, the physical and mind-force energies of the so-called living and the dead working together! As such my life has been for me (though in no way a bed of roses) and for others a source of information, advice, evidence of survival and healing, for which I sincerely, gladly and daily thank God and Spirit.

Finally, I hope that I have pointed the way but that is all I can do and the rest is up to you, as an individual, to take it, or leave it, as you will. Safe to say it has, anyway, been for me, (and still is) a long and winding road, but it has been (and is) well worth the effort of beginning the journey and continuing onward towards Light and Truth. And may your God go with you...

HELPFUL NOTES!

(On What is, is!) *Be aware and know that "what is, is" always is, however tempo-rary! For instance, taking a playing card and tearing it in half changes the "is", wrought (in time) by your action. You may be quite adept at repairing things even to the point where the repair appears to be invisible. Even so, the molecular struc-ture of the card has been changed and therefore the new "is" is, the last "old is" again having changed, wrought by your further action of repairing the card.*

In consequence, "what is, is" has validity only during any unchanged state, which in itself is a non- starter. It has to change due to time moving on for, in that time, it has aged, however brief that time may be! Another example; what is hot is hot and what is cold is cold, but these too are constantly undergoing change for as the ice melts so the fire cools and vice-versa! Nothing escapes; everything con-stantly changes! Notwithstanding, it can be argued that the real "is" is the excep-tion for, however fleeting, the eternal now is manifest as, in reality, there is no past, present or future!

(On east/west cultures) *Students are advised to remember that we in the western world cannot commit so easily to earnest deep meditation as do those in the east. Over many generations these peoples have had such things instilled into them, by now perhaps these might even be a part of their genetic structure. Honestly, how many of you westerners reading this would like to have to drink bad water every day with all that this entails, exist on just a bowl of rice a day for sustenance and disregard flies covering all of the exposed parts of your body and, in particular, take no notice of them drinking the fluids from your eyes? And how many of you would obligatorily arise at dawn each day to exercise and or to worship?*

Such things come naturally to eastern cultures, especially to those who seek holiness. Pain disciplines, most times self inflicted too, are the norm, e.g. walking on hot coals, piercing the skin with skewers and hanging weights from them, chal-lenging venomous snakes and insects to bite and so on! Often fasting for days on end in meditation up in the hills, virtually naked and exposed twenty-four hours a day, come what may, to the elements. Shall I go on...?

PART THREE
Self Help!

THE DIY MANUAL FOR BUDDING MEDIUMS

Chapter 1

Throughout our lives we come across all sorts of different trades and professions and just when we think we have met them all, up pops another one! If I am interested in a term or word that someone mentions during a conversation and I do not know what it means, I wait for either a pause in the conversation or speak to them alone afterwards. This stems from having an inherent curiosity and a particular appetite for words that may expand my vocabulary.

One such opportunity presented itself recently when a guy I was speaking with mentioned that he was a technical author and subsequently, I asked him to explain. He said that he writes DIY manuals on whatever was required; cars, aeroplanes, radio and television for instance. Mediumship of course, and neither is this part of the book specifically a "technical manual" in the accepted sense, but nonetheless, I still thought it an appropriate title.

However, unlike technical authors, I do not have instant reference to reams of "bumph" from which I can research and collate my material. Nor can I pick up a telephone, when necessary, to ask a manufacturer to clarify a point. True to say, data to which I have access is available from very able guides and helpers but the requirement here is that I must be, when writing, "tuned in" virtually all of the time. This though means that I have to expend far more energy and time than I would if I was just perusing notes or picking up a telephone!

So although I take full personal responsibility for this book in toto, I am also acutely aware that the manual may well prove to be the most difficult part to write. Some reasons for this, like those above, are obvious but the main one, being patently so, might quite easily be overlooked.

Sat here at the keyboard, apart from the mental thoughts and comments back and forth with my helpers, I spend the time "talking" to a PC monitor; so, in "reality" I am talking to myself. When teaching students in a live situation this does not occur because the tutor endeavours (or should anyway) to automatically create a two-way flow of interest, prompting questions and answers, resulting in a worthwhile exchange of ideas and information.

If schooled correctly from the beginning students will (hopefully, and should always, if they remember my words on challenging) immediately ask about something, as it is said, that they do not fully understand. If anything is misunderstood, or, for whatever reason, requires further explanation, even to only *one* student in the group, such explanation, in deference to that student, should be forthcoming. And until he or she fully understands to their *own* satisfaction, it should be explained over and over; then, if necessary, re-hashed again until it is.

Instructors should make every effort to elucidate, expanding their themes, sieving both their own words and the words of their students, which should result in much more all round satisfaction. Certainly it is far better than students and tutor merely politely reaching the sort of unsatisfactory compromises that can occur when tutors *do not allow* interruption to their flow. Denied questions at the time, these go unasked mostly due to embarrassment or forgetfulness. As such, opportunities for answers being received, not to mention parts of the lectures, are totally negated, unlearned, mislaid or lost.

What should be understood is that almost invariably these questioners will often want answers to what other "pretend to know" students, for fear of being thought dumb by the rest, would never ask! So all power to these classroom "heroes" for having the courage to question and not caring what others may think of their "stupidity".

Know that mediumship does not simply stand or fall on levels of pseudo puffed-up education or intellectual thinking! The poorly educated are never automatically dismissed by Spirit! So not being concerned with, or fased by peer pressure, although they may take a little longer to absorb something, it may well result in *their* mediumship ending further up the spiritual ladder than the "collegians" could ever have envisaged!

From the foregoing it will be seen that, in the solitary writing situation, unless one is totally professional, one can easily fall into a trap. Explanations can become long-winded, tedious and even boring. As such, I have made every effort to keep the text interesting, logical, sometimes amusing and always minimal! Something else that is not immediately evident to amateur writers such as myself, maybe, is that the written word carries, to a greater degree, more responsibility than the spoken ones. After all, whilst yesterday's news or TV programmes may quickly be forgotten, once the written word is published, it enters, in *solid* form into the public domain and, from that time on, virtually anyone has access to it, with all that this implies.

As people have different learning abilities, their ability to absorb knowledge must also differ. Accordingly, I make no apology for setting out as simply as possible the methods I employ when conducting circles, etc. hoping that all readers will recognise, absorb and use! After all, when I opened the "Oasis of Psychic Development" all those years ago the prime initiative was to teach. Therefore I sincerely hope that my words within these pages will succeed as the natural heir to the set aims achieved there and which today continue in my new centre in Spain.

Before moving on consider the following scenario and learn from it what you will.

A family of five, say, father, mother and three children aged four, eight and twelve years of age respectively are watching television. Whilst watching *and paying attention*, although they all see the same pictures and hear the same dialogue at the same moment, each person will have received and will relate afterwards, in accordance with their level of intelligence, a different input.

The content is of no importance here either for our experiment! Rest assured that whatever type of programme is seen together, each of them, should they be asked separately, will almost certainly give varying accounts of the programme viewed. And this will be irrespective of age difference and or of being adult or child! For those of you who doubt my words, I stress it is also a safe bet that the mother and father will also tell of, and subscribe to, differing versions of what they have just watched.

Similarly, independent persons witnessing an accident, a burglary, a mugging and so on will, all too often, when recounting what they saw, differ with others at the scene as to what they will say occurred. It may be that the witnesses are of roughly the same age and mentality, when one might expect to find a correlation of the happening. However, this rarely proves to be the case, as almost any investigator will concur. It is not solely the witnessing of bad incidents either because the same thing happens when watching pleasant events too. By the same process, in psychic and mediumship development, each person, even though they may be "seeing" the same thing observes, learns and progresses in their own way and at their own pace.

I thus assure all readers that such inequalities must and do exist among us all. Indeed, the impossibility of all persons being on the same level of learning and thought is an indisputable fact of life. By definition it is this that disqualifies and absolutely destroys the debunkers old argument of mass hysteria in Spiritualist physical séances and Spiritualist Spiritual healing sessions*. But equally, this in no way disqualifies *anyone*, however much they may see things from a much broader or narrower perspective, from progressing in their quest...

*As opposed to, for example, evangelical and Pentecostal purposely intentioned hysterically enhanced healing sessions.

Chapter 2
THE IMPORTANCE OF TIME

An old chestnut frequently trotted out, often by psychics and mediums who ought to know better, is the claim that there is no time in the Spirit World. My spirit teachers have always disputed this and have many times shown it to be wrong. On receiving a postal reading for instance, I never immediately open it. As instructed, I always tune in and invariably receive a date and time when I should effect the reading. Oftentimes these appointments are days and even weeks ahead!

This alone, for me at any rate, indisputably demonstrates that there must not *only* be measurable Spirit time but that they are far more conscious and understanding of *ours* than are we of *theirs*. It also more than suggests that in order to marshal the links (evidence) a lot more goes on regarding the arranging of these than most of us seem to comprehend and however brief or long it must take time! It demonstrates too that our spirit friends and loved ones, just as when on earth, do not, simply at the drop of a hat, appear at a sitting or public meeting. It also shows that certain arrangements have to be made in order to have good sessions, taking time to do so.

The alternative argument that may be put forward (that of a medium linking virtually instantly on meeting someone by chance) only shows two things. (1) That the medium is "open" all of the time and encourages the invasion, for various reasons among which are ego and or the inability to "open and close" at will. (2) That the entities were within hailing distance at the time when we find them almost attached to the recipient's aura. This happens more when loved ones have not been long in their new environment and still cling to familiar things. Others (those that haunt or are lost for example) have not yet found either their place or what they want to do there.

Other mediums, perhaps more airy-fairy and or inadequately trained or developed will also claim that spirit are often too busy, or anxious to move on to want to bother with those who are left behind. Mind you, they couch their terms more cautiously and kinder than this but the implication is clear! This is sometimes true of the loners in spirit (or haunters who, in their wanderings, are unaware that they are causing problems) who feel that they have no reasons nor persons to contact anyway. In the normal run of things however, e.g. regarding loved ones, I would never make such inaccurate or insensitive statements.

Not picked up by some sensitives, nor that they should *clearly* understand or even consider its significance and importance, while others yet will simply disregarded both, is another time aspect. In many too it has never even occurred that such things are of any consequence! It should be realised by all (and *known* by *all* mediums) that when a sitter is early or late for their appointment it can never be as successful as when they sit at the appointed time; and the same is true of public meetings too.

We still in the body, in our apparently solid world often think transparently about Spirit! Consequently it does not enter our heads, unless we take the trouble to find out, that they too are sometimes caught on the hop! Too early, they may not have yet arrived in the "vibration" that is so necessary for the production of good evidence and sittings as a whole. And the reverse is also true when, just as unhappily for all concerned, they are unable to maintain the "vibration" any longer and accordingly have to leave.

In the event then, I affirm as above; Spirit knows and respects *our* time! In turn we should also respect them more and *know* that sittings and even meetings, unless they begin on time, are never as successful as those that do. Therefore it is imperative that *all* mediums (if they claim to acknowledge personal responsibility) become aware of such anomalies. Further, that on acknowledgement they also accept the obligation of explaining them much more often and far more clearly to their public.

Spirit time, functioning as it does in a different dimension to our physical world is *of course* differently structured to ours but this should not lead us to deny its existence. Equally, we are neither obliged nor required to have to understand its workings. It is common knowledge that the average person cannot explain how a very basic electronic gadget's innards function, yet they can still operate it! I know and have proved that Spirit easily relates to our time scale and that satisfying, rewarding and evidential sessions require only the right attitude. This means that all participants should have an enquiring, open mind and infuse a friendly, congenial atmosphere into the proceedings. (All things being equal, sceptics are OK but do not waste your time on debunkers.)

Logically, viewed in real terms, it can be seen that we simply utilise *our* time scale as a convenient vehicle by and through which we move from one place, situation, condition, etc. to another. Most of us also rush about trying to *save* it, when most of the time our actions often result in the wasting of it. I repeat; *circle results are intrinsically dependent on attitude, the mind-force capability and conditions ("vibrations") during the sitting and not on the timepieces we so often love to hate.* Therefore, results are not dependent upon us and Spirit having to synchronise our watches! Far more important is our determined desire to learn and understand, with all that this infers and entails.

Again, logical reasoning will show that when we visit a venue either as demonstrator or potential recipient, our spirit friends *must* be aware of time. If it is not so, then we have to conclude that they continually "hang around" ad infinitum, waiting and hoping that we just might attend one some time. If that is the case and the desire is strong enough, we will find them sticking to us like glue twenty-four hours a day, every day! Then, if *this is true,* it will mean that our privacy is nonexistent! Obviously surely, one sees how illogical, inconvenient and perhaps embarrassing this could, no, more likely *would* be, for all concerned. Worse, it could possibly, in some cases, lead to obsession and even possession by unhealthy, negative, mischievous or even malevolent entities!

Patience may be a virtue, but who among us would wait indoors *all day, every day* sometimes for weeks, months or even years in the hope that someone might just condescend to drop in on us? Of course it is ludicrous, as are quite a few other myths about Spirit, psychic and mediumistic matters!

When demonstrating, on more times than I care to count, I have spoken of a contact describing a certain *time* and *day* when so and so had occurred. At other times they refer to a *coming* event or occurrence. Affirmation of such statements by recipients confirms that entities are not only aware of our time but can also pinpoint the moment exactly! Many other examples abound, but I am sure that by now, on consideration, you will find yourself agreeing that time must be just as important to Spirit as it is to us, *whatever the scale.*

In concluding this piece, I point to something that has long been recognised and acknowledged by psychologists and the like which is that we are all creatures of habit. Equally recognised is that good habits are harder to learn than bad ones. So from the beginning I urge that you understand that only good habits in all matters concerning any and all interchange with Spirit are well worth acquiring. Habitual exercises too are important to both psychics *and* mediums; indeed I would argue that some of them should be regarded as essential!

Let us begin then by acknowledging and understanding the importance of developing the habit of *punctuality* in all our spiritual endeavours. Irrespective of how trivial these may appear to be at first sight the same rule of thumb should apply. It is not only a question of good manners and respect for Spirit, not to mention common sense, but also to other persons (members of your circle for instance) all of whom are facets of, and participating in, your most sacred search.

For instance, "a", "b", "c" and so on are always punctual, arriving before start-time so that they can settle and indulge in a little social intercourse. This allows our auras, (magnetic fields), our "psychic juices" if you like to mingle, which encourages close companionship. Then they will still have time to sit for a few minutes in quiet contemplation on the coming circle. But when one or more of the other sitters are frequently late, they usually arrive out of breath and offer up the same old tired excuses. Some frustration and animosity can creep in and probably will, given (that word again) time. Once this condition is present it can quickly deteriorate into a cancer, which spilling over, can destroy and kill off what might have been a circle with real potential. Believe it; indeed *know it!* These sorts of things are definite no-no's for the production of anything of a good nature spiritual or otherwise, often leading to some very unpleasant events. Such happenings sometimes go beyond the emotional falling-out of one with another too.

So, this is the last thing I will say on *time* here! If you are not guilty of this make sure that the *time* does not come when you are. On getting to the venue early use your *time* wisely and therefore usefully. On the other hand, if you are one of the tardy ones, long before dissent fills the air, make the last late *time* the last *time!* Solemnly promise to Spirit, the other circle members, the medium in charge and to yourself that in future you will be on time, for both here and in Spirit, *time* really is of the essence.

Finally, the last thing you want is your round circle to become the square ring! So, forget *"time-out"* and leave the in-fighting to the professionals; to those who enjoy such sport!

Chapter 3
SIMPLE BUT EFFECTIVE AND
NECESSARY EXERCISES

Buddhists, among other religions, practise chanting, a form of exercise to promote well-being and spiritual grace but I have found that one does not have to employ any particular profundity of thought or phrase. My conclusion then is that it is more beneficial as a learning lesson of self discipline than the actual chant itself. So, as they say: "Whatever turns you on!" I advise therefore, as an aid to concentration and self-seeking, that you pick your own fancied particular "aum" and chant away.

Apart from the somewhat obvious mystical connotations such things usually suggest, I would point out that for centuries past Yogins and the like also practised breathing and colour exercises. Still today, by using such proven, beneficial exercises they are able to store prana, (energy or power) for use later, in the physical body. When spoken of by my helpers I found myself both interested in and attracted to the idea that the "flexing of the muscles" could be so easy and accomplished virtually anywhere. Accordingly, I gladly pass these on in the certain knowledge that many of my students, and patients too, have benefited so positively as a result.

Medical pundits readily agree that it is good for everyone to breathe more deeply for, in general, we all breathe far too shallow. Giving, as it clearly does, greater dispersal of oxygen throughout the system it can only be beneficial. It is however, at any and all levels of development, particularly more so for psychics, mediums, seers, adepts and mystics. Practised at any time, anywhere, it is an excellent aid but more especially prior to undertaking psychic work of any kind. If I feel underpowered before taking a private sitting or public meeting for instance, I always exercise as required, either (or both) the breathing and colour-filling exercises that follow.

It is also good practice before a circle of *any kind*, but more importantly before the student developing circle session. In these the most commonly occurring phenomenon sought is the mental kind. Found on the blue end of the psychic spectrum these are, among others, clairvoyance, clairaudience, psychometry and inspirational speaking.

These though are of even greater value when attempting any physical phenomena. It is also *more* necessary here for such phenomena are on the red end of the spectrum. Physical circles and séances, requiring far more energy, is drawn from *both* sides of the veil to produce good and positive results. In such are found for example, table rapping, tipping and its levitation, direct and independent voice, electronic voice phenomena, inter-trans-communication, microphone in the box experimentation, materialisation, transfiguration, levitation of other objects, including mediums, healing and so on.

This exercise is, like all of them, very easy to explain and use! For this you simply work in a ratio of four, eight and two. OK? First, breathe in through the nose, counting to four at a speed you find relaxing. While counting at the same speed to eight, hold the breath. Then, still using the same speed, blow out through the mouth for a count of two. At first you will find it difficult to keep to the timing, especially after a few breaths, probably wanting to breathe out more air than you count. This is mainly due to breathing "high" to begin with, filling only the chest cavity but in a very short time you will begin to breathe "lower", as singers do. As you do you will find you can increase your numbers (in full flow I can get to 32, 64, and 16) with the entire process becoming more natural to you.

You may practise anywhere, walking is good; when doing so I find it most relaxing. Be warned not to overdo the numbers in the car though, keeping them to a minimum. Reserve the higher ratios for another situation as sometimes one feels a little high. The lesson is obvious - do not try to rush your own progress; remember up until now you have probably been breathing at less than half capacity! I would add that you can do this either in conjunction with, or before, or after, or even independent of the following colour-filling exercise.

The colour-fill is valuable as a "builder" both of energy and confidence for it gives to one a feeling of healthfulness and well-being. In this I take a colour, in my case it is nearly always a pale pink (that of candy-floss) but sometimes I employ a mixture of pale green (that of mint ice-cream) and pink. Healers often speak of colours as having a particular beneficial effect in their work, but here we should pause and consider for a moment, or even several. They will and do comment on the value of colour but there are different schools of thought as to what these might do and mean! Thus certain discrepancies occur, among which are that one might argue that red, yellow, or whatever is specifically for a particular condition, while another will argue as strongly that an alternative colour is better.

Notwithstanding, logic, experience and common sense tell me that every person cannot like *all* colours. Therefore be it employed by or for a patient, a trainee or even a developed healer, we should question the benefit of its use in such cases. I also believe that we see colours differently and I muse often on the idea of wondering if I actually see what others see and vice-versa! For instance, how do I really know that what I see as blue another person sees what I actually see? They may be seeing the colour I see and recognise and call red, having been taught thus and have always known, as blue, as red, or grey, or whatever! It follows surely then, with due respect to opticians, that we may perhaps not only see colours but shades of them differently too.

Picture, if you will, a person born on an island t, an unsighted couple. How does the child learn the names of, or what to call the colours *he* sees? Eventually, both parents die and the youngster has to fend for himself until one day a lone yachtsman arrives and rescues him. He then teaches the lad the names of colours but only as *he*, the lone yachtsman, sees them! Do you get my point?

These are some of the reasons why for many years I have regarded colour as a very individual thing. So whatever colour one chooses for a particular event, be it dress, exercise or healing, I feel it is as good as the next; results and one's own choice are what counts. If one likes black, yellow or even sky blue pink and it feels comfortable and suits one and produces the required result, why worry? It is really a case of experimenting with the colour that actually appeals to you and working from there.

Much of what we do is with the hands, from gesturing and indicating to constantly using them in all of our everyday tasks. So the logic here is that if you are "giving out" through the hands then this is where you should receive the in-coming flow of colour. So for the colour-fill exercise first imagine that you have automatic taps on both feet. (The design and quality, as is the colour – purely personal!) On your instructions, these open and a pump on each foot immediately draws out all of the discoloration (dirty sludge if you will) from within your total frame.

Keeping a free-flow of "fresh clean water" entering through the hands and out through the feet try to visualise your body being flushed through until the water is crystal clear. When this clarity appears in your mind's eye, let the water flow out through the toes and, with the operation completed, feel the automatic taps close. (You will not need them again unless and or until you feel that this part of the exercise, at some time in the future, has to be repeated.)

Now imagine your *own personally chosen colour* to be filling up your entire body, entering at the hands and passing up the arms, dropping down through gravity to your feet. Mentally watch your body filling up and when it reaches the shoulders, continue the in-flow until it reaches the top of your head. Full up you should now *experience*, not simply *imagine*, the feeling of contentment and energy within you! A little practice enables you to perform it at will and the validity of the exercise becomes self evident when you feel *immediately* the benefit gained. As a rider I add that you may find it better (unless you pick the right one at the start) to experiment with different colours. Experiment if necessary with different ones until the colour response (the desired result) is actually felt, for then you will *know* it is the right one.

The best exercise in bringing about a feeling of tranquillity and spiritual awareness, the basic purpose of meditation, is to visualise, then create, your own favourite scene. Build it and hold it in your mind to the exclusion of all other material, or for that matter, spiritual matters. Forget all the tranquillity claptrap uttered by some instructors for we each find our own particular as we work. (See e. of ch on adverts for courses.) I also find that if a tutor sets strict parameters for such personal endeavours they all too often become, for some students at least, a stumbling block. (See e. of ch. on "quietude" pros and cons.)

I would suggest that students initially choose and endeavour to become active or passive within their scene, as they desire - after all, it is their scene! Once you become part of it, drink in the surroundings; enjoy being there – and if you do not feel completely happy, then get out and start again. Then try to aspire to your spiritual potential, asking that you may receive answers to your questions and or problems. These may be either material or spiritual queries and though it is all too often difficult to receive answers, I urge you to persevere, for there always is one and sometimes you are not even aware that you have received it until it steals up on you!

For the record this scene may be anything you choose but to give you an idea mine is a large field of long, swaying, rich green grass, under a sunny, cloudless sky and it is comfortably warm. I walk into the middle of the field and, lying down, I drink in and enjoy the solitude. But that was just the beginning of my visualisation for over the years the scene has become more substantial with extra bits added. Today I see a lane leading to the field; there are wild flowers either side of the path; then I come to the stile. I climb over and enter into the field proper.

Through constant use over the years (and watch for this yourself too for remember everything in the real world grows older and different) both path and stile, now aged through years of use, have become well worn. Comparatively recently too, on climbing the style, I now always see Tuan in the middle of the field, cross-legged, but about a metre above the grass. I sit opposite him and upon crossing my legs I too ascend, totally weightless, to the same height; magnificent feeling!

However, I learn most of my knowledge while in the sleep state. In consequence, for more years than I care to remember I have not felt the need to meditate on any sort of a regular basis. Notwithstanding, I recommend it, in moderation, to both novices and advanced students. I caution you however not to meditate for more than about a half-hour session at a time. Further, never meditate more than a couple of times a week. Later, as you develop, you will have no actual need to meditate to learn, for, if approached correctly, it will not only become automatic but "instant" as well!

In qualifying this down-slant to meditation, I have to report that I have met many long session meditators and, almost without exception, they all appear to be exactly the same mentally, i.e. often not quite with us, if you know what I mean! I must therefore conclude that meditation over too long a period and or too many times a week and, in *extreme* cases, *too many times a day*, can produce very dramatic consequences.

The continued for years "I always have two or more hours a day sessions" appear to convey an attitude of withdrawal from the real world, (remember my helpful note on east vs. west, e. of Ch. Three, Part Two?) being in a sort of half-awake state much of the time. For the rest of it they seem to be living more out of the body than in it, thus producing an effect that is detrimental both to themselves and to others with whom they may come into contact. As "The Manna Group" has said on occasions of and to such persons: "You can aspire to the enlightened ones but you cannot live with them!"

There are three other exercises that I always teach to students and these are as follows. To assist your "tuning in" once you are ready to begin work, forming a "y" shape, put the hands together, palms touching, fingers extended and apart. Then rub your palms together hard until heat is generated to the "burning" point. As that happens, quickly separate the hands and, holding them apart, find the "balance" point. They should react, one with the other, as if there is a spring between them. Do not attempt to find the distance mentally by just *thinking* the position. Let the hands do their own thing and allow them, via a calm emotion, to find the distance *naturally!* Practice often and the heat level and balance between them will quite quickly be achieved. It is by and through this operation that the *inspiration* centre is opened.

The aura is affected by emotions in one's life right across the spectrum of thoughts and actions. From shallow to profound, from both others and oneself, positive or negative effects occur. In very real terms though, this particular exercise is different for, in essence, it *always* produces both a positive *and* negative effect. In adjusting the aura, it enables one to react *positively* to the *negative* quickened "vibration" used in mediumship and, thus attuned, it works to the mutual advantage of Spirit and oneself.

Next find the "third" or "psychic" eye by placing your middle finger in between the eyebrows and, immediately below, at the top of the bridge of the nose, search out the small cavity. Then pressing fairly hard in and upwards (but not so hard that it is painful) imagine your finger is passing through the cavity and coming out through the crown of your head. Do this about three or four times when, by your actions, you will have opened your *psychic vision* centre, thus enabling your clairvoyant level and or other mental faculties to function. (It appears that I make a distinction here but in fact these exercises work equally well with the initial development of *all* and *any* mediumsitic talents, mental or physical.)

The third and final operation is to go to the thyroid area of the throat and, using the forefinger and thumb grasp, yet again without causing pain, the hard part. The Adam's apple is of course so named because it is more prominent in males - but do not search too hard for it ladies, simply grasp the oesophagus - it will still work! Then twist an imaginary screw about ten times in a clockwise direction, imagining that it is passing through the throat and emerging at the nape of the neck. Students who feel or hear clicks with these turns should not worry for it is quite safe but those that hear nothing should not worry either! Now you have tuned in, for want of a better expression, your *interpretation* centre.

From the foregoing three simple exercises you will see that you now have inspiration, intuition, seeing, hearing, feeling and interpretation, all you require to begin developing your mediumistic talents. Like the breathing exercise, once you are aware of the value of such things, they become virtually habitual. (The intuition part is a starting point only – you will use it when working as a psychic only, e.g. reading auras)

Soon, after practice, before you begin circle or whatever, you should find yourself performing the exercises naturally, without prompting, regarding them as a normal part of your start-up process. Later on, through the emergence of your more progressed soul mentality, compatibility, and integration with your helpers, having progressed sufficiently, you will begin to feel that the necessity of physically performing the exercises is not quite so important. Later still, they appear, or you will actually be told, that they are no longer necessary and will cease altogether. This is because these are effected automatically by our d/k and helpers for the aforementioned reasons.

On concluding your session do not forget to close these centres, an essential part of these three exercises when developing. (Later in your development as with the opening so will closing become automatic.) So, meanwhile, to close, (1) Simply brush your palms, one against the other, thus discharging your magnetic link. This indicates to Spirit that your session is at an end (Remember, they do not get tired and are always ready!) and the aura reverts to its normal magnetic field ratio. (2) Bring the fingers downwards over the third eye position, imagining that you are closing the "eyelid". The last thing you want is to go about "seeing" all of the time! (3) "Unscrew" the neck position; thus preventing continued interpretation of that which was being fed from Spirit.

Meanwhile practise is very important for it brings about a knock-on effect producing a more positive response from Spirit. Why? Because these three simple exercises all contribute in exciting one's own electro-magnetic field, creating a quickening in the aura. This, of itself, is sufficient to power up and trigger off the inspiration, intuition, vision and interpretation. It also sends out signals (vibrations) displaying our willingness to work with Spirit when our door-keeper and helpers react accordingly. Thus it is that you can work when you want to and you do not need to be, indeed you should not be, open all of the time. (See e of ch. on "twenty-four hour" mediums)

In opening up and operating the physical talents, as opposed to the mental ones, Tuan and others have taught me that spirit helpers initiate the opening of such psychic centres as are required for the particular function the medium is performing. They will by then have already been "in charge" of the three previously mentioned and there are three others that will now come into play. These are situated at the crown of the head, the base of the back of the skull and the solar plexus. (See end of chapter, on new phrases for old - are they just considered chic?)

Thus, when we sit for physical phenomena, including healing, opening and closing is also automatically undertaken by our d/k and helpers wherever and whenever it is necessary. I pass on to readers however that there is no extra gain (even perhaps the reverse in fact) in opening all of them (seven common ones in all) either for meditation or any of the mediumistic talents.

The exception to this "opening and closing" is possibly (although by no means a necessary requirement) in the giving of magnetic healing when experienced healing mediums need to turn on and use their *own-source* full energy (power). After a session care will be taken by helpers however to initiate and restore their energy levels and to close the centres down. If this is not undertaken the result may be that they will be left feeling below par and also, in some cases, it can lead to depleting illness. Either way it is absolutely *essential* for, at the very least, the medium could well afterwards be under-powered with lowered magnetic responses in the aura. In extreme cases too the healer could be *taking* the life-force from the patient rather than *giving* it! Also, as a rider *never* give healing through the heart chakra as this can, after a period of habitually doing so, lead to, and cause arrhythmia (intermittent heartbeat) in the healer.

Many schools of thought put forward complicated theories about opening and closing the chakras. The "pundits" proclaim that we should open them all at the start of our session, whatever that may entail and close them all at the end. In the same breath however, they also state that one must never close the crown and base chakras! They cannot have it both ways! Many who profess such actions are also sublimely unaware of what dangerous territory they are treading. Are they so obviously unaware (or do some not care that much?) that students, left to their own devices outside of the classroom, might easily become jeopardised? I therefore make no apology for writing that many of these "teachers" themselves are simply book-read enthusiastic amateurs and really do not know what *they themselves* are *actually* doing, never mind teaching! (See end of chapter, on chakras and healers.)

Consequently, I am impelled to especially warn novices of the inherent danger of casually opening up the chakras, nor indeed, in any way just casually inviting *any* kind of spirit participation. Doing this is like opening your front door. Then, hanging a notice outside you proclaim to all and sundry that they may enter and take anything they fancy; or treat the place in any way they wish. It must however be recognised and always remembered that Spirit is in abundance by comparison to our wee selves.

Know that once one casually opens that door (ouija board players particularly take note) or just simply dabbles, entities can come through in all shades and levels of intelligence, morals and credibility, etc. Without fear of contradiction, I tell you that as highly developed as I presently am, I would never just "play" with the chakras, nor ever treat Spirit or casually "play" in any way whatsoever!

Another old fashioned precept that needs revising and explaining more fully is the "famous" (or infamous) sitting position. For years so many presiding mediums have insisted that everyone when attending any mediumistic happening, and especially when sitting in circle should sit solely in one position throughout the session. They insist on members sitting upright, with their feet on the floor. The legs must be bent at the knees, with the hands, resting on them, palms uppermost. Any deviation, even a scratching of the nose can provoke an immediate rebuke from the medium in charge. This may be an accusation of the culprit being inattentive, of fidgeting, or even being bored with the proceedings! But for me the ol' logic is at work again folks! Therefore I have to say, in the words of Ira Gershwin, "It ain't necessarily so...!"

I would by explanation of this statement point to the public stance of those very same mediums. At public meetings these same will, quite readily and happily, never examining the sitting or hand positions of their audience, go through their public demonstration without even one tiny comment regarding same! Equally, I am sure that they do not impose such impositions on sitters who are usually paying them for a reading - get the point?

However in qualifying the sitting position, slouching in an overstuffed armchair is definitely not recommended and the better choice is an upright dining-room type of chair. The exception is when a person is sitting solely for the development of physical mediumship. In due course a chair with arms will probably be requested by the control. This is so that the medium can be more easily restrained (often a requirement by Spirit to ensure that the medium, during a séance, cannot be accused of moving objects, etc.) when it will be easier to tie his or hers wrists and ankles to their seat.

The reason for using upright chairs is more obvious in acknowledging that in the hurly-burly of today one is likely to be far more attentive, whereas in an armchair, especially after a hard day, one might easily drop off to sleep. There is not though any *hard and fast rule*, especially with newcomers, about actual sitting position as such. It is *not* essential that one keeps, from the outset the hands and legs in one fixed position throughout the session. It is however very essential that one keeps an open enquiring mind.

I stress that although upright chairs are *not* the most comfortable of seats, better results are definitely achieved by their use. Hence, initially anyway, in my circles, members may feel free to choose their preferred choice of sitting position. This has proved to be far more agreeable to all attending than having to sit with a real fidget bum! It almost always provides a pay-off too for within a few sessions, more often than not, the sitter automatically tends to adopt a relaxed, upright, yet comfortable position. The hands now rest easily on the knees with the arms relaxed and bent at the elbows; the feet, generally, are also now slightly apart on the floor. Eureka! The sitter has quietly and comfortably adopted the recommended position, accomplished without any pressure from me.

The conclusions reached by casual observers for this change may be that the sitter quickly feels (consciously or not) that the others are tending to "receive" and or "see" more. Natural peer competitiveness lends thought to the idea that the others, perhaps because of the way they sit, appear to be pulling ahead, so, accordingly, they adjust *their* position.

However, although this may be a contributory factor it is not the prime reason. This is a disciplined action initiated by the sitter's spirit-helpers, having, as it were, crept up on the sitter's thoughts. He or she is suddenly aware that they are not only now sitting in the "preferred manner" but actually finding it, as time passes, more and more comfortable. The reason the helpers do this is that in the circle atmosphere they find it much easier to "impress" images, etc. on the mind of the sitter. Also sitting this way and particularly with trance, the spirit helper can more easily take control of the body and use the vocal cords to their mutual advantage. (See e. of ch. on peer pressure and ground rules for sitters, etc.)

The last part of these exercises I wish to draw attention to is the attitude of mind. Never be afraid or fretful about "giving off" (exercising) what you receive for fear of ridicule or whatever. I have "seen" many times when leading a circle the strangest things "placed" there for students' mental observation. Spirit helpers have "projected" such objects as a large toothbrush, coloured discs, clowns and even baby elephants! Early on in a new circle, on enquiring whether any of the members had "picked up" anything, almost without exception I receive a negative from everyone.

Why do sitters not say what they are seeing when such image-exercises as above are presented by the spirit circle leader? When challenged, until they very soon know better, they might comment, for instance, that they did not want to look stupid by mentioning such inane things. Usually, continuing, they will say that they had always thought that they would see only "spiritual" things. I would then explain that what they pick up from Spirit, in a protected circle at least, *is* Spiritual, the whole idea being that Spirit wants us to "give off" whatever we see, however stupid, unreal or down to earth these may seem. (See end of chapter, on odd bits and bobs I have received.)

Do not worry either if you apparently keep getting a "no" to what you are receiving as we all have to start somewhere. So metaphorically speaking, to crawl is a progressive step towards walking and is far better than sitting on one's bottom, a security thumb stuck in the mouth bawling I can't! There is a desire in all people to achieve goals in whatever activity or pursuits they engage in, so remember the advice I touched on in Part One about bus and train evangelists. You will of course make mistakes and will have your "downs", but things worth having are not easily wrought and believe it, the "ups" are well worth the wait.

You are in circle or studying with the express purpose of learning! To sort the wheat from the chaff is, of course, at first anyway, very difficult! Equally important; remember that your helpers have *learning problems* too! Further, it should also be remembered that it is not always you, your d/k or your helper's fault! Far too many recipients seem to fall into a non-remembering mode when "given" something. They either cannot recall the name(s) or do not even have that knowledge until they check out the evidence!

This too is an exercise, albeit sometimes a very frustrating one, in practising your ability to receive and for Spirit's ability to send. As mentioned above, the Spirit helper(s) is learning too so like most things, practise is not only valid, it is very necessary if you want to become better at what you are doing. Rest assured however that when that time arrives and someone says yes, especially if you can expand on the original piece of evidence, you will get a buzz like never before. As your confidence builds, so will your *ability* become *knowledge* and suddenly, as the saying goes, you are off and running...

HELPFUL NOTES!

(On adverts for courses.) *A gentleman told me that he was taking a correspondence course on meditation and the very first exercise was to visualise three cats speaking to him, but having an inherent phobia of cats he found this impossible. On sending in his report he was chastised by return of post by the tutor for not dismissing his phobia out of hand! He responded with a request to change the format; flatly refused! He then requested perhaps a refund of some of the two hundred pounds he had paid up front! Protracted further correspondence has produced no result whatsoever! My response and comments are not printable! Learn from that - such people are out there - con merchants trading on those foolish enough to fall for the magazine advert blurb! Be warned! Request that they send you at least a titbit before you part with any money!*

(On "quietude"- pros and cons.) *Having such a varied interest in and knowing thousands of melodies and songs I cannot work with music during healing sessions. Noisy chit-chat and other extraneous sounds do not bother me but since there are only seven notes to write with, I find myself distracted by the music. On hearing something I almost always recognise a cadence or chord sequence of something similar. Then I find myself searching for its "twin" and wondering how much was inadvertently "pinched" and how much is original.*

(On chakras and healers.) *I do not advocate the opening and closing of all of the chakras at all and certainly not by novices. However, many healers actually perform this opening ritual (but that is all it is) every time they work. Then afterwards they close them all down with the said accompanying "ritualistics" but this practice of itself, is a contradiction in terms and action! I write and explain about this more fully later but as already stated, your helpers, as do mine, will do this automatically for you as you develop. Why is it then one wonders does this not happen with these healers? Well, in fact it does but they are either not aware of it or they persist in their very unnecessary ritual. Sadly some, as do many mediums, act out the syndrome of the "them and us" in pretending a mysticism of Light and Truth for sheer self- aggrandisement and nothing more!*

(On "twenty-four hour" mediums) *Such as these very often burn themselves out, or die young, or both! So why do far too many feel that they have to work twenty-four hours a day? Well, a d/k cannot impose upon the freewill of their charge; they can only advise, not command and the converse also stands. Many mediums do not even acknowledge nor recognise or know their d/k's or helpers and side-step this important protection, going direct as it were. Therefore the d/k, unable to impel their charge to cease or at least take some breathing space, cannot stem the flow of "unwanted" entities entering the aura of their charge. They can also be, to an uninterested and or unsuspecting recipient, sometimes nothing more than a pain in the proverbial! In consequence they are wasting their valuable talent, something they should use with very great care and caution. To coin a phrase (never mind if you don't use it, you lose it) if you abuse it you lose it too! (Remember what I said about "bus and train evangelists" in Part One?)*

(On new phrases for old - are they just considered chic?) *In earlier times these were called psychic centres (of the psyche). Today, more because of the accelerated influence of eastern meditation and gurus, martial arts, the so called new age wallahs (or should that be Wallys) and the interest in alternative therapies, to name but a few, it is more fashionable to discover new names for old products. Among these are tuning in to one's d/k in quiet contemplation/meditation, trance/channelling, psychic centres/chakras, power/energy, sitting with one's feet on the floor/ grounding and so on.*

   One might say well I guess a rose by any other name! What is my response? The hell I do! It simply confuses the up and coming adherents and young mediums! For example, when asked to explain channelling a student told me recently that it was using meditation for linking with one's guides as opposed to one's self-awareness. When I mentioned trance, simply because she had read the wrong book, she went on to say that it had nothing to do with trance! And my comment? Well-well-well!

(On peer pressure and ground rules for sitters, etc.) *Another thing to "exercise" or perhaps that should be exorcise, in your early days! Always endeavour to put aside peer pressure and competition when undertaking or participating in anything of a psychic nature. This is particularly important for all sitters, be they workers or recipients. Healthy competition is good, but undercurrents of any kind will definitely undermine good performance, resulting more often than not in failure.*

   An example of this, seen all too often is the medium being blamed for a bad sitting when in reality it is the sitter! Having no regard to punctuality, respect for Spirit and also suspicious and untrusting throughout, they virtually predetermine the poor results! In this way, allowing for the fact that they may be doing some of these things unwittingly, they still do not, indeed will not, allow the medium to work as the Spirit moves them.

So remember, when you make appointments instil upon sitters the value of punctuality. On arrival, state your parameters, that is ask them for an open mind; to say yes if they understand and no if they do not. Try to ensure that they speak up with audible responses and not just a nod or shake of the head. Explain, using the analogy of a telephone conversation, that if all they do on the other end of the phone are nods or shakes of the head, the other person hears nothing. Consequently, the other person, hearing nothing, assumes that the phone is out of order and simply replaces the receiver! This is particularly difficult for someone like me who either closes their eyes and or does not look into the face of a sitter while working. Another must! Always work positively and try to avoid asking questions unless it becomes absolutely necessary.

(On odd bits and bobs I have received.) *From the rostrum of some very famous halls and churches in different countries, but in England especially, I have seen and given off what appear to be the most ludicrous things. These range from a man dancing with a bear to a Salvation Army man, in uniform, who was an alcoholic! A woman drowned in a puddle to men taking out their false teeth and a man playing the piano in the nude! I also tell students that these are but a few of such "seen" things. So that which may appear to be stupid to the psychic student (or even a medium) and totally out of place may well be very vital evidential proofs for recipients!*

Chapter 4
THE FORMING OF CIRCLES AND THE
CONDUCTING OF SAME

In Greece, standing as a testament to its existence, are the re mains of perhaps the most famous "circle" of all time, the Oracle at Delphi. This nation's rise to the heights of sublime magnificence is attributed by historians of antiquity and legend mostly to the knowledge and advice of the *voice of the unseen oracle*. One thing certainly evident is that the Oracle more or less ruled and influenced everything Greek for more than a thousand years.

It was called upon to answer questions from the flood of petitioners seeking answers to problems on pretty well anything from family disputes to the where and how a temple or building should be sited and built. It also gave out advice on matters of trade, state, law and order and even how, when and even *if* battles should be conducted. Carved above its portal for all to see was the same brief sentence as that on the Sphinx in Egypt: *"Know Thyself!"*

The Greek Arts, Classical Culture, Sublimity of Truth and the breathtaking grandeur of their temples; the elegant grace and the ennobling and perfecting of the physical form of this bygone civilisation, have, in reality, left their mark on all of the western nations of today.

The group leader was the positive Hierophant or High Priest. Also present was the High Priestess or female medium, two maidens or children and the negative male medium. Four other negative males and five positive males made up the total. All participants took their places according to their temperament, arrived at through magnetically grading their abilities.

The whole formation was crescent shaped and everyone faced the East. The High Priest sat and or stood, as was necessary, at the half-way position, in line with the oracle itself. Sitting either side of him, in order of rank and magnetic temperament, each of the others sat progressively nearer to the oracle as did the High Priestess and the two maidens or children. A brazier of fire and incense and a large vase of pure water was also always present.

In those far off days, in much the same way as a shaman passes on their secrets to initiates, all participants were selected by the mediumistic priests. These were claimed as affinities with themselves and was considered by the parents to be a great honour to have produced such offspring! Accordingly, they gave the child up, accepting the will of the Gods. They also rejoiced in agreeing that, almost from birth, the baby boy or girl would become a temple dweller where they would live until they died. (This would by all accounts be from natural causes if they made the grade or earlier, probably from poisoning, if they did not!)

Cloistered thus, they were tutored, fed, clothed and probably brainwashed too in and for their selected, or as the priests would own, their predestined tasks. They rarely ever came from wealthy or influential families either. One or more would be trained as the "voice" so the reasons for choosing poor kids were obvious, the foremost being that once trained and initiated they could, if desired, have commanded, through the advice dispensed, enormous power.

As well as the one trained to speak, a lower class married woman of mediumistic quality, known only to the High Priest, would replace a sick "voice" or even, if he wished, for reasons known only to him. Leaving her family to work in the inner chamber of the oracle, she was sworn to secrecy and remained anonymous both before and after. However, she only actually worked for about a month in all and then returned to her family. Most of the year was used by the priest and protégés group in preparation, through prayer and meditation, for the one month of celebration of the festival of enlightenment and counsel by the "voice" who only spoke for that short period each year.

However, a wealth of information exists and is easily available regarding this incredible phenomenon. For this reason alone I do not wish to dwell upon it. My reasons for mentioning it are (a) to illustrate that mediumship did not arrive with modern Spiritualism as many appear to think. These include Jehovah's Witnesses, Baptists and even some Spiritualists to name but a few and (b) to draw a parallel with the circles that are conducted today.

In this last regard the problem of sitters' temperaments, at least initially, is not normally considered and *certainly* not by consciously balancing them magnetically! (A good medium in charge will consult with the Spirit circle leader however and asks where sitters should sit, which is actually another way of magnetically placing them.) Neither do we worry particularly as to the number of people in the group. Needs must, so basically ours depend more upon room size, the medium's or group leader's decision, capabilities, etc. We do not sit in a crescent shape either and society does not place virginity on its previously regarded moralistic and political level. Further we certainly, even if we wished it so, could never insist that virgins must be part of our circles! (See e. of ch. on looking into and beyond the veil.)

The word circle itself simply illustrates position, that is a circular formation of the chairs of the participants taking part. So first I caution all students to understand that there are not only different kinds of circles but different levels of circles too.

Open circles, under the auspices of a medium in charge, are usually held in Spiritualist churches or halls. These take place in normal light and are mostly unrestricted in numbers. Almost anybody is welcome to attend and the leader will invite sitters to expand on or demonstrate their psychic, mediumistic and spiritual talents (gifts). These may rest in inspirational speaking, clairvoyance, healing or whatever. Occasionally, if the medium in charge allows it, someone may be allowed to go into trance but it is not normal to encourage it in this environment. The exception to this is when a medium's quality is known to the leader and, calculating that it would be of benefit to the circle, they may allow the trance session.

In churches too or perhaps in private houses you may have the opportunity to attend a *physical circle*. In these one experiences, depending on the type of mediumship and séance demonstrations, transfiguration, direct and independent voice, materialisation, psychokenesis, apporting and asporting, etc. This last is very interesting, with not only objects being removed from the séance room, but the medium too!

At one such I attended, the medium was securely searched and tied in his chair with rope. The lights were extinguished and to our utter surprise, some minutes later we heard him knocking on the outer of double locked doors, calling out to be let back into the séance room! It transpired (told to us by his control) that he was dematerialised, passed by Spirit through the *double locked* doors and then, rematerialised, he was gently brought out of trance. Finding himself thus, he of course took the appropriate action when, a short while later, with the inevitable comments (like "follow that!") the séance continued to its conclusion.

Others I have witnessed and Bill Olsen in particular, have been levitated in red light. I also remember another séance at Bill Sylvester's house in Lewisham, London when the little girl control banged the metal trumpet (megaphone) so loudly on the ceiling that he pleaded for her not to spoil his new decorations. She assured him that it was not damaged in any way and afterwards, whilst the trumpet had been completely smashed flat by the force of the blows, the ceiling was completely unmarked!

However, I am not aware of any medium demonstrating such talents publicly per se! Such "public" séances will usually number, in total, up to about forty maximum of carefully vetted persons. The exception is public transfiguration séances which are often demonstrated *very* publicly before much larger audiences.

In all physical séances however, restrictions and precautions are vital to the safety of the medium. In the event of somebody acting stupidly, a medium might well be physically harmed. So as far as is humanly possible the medium must be protected throughout. Séance organisers therefore (and mediums too for that matter) should be acutely aware of such eventualities for these can result in psychic burns, internal haemorrhage and, in extreme cases, even the death of the demonstrator. To my cost I can personally attest to this type of thing happening at a physical séance.

I was conducting a public transfiguration séance at, of all places, the College of Psychic Science. An idiotic man, one of their members no less (who should have known better) shone a torch onto my face. Today, some thirty years after receiving the burns, I still often have soreness and scurf build in those damaged areas. Worse though, at the time, I also suffered an internal haemorrhage for six weeks! So whilst I accept that organisers cannot actually strip-search people they and or the medium, before each séance, should rigorously point out the dangers that can result in abuse of any kind.

For many years and many hundreds of times I demonstrated transfiguration (see section on this phenomenon) all over the UK. The séance is held in a completely blacked out room, hall, church or whatever. The only light source is a low wattage red bulb aimed at the face of the medium. In the groups, depending on the accommodation, there would usually be about twenty persons. In public séance they mostly numbered about a hundred but many times there were at least double that!

Worthy of mention too is the growing interest in experiments and evidence emerging from Electronic Voice Phenomena and Instrumental Transcommunication, known as EVP and ITC respectively. Not generally known though is the fact that experiments have been conducted by a few dedicated souls since the 1950's! It is due to the efforts of these experimenters, scientists and technicians on both sides of the veil that today, in its simplest form, EVP at least, is quite easy to set up.

Thomas Edison is credited with being the first person to experiment with electrical contact (no pun intended) and in the 1920s he endeavoured to build, unsuccessfully it must be said, an apparatus to communicate with Spirit. However, he is still in there fighting his corner (as are Konstantine Raudive and William O'Neil among many others) and has actually not only written communications via the computer but has managed also to produce his picture through the same (sorry, again no pun intended) medium. For the record too I repeat here that both Josh Joplin and Raudive, as have others, also held quite lengthy telephone conversations too!

Sitting with my present circle members we have had some quite good results and success with this and we would like to see more people involved. I would like more time and money to go further into ITC as well. Basically, so I understand, this means putting a modem into one's computer and also probably going onto the Internet system. But on being introduced to the net via a friend's PC, I found it to be too time consuming for my liking.

Nevertheless, I really believe, though with some reservations, that this might well be the foremost of the next Spirit generation's form of communication. I do not claim however *certain knowledge* of these phenomenon and therefore can only hope to whet your appetite. So those of you who might be interested will, therefore, have to make your own individual enquiries. This can be done by following up on the many articles produced in the various readily available psychic publications.

There are also specialising circles normally referred to as *"closed circles"*. These are mostly found and conducted in private homes or Spiritualist Churches and fall into three main categories. 1. The developing circle which is mostly broken down into the novice, intermediate and advanced. Some though, as in mine, run together, a mixture of all three levels of study. 2. Specialising circles such as the physical, healing, and meditation ones that can also be broken down, that is, mixed as to need or desire, as in the development circles. 3. Not quite so prominent today but still run by some groups are rescue circles. (See e of ch. on rescue circles, their pitfalls, dangers and possible consequences.)

Mediums oversee most circles, their main function being to control the proceedings and to encourage the members in their development. In my circles there is no distinction between the level of *any* of the members, novices *or* advanced and I find that mixing the ingredients thus is actually more fulfilling for the members. In these, interestingly, many who think they are advanced will sometimes find that they are not so far ahead as they thought and no, this is not a big-headed comment, for each time *I sit* I too also learn something new!

As in my own case (mentioned in Part One) I find, and not all that rarely either, within a few short sessions complete novices are working quite well in their particular bent. On the other hand the long term "more experienced" sitters will often be the reverse taking longer than they expected to advance their development. They generally comment that the standards and disciplines that I work to in circle are more advanced and out-think others in which they have sat. This makes them realise that they have to unlearn some things, usually bad habits.

One of these, perhaps the cardinal sin, due most times to them being too embarrassed to speak out in circle, *is pretending that they understand and know what is required.* Such pretence will often tend towards their feeling out of it, uncomfortable; so it is very important to speak out. Undoubtedly though and far more important is that these circles will lack cohesion. Yet all they need is to have some point(s) explained to their satisfaction when such feelings will melt away! So whilst assuring them that this is in no way to their detriment, I prioritise the need for us to get together, possibly even in private, to reassess their progress. Inevitably my opening gambit is to stress that the last thing they should be afraid of is to state their lack of understanding in or out of the circle!This is why I set the parameters as I do, running a circle as if the sitters have *chosen a family of which they want to become a member.*

In some circles a developing medium may be sitting, for example, for the production of physical phenomena or for that matter it might be the medium in charge developing this talent. Accordingly, the medium and sitters will be dedicating all their circle time and energies solely and exclusively to helping to develop that sitter's physical mediumship talent. In others the session is split when the development of all the sitters' talents takes up the first period with the second devoted to the specialised development of just one person.

The distinction between the two is that the medium controls the (all sitting) general circle development. He or she imbues and distils the methods and skills they will recognise, absorb and use in their search for knowledge. In the physical or split session however, once the controlling helper works easily through their medium's body, the leader will generally hand over the reins in deference to the control. Mostly, from then on, the control virtually takes over explaining, directing and deciding how to proceed in order to achieve good results with and through their medium. Nevertheless, still in charge and responsible, the circle leader will (or should) still maintain ultimate overall control.

This is more evident in physical work for as well as the main control there is often a group working as well, each member responsible for their own particular job. Collectively, they are responsible for developing, mixing and moulding all of the ingredients necessary to the mediumship of the medium being developed. Some of these might be, for instance, chemical balancing of the medium's bodily organic systems for the production of ectoplasm. There is probably an electronics engineer(in Spirit) who will tune in the spirit frequencies for the production of sounds and voices, etc. that might come through microphones. These in turn will be produced via voice boxes that are constructed by other "engineers" and so on. Remember, whilst everything, in *all* séances is experimental nothing foreseeable in advance is left to mere chance!

Ask the average person why they want to sit in circle and almost without exception they will say that they want to learn about Spirit and or develop their psychic and or mediumistic potential. Never have I heard a rank beginner say that they have, or even feel, an inner driving need, that of the desire to work with Spirit, to serve their God and our universe. The day I do I shall give thanks that I have been blessed in being sent such a student to teach. Even though this may not strike us at first, I stress that such motives should be our prime movers for wanting to sit in the first place.

Endeavour always to seek out and to sit in a quality, solid, all-round (no pun intended) developing circle if you want to gain in-depth knowledge and experience of psychic, mediumistic and spiritual matters. The closed circle definition, since they are often difficult to get into, also applies here. But as members find their niche, or not, in this or that one (staying, leaving or moving on) places do become available. So it is good to keep your ear close to the ground and to make your desires known to the folk around you and more especially at Spiritualists' meeting places.

On the other hand if you simply want to test the waters then the open circle is perhaps the best starting place for you. Follow this by joining a novice (or beginner's) circle, usually overseen by an interested medium and formed from such groups as open circles. In the event, whatever circles you join understand that commitment, dedication and humility is necessary, together with regular attendance and punctuality. These requirements not only make for faster progress, they also benefit our d/k's, spirit guides and helpers, ourselves and our planet as a whole.

Disciplined, well established circles will be presided over by a very competent medium who possesses an all-round knowledge of the different psychic and spiritual talents (gifts). However, this does not mean, nor is it a necessary requirement, that they have to be able to demonstrate such talents themselves. Their experience may well have arisen either by studying and observing other mediums at work in circles, or by their having received such knowledge directly from their door-keeper and or spiritual teachers.

Good mediums will be, or should be, eclectically didactic but *never* pedantic, petulant or act as know-it-alls! Quality mediums, steeped in spiritual knowledge, will always control the proceedings without having to be a dictator, even a benevolent one! And it is *because they possess this extra spiritual knowledge* that such circles are safer and will progress more rapidly than others conducted by less competent mediums or lay persons.

There are of course mediums and non-medium circle leaders who will also be acutely aware of their limitations and as such will teach accordingly. This is because they *know* the limitations of their knowing! Unfortunately too, there are those who profess knowledge but they are unable to demonstrate it. They have probably read a few books and, in six easy lessons, think that they have learned it all! Just be aware that many of these "teachers" simply run circles solely for financial reward or to feed their ego, or both; but if this is your bag, then so be it. If however, you do not feel comfortable with your tutor then start to think about alternatives; or to quote another of Tuan's sayings: "If in doubt, don't!"

The savvy genuine, not merely emotionally-driven students though become, or are, the *real* enquirers of Truth and Light. Thus it is that these should, indeed will, quickly become aware of such insensitive discrepancies. Perceiving these early on, together with their own unsatisfactory progress, they will be imbued with, among other emotions, a frustrating sense of lack of achievement. Realising the often intended obfuscation by the leaders of such circles they will soon leave such gatherings being not so easily fooled or persuaded as others.

Endeavour therefore to be always alert as to what is going on and taking place in *your* particular circle. Remember, like everyone else, you *also* have access to Spirit! Be unafraid; do not simply believe; always question the question and then question that question until you *know* that you understand! What you cannot believe from within, you will never believe from without says Tuan! Therefore, in deference to modesty or polite custom do not just simply accept in *belief* that which you do not *know*.

Since my revelation, described earlier within these pages, I have always, throughout the years, preached and spoken of and used the term of door keeper. Prior to the beginning of my public work, others who *did* these things had, to the best of my belief, always called d/k's guardian angels. In the event then it appears that I must have done something right for today one finds that the use of the door keeper form of address is far more commonly used and certainly by those mediums who acknowledge and are interested in such facets of spiritual philosophy.

For me the recognition and quality of acknowledgement of d/k's and helpers are both polite and correct. For those who do not subscribe to such philosophy or are unaware of this help so near at hand, I have to say that they lose much (see comments on this in later paragraphs) both in protection and spiritual advancement.

N.B. So do remember that even if *you* are given, with evidence back-up, the name of your d/k or helpers not all mediums acknowledge d/k's never mind know their names. If your circle leader is one of these, then you must make your own mind up about what to do and how to broach such things and act accordingly. (See e. of ch. on door keepers.)

Right from the start in my circles and public teaching I always endeavour to make my sitters aware of the importance of their door-keeper. Sometimes students, previously misled, comment that all the work, indeed *everything* that they do is controlled and effected by their doorkeeper! This clearly displays an imposition upon one's freewill and if this is happening it clearly demonstrates dark influences, and not light truths; in short, an inversion of Natural Law! Thus the scenario presented is that of a "war" being waged for superiority of "brain control" conditioning between the d/k and their charge. However, Natural Law shows that the exercising of freewill is reciprocal and therefore such attitudes as this cannot exist between loving souls, discarnate or otherwise, and ourselves.

They also erroneously state that their d/k *always* controls them during trance! No way! On very rare occasions, when the conditions are as *near perfect as possible* a d/k, leaving the "door" in charge of another helper, just *might* control their charge. However, they rarely, if ever, do so and *never* control anyone other than their own charge.

This is simply because their job, as one's only personal guide is to guard one's psychic door. Helpers and higher guides on the other hand are given permission from a "10" d/k, (I write on d/k scoring later) allowing them to control and/or work psychically with their charge. To *guide* and *protect* their charges on their incarnate journey is paramount; not to *trance* mediums, even their own! Our d/k's commune directly through our minds anyway (often confused by us as talking mentally to ourselves) so there is really no need for them to trance anybody.

A prerequisite by Tuan and the Spiritual circle leader (see later on "floating helpers") is that all d/k's are, on sitting in my circle with them, in total accord with their charges. If they are not as strong as they should be (a ten out of ten score) their first requirement is to gain full spiritual protection knowledge. The way-with-all of this is given to them by Tuan but d/k's, like all of us, learn at different speeds. It follows that some will "10" in days or weeks but some actually do this in a few hours! Once gained they will have the power to turn away from the "door" of their charge any unwanted or disallowed entities. The d/k's also form another circle of protection around ours and this should be the first initiative in any and all circles. But their job is more easily achieved and done well if they are of one mind, strength and purpose.

Consequently if their indentities are unknown to any of the sitters these should be sought, on their behalf, by the circle leader. All good mediums should be able, as I do, to sit quietly during the interval between circles and mentally (telepathically) link through their own d/k with the members' ones. He or she tells Tuan (who of course tells me) about them, usually stating or confirming what they had or had not already known. These include events and happenings in their charges' present lives from childhood until then and of course their d/k's name and nationality. This I relay as soon as possible, usually privately, to the circle sitter giving them the requisite information.

Until I *have* established that their door keeper is a "10" I do not encourage students to link in when alone, either to tune in with, or to speak to Spirit. Once achieved though I urge them to ask of Spirit that, especially during circle time, they may be "gainfully employed" both psychically and spiritually. To achieve results it is obvious that Spirit and students must dedicate time and energy to turning up for, and sitting through, each session. In this too I always suggest that students make a kind of pact to dedicate time and energy and to sit for a number of sessions, say six to ten for example. Then, if, at the end of that period, they feel that they have not advanced at all nor gained in any way from their experience of circle, it is for them to reconsider their options. (See e of ch on making deals with Spirit.)

As the circle leader I gently discourse on the need for harmony in the circle emphasising that it is the keynote to the success of any gathering. Harmony is the basic foundation, in a séance of any kind, from which Spirit Truth and Light springs! Crossing as it does, *all boundaries*, it is patently obvious just how important it is to prioritise it. Accordingly, as soon as possible I set about creating and establishing it firmly in the sitters' minds.

I discourage early on the idea that anyone should feel that their talent is, or even may be, a "better" or "lesser" one than the next. So, from the beginning, I make the point that we are all pupils and will never be masters and that this includes me. I also set about creating a "chosen family" atmosphere, based on the old premise that you cannot choose your family but you can choose your friends.

Thoughts and emotions such as jealousy, dislike of one or another of the sitters by anyone, together with greed, selfishness, etc. must all be put aside. Any disagreements, discussion and the like on such inharmonious things are destructive and should be kept, at the very least outside of the circle and, better still, of the whole session time involved. In this way we create the best of both worlds and with the results endorsing the actions, love and harmonies become quickly established. Mind you, logic and common sense will show us that if these things do not become apparent in the early days, then the circle is unlikely to prevail and is probably doomed to failure anyway!

As an experienced circle leader I am able to use a measure of subtlety. In this way I am able to naturally encourage healthy competition without upsetting anyone. After all, better or lesser, as above, are only words; actions are what really count! Remember too that *all* talents, without exception, are from the God-head. Even so, what we do about becoming a computer buff, cowhand, politician or anything else is intrinsically up to us and equally, depending on our psychic potential, that includes good, solid mediumship!

I am only there to help and inspire the sitters but I *cannot*, nor will I ever try, to *make* them work if they do not wish it. In the same way if someone wants to leave the circle they are in no way expected, unless they wish to do so, to give me or other circle members their reason(s). Equally, I make no attempt whatsoever to try to persuade them to carry on! In other cases I will, if I feel it is to the general detriment of the others, also ask them to leave. Age and gender also is not that important either...

In public meetings and more especially today, there are folk of varying age and sex. Nobody stands at the entrance asking for proof of gender or age group! Yet, when running a circle, all too often there is an insistence by some leaders to do just that! In a perfect world maybe...! In reality though, the number of sitters is dependent more upon the accommodation available and the medium's knowledge in the running of a circle. In the real world the age and gender of participants are also dependent more upon supply than selection or demand.

I have known circles of just three persons and any combination and at the other end of the scale, particularly in open circles in the old days, as many as three hundred! I have had circles with as many as twenty-five regular sitters which can be a bit much. So, when given the choice, I personally like about thirteen including myself which, for me anyway, is a far more comfortable number to manage and control.

Numbers of sitters therefore are not that important and can really be any number, within reason. Mainly though it is up to the medium in charge and his or her ability to control the proceedings. Gender and age is equally unimportant although a balance of the sexes is preferable (but again not essential) for it does help in the interchange of ideas, progress and congeniality of the group. This is particularly in evidence when, both during and after the session (and here the medium may choose to join in or just listen and then perhaps sum up) discussion among the sitters takes place.

Like me, I guess almost everyone has met the young "oldie" and the old "youngster". Many young people are also old souls whilst many older people are young ones and vice-versa. It is when and if we take such factors into account this whole gender versus age thing becomes academic! It is not anything like as foreboding or compulsive as might at first be imagined. More often than not too, sitters are "found" and brought together by Spirit. Consequently, with harmony, regular attendance, punctuality, dedication, and so on as I have described, good solid circles will thrive and progress. Believe me, all the periphery paraphernalia is totally unnecessary having little or no factual substance!

Although, of course starting and finishing times of circles is important, I mention it only in passing as these are self-adjusting. For instance, those who work a full day need to get home and maybe have a light meal before attending; some may have to come straight from work. (Tip! An egg or two beaten in a large mug of milk with brown sugar added is ideal before circle It is both sustaining without making one feel bloated and is a big help in producing the structure of ectoplasm.) Others yet will easily be able to fit in with the arrangements made. Time should also be set aside before (to settle down) and afterwards as a bit of social intercourse over a cup of tea or coffee works wonders for cohesion of the circle. Accordingly, all things being equal, the best day or evening for the circle and the duration of it is automatically resolved.

Ideally, it is better to have a room set aside for all séance work and some mediums will insist on this being absolutely necessary. Whilst agreeing to the ideal, this argument (as do many others of the ilk) falters if looked at dispassionately. After all, in today's crowded world most folk cannot devote a room in their home for such exclusive use as séance! (See end of chapter, on definition of a séance!) Therefore, for practical reasons alone, this is mostly a non-starter!

The format of the circle is initially the prerogative of the leader. However, as progress is made things are likely to adjust or even change dramatically, especially if one or another of the sitters stands out as more mediumistically endowed than the others. In the sense that they might require special sitting conditions, e.g. physical mediumship requires, at least initially, a pitch dark fully blacked out room, they will have to be regarded as "special". This might lead to sitting as described previously, that is from a normal, all-round circle to a split, or even a specialised one. The members should have an equal say and elect or not as the case may be, to change the format. When, or if, agreement is reached then the necessary instructions and adjustments can be made by the medium in charge.

On the other hand, individual choice being the issue here, if just one negative response is forthcoming, then the medium might well decide to run two circles taking perhaps those members who wish it from the main circle, the other specialised and different type of circle is established. This though needs careful thought and steering but it can, and mostly does work. Here sitters attend the whole session to develop only one or maybe two sitters. Fully explained previously, since the choices were individually made, the harmony between the members of *both* circles therefore should be as was, in essence, unchanged.

Visualisation and the exciting of the imagination are points from which all development of psychic happenings' spring and pour forth. In my developing circles students always sit initially for the production of mental phenomena. To this end a blue light, which is on the ultra-violet end (the mental phenomena end) of the spiritual spectrum, is employed. This will quickly lead on to the exercising and expanding of the sitters' intuition, a fundamental part of our spiritual selves. From this I lead them to the doorway of their psychic side. Then very soon after, when they move further forward, I will allow that door (remember "10" d/k's) to be opened. This in turn opens up the two-way communication so vital to the moving forward from psychic ability to the development of any mediumistic potential and knowledge.

I try to calm everyone down at the start of each session by speaking quietly and encouraging them to relax. I tell them to try to put all of their material problems and thoughts outside the circle. Then, after a couple of minutes I establish the thought of the circle being surrounded by a large tube. Each person makes an effort to build this (materials are irrelevant) by looking, with eyes closed across the circle and imagining "our" part being constructed. The tube, at will, because it is "magic" may be pushed out by any member if it becomes claustrophobic. Equally it is totally impregnable and impossible to penetrate from without by anyone or anything material or spiritual that is of no use to or unnecessary in the circle. This means that the only way into the circle is down the tube from above and that is where we are aiming our thoughts and feelings. (See end of chapter, on breaking circles.)

I request that they close their eyes and "see", visualising the curved shape of the tube behind the folk opposite their sitting position. As each member, including myself, does this, it creates a completed tube and circle. Next, still with their eyes closed, "looking" across the circle they mentally move their eyes and minds upwards when the tube becomes, the farther up they "reach", brighter and brighter. (Here I ask them to lift their heads gradually when the blue light bulb, now in "vision" as it were, obviously gets brighter through their eyelids.) The ultimate goal is to visualise a bright, warm, iridescent non-blinding comforting white-pink, cloud-like substance. This, lighted from within is so strong that one may walk in it or languish upon its cushiony layers. It is here that we find Evolved Spirit, Light and Truth!

Once accustomed to this seeing the light at the top, I actually get them to visualise travelling bodily up the tube (again method of doing so is not important but mental levitation is about the best one) and then to bathe, sit or lie on and or in it and to look around as well and then to report what they see.

Going up the "tube" mentally it is easier, figuratively speaking, to aspire to the top rung of the ladder than it is to step onto the bottom one. This is because standing in the comparative quagmire of the lower spheres, surrounded by more down to earth entities, it is like having to fight one's way through a crowd to even reach the ladder! There too one may find oneself burdened down by others who might well cling, parasitic-like to you, looking for a free ride upwards. The result is that one may well find oneself unable to reach even the next rung! (See e of ch. on the "ladder" versus our loved ones explained)

Another thing! Remember here that we all develop at a different rate! Some students though will sit "forever" and for various reasons will almost never develop anything! The cause most common in such cases will be the conflict within, virtually an immovable barrier. Trust in themselves and Spirit is lacking sufficiency, so they cannot accept that thoughts are anything other than of their own making. They find it impossible to understand that thoughts arrive into their mind from an external mind-force-energy without being aware of it consciously. Because they do not feel it, they can only accept that it is imagination; to them, it could not have come from any other source than themselves! Encouragement or even cajoling by the circle leader will prove to be of no use. Such sitters are classic examples of the "piano-learning syndrome" mentioned earlier within these pages.

However, it takes all types and these "non-starters" might still become a valuable asset to the circle even though they may show no psychic progress in the accepted sense. If they wish to continue to sit they may well, in time, find their feet as healers who, incidentally, are, all too often, not clairvoyant, at least not initially. They may also, for want of a better expression, become "professional" feet on the ground observers, or recorders of happenings, or perhaps even "power houses".

These last can be invaluable to gatherings of any kind for novices, psychics, mediums, and ordinary folk alike. This is because they naturally have lot of power (energy) flowing through and from them. If it is needed, it can be drawn off without them suffering physical loss of any kind. In much the same way one starts a car through another using jump-leads, power goes from them to others. In simple terms it is the personification of an invisible interaction. This is generated out of harmony and love from all concerned souls, both seen and unseen, for nothing dies and least of all the power energy.

At this point I used to do the absent healing but now this is done at the end of the session. This is because on tour in England recently I noticed that at some venues the happy vibrations dipped as the healing prayers were said. Then I had to work at raising them again! So, placing our right hand over the next sitter's left around the circle we link hands.Then, in turn each member mentions the names and conditions of folk needing healing. It is agreed too by all that better results are being achieved and that the circle vibrations remain brighter throughout.

Next a member, or myself will open in prayer for I think it necessary that all members become used to openly speaking aloud. After all, if or whenever they demonstrate in public it is impossible without speaking, prayers included! So it is not only a good way of introducing this but it also imbues in sitters respect for their circle companions, both seen and unseen.

Words as such though are not important; nobody is required to be a priest or poet; and anyway, neither insincerity nor pseudo piety wash with God nor Spirit! So do not worry, short or long, whether opening or closing, let your prayers come from your *heart* not from a book. Originality always creates far more impact, credibility and response! It also promotes the move towards a cementing of others' and your own power (energies) more rapidly. This soon leads to the realisation that you are, in your own way, an integral contributor to the circle and are just as valuable and important as anyone else, including the leader!

The foregoing reminds me to point to another "piano playing syndrome" constant. It is that *everyone* is psychic in varying degrees and each may have the occasional psychically based intuitive flashes. Using psychic ability for *mediumship* however, by definition, means that one is able to communicate, and indeed, commune with Spirit as well! Not counting mine received and given thousands of times, a wealth of evidence abounds, standing on its own as proof of this! So remember psychics and mediums are intrinsically poles apart in the actuality of what they do and operate!

Elsewhere in these pages I explain how virtually everything we have ever learned comes to us extraneously, that is from the media, books, our peers, parents, teachers and etc. Yet the hardest lesson to learn (hence my repeating here) is to remove from one's thoughts that what one is receiving is *also* extraneous and not, *repeat not*, one's imagination.

This does not stop just at clairvoyance either! The whole development of the psyche spectrum falls victim to the same idiosyncrasies. Indeed this fault will often hold back many who might otherwise move forward far more rapidly in their potential development. So *know* that the sooner you *lower* the barrier, the sooner will your mediumship blossom, quickly supplanting your psychic ability and you *will* move ahead. So I tell students; *do it* as soon as possible! Better still, right from the beginning make the "this is my imagination" thing redundant; better yet, obsolete, non-existent!

A question asked of "Running Waters" the spirit circle leader was how does one know? He answered very simply that if we see the picture first it is Spirit; if we think about it first, it is us! You may be washing up for instance and suddenly you have a strong flash in your mind's eye of a loved one you have not thought about in a long time. You should acknowledge their presence happily and thank them for popping in. However, if you are thinking about that person and their image then enters (is conjured up by you) your mind's eye then it is you! It is easy, you see - and if you ask me how to get better at it, I reply with three words, practice, practice, practice!

I constantly stress therefore that all students should, initially anyway, go with the flow, as the Americans say. I also tell beginners not to try to decifer if what they are receiving is from themselves or not; such thoughts will only block inflow data from Spirit. Once this "flow" is allowed, it will be automatic, like the "sitting position" mentioned earlier. In less time than you might think, Spirit will interact through the intuitive areas of your brain. When this occurs, convinced by the recipient's responses to evidence previously unknown to you, the certainty will be that it could not have come from you! The conclusion then must surely be that it is from an extraneous source. Once you engage and recognise the essence of the intervention and assistance of Spirit, you will also, from then, on more easily coexist with these fine faithfuls.

I teach, when demonstrating publicly or privately to always go that extra step in one's delivery and deliberations. I encourage the pursuit of "clues" shown and or given to them from Spirit. The secret is first establish the contact; this may be by name, description, health condition, etc. when the loved one was in the physical, etc. From then on endeavour, like a detective would, to ask questions (but only of Spirit), to delve deeper. Seek out the evidence the recipient is not thinking about, things requiring the sitter to rack the brain and memory. Seek for a gesture or habit that the entity had when in the body or a subject or thing they talked about, liked or hated even! Maybe long forgotten by the recipient a loved one may relate an anecdote, family or friends' names, dates, places, nearby landmarks, etc. Believe me, when you are on the right track and have a good contact the evidence *will* flow.

However, not all contacts are live-wires, delivering the evidence like some enthusiastic errand boy! Some will not have as good a memory as others either, so one has to be doggedly patient on occasion. Also, like on the earth-plane you cannot *like or be liked by everyone*, so *you* may not be the best link for *them!* (see section on mediumship talents).

Notwithstanding, I hope that, like me, even after all these years, you will feel that wonderful buzz as you deliver more and more evidential points. I state categorically that the day I cease to be amazed by Spirit's ability and ingenuity often amusingly coupled with ingenuousness, I will retire! Further, I would advise anybody else who feels blasé about their work to do likewise!

When very much more experienced in rostrum work, you may well find yourself telling a contact to stand back and to let someone else come forward. You might even, depending on how you work, find yourself telling a confused entity to stand back, sort out what they wish to say and to come back "in" later. Remember, you are there to deliver the best, the fastest and the most evidential demonstration of which you are capable. As such democratically, you cannot afford the delay contacts can cause who do not link solidly; indeed, you are virtually obliged to move on. Do not get trapped in labouring away at a lost cause and end up boring the pants off everyone concerned! (See end. of chapter, on explaining talent errors.)

Understand clearly and precisely that "seeing" and *seeing* are distinctly separate and different, the one being mental and the other physical phenomenon! So do not worry if another person says they can "see *and* hear" and you can only "see *or* hear" or neither, for if something is physical in circle, etc. you will see it anyway! No, your gift (talent) may not lie in "seeing" or "hearing" but in what some will refer to as, perhaps, the Cinderella of the three, that is, clairsentience.

Clairsentience takes many forms, feelings about people, animals, property, atmospheres and so on but I will write here on one other form of it, namely psychometry. Its application in developing circles is probably more easily developed than the other facets, simply because the modus operandi is easier to promote. Simply by asking the members to provide a personal article and taking it from them, the scene is set for the budding psychometrist. Ensure that these have only been handled by the owner and that prior to arrival that it was not handled by anyone else. Articles brought belonging to someone else are placed by *that owner* personally in an envelope. The information received is recorded and subsequently checked for accuracy, evidence, etc.

Those participating take an object and endeavour to feel impressions (mentally) given off by it. These initially might well be things that have connections to when the object was handed over or put into its envelope. Do not worry if the person does not remember what you "see" for we all do many things somewhat subconsciously and or automatically. These not registering as being an important enough, storable thought may well be remembered later, rather than on instant recall.

Equally in all honesty we are all hoping for that mind blowing piece of evidence that gives us our clincher. So household chores and so on are farthest from our minds but *not if something happened at the time!* For instance the phone or doorbell ringing when someone you had not seen or spoken to for a while is calling; maybe you broke a nail or knocked over an ornament, whatever! The student might have been about to say such things and could maybe have delivered a good reading but the recipient, with spontaneous negative replies, "blocks" their concentration. So receivers should not be so quick to refute what is given, keeping an open mind and storing that which at the time is not "known" only to find later that the psychometrist was right on the ball. Moral? One should always listen and not just hear and more especially in circle!

When trying this just move at your own pace but give off what you "see" or "feel" for though it means nothing to you (and why should it?) to the recipient it could mean so much. As in all mediumship, the truth is that you are not linking with *the person!* You are like the telephone operator, the link being via your *spirit helpers* and the recipient's contacts through to the recipient; *you* are simply able to make the connection and pass the information. After some practise, you will also probably move on to another facet of mental talent development. Often the holding of an article is just another comforter, another way, like the pad and pencil, of focusing on your particular.

Those who do go on to demonstrate psychometry in public can often become somewhat like an agony aunt because the level of psychometry is generally more slanted towards personal details and advice on situations in recipients' lives. It is for this reason that demonstrations are mainly found in Ladies' Guild meetings, mid week, in the afternoon and if you enjoy this, then why not? I have to stress though that compared to the other mental talents it really is, as I have said, the Cinderella! Psychometry is also employed in working with flower, sand and coloured readings. These can be quite interesting sometimes and though *I* find them rather quaint, in many ways they have their place, often displaying and performing a somewhat useful function.

The true dedicated and natural psychometrist can take off the layers of history of an article right back to its raw state. There are however, very few who train up and exercise this prerogative, principally due to supply and demand. After all, most folk are more concerned about the future and have only a passing interest in history, another reason for psychometrists reading the way they do. They prefer I guess, to leave other proofs of survival to those who will.

The other caution is that many psychometrists only use their psychic ability, working through their own intuition. So I reiterate; if you have the talent and the desire is strong enough you *will* move from psychic to medium. It is then that Spirit and you undoubtedly conjoin, for the one, however long it takes, surely follows the other.

Another good lesson to learn, right from the beginning, is to develop your own exercises as well as those already described. One such is to devote some time *between* circle nights, preferably when you are *not* tired, to "open up" as described and "tune in". (This is something students do not seem to do naturally yet it is vitally important to their progress). Link through the prescribed methods and endeavour to work with your own d/k and helpers but *do not forget to close down at the end of your session!* Also remember to *disallow* any trance work unless and until your circle leader says anything to the contrary.

Early on in your development, it is through these "exercises" that Spirit and yourself are motivated to action, building a closer co-operation between all parties concerned. Such linking-in is essential in my circles as I often set homework. For example, I might ask a question silently and between times they have to tune in to Spirit seeking the answer for the next circle session. Readers might be surprised to learn that most answers often coincide, or at the least, have a relativity.

In the same way, if they have a problem, I urge them to sit in their "thinking chair" or lie in bed. I tell them to link in and ask for the solution, narrowing it down to should I do a, b, or c? Immediately, one or another will be forthcoming - he or she may not like the answer Spirit "give" but this is when the trust (not faith or belief) in Spirit come into its own. Go with the flow and in hindsight you will find that it was the correct decision for and at the time.

Another way of doing this is to ask for an answer before you go to sleep. During slumber your d/k or a consensus of opinion of helpers works out a solution and you receive it, implanted, courtesy of Spirit, in your subconscious. So if you wake up in the morning with an impression of what to do next, go with the flow!

The foregoing examples should show and reveal how tuning in is not quite so difficult as many would have you believe. For the doubters among you, I have to agree that it does not always appear to work but to you I say that no, or not yet are also answers! So try again and again *too* if necessary! Practise, like anything else, will help to make the answers come more regularly. Then you will become aware of a whole new dimension of thought, the result of the infusion of spiritual knowledge and will now *know* far more than you previously *believed!* This awareness, if nurtured by your tuning, will grow! You will then receive and experience the wonder and tranquillity which Spirit so truly and lovingly brings and bestows. (See e of ch. on the voice we know)

More often than not though they use the easier method as follows. These sorts of things are kept secret by many mediums who indulge in, and enjoy, lesser mortals polishing their vanity and is, in all probability, the main reason for such anomalies. For whatever reason though, in many cases they are never openly talked about, not even when around other mediums, yet so many use this method in their work. But should such mediums come clean, the pseudo mystique they build around themselves when speaking of their guides and helpers might well rapidly dissolve away. Even worse (for them) though, their "disciples" might fade away too!

It is not so difficult for students to accept the concept of d/k's and helpers talking to us in "our own voice". After all, Spirit transmits virtually all communication to us telepathically and this works both ways. If it were not for other recipients, almost invariably our *own* spirit communication would be silent, heard within our minds, which when alone, it mostly is anyway.

If telepathy is not used and is not the answer, then how are other mediums and myself able to speak with entities (not knowing their native tongue) who only speak their own language? Well, I would also suggest another point; there is a form of international spirit language but telepathy is still demonstrably employed. Such language is often used by me in circle to talk to a control so that the student is not persuaded by spoken, understood words. Strange too for though I do not *know* the *words* used, I *know* what is said. (A combination here of telepathy and the spoken-word?) What is more, the controls do too, for implied aloud or mentally, they respond accordingly! Language notwithstanding, the conclusion must be that telepathy plays its part here too! (I also ensure that students will not be influenced verbally when sitting for trance. As such they are only referred to by others as "this one" or "that one" and *never* by gender or name!)

An inappropriate phrase might seem out of place here but I have always been taught to "tell the truth and shame the devil". So I honestly and without reservation reveal that when working in public I also often hear my own voice in my head. The clairvoyance or whatever is delivered in this way by Spirit giving names, etc. and I state that this is in no way unique! I assure you that many, many times we mediums also "see" without "seeing", "hear" without "hearing" and "feel" without "feeling" and we also "hear" and or "feel" our own voice dispensing information.

It really is not so strange to accept! After all, most folk talk to themselves at least some of the time and we all hold mental conversations in our heads, especially when alone. You must have noticed too that in disagreeing mentally with someone the discourse goes our way and we always win the argument.

To illustrate why they use our voice and not their own I take the following example. Imagine you are lost on a road at night. You ask Spirit as you speed on right, left, or straight ahead? Immediately, if you are *listening in*, you will mostly mentally hear your own voice utter one word and accordingly you will turn right, left, or carry on as per.

Now take the same sort of thing and try to listen to Spirit direct. Unless you are extremely fortunate (in the sense of which I am illustrating) you will hear your helpers, relatives or whatever, procrastinating somewhat! Inevitably, each having their own opinion, in no time at all, the turning or whatever is passed because you are listening to the *back and forth discourse.* Until you learn better, somewhat because you expect it, you believe this is the only way! Hence in waiting for such discussion to conclude, the initiative will often be lost!

The fact is that Spirit do not actually discuss things in the same way as we do. Still in the mortal coil, we would think, if we did not know better, that they do not really think things through and literally reach decisions instantly. They do though carefully consider issues but their thought processes are many many times faster than even our "quick as a flash" thoughts. I myself often receive the most complicated and long answers to recipients questions without seemingly, thinking out the reply at all! But I am not suspicious or nonplussed for, unlike many of my contemporaries, I have taken the trouble to find out how it is done. So, I reiterate; Spirit works almost always in the telepathic mode when many words can and are conveyed "instantly" to us.

In view of the explanations of the three "clairs" one easily understands, realising that students and even mediums may only be linking in through one of these, i.e. "seeing", "hearing", or "feeling" in the *pure* sense. Whatever, I can and do assure students that mediumship is very much a case of horses for courses and frequently impress upon them not to feel hidebound or disappointed that they are only going in one direction.

I recommend that some will find a pad and pencil useful; it can help a lot in developing one's talents. So try this, especially if you have a bad memory, or cannot, in trying to explain a particular point that your recipient does not understand, hold the input you are receiving. Others work from and need (a) a focal point and (b) to write as they see, hear or feel enabling them to put down their impressions so as not to lose their concentration. I personally know mediums, and have heard of others too, who doodle or scribble while they work. So, try it yourself for this method may evolve and be right for you.

To others I suggest that they take the hands of a recipient for a half a minute, which is of equal value to the doodling. It is something many other mediums and I always employ in private consultation; indeed, to amplify a link I have, on occasions, done this in public meetings too! I therefore openly endorse and encourage, without reservation, *any* method that produces good, positive mediumship results.

In can be argued that this hand clasping links one closer to the recipient and this is true. It is important to remember though that one links closer to the aura of the recipient! So early on I instruct students to *know* when they are reading the aura (using the psychic faculty only) and when they are using mediumship. Remember that with the inexperienced psychometrist such aura over-lap can also occur. So, novices should pay careful attention when demonstrating this talent to ensure that they know which is which.

So how do we know the difference?

A good clue results in the observing of demonstrators. Say for example one establishes the initial link by negatively asking a recipient *if* so-and-so is in Spirit, not that so-and-so *is* in Spirit! The recipient, acknowledging the negative "spirit" link, thinks of that person immediately and builds a "picture" that can be "seen" in the aura. The person's thought-o-graph and or the "picture" in the aura field is picked up by the sensitive, using telepathy but only psychically and not mediumistically. Sadly, unintentional though it may be, knowing no different (bad training habits) they will continue to give "evidence" by reading the aura only. But this does not prove survival!

Not always, though far too frequently, such demonstrators will go into an over-long drawn out description of a loved one. Going on thus they are simply building on the recipient's thoughts and whilst the experienced person will probably recognise this for what it is, the majority will not! A round, square face, not too fat or too thin, not too tall but not short and so on is neither here nor there. But to stipulate, before you ask a negative question of a recipient, that your contact had for example a handle-bar moustache or one eye, or a finger missing, etc. is, *if it is so*, hard, irrefutable evidence!

Remember too, your job is also to hold the crowd and to give them an enjoyable public group or meeting. As such long descriptions are time consuming and they will actually bore the pants off of the rest of the gathering. In private this might be (and sometimes is) OK but *only* when the entity is actually *from Spirit* and *not* from the sitter's *imagination!* The moral is to be *positive* not *negative*, to make statements and never to ask questions of your recipients, unless it is absolutely necessary.

On the other hand question the entity mentally if you appear to be stuck on a point but continually seek out evidential facts. Do not "pad out" your work by telling a lady that which can obviously be seen by all. For instance a medium will say that a lady needs to do something with her hair (which looks like a poorly constructed bird's nest) and, as everyone can see this, why state the obvious? *Get your evidence first* and her mum can talk the hair later! If, though mum says that she was around on a particular day and time listening to the recipient discussing it with a friend, sister or whatever, then this might well be the route to take. Such facts are clearly far more evidential proof than the single bland, obvious comment;

then getting confirmation qualifies and clinches your mediumship too. (See end of chapter on more about reading auras.)

The aura versus spirit contact becomes even more apparent when one examines the psychic spectrum of talents (gifts) more closely. For instance, initially healers will more often pick up patients' conditions from their auras (psychically) than clairvoyantly, (mediumistically). *If trained correctly* that healer will recognise the signs and accordingly, the aura reading will be developed to the full, be left behind, or at least take something of a back seat.

If the latter is the case then they will begin to perceive far more through mediumship-sensing, rather than mere psychic ability. Better yet they may well use one or the other or even a combination to arrive at the diagnosis. The reason is that the Spirit helper (via the d/k) and healer, now being more compatible, decide to move forward. They experiment further and this assists in the clairvoyant faculty blooming and developing accordingly. As both sides of the veil (helper and medium) gain in knowledge and experience so will facets such as these become more easy to use.

In many cases too the clairvoyant faculty of the healer develops somewhat differently to that of the *normal* clairvoyant. He or she may "see" only *anatomically* for instance and though patients' loved ones may be within the "vision range" they are not automatically "seen" by the healer.

This is because the clairvoyance is primarily developing in direct response to the healer's own potential. This contrasts with the more commonly held, but equally erroneous narrow one, that is of seeing spirit entities and going on from there. I am of course aware and hold to the concept of clairvoyants primarily proving survival via the evidence produced but I also know that they use it in different ways. So for what it is worth to students please note that my teachers say that in healing sessions, except where it is beneficial to a patient's condition and healing ministry, giving "messages" is basically wrong. Quite apart from it being the wrong time and place it also "steals" the power (energy) which should and must be used solely for the benefit of the patients healing process.

Eventually this alternative clairvoyant path will probably lead to full diagnostic abilities and practice, which my spiritual teachers contend is the correct direction to take. They consider that the opposite view of non-diagnosis under any circumstances, or of ignoring the warning bells ringing in the healer's ears, is not only wrong but can be, potentially perhaps, far more dangerous. Personally too, I always prefer having *quality* of talent rather than, as is the case in many instances, *quantity of persons* ministering unto patients. It has to be better to have more of an idea of what is wrong with someone than just laying on the hands in the hope of treating pain without any anatomical knowledge, insight or lack of referral to a doctor, etc.

Often a healer might think (or say to others even) why has that little ache or pain that has had so much healing heaped upon it at each session not got any better? Found alas, much too late by a specialist to be cancer or some other equally bad condition, to coin a phrase *the healing was a success but the patient died!* In agreeing that good spiritual or magnetic healers *might*, variously, refer a patient to their doctor if they are in doubt, I know that good diagnostic ones, should it be necessary, *always* will.

Whilst the foregoing paragraph displays one reason for a healing failure (the obvious non-diagnosis) a patient may, just the same, be given a whole bunch of healing sessions without any apparent response. The causes for this are varied and can be, for instance, as follows. It is a medical fact that with health conditions of all kinds, while most folks *want* to get better, others, for whatever reason, do not! There are those too who perhaps may not even have a terminal illness, yet they are beyond known medical help and will, in all probability, *never* get better. Some may also even "die" and for no apparent medical reason!

Karma also comes into the picture here but I do not wish to digress too far from the subject of circles. As such, I will simply state that Spirit has taught me that healing can only be given in accordance with the patient's soul progression. This means that karma-wise "medical" principles may well apply, but from the spiritual, rather than the physical standpoint. Thus is indicated the soul position, that is to heal the physical body or leave it wanting, for example, with lameness, loss of a limb or a protracted illness. Or, the soul may wish to withdraw altogether and return to Spirit. (See end of chapter, on "clubs" and cliques, etc!)

Quite apart from the mental phenomena experienced, students may see other things too in circle; flashes or rods or globes of light even cloud-like patches (ectoplasmic composites). One might experience a feeling of someone gently blowing into one's face. Equally, one can experience what is termed psychic mist or rain falling on one's hands or face. It is quite realistic and as one might expect, it is damp, or even wet! One can experience being touched, a hand on the shoulder head or knee, for instance and, especially when sitting for trance, one or another often feels exactly as if they have walked, full faced, into a cobweb!

Most of the aforementioned is often seen physically and felt simultaneously by more than one sitter. Here the viewing is more through the emotion than through the brain, the outlet being more physical than mental. A sudden drop in temperature is also very common, especially around the legs and feet. This last, together with the cloudy substance, the mist or rain, and itchy noses particularly, are more prevalent when specifically sitting for physical phenomena.

Such things may spook a sitter in the early days, even more perhaps when a circle is *not* sitting for physical. Consequently, I take pains to impress students to realise that we are *not* sitting alone. I repeat this message over and over for several weeks until I am certain sure that everyone is confident and trusting of the protection we receive in and out of circle. Apart from reminding them all that the d/k's are (naturally) always present there is also always a Spirit circle leader complementing the earth-plane circle leader. Equally, helpers of the sitters will also complement them; often loved ones and friends are invited also.

Spirit circle leaders are specialists, schooled in the running of circles, engaged for the duration of the circle sessions and assist accordingly. They are usually one of many experienced, floating helpers (see guides and helpers). The medium *will* link and speak with them both in and out of circle but rarely are they one of the circle leader's personal helpers. Indeed they will also probably be leading other circles in other towns, perhaps even in other countries! And though there are also many other spirit entities within the tube, our helpers and loved ones, etc. it is not the prerogative of the Spirit circle leader to decide whether or not they are permitted to enter.

Since every entity in a strong circle is vetted by the d/k's, it is *they* and *not* the Spirit circle leaders who decide. D/k's know far more about their individual charges than the spirit circle leader and this is why those leaders readily defer. Thus the d/k's, because of their power and control, automatically rule out any unwanted or unhelpful entities penetrating the tube (circle) and more importantly, their charges becoming vulnerable in any way. My circle members d/k's are instructed, as aforementioned, to reach the more subliminal state with their charge. Once fully in accord with them, they can offer one hundred per cent protection from such unwanted entity intrusion, not only during circle time but around the clock as well. (See e. of ch. on using language and voice.)

From the beginning it is vital that all students are made aware and become aware that psychic talents, spiritual philosophy and the workings of Spirit cannot be learned in the same way that children learn the multiplication tables. This is the first lesson they should take to heart very early on in their studies for this might well avoid disappointment later.

Always "open" any session, including meditation, with prayer. Ask of your God and Spirit and *know* that you will receive the protection that genuine, good souls offer you in mutual love. Then, sitting quietly, opening your mind, look within yourself, and *expect* Spirit Truth and Light. (Do not worry, you are not required to see these or even know what they are at this stage but aspiring childlike to gain knowledge is very necessary. Indeed, it is through such aspiration that knowledge, certainly initially anyway, assuredly follows).

Ask for, and *know* that you will receive only the highest and the best of their wisdom, both consciously and unconsciously (e.g. in sleep state) protected from the wanton intrusion of lesser developed entities. Afterwards thank them, as you would any friend, for their unstinting help. This holds true if you have received only a very little, or even feel that you have received nothing. But if you have been paying attention, you know that this "receiving nothing" is a misnomer anyway and is not blind faith either. It is, at the beginning, an acceptance of your own inability to recognise and absorb what has been given. In accepting this you will surprise yourself later, realising that you actually know more than you did previously, so you must have learned! As mentioned earlier, terminate your session with a simple prayer too.

To have a sense of humour, a desire to stand up in front of an audience and to be something of an extrovert is an advantage to the demonstration of mediumship. I have had sitters in circle who, readily accepting that what they are receiving is not their own imagination and not being afraid to state what they "get" have begun working in public very quickly. True to say I might, at first, have "held their hand" but there is no shame in that!

They may stumble a bit in the beginning, especially when they give unrecognised evidence or, worse for them, misunderstood information, but it is all part of the learning game. Recipients though, especially when a novice has given them something, will often take the trouble to report back that they have found that which they were unable to place at the time. But such things become easier to live with as novices become more confident of their talents and of course more highly attuned. (See end of chapter on the "them and us" attitudes.)

It is the lack of aspiration that prevents many ordinary folk, psychics and even mediums too from receiving true spiritual knowledge and philosophy. It is mainly through ignorance, but sadly often also through swollen heads (the "I developed years ago dear" syndrome) and laziness as well, that these stay on lower-sphere-levels. Picking over the scraps of moth-eaten, old fashioned and no longer logically valid ideas, they continue to proclaim such things as philosophy to any who will listen.

Philosophy itself presents an ever changing kaleidoscope of new ideas and propositions. So what was good for yesterday, today may require reassessment, and indeed, it might even need the same again to morrow! Therefore redundant philosophy and ideas if left to stultify can and always will make a circle's progress that more difficult for all concerned. However, freewill, God given as it is, means that we can stay where we are, in circle or not, if that is what we want. But it is wrong to want to remain static, stubbornly believing that we know it all; all that happens is that we remain uninformed or updated, idly languishing in a lower and possibly negative vibration.

In fact, with such an attitude, why sit as a circle anyway? It sounds facetious but in the event, one may as well revert to the ouija board, for its level of communication is about the same! Such people as these might claim they *are* progressing but this cannot be with minds that are stilted. Haughtily throwing back the head they declare their superiority in the field of matters psychic and spiritual. But I assure you that progress is plagued by not moving one's *ability* onto the *knowing*.

In spite of, or perhaps because of the end of chapter helpful notes, be as acutely aware and alert as I. *Know* that ability without knowledge is like a boat without a rudder. *Know too* that there are many souls, both in and out of the body who are very progressive so ever strive to seek them out. Highly evolved spiritually, they are only too willing to impart their continually updated knowledge to seekers of Truth and Enlightenment.

The willingness and desire or not to learn are painfully obvious to them (they will not cast their pearls before swine) so they will not look to you unless you display your interest. So only those of you who are sincere and intrepid seekers *will* learn and be *amply* rewarded in the certainty of the growth of your own spiritual awareness and progress. However, there are of course all shades of "entity character" from the lowest to the highest. So be sure to set your parameters accordingly, remembering that like attracts like and therefore as you seek, so shall you find!

I reiterate! Endeavour always (and continuously) to reach out, childlike to your loving father (the God head of Spirit) to receive of the highest and the best of Spirit. *Make it an ambition, do not just hope, for hopes are simply dreams! Know that ambition brings its own reward, but only if you positively reach out for it! A positive action, especially to Spirit, brings a positive response! So do it, and the results will be quite beyond your wildest imaginings!*

Imagination is a vital contributor to a medium's armoury. Without it, it is like David fighting Goliath in an area barren of stones. Unprepared thus, the sling-shot is useless! So I make students very aware of their own imagination, explaining over the first few sessions to treat it as a tool not an enemy in circle or, for that matter, any other place. Then once identified thus I ask and encourage them to try to move beyond it.

I explain that much of what one sees in circle is physically visual but many things are also "seen" mentally. Overshadowing for example can be either but is often "seen" more mentally than visually, especially in the early days. On the other hand, with transformed states the features alter and as such are seen far more physically than mentally. Full transfigured trance states, since ectoplasmic masks are employed, are *always* seen physically. (This is more readily seen if a member or the leader, as in my case, is able to demonstrate these various states.) Obviously then it is seen to be vital to one's own development and, just as importantly, to the circle as a whole to *say what one sees.*

When an entity overshadows he or she will appear anything from eighteen inches (450 cms.) in front of, or to being completely in line with, or even seemingly behind the features of a sitter. This last presents a singular phenomenon in that the sitter, from head to waist, disappears. The furniture, wall or whatever can be seen quite distinctly, exactly as if nobody is occupying the chair. Keep on looking and the entity will endeavour to show itself, replacing the sitter. Often seen too is a face turning or moving *in front of the sitter's* when the two are simultaneously observed. These are not trance states, though they equate with them somewhat in that the one will often supplant the other.

The best way to see this is to half-close one's eyes and to look *through* and not *at* the person you are watching. (Concentration here is a contradiction in terms for doing so in its defined form will often result in one not seeing anything!) The better feed back is produced therefore more likely and more often too by observation more than a super concentrated effort. And this leads us nicely onto another facet of the "it is my imagination" thing...

For instance, if you are a potential trance medium and if what follows sounds familiar when you are trying for it, then you are doing it wrong! Most students at the beginning of training will try to record the moment of going under control; wrong; that will only "awaken" you again! If that fails though he or she will probably be well on the way to trance, only to begin worrying then that they might sound stupid if they open their mouth!

Understand that, if and when you do speak, you will please all the other members of the circle. Feeling that they have helped to encourage the entity to take control and to have been successful gives a boost to everybody on *both* sides of the veil. More importantly though, you will, no doubt, politely surprise yourself! So at this point, I want to explain more fully the way forward to the trance state.

I practised clinical hypnotherapy for some twenty-seven years and trance states for many more. As such, in defining it, I am able to fall back upon my own experience. It is *absolutely like hypnosis* in that the levels reached are indubitably parallel in almost every respect. A fully co-operative hypnosis patient may well find that though they are totally conscious they are unable, or, more correctly, have no desire to control what is happening to them. (Note! Subjects will only receive according to their own moral conditions and will *not* respond to any suggestion *except* these! One should know too that anyone, except imbeciles, deaf mutes and babes in arms can be hypnotised and further, that the more intelligent a person is, the easier they "go under".)

Spiritual trance, like the hypnosis one, is a subliminal state and operative at all levels of consciousness. So, once induced into a very light state and depending upon the degree of trust in and co-operation with Spirit, it is possible to move through to the so-called unconscious (the deep trance) state. The significant difference between hypnosis and trance state is that one does not audibly hear the voice of the "hypnotist" when working for spirit control as one does in the physical hypnotist's session. Apart from inspirational control, depending on the depth of trance-state, one leaves the body in various ways. In my own case I "go out" through the back of the neck just below the medulla. I then position myself some feet above and to the rear of the entity controlling my body. Basically, apart from when I am taken deeper or drift away (my curiosity again) I am always there listening and watching. Other than this I take no active part either in what is being said or any movement that may occur with the controlling entity, e.g. standing up and or moving around. So although some schools of thought declare that entities do not take possession of our bodies I cannot cede to this concept. I *know* that I am out of mine for though I leave in a different way, it is very like the same as astral projection. Further aura photos taken of me show that the aura registers quite differently to when I am in the normal state.

In recent years some tutors in seminars and workshops I have attended appear to have trapped themselves in a metaphorical New Age "hypnotic" web. This is probably due in part to the influence of New Age books and alternative therapists found today in Spiritualism. Some of these have, with due respect, somewhat insidiously crept in through our back door. In theory this seems, though somewhat clandestine, still OK, for whatever door they enter they are, at first anyway, welcomed! Problems soon arise however, one of which is that more than a few of these also claim the title of "medium" when it should be "psychic". Undoubtedly psychics and the mediums are linked but they are not (as I clarified earlier) one and the same. So though all too often spoken of in the same breath, intrinsically they are poles apart. (See section on mediumship.)

In trance courses I have observed tutors using, possibly due to some "New Age" influence, both hypnotic and meditation suggestion. In the hypnosis treatment room these two, run close together, can and do result in being therapeutic. But this route must not be taken with trance students! It does nothing in helping them towards control by Spirit; quite the reverse in fact, for though this can promote a subliminal state, it is not the right one! Such states cannot produce the genuine *spiritual trance* (meaning the sense in which this is generally understood, that of a spirit entity entering into and controlling the body of a medium) when attempted solely through hypnotic or meditative suggestion by earthly tutors.

Such methodology could result in, and simultaneously too, an overwhelming number of students becoming hypnotically or meditatively entranced, when the tutor might well find that they are out of their depth. The ensuing panic of the tutor is easily seen for, unwittingly, they have put most or even all of the students into deep meditation or hypnosis trance! Unable to manage or control the situation, the session could well go into warp drive! Imagine the obvious consequences of what would happen if the media got a hold of something like that!

(True trance state comes *only* through input, i.e. suggestion from Spirit controls, and this is always subject to and under the auspices of the d/k who allows the entity to control their charge. In the circle (séance) situation the leaders on *both sides of the veil* fully co-operate together. If they all *know* their job they will correctly guide all of the spirit entities accordingly and these will patiently wait their turn which automatically eliminates the possibility of a multi-trance situation.)

Such hypnotic suggestion from tutors as aforementioned can also lead, on the part of the students to self-deception, resulting in unconscious fraud. Unfortunately, using such verbal suggestion students might, simply through imagination, reach a "spirit control-state" that they have simply created! Whilst this may amaze the uninitiated onlooker it is, in fact, but an unwitting sop to the tutor! Worse, it is a dismaying and potentially disastrous occurrence for the Spirit controls and teachers, not to mention the student!

Armed with this new found "knowledge" of "spirit trance" these, after just one or two short sessions return home. Badly taught and thus misinformed and unchecked they cannot wait to tell anyone who will listen that they are now a trained trance medium. Worse, they will, at the proverbial drop of a hat "bring through" a chief, an ancient prince or noble of some long lost indefinable, *non-provable*, culture.

For instance, various "famous" (or infamous) mediums claim as their "guide" speaking through them to be Joseph of Aramathia! Handed a transcript recently of a "trance" talk by him on spiritual wisdom I confess to being totally unimpressed. The standard of "philosophy" did not, as I would have expected from such a personality, stand alone! It was simply a concoction of worn out clichés and of such a poor quality that if it *was* him, he need not have bothered! After all, should we not expect him to be of a very high order and to be have an incredible level of Spirituality and enlightenment? And if it *was* him why use his given name?

It is my understanding that highly evolved souls, having become more enlightened have no further desire or need of their personality, nationality or given names as for instance "The Manna Group". If such a famous biblical character did control they would act accordingly. If therefore entities control and say such things then it is virtually certain they will be impostors! This would mean that such entities are (a) suffering from delusions of grandeur; (b) earth-bound in the lowest of vibrations, and enjoy getting their kicks this way or (c) the mediums are kidding themselves that they are in trance. Far, far more importantly it stretches credibility to the limit. To even think that *anyone*, leave alone *J of A*, has not progressed beyond the very lowest of spheres after making their transition so very many years ago defies belief.

If in fact he was Joseph, then by coming through as himself, it would patently display that *his* progress is sadly lacking! He would surely be in much more profound spiritual company, part of a group on a very high plane of Truth and Light and not simply name dropping! I wonder why it is that such mediumship never produces Fred Bloggs or Charlie Farnsbarns to address their acolytes? The conclusion must be, sadly, the medim's own brain-influence and ego, which is self explanatory.

We might also ask why and how did trance suddenly become channelling? Easy! It is yet another alternativist, so-called New Age term, adopted by some Spiritualists because it sounds more mysterious! Such things are one of the ways that many of these alternativists spread their smoke-screen over an unsuspecting public who pay them good money, only, in many cases to be out-foxed by them! This word has now moved on to embrace inspirational impression, healing and a multitude of other actions - a very confusing definition for the novice to grasp, so take my advice and stick to the word trance.

Watch, as I do so-called world experts on TV programmes. They spout such things as: "I am able to see the energy colours around a person changing constantly" (From yellow to sky-blue-pink with black and white dots on?) Another: "Sit down and we will see whom we can channel through you!" In a recent programme a reporter tried to get Moses through! The "channel assisters" were (would you believe) astounded when nothing happened! I tell you Moses is about as likely to control anyone, let alone a hard-nosed interviewer, equally as much as he is likely to walk into a Woolworth store for a writing pad to jot down a new set of commandments!

(Remember, workshops and seminars are still, by definition, *séances*; simply glorified open circles and I repeat, normally, in open circles, trance work is minimised! Therefore a lot more investigative energy is required by tutors and organisers of such things to decide whether or not potential students have the necessary mental and physical balance for undertaking such work.)

The foregoing may still appear, at least to the uninitiated somewhat very innocent and entertaining. They may not see in my words the underscored evidence of spiritual or philosophical guidance. However, be very aware that my words are dictated from true souls and these point more to the danger of dabbling, often the result of an innocent couple of days, or weeks seminar. Under "shortfall" tutors such novices may well continue to practice as possible unconscious frauds. Potentially more dangerous though, they are also blissfully unaware of the maxim "Beware the door you open that you can close it again!" Sadly then, what might well have been a potentially fine medium soon may become dismayed and or give up in despair or fright; or even, when the penny drops, in total disgust.

With such persons blithely skipping down a possible, or even probable, road to disaster, I also take to task those tutors who pronounce that entities cannot control us unless we give permission. Standing as an authority in trance courses (if you cannot trust the tutor who can you trust?) they state *categorically* that since *no* permission is given, this alone *proves* that possession does *not*, and therefore *cannot*, exist. Thus, misinformed, when students return to their everyday life they are totally both unprepared for, and *unaware of*, the potential dangers.

I have to say that this last little gem proffered by tutors is utter balderdash, absolute rot! In very well run situations conducted by very competent mediums precautions are taken to ensure that this *does not happen*. But this is far and away a different thing to stating categorically that it *cannot* happen! To believe that obsession and or possession *cannot exist*, one has to be the proud possessor of the finest rose-tinted spectacles ever produced!

Without fear of contradiction I state that I have personally dealt with many obsessions and possession cases where the cause has been, among others, due to depression and or dabbling in psychic matters. Further, I would shout it from the roof-tops that not one of these *gave* their permission! So I caution *all* students to enter into *any* psychic quest with their eyes open and their feet firmly on the ground.

In the section on obsession, possession and haunting I will explain this more fully. It is enough to state here that I have dealt with all kinds of cases in my time. Many of these have been for the sake of argument, "normal" hauntings. More worrying though is that I have also dealt with many cases where complete novices have been in all sorts of psychic troubles. Mostly this has been through dabbling in the occult (playing with ouija boards for instance) and "calling up" the dead. (See end of chapter, on suitability of students, etc.)

Schools of thought vary quite a bit on how to conduct circles. Some hold to the view that there should always be a competent medium in charge. At the other end of the scale others claim that any group of people may sit in safety whether a medium is present or not. However, one can only speak from experience and I feel compelled to state that I subscribe to the former group for prevention is always better than cure.

Although by comparison to other peoples' pursuits there are not exactly a plethora of mediums, good bad or indifferent, the problem really is not as difficult as one might imagine. There are Spiritualist or at least Spiritualist related churches in most towns in UK and in many other countries too. Spanning a very broad base, interest in the spiritual counterpart of existence is also growing throughout the world, so, if you are that interested, keep your ear to the ground. Be persistent and if you are also prepared to do a bit of leg work you will soon search them out!

The difficulty is not so much in the seeking either it is more in the finding! Ideally, a group requires, basically, a person who feels the need to teach. They must also have the potential for compatible and companionable reciprocity with the group and most of all be knowledgeable in their field. But I can only reaffirm that if the desire is strong enough the way will be made clear and the intrepid searcher will inevitably be led accordingly. Start as you mean to go on: with a definite continuum of a positive attitude and an enquiring, open mind. Prayerfully ask (also positively) that you receive that which you desire in your quest.

Nevertheless if, in spite of my recommendations, a number of you decide to sit as a circle and you are unable to engage a competent medium, then a member must be chosen to be the leader. They will have to take full responsibility for the circle and all that it entails. Also they will not, unless the others agree that someone else can take the reins, be able, during circle, to sit for their own development. However, I reiterate! If the desire is strong enough and the need is sent out as an appeal to Spirit then, in the event, your "guru" will come to you, and often too, in a much shorter space of time than you may think.

There are no hard and fast rules to development but pointers can be learned from those more experienced than yourself. So for mental talents, initially try different methods of approach, the pen and paper, the taking of hands or an object. Great value is to be had in discovering one's particular focal point but you may find yourself actually resisting the use of one! This is OK too for, in fact, yours may be more subtle in that the non-use of it may be your forte! All I can say on focal points is that *if it works for you*, then do not try to fix it! The simple expedient for good sound all-round mediumship is to be honest, friendly, happy and relaxed. In this way you will earn respect from Spirit and your peers and live to fight another day!

Although I have covered the talents in the foregoing, a short summary of do's and don'ts will not go amiss. The three "clairs" stand alone as the main-stream mental talents and each has its place. Do not expect, nor be in any way dismayed if you only begin with one or another of these. Remember, in attaining any skill, practise is of paramount importance but make it always positive, regular and disciplined. So there follows ten little reminders to help you on your way.

(1) Never force yourself, your ideas or thoughts upon others (especially watch your ego here) and never become obsessed either with your development or any spiritual work. (2) Childlike, *go with the flow*, knowing that Spirit is *not* using *you* or *you* them; you are working together to achieve the same results. (3) Always endeavour to recognise, absorb and use! (4) Ask of your God and helpers to protect, guide and teach you throughout your endeavour. (5) Open up, using the appropriate inspiration, vision and interpretation exercises. (6) Give what you get through whatever "clair" or talent is operating at the time (and do not even pause to analyse which it is, just get on with it.) (7) Make statements and if you seem to be wrong then question your spirit contact for clarification and, unless it is absolutely necessary, *never* ask questions of recipients. (8) When you feel you have run your gamut say so; do not fluff or flannel in an effort to make something fit! (9) Use the exercises (initially anyway) to open and close. (10) Irrespective of your good, bad or indifferent "performance" say a short prayer of thanks and look forward in eager anticipation of a better next time!

HELPFUL NOTES!

(On looking into and beyond the veil.) *Doubts have existed in some minds as to whether it is right to look beyond the veil. Among the reasons are the hierarchies of orthodoxy who, for centuries, have suppressed any and all attempts to do so, calling these, among others, blasphemous, seditious, heretical and sinful. (I have covered this more within these pages). However, by what ever label, the principal reason is the fear orthodoxy has instilled into the masses over the centuries. By promoting a wrathful God and fear of the unknown, not necessarily in that order, thus was incorporated their greatest weapon. They constantly held in check any free thinking by the uneducated by exerting dogmatic pressure and power, cajoling and brainwashing the masses into submission.*

Many of these "sheep and goats" still hold to the belief (hope) that the priests must know. So just in case they offend them and thence their God, they dismiss any alternative to that which is still, even in today's enlightened times, forced upon them! Yet, after the Sunday school and possible choir-boy stints, from then on most only attend funerals, weddings and christenings for the rest of their lives!

Others of course contend that we should not "dabble in the unknown" and I heartily endorse this view. However, serious investigation and non-obsessive, down to earth study cannot be called dabbling! These are different matters entirely and in reality of course, everything is unknown and "behind the veil" but this should not, nor does it, prevent the search! Intrepid scientists, doctors, engineers, inventors and others continually dare to reach beyond the pale. Eventually they uncover the secrets sought for so long, mostly to the benefit of the planet! In consequence, I see no difference at all in undertaking the spiritual search.

I contend that if God and Spirit had determined that we should not communicate with a world of being unseen by ordinary vision, it would be impossible for us to do so! Indeed, it would be impossible for us to find the veil, let alone to be able to lift it and see the wonders that lie beyond! And since such communication does exist, it is proof positive that it is not only allowable but desirable, ensuring that we should all be partaking of it! Sad to say though, for centuries, orthodoxy has labelled anything other than blind acceptance of their doctrine and directives as sinful.

(On rescue circles, their pitfalls, dangers and possible consequences.) *Maybe I have been unfortunate in running across participants engaged in rescue circles for I have to say that those I have met, more often than not, seem to be a little strange. They most always seem to be depressives, definitely unlearned in the ways of Spirit, off-beat and or eccentric to boot! They tend to regard such circles (and themselves) as being very special and even self-gratifyingly invigorating.*

The explanation for this seems to stem from the fact that they love to talk about what (never who) came through last time, especially to others, "less fortunate". These cannot boast of the same "entertainment" for often that is how the "rescuers" view it, though they would never openly say as much. More importantly though is their claim that they are searching for lost souls (their phraseology, not mine) and having once netted one, they set about "rescuing" him or her.

This at first sight also looks and seems very commendable but the trouble is that many of these do not want rescuing! However, the members "vibrations" set up in such circles almost invariably rule out any kinds of differentiation. By definition they are openly inviting souls, come one, come all, back into the physical dimension. But these are quite capable of, and often do, escape through what might be termed a tear in the veil. Thus rescue circle members can find themselves and others within their friends and family sometimes entrapped by the more powerful (energy-wise) of these but unfortunately, it does not necessarily stop there!

Thus ensconced in the physical environment again these entities more often than not prey on others totally unconnected to circles or psychic matters. As such, they can and often do, unless completely controlled and or exorcised, begin wreaking havoc among unfortunate folk in the world at large. They can (and also do) obsess and or possess unsuspecting persons in the physical. The motives for such inva-

sions may be, to name but a few, depression, spite, anger, mischievousness or malevolence. Perhaps worse, it may be simply from the desire and or the sheer delight of experiencing again physical things through a body when its dominance is far more aggressive and effective. (Do these quotes sound familiar? "I don't know what came over me" - " I was told to do it by a voice" - "Everything went black and then I came to." Read more in section on hauntings!)

It is imperative therefore that such sitters are very physically and mentally strong and that they know how to completely control, all of the time, each and whatever kind of entity that enters their circle! Apart from what I state above (those who slip through) rescue circles often set out to encourage trance states to bring these entities "through" and in many cases, the whole thing goes pear-shaped!

In reality, it is the same sort of situation a well trained and knowledgeable exorcist runs up against but any similarity ends there. The difference in rescue circles is that the entity was unable to break through and therefore incapable of haunting in the first place! Having been brought by invocation and or invitation however, sadly, due to the inability of the circle to control the situation sufficiently, far more are released back into the earth's vibration than are rescued!

It is these, not returning to their own place, either because they do not know how, or they choose not to, who often plague other poor unfortunates who are still in the body. Some of these, though by no means all, begin hearing voices and or taking on what are called multi-personalities. They are then frequently mis-diagnosed as schizophrenic whereas in reality, these are actually being haunted! Would that expert exorcists were allowed to treat these patients for many could be, and would be, effectively healed overnight!

I therefore most earnestly urge any reader or their friends who are either involved or are invited to join such circles to cease immediately or decline accordingly. I assure those who do not decline that though it is not a hard and fast rule, the consequences can, more often than is desired, be horrendous in the extreme.

Finally, I know that there are countless souls in Spirit, dedicated to this very task anyway! These can more ably effect such rescues too, being of a much higher vibration than we mere mortals! Equally, my own spiritual teachers have always taught that there are quite enough "lost (physical) souls" here on earth to go around without scraping through the quagmire of the lower spheres, heaping even more upon us from another dimension!

(On doorkeepers) Of course we all have guardian angels (d/k's) but most folk in the world do not ever consider, recognise or even understand, except in a very superficial way, that they even have one. This is simply through a lack of Spiritual education and orthodoxy telling us that they are not personal to us and that they all have wings, halos and harps!

It is also true that many Spiritualists, mediums included, do not even know (or seem to care either) the identity of their d/k! Further, of these, lacking knowledge, or perhaps for other more obvious reasons (remember: "Ain't I great when I dem-

onstrate?") walk around "open" much of the time like an optimistic fisherman on a pond, barren of fish, the "just in case" syndrome! Totally unaware of psychic attack for example, they can and often do, cause damage to Spiritualism, the recipient and themselves alike. The cause is due to the unrealising and or the disregard of a mischievous entity slipping through the "door" and giving them a lot of misinformation without qualification. Most times these are the "off the cuff" advisers on how to rule one's life (or the predictors) whom, if they are found wanting or wrong, simply blame Spirit for the error!

This is another failing of the system in that I feel it has never been considered important enough to worry about by most of the leading lights. The accent has always been more on what entity is controlling or is handed down as evidence by a medium and not its status or function! Lacking in this awareness and knowledge has also resulted in many mediums erroneously and or blindly believing that their d/k even gives them the clairvoyance or whatever! Knowing no better, they are simply unaware of the function of this guardian (and God knows they should!) for most have never even bothered to ask Spirit what they are or to clarify their function and position!

Another thing is that d/k's are our only personal guides! So the difference between true guides and helpers should and, I feel, must be defined. Surely our d/k's and our helpers are as important as any other spiritual matters we learn of in the psychic, mediumistic and spiritual field and certainly enough to acknowledge and understand the functions they perform – aren't they?

At the risk of being pilloried by my contemporaries then, I pen just a few examples of those who are still wrongly referred to as guides and not (which is what they really are) as helpers. Maurice Barbanell's Silver Birch, Ursula Roberts' Ramadahn, Leslie Flint's Micky, Ivy Northage's Chan, and Nan Mackensie's Running Water. Of course Gordon Higginson's Cuckoo, Paddy and Choo Chow are also referred to in the same way.

He and I discussed the guide versus helper thing on a couple of occasions but his attitude, in all fairness to him, was, like mine, intransigent, so we agreed to disagree. It is common knowledge of course that Gordon was trained by his mother, an excellent medium herself. So his position was perhaps in deference to her teachings, whereas I deferred to my spirit teachers. But like her and those truly great mediums mentioned here, almost everybody in those days referred to all spirit helpers, and especially controls, as guides.

Seemingly they never felt the need to ask for further explanation of the contact's "title", accepting them for what they were, or more correctly what they thought they were. Further they would claim (and some still today say) did it matter? It matters because bad habits are easier to learn than good ones! (I respectfully point out that the Christian teacher Jesus never said he was God incarnate or the only son of God. It was others, many years after his transition who thrust this mantle upon him; look where that has led over the last two thousand years!)

These things, let us face it, because nobody bothers still prevail in Spiritualism. Sadly, such misnomers, either loosely attached or unverified, have been carried forward to the present, with many still incorrectly labelling our discarnate and loving teachers and friends. So like so many other misplaced actions and attitudes and misused words in Spiritualism I, in my small way, try to clarify these whenever and wherever possible.

The main distinction here is that a helper controls, either mentally or through the body. A guide is normally one of a group and their words are the result of a combination of wider thinking and philosophy. These are visitors from higher spheres who, for want of a better phrase, might be termed as mentally and spiritually above the normal "active" spheres. Their sole dedication and function is to teach and to guide the earth-plane in general, not just individual mediums. (See later on reference to The Manna Group.)

(On making deals with Spirit.) *Unfortunately, another misnomer is that one should not bargain or tell Spirit what you want. At first sight, in principle anyway, many might echo "and quite right too!" Prayer-time however ably demonstrates that such argument as this is negative, even defunct! After all, virtually every Spiritualist gathering asks for healing, guidance and protection, often expressing the need and necessity for same. So where is the logic in arguing that we must never do so? Indeed, is asking and expression of need so far removed from telling? As Tuan says: "Without logic it has no substance!"*

It has been demonstrated countless times that Spirit are patently and acutely aware that, by comparison, our time here is pathetically short. Therefore they willingly accept such bargaining and are not at all offended! Indeed, it also promotes a more strident effort from both sides to bring about mutually desired results. In the event, if you still feel that you have made no progress in any direction and are finding little or no enjoyment to boot, then consider whether or not you wish to carry on in situ or maybe look for alternative spiritual sustenance elsewhere.

I appreciate fully that it is not easy, especially if you are a novice, to know what is right for you personally, especially when it has perhaps been very difficult to begin your tuning in anyway! You may feel too that it took you long enough as it was to find your present circle, so is it that wise to simply exit? But really, honestly, I stress that you should not worry unduly! Experience shows that Spirit themselves have a habit of bringing about, on your behalf, any changes required and or considered necessary in a calm and dignified manner. For instance, if you are not consciously aware of your own unsuitability, they will implement a situation that will make it necessary for you to leave that environmental condition. And this will most always be without any ill feeling or rancour from other circle members, the leader, or yourself.

(On definition of a séance!) *Novices and some others might also be surprised to hear that circles, like spiritual meetings of any kind, are, in essence, séances! Chamber's dictionary defines a séance thus: a sitting, especially of psychical researchers or Spiritualists. So, by definition, any and all private sittings, closed or open circles in the dark or subdued light, or even in a well-lighted church or hall are all séances!*

(On breaking circles.) *Interestingly, in the old days we were told that we must not break the circle under any circumstances. I questioned the inflexibility of this with my own spirit "crew" who answered by producing "the flexible tube" making, if necessary the breaking thing a non-entity! So now, if someone wants to get something from outside the ring of chairs, or simply stretch their legs, or even go to the loo, they are able to do so by simply mentally pushing the circle out accordingly, just as if it was a real, flexible, elastic tube! Mind you, such actions, though not frowned upon, since sometimes they are unavoidable, are also definitely not to be encouraged.*

(On the "ladder" versus our loved ones explained) *I stress, in mitigation, that in no way am I denigrating the messages received from loved ones who have made their transition. I do hold though to the view that this kind of contact is, basically, better made from the platform. Its validity in a circle is justified of course, but only when it is demonstrated by one or more of the developing clairvoyants, etc. or for the leader to make a point. (It should not do the rounds in a circle purely for the members' and its own sake, as if the circle is some exclusive club!)*

And when they are allowed into the circle by our d/k's and the spirit circle leader, try to get these contacts to give irrefutable evidence and not just a message about the recipients hair or whatever! From the beginning I always teach that one "gives off" in a positive way, never negative. For example "Your mother is here" is a positive statement! The equal and opposite negative one is "Is your mother in spirit?" The distinction is clear in that it is a medium's first obligation to prove survival, so be sure that you start as you mean to go on; develop positively!

By way of further explanation of positive clairvoyant, etc. attitude, another tip is to ask the contact for something the recipient is not thinking about. After all, the last thing you want is to have somebody walk away saying that what you told them they were thinking of anyway! (See unconscious fraud in clairvoyance, etc. section.)

A particular problem, the catch 22 situation, can also arise in circles! One can only give fellow sitters a certain amount of evidence before running out of information from their spirit friends and relatives, etc. Sometimes the budding medium will feel frustrated in not being able to move forward, especially if they have come on well. In such cases the student may feel an overwhelming need to try to work publicly.

If the leader thinks that student is ready (and know that it is a whole new ball-

game to go public) they will try to arrange for some fledgling work on the platform with themselves as back-up to the novice. They may even ask another medium to accompany the student in order to assist if, or when he or she becomes stuck. Notwithstanding, a good leader will know when students are ready so do not be too discouraged if your request is turned down once or twice.

(On explaining talent errors.) *When demonstrating, one does not have to concentrate to "see" so that you can spend ten minutes describing a person. This person is generally only known to the recipient who, surprise, surprise already knows what they look like! A gesture, habit or distinctive feature is, in reality far more evidential and keeps things moving smoothly along! Also one has to be careful that one is not inadvertently "reading" the recipient's aura and "picking up" the description from there!*

In working with students in the pursuit of the three clairs, I, like others sometimes make the mistake of speaking of these in one breath. I correct it immediately by stating that, in no way must they be regarded thus per se. It must be clearly understood that the one does not automatically propel, or even prop up, the next; each is a talent in its own right. Indeed, to develop all three together and at the same pace is rare and most will only develop one or maybe two of them simultaneously.

Once one begins to "see" or whatever, they tend to linger a while developing in that area alone. If they do move on to hearing and feeling, (sensing) the time lapse can be either long or short. This depends upon the compatibility of the helpers and their talents too and also has to accord with students' own ability to develop the alternative(s) to that first discovered.

Notwithstanding, many folk, mediums included (who should know better) still believe that a clairvoyant is also automatically clairaudient and or clairsentient. Some also promote the notion that one must develop mental mediumship before they can become a physical medium. This is yet another spurious pronouncement, totally without foundation and I state categorically that it is untrue! The one is definitely not contingent upon the other!

Logic alone should define your understanding that these are separate and different talents anyway since they are at opposite ends of the psychic spectrum! And if they are, as inferred, one and the same, then all mediums would be both physical and mental exponents and they clearly are not!

Types of energy levels and chemical balance of humans intrinsically, to a very great extent, also vary. As such, the artisan who naturally uses his hands to perform his particular tasks is vastly different to the chartered accountant or barrister, for example. The one employs physical energy, the other mental, while surgeons clearly demonstrate the employment of both! Given the right conditions and circumstances, of course, some would be able to do both jobs using both energies. However, they would always favour one or the other in much the same way that a lame person favours a bad leg.

OK many mediums have more than one string to their bow! But even so they have to be the "right tool" for the job, compatible with a suitable spirit helper and having the time needed to sit and develop these. It also requires the medium to have both the talent and an almost aching desire to want to go the distance! I will only add that, as previously noted within these pages, a belief of, or in something, pre-supposes that it may not be true. To know however... hence my qualification of same! The moral? Seek these things out for yourself and rationalise them logically through until you feel from within totally satisfied!

(On the voice we know) *The most easily recognised voice we know is our own. This is the inner voice ("Spirit moving us") that many speak of as that which should be sought out and to which we should listen. It is not, as you might imagine, some fanciful voice booming up from deep within ourselves. Those who tell you that they always hear their d/k and or helpers drumming away at them day in and day out are not quite correct and, perhaps, in some cases, even a little untruthful. I do of course speak directly to and with my d/k and helpers; indeed it would be strange if, after all these years, I did not but they, most often, use my voice in my head!*

(On more about reading auras.) *Whilst agreeing that the two can run together in reading the aura one is not proving survival through mediumship, one is only prov-ing one's psychic ability. In the strict sense the linking here is only into the person-ality, thoughts, health and emotional conditions of a recipient. The problem with it is that if someone is thinking about a particular loved one and is desperate for communication the reader may well pick up those thoughts. Often this is the case both in private readings and public demonstrations. Giving a description of that entity, the conditions that caused their transition and so on solely via the aura, however skilled, nevertheless gives a lie to what is actually happening.*

The problem with this type of demonstration is that many will go from such meetings blissfully unaware of what had really taken place. Exhorting the person's "brilliant mediumship" (intentional quotes) they will tell any who will listen that the "medium" (only sadly a psychic) was so very good! However, as already stated a discerning, experienced medium will know, from their own mediumship, the dif-ference.

I am not in any way denigrating or knit-picking such persons' psychic ability; indeed it is a valuable asset and has its place in development; indeed healers often work this way. I too read auras both in public and in private but I also link directly with Spirit. However, I always explain and demonstrate the different techniques involved and employed, whether in private or in public. It must also be said that, as a matter of expediency, many operators at psychic fairs and on the end of piers mostly work through the aura and not through Spirit.

Finally, I defend its use and confirm that it is still a valuable talent! One exam-

ple is when meeting sitters. Having 'phoned and said they were at the kiosk, for some reason best known to themselves, by the time I arrive they have moved! I then often have to seek them out by searching the auras of the folk in the vicinity to establish who is mine! Often too, would you believe, they have wandered into the adjacent supermarket and I have to do the same thing!

(On "clubs" and cliques, etc!) *Thankfully I am not bound, held like so many others, in a sort of "spiritualistic time warp" by or through the persuasive writings of others. I am though more than a little dismayed at other Spiritualists' adhesion to the narrow path they tread in their search. I agree that their voyage is much more comfortable and therefore easier to travel. But this should not sit well with them and they should examine more profoundly their somewhat static, narrow perspectives. It is to be hoped that they would have (and still might have) discovered the truth. That their thinking runs parallel with their solid stubborn disinclination to continue to sit in concourse with Spirit, in or out of circle! They also think, quite erroneously, that they do not have to as they are "fully developed" (intentional quotes).*

I am therefore thankful for my extensive experience and bless my spiritual teachers for taking me in hand at such an early age. This has allowed me to continually absorb updated input from my d/k, my helpers, the "Manna Group" and other wondrous souls. By such education and my resistance to becoming a "club" member, I have always been freelance. I am also now too old (in my 21st. incarnation) to be afraid or worried by the establishment. Thus it is that I feel justified, more than able, and qualified too, to state that which I know to be true as follows:

The real reason for the banning of diagnosis in spiritual healing is, in reality then, not simply because of the law! It is more the case of the healing pundits' examining bodies themselves being unable to mediumistically or medically diagnose! These, like so many of our Spiritualist ministers, examiners and tutors are not, in the main, in-situ because of their knowledge and wisdom. Many of them are there because of their "politics" of, and whom they know in the Spiritualist "clubs" and cliques! After all, there were diagnostic healers and every other kinds of mediums for that matter long before there were mediums' proficiency examining boards, healing federations and such!

In the main most of these boards have set themselves up as prosecutors, juries and judges. More, in some cases they also take on the mantle of persecutors, acting as both censors and censure! In doing so they imply, to name just some of these, and that they dismiss, out of hand, people like Edgar Cayce, Mrs. Osborne Leonard, Douglas Johnson, D.D. Home, Alec Harris, Bill Olsen, Frank Leah, Jack Webber, Bertha Harris, Leslie Flint, Joe Benjamin, Harry Edwards, Ena Twigg, Maurice Barbanell and Doris Collins! The implication goes further too - that such outstanding mediums as these, in the examining boards' scheme of things, actually count for nothing! By definition alone, the further implication is that such truly great persons as these have, apparently, simply because they did not toe the party line, contributed nothing to the Spiritualist cause either!

I have known many of these finely tuned sensitives and have worked with many more too numerous to mention here and I gladly testify to their abilities. Indeed, I will go further; I think they are more worthy and more qualified than many of those sitting in judgement today and, for that matter, of those who may sit in judgement in the future too!

Again I would point out that this attitude is not taken from an egotistical know-it-all standpoint but from a spiritually guided and common sense one. It stems from an innate and incurable desire to continue to learn, plus an equal desire to want to impart more and more of the knowledge I have gained. It is about seer-ship, that of having real insight, coupled to a continuing observation, clear-sightedness and discernment of Spirit. This too without ever becoming at all obsessed in my journeying, or having become "fully developed" on the way.

Scientists and medics tell us that there are no two of anything exactly alike in our world! Surely this displays an equal truth which is that this is not an accident but an intentional, obvious miracle. Also that, for the very same reasons, although we cannot develop mediumship or anything else at exactly the same rate nor in exactly the same way there is only one way to go. We should therefore know that we have the ever present backing of Spirit and the God-head. Each of us should therefore invest time and energy, fiercely imbued ever with the desire to learn, in a continuing search for Spiritual Truth, Light and Knowledge.

(On using language and voice.) *Some readers may think that if Spirit teachers traverse the globe visiting circles, they must speak many different languages and this is true in principle, but remember they communicate via telepathy. The reasons why they do not speak a foreign tongue through a medium of another country, say Japanese through an English medium are simple. One is that the purpose of a control is not to show off but to instruct or demonstrate the medium's talent. Apart from this, the medium's own brain is used both in inspirational and trance communication which can, of itself, lead to difficulties by both communicants.*

It is often seen that the control also experiences difficulty with the medium's native language. For instance, Yu Sin my healing control, even after some fifty years always says gooder, instead of better! Imagine then, in using the medium's brain, as they do in trance, the tussle they might experience holding the body as well as trying to speak in a foreign language through their medium! Further, unless somebody in the group can speak the same tongue it might as well be gobbledegook! It is therefore, most times, obviously a waste of time and energy of all concerned.

In several cases another language has been spoken through various mediums but it had more of a purpose than mere clever-dick-ness! There are well attested cases involving psychic researchers when a foreign tongue has been used to dem-

onstrate the power of Spirit. Too, more often than not, many of these mediums had never been farther than the end of their gardens, never mind abroad! So unless the control is making a point as say, in research experiments, it is of course easier by far to use the sensitive's natural language. Lastly, remember that not only is the brain involved but also the lungs, trachea, vocal cords, and larynx. Then the articulators being the teeth, palate, lips jaws and tongue also have their part to play! In the case of control, all of these are required to adjust in accord with the voice and pronunciation of the medium! The proof of the pudding... ask a bass baritone singer, at the drop of a hat, to sing soprano - get my point?

(On the "them and us" attitudes.) *In my experience there are too many mediums who give the impression of this and whether or not they are given inadvertently is of no consequence! Either way, intended or not, such truculence and or egotism is definitely out of place in, and out of step with, Spiritualism!*

Having been out of the public limelight for some years and living in Spain, I recently have done something I have never done before to wit, attend a few seminars and workshops. The idea was to update on the present scene and I also hoped I might meet some old and new friends. I hold no bias, quite the reverse! Yet consistently I witnessed the same old run-a-round from people who thought I was a new face, just on the scene! But for me this smacks at their lack of real knowledge to not be somehow, in some way, aware of another medium in their company!

Well, not quite the same run around for my experience and mediumship observed just how much more pronounced these are today and more especially in some of the tutors of workshops and seminars. Puffed up with their own importance this is mostly out of all proportion to their spiritual scholarly learning.

Standing back purely in an observing mode however, other things surface and are even somewhat more ominous than hitherto. The previously held "I will not tell them all I know or they will be up there instead of me" stance is now conspicuous by its absence! The "them and us" in the previous sentence still prevails, they still only teach so much. Now though it is for very different reasons! Subtle in presentation, those of us who have half an ear can see that the object is to engender the notion that one must always take future "instruction" courses to if they want to learn more! It follows that another course means extra money for it and often accommodation too!

Without fear of contradiction I state that there are two principal reasons for this. (1) Some tutors are deficient in the knowledge of their craft; many of them probably cannot even tie their own shoelaces! (2) It keeps a small band of tutors, members of an ol pal's club, on top of the heap, cushioned from the other, lesser mortals, horning in on their pickings! Sadly too, it must be said that they also selfishly guard their secrets, even from one another - how Spiritual!

In case those among my readers get the impression that I feel left out or neglected, I restate! I was never one for clubs or associations; I have always been freelance! Many times Gordon Higginson, the late president, and others asked me to join the S.N.U. but I never did. Indeed, though an approved S.A.G.B. medium, I was never a member as such and I only ever did one reading there; it was in the café for Donald Sutherland, the Canadian actor.

Actually, since their mediums' fees hardly covered my train fares at the time, the only work I ever did there was my audition, under the late Ralph Rossiter in 1967. For this I had to take six each of private readings, groups and public meetings. Later collated, the findings and I went before a committee and one earned or not their accolade, (as did I) of "approved medium", something of which I am proud. In mitigation, referring back to testing boards, I knew on applying, that they worked in a professional way and I accepted it as a part of one's job application. Today though, more is the pity, I understand that one just applies, is given a job and begins work!

For the record I am acutely aware that jealousy, hatred and greed are emotions that are self destructive. As such by sheer will power (and it has to be said, not a little help from Spirit) I abandoned them around the age of twenty-two! In consequence they are not numbered among my remaining vices! So I can coldly assess and criticise constructively those of my contemporaries without rancour of any kind.

Equally, with some fifty years experience of most phenomenon, much of which I have demonstrated myself, I can also state, hand on heart, that I have never taken the "them and us" attitude with anyone! I have always happily dispensed my "secrets" to all and sundry when they have genuinely wanted to gain in knowledge, the only proviso being that they began the discourse!

(On suitability of students, etc.) *Recently attending one such seminar, I was surprised to discover that nobody was vetted as to their suitability, psychologically or otherwise for the trance groups. No restrictions were placed upon sitters nor were any questions asked; it was simply a case of come one, come all! Sadly too, it was under the jurisdiction of a well respected organisation and a well-known medium. Mind you, to note that the charge was also quite substantial for these tutorials probably says it all!*

Clearly however, whilst I applaud the notion that Spirit is open to all, reason must prevail. If and when there are such lax attitudes, the "open to all" thing remains questionable. Many folk are absolutely wrong physically and mentally for development, and for that matter, any religious study. So before they enter into such pursuits they must first be healed of their own inadequacies! So, as I see it, to say come one, come all, is simply a prostitution of a very precious jewel in the crown of Spiritualism.

It is imperative that seminar vendors recognise that they must be far more discerning and particularly in instruction on trance. Indeed it might be wiser perhaps, in many cases, for the tutors to go back to school and learn more themselves!

This would at least make them more aware and would help to replace the some-what lackadaisical attitudes and practices that can be, and often are, potentially dangerous.

I myself spend quite a bit of time talking alone with new students and also with Spirit in obtaining guidance as to whether they should come into my group or not - money here must never be the motivation!

Chapter 5
TALENTS FURTHER CLARIFIED!

I have written about the three "clairs" yet I feel I ought to explain a little more about clairsentience. Regarded by some as the Cinderella, it also strikingly differs in its own way from other mental talents because impressions received are, in many, or even perhaps most, instances less relative to the "dead" than the living.

Feelings often reflect and explain "strange atmospheres" in a property for example. Upon entering, one may experience, among other things, the shivers, depressed or happy feelings. Such things *can* be felt and often are, by both the convinced person and the self-confessed non-believer. Also experienced are transient atmospheres such as is often found in hotels, a sort of unlived-in feeling for instance.

Persons knowing nothing about psychic impressions cannot explain them and these may only be minor or fleeting flashes anyway, recognised as "spooky", yet they are still sensitives. In the main the "vibes" are intuitively felt and are often the emotional imprints that previous occupiers have left behind. Mostly though, the "mood" passes and is dismissed with the idea that once they "put themselves into it, in no time at all it will feel like home!" The former atmosphere is then overlaid, or perhaps added to, by *their* imprints, unless of course they have inadvertently opened a door (see Hauntings). Mediums, on the other hand, will mostly be able to go that one step beyond when, using their skills, they will, if sufficiently knowledgeable, distinguish between the emotional and or the entity (haunting) disturbances.

Another clairsentience facet! How many of you, on entering a room, even though all appears to be normal, are immediately aware that an atmosphere prevails? Greeted by happy faces is of no consequence for you know somehow that before you arrived there was some dissension. At other times, not knowing that you were coming and in spite of the warm Hellos you know that they had been discussing *you!* But you are not naturally paranoid; you simply "feel" via your psychic clairsentience faculty, their auras! (This can be very handy when your investment broker or bank manager is not being honest with you but it also has a down side! Maybe, attracted to someone, you feel that they do not like you! But look on the bright side - at least it saves time.)

The following actually happened, dramatically illustrating the emotional, as opposed to the spirit entity side of this phenomenon... A friend of mine wanting to remove went to an estate agent she knew and he affirmed that he had just what she needed. He knew the absent owners he said and had the keys there with him and normally would accompany clients. But since he knew her, giving her the keys he said to ring the bell before entering in case anybody was at home.

On arrival she did as instructed - no answer! To make sure she repeated the operation a couple of times more but with nil response, so in she went. Much to her surprise she heard raised voices upstairs and, accordingly, called out several times but to no avail. Thinking that they had not heard her, she continued calling more loudly as she mounted the stairs. On reaching the landing she saw through the open bedroom door a man and a woman, the source of the shouting, obviously involved in a very heated argument but she could make no impression upon them.

In an instant she saw these as "ghosts" and in even less time she fled the scene! After getting over her shock somewhat she returned to the agent's office. Declaring to him that the house was haunted she related what she had seen, describing in detail not only what they were wearing but also the words she heard.

As he listened his mouth fell open and his eyes grew wider! When she paused for breath he told her that a nephew and his wife owned the house. What she had described he said was exactly what he had told him had occurred prior to the wife walking out and into the arms of her new love. It was why the house was being sold and that the argument had been just a couple of days earlier.

Speaking to me about it that evening I was able to explain the phenomenon to her. Of course these were not ghosts in the accepted sense! She had picked up an incredibly intensified emotion, so strong that it had impinged itself on the atmosphere and had had no time to dissipate especially as nobody had been there, not even the agent, since the occurrence. Until then, totally unaware that she was sensitive to such conditions, I explained that she had unwittingly tuned into the same "emotional wavelength" as the couple; not knowing any different she assumed that they were "dead people!" Many readers, not as fortunate in possessing such high levels of talent as she will, just the same, understand a little about how she felt during this experience.

As this anecdote is true I will not name her but I can say that she is a very level-headed, serious enquirer into psychic matters and at the time was very involved in the Grimsby Spiritualist Church. (Incidentally, serving the church that week-end was why I was in there in the first place.)

Notwithstanding, every case has its own individual aspects and requires, before jumping to any conclusions, intensive common-sense investigation. It should be overseen by a competent experienced exorcist when that medium will easily be able to differentiate between what is a discarnate and a incarnate happening. In short, for want of a better term, what is a ghost and what ain't!

So we might conclude that clairsentience is not quite so much of a Cinders after all for it also has wide ranging uses! It is just that mediums, when demonstrating, rarely mention it because it is not so obviously portrayed. On the other hand, when a medium does differentiate, declaring that they are seeing, hearing or feeling such and such it goes almost unnoticed. Common politeness alone prohibits members of the audience from interrupting at that point, asking for an explanation of everything that the medium is doing.

Mediums too, unless there are Q and A sessions rarely explain *any* part of their work. As is expected of them, they just get on with the clairvoyance or whatever! But if we are to move beyond the message only standard, this too surely has to change. The easiest way to begin is for more and more mediums to invite, as I do, both spontaneous interruptions and previously written, unsigned questions. It means that embarrassment in asking aloud is avoided as nobody knows who has put the written questions and the response from Spirit more than equals that of the enquirers.

In the meantime however, do not just sit there *hearing* because the medium is not addressing you personally. I know,'cos I've observed 'em from the rostrum, that many "switch off" when the clairvoyance begins because they think that philosophy is paramount per se. But one should also *listen*, observing throughout, to the best of their ability, exactly what is being said and done for demonstrations often reveal hidden philosophy gems - so "He that hath an ear..."

Thus observing, listening and also trying to differentiate which "clair" is being used will exercise your own physical and spiritual faculties. In doing so you are, until you know better, unconsciously reaching out to Spirit but in time you *will* feel the more intimate, closer alignment and co-operation with your *own* helpers. Consciously or not, if the desire is there, then those talents for which together you strive will unfold and begin to develop. But if for whatever reason your mind is closed then development, in proportion to that closure, will only stagger on, disappointingly unevenly.

Other things too need more explanation and I begin with the four types of guides and helpers. These are set out as dictated to me and are not, therefore, meant to infer any kind of order, rank, or importance. As totally free agents "mine" are also in no way bound to me; they work *with* me, as I do with them, *solely* by choice! Whilst it is this that ensures mutual harmony, compatibility and love, it also means that either can split from the other at any time without rancour of any kind. Further, they do not work, nor are they limited to any kind of a one-job-bind as a d/k, healer or clairvoyant, etc. Like folk in the body, they often take on other different tasks and challenges as, if and when required.

THE DOORKEEPER (guardian angel) is our *only personal guide* and is "born" with us and "dies" with us. Our d/k may (or not) have been travelling with us prior to our present incarnation and may (or not) continue to do so at our transition if, for example (two way freewill operating) they or we have other Spiritual paths to travel. The Manna Group say and I have never heard anything to the contrary in nearly fifty years of experience that these are almost never relatives or close friends of their charge's family.

They are also acutely aware of something they strive continually to alter which is that most folk still lack the knowledge that they are able to safely communicate with, and receive help and advice from their d/k. Orthodoxy in many religions still decry (for their own ends) any communication with the other dimensions claiming it to be the work of the devil, another man-made image like the big man in the sky only this one lives somewhere, as yet undefined, below.

The d/k's "sacrifice" insofar as it goes (for this chosen chore is a part of their progress too) is that they have dedicated themselves to assisting the spiritual progress of their charge, namely a soul in the body. Wherever and whenever possible, acting somewhat like a speaking signpost, they offer advice and direction to their charges in their earthly journey. Such advice is communicated telepathically and, in general, these are received mostly while their charges sleep. Registered thus in the sub-conscious, equally we think these to be our own thoughts and not given to us from without, in this case by the d/k. It is simply another instance of non-conscious realisation of learning from other sources than our own minds.

Nonetheless, this does have some effect and charges will often resist the temptation to do something without consciously knowing why. So the fact that most folk are not aware of their d/k does not detract from them having at least *some* influence in their charge's progress. Also true is that many d/k's become despondent when their charges constantly rebut their guidance. Some will even be found tearing out their "spiritual" hair at some silly thing their charge is bent on doing. But remember what I said about d/k's often being only 2 or 3/10? Well, they too learn by experience which means, in many cases, that by trying harder, like Tuan, they will also make the 10/10 grade!

HELPERS are personal to us only insofar as compatibility and suitability one with the other work to mutual advantage. For example you may wish to develop clairvoyance but you may not possess that talent (think of the "piano-playing" syndrome) and your d/k, being more aware of your particular bent, will still search out on your behalf, a Spirit counterpart to your aspirations, even if only to prove a point. If after a while, although you seem to be getting nowhere, the helper may be coming along much faster than you so they cannot be blamed for wanting to move on to work with another more compatible soul. (Therefore seek out the work that you are able to do and surprisingly, once begun, other talents may follow. Lesson? Intransigence with Spirit does not cut it.)

Consequently such helpers will give notice to the d/k that they wish to withdraw. I have had many a novice tell me that they "used to have flashes and so on but now they get nothing" but it is only a simple case of suitability for the job in hand and or d/k protection. So obviously students should try to discover their own particular and work towards an end in achieving a good standard in it. Remember we all in the main would like to be something else but that does not mean we should settle for what we are for nothing is impossible if you reach far enough.

Footnote! Long standing helpers sometimes, for various reasons, move on too! Funny Eye, who worked with me for all those years in transfiguration séances has advised me of his new station. Since I can no longer produce the energy to formu-

late sufficient ectoplasmic substances to practice this talent, he has moved on and up to a soul group like the Manna. The brief in his group is to collate and gather both information and helpers, including chemists, scientists and doctors for the promotion and production of a new era of physical phenomena mediums.

FLOATING HELPERS are those who control varying tasks like Running Waters, the Spirit leader of many circles, including my present one. Others just "move" into the aura for a particular one-off or more job, as did Will Gaines (see reference Page 1) with the cover picture. Vera is a f/h, a fantastic speller too and assists me in the operation of planchettes, ouija boards and table rapping. As in all my mediumistic work, by making the appropriate appointment via Tuan she will respond accordingly. She also works as an adviser, operator and extra helper for automatic and inspirational writers. So the next time you are working at this, ask not only *who* is communicating but also *who* is operating! This might well explain why mum, dad or whoever could not spell when on the earth-plane, yet now spells perfectly. They still cannot spell they simply dictate to a "Vera" and if you bother to ask, you will be told who.

"THE MANNA GROUP" who have contributed so much to this manuscript. These are a number of highly evolved souls who have left behind their personalities per se and no longer desire to use their personal given names nor cling to any nationalistic tendencies. Consequently, when manifesting, they only ever use the chosen group name. They came together many, many years ago, drawn one to another, with like desires and purpose. Forming a group, in much the same way as starting a club or organisation on earth, they constantly unequivocally pool their on-going learning, knowledge and power.

They are pledged to the teaching of unbiased philosophy and easily learned instructions on how to open and develop the many spiritual talents. They are also dedicated to the endeavour of trying to make the earth-plane a better place to live in for all humankind; indeed, for all living things. Thus their prayer is that the journeys we take through it during our spiritual progression towards Light, Truth and Perfection may be more quickly and readily attained.

They give, as required, both philosophical and logical talks and readily answer, without hesitation, the most difficult of Spiritual questions posed. These, the same as everything else they do, are explained in a very simple, down to earth manner and as such the answers are easily understood.

By their words shall ye know them" is absolutely applicable in their case but they are *nobody's* personal guides! These are *teaching guides*, real true guides and not helpers who are so often erroneously referred to as such. The Manna manifest through many mediums throughout the world, dispensing knowledge, both through trance state and inspirational impression.

I, as one such instrument among so many, feel extremely privileged and grateful to them for the years of sacrifice they have made. I thank both my God and them for the truly incredible amount of things I have learned. More than this I feel deeply humbled to have been entrusted with such an array of wonderful words of wisdom and profound knowledge. I also feel privileged and honoured to be able (and to have been so) to pass on so much of what I have learned to so many other seekers of Truth. N.B. Many similar highly evolved souls-groups, organised in much the same way, constantly help mediums, who are aware of their group, throughout the world. Their purpose and endeavour however is always the same. They are purely Spiritual teachers, guides who reach out to all who desire to learn of True Spirit and Light.

TRANCE WORK is often misunderstood. Novices usually feel, when entranced, that *their* helper should say something quite profound. It is yet another misnomer to expect or even to think that all helpers are philosophers! Most are spiritually not so very far removed from our own sphere or dimension. Indeed primarily it is because they are so "close" to the earthly vibrations that they can help us develop *our* mediumistic talents. They too have to learn and still being a little "of the world" they are able more easily to connect with their mediums and our loved ones.

Levels of trance too are not necessarily in proportion to the work a helper or guide does either. For example one can be in a very light trance and or any degree through to a deep one and still connect with a highly evolved soul of guide status. Equally, for want of a better term, simple down to earth spirit assistants can be invaluable in assisting mediums in any and all kinds of demonstrations. So via the medium's brain processes "ordinary" contacts or controls will deliver their "earthly" words or deeds accordingly. Equally highly evolved guides (philosophers or not) may not be much good (if at all) at levitating trumpets, materialisation or direct voice etc. It is just another facet of the "piano-playing" (or harp perhaps?) syndrome.

In qualifying my earlier statements though, this in no way detracts from always aiming towards the highest and the best! At first glance one may think that the child helper for example does not seem to be so highly evolved as the soul who comes with great teachings. However, it is as well to remember that we cannot (and *must* not) judge spirituality solely by earth-plane, jerk response, perspectives!

Remember too not to allow others to hassle you or cloud your judgement into believing that one depth of trance state, helper or guide is necessarily better than the next. Work from the base of "To thine own self be true"; and I tell you this! Sincerity will always outweigh bigotry and peer pressure if you will hold to your ideals, for in the holding you will gain True Spirit help.

Students, if they have read this far, will know that **PHYSICAL MEDIUMSHIP** (healing apart) takes far longer to develop than the mental kind. I also stress the importance of effort and dedication on the part of one's fellow circle members. Certain requirements and disciplines are absolutely vital for the medium's and the circle's on-going progress. Many of these, though listed here here are basically for initial guidance only. This is because the physical mediums' controls will almost always have certain idiosyncrasies, quirks or whatever, thus establishing their own individual format for working in the circle's development and séances.

Although the setting up has already been covered in the Forming and Conducting of Circles section, even more stringent here is the total commitment and regularity of circle sessions – an absolute must! As with any circle, numbers depend on the supply and demand factor and the size of the room but more than these, *everyone has to be profoundly content with one another.* The room must be completely blacked out with not even a hint of light penetration. (This can at first be sometimes a little foreboding but *know that you are blessed to be even sitting there, so never fear.*)

Later a dim red light, usually controlled by the medium's spirit helper, may be requested, the better type employing a dimmer switch. Other things, e.g. microphone in the box, tape recorders and even infra-red cameras may be requested. But nothing must be pre-empted - all such requests and guidance hangs on the lynchpin of the spirit group working with the developing medium when all additions must be solely via *their* prerogatives. N.B. During the circle session, since "physical" is on the red end of the psychic spectrum *none* of the mental talents should be used or even entertained; reactions, observations and feelings should be physically seen and felt. Try then to "feel" via the emotions, if you will, rather than through intuitive impressions.

If objects are moved about they can be seen by applying luminous paint sparingly for example by dotting small balls, bells and kiddie's tambourines. Plaques, usually of light plywood and about one foot (300cms.) square are also useful "lights" but these of course should only be painted on one side. All should be placed as directed by Spirit but in your eagerness, do not overdo it as (a) valuable space can be cluttered up (b) materialised entities sometimes invite members to personally greet or touch, so clear areas must be left in order that movement within the circle is not disruptive and (c) luminous paint (you can always add more) provides more light than might be expected!

Personal hygiene, a stomach containing only a very light meal (or nothing at all) and loose fitting clothing is also desirable. Watches should never be worn in circles as the power can easily make them falter or even break down altogether! (Budding healers take note here too!) Building up of ectoplasmic material in the circle should not be interfered with as it is easily destroyed and can cause discomfort or harm to the medium as it forms. Therefore avoid, at all costs, the desire to brush away the cob-webby feelings on the face and bare parts of the body; this also goes for itchy and feather type tickling sensations. The sitting position is far more important in physical séances as well, and fidgeting is a definite no-no!

The atmosphere must be congenial as well as harmonious and a level of levity is in order too - a mini-party mood should be created, singing being a good way to keep it going. But this should not be over-loud as something, e.g. raps, objects moved slightly or even voices may not be heard! Keep the proceedings lively throughout and do not allow things to go flat for this can cause "troughs" which in turn can lower power (energy) and such occurrances are wasteful to all on *both* sides of the veil. More importantly, it means that what may have been built or is being stored for use later in the séance is wasted or even lost altogether.

Report any physical thing, being touched for instance (the head, shoulder or knee seems to be favourite) or any other previously mentioned phenomena (see Forming and Conducting Circles) and request a repeat of them.

Have quiet background music to help with the singing and also try to tape record the sessions, one reason being that often sounds and voices not heard at the time are recorded on the audio tapes. (Just recently none of us sitting heard anything unusual but on playing the tape, a minor explosion is clearly heard in the room. I also have a clock with a rather loud, regular tick going during séances, thus ensuring that any tape, as proof of occurances, cannot have been edited, except by very expert professionals in the field.)

(Voices in particular record more frequently with EVP. At the time though nothing is heard on play-back the replies to questions are there. A friend, Alan Taylor, for many years the host of the TV show "Mr. and Mrs." recently made his transition. Just two weeks later we had his voice on tape answering *and a bonus* near the end, for *without* prompting in any way, he whispered his wife's unusual name - "Olga!" - not exactly yer common Mary, Liz or Nellie is it?)

Finally, as in all séances, harmony and love are the keynotes and therefore, good, positive results really do depend so much on what goes into the effort. Expect too to sit patiently for, unless you are extremely blessed, no circle, but more especially a physical one, is going to be an immediate overnight success. I can only add that if you are so blessed, then thank your God and Spirit and treat your circle with the reverence and accord it deserves.

ASTRAL TRAVELLING. As with all other talents it is imperative to set your parameters so begin as always with the exercises as previously prescribed. First though, make yourself comfortable and be sure that you are not going to be disturbed. Take the precautions I wrote about earlier when referring to meditation and trance. In short, ensure telephones and doorbells are rendered impotent and that the cat is out, etc. etc.

Now, having "opened" and lying on your bed or couch as the case may be (lying down for me is better than sitting or lounging) breathe as you would when settling for sleep. At this point you need to be aware of four things (a) the *knowing* that it is possible to exit the physical body and to and return to it, at will (b) what you are hoping to achieve, e.g. destination, learning and so on (c) that your d/k and or spirit helpers will be either travelling with you or surrounding you with love and power so that you can go solo and (d) though you may not see them, you may feel (their exercises regarding protection) the peace and energy. Of course, as with the sleeping position you also need to be comfortable and warm. OK; now the object is to leave your body but remain, initially anyway, *fully* conscious as you effect this. (Later, as you become more used to travelling, you will not need nor have the need to stay "in touch" with your body and figuratively speaking, you will "unconsciously" travel.)

Tell yourself, *if necessary*, over and over, that you are unafraid and simply attempting to do consciously what you normally do each time you sleep! Any feelings of moving out can be a bit hairy to begin with but know of your d/k's protection and look forward to the exciting experience and journey. Trepidation at the beginning is easy to explain too for one moment you are in your body with your eyes closed, breathing normally and the next you are likely to see yourself hovering above yourself! But it really does become easier and more rewarding and exciting too!

The strange thing is that even if you are facing the ceiling, you *may still see yourself* just as if you have eyes in the back of your head lying prone on your bed! The reason is that you are no longer seeing as in the physical body; your perception is the "all-around" extra accentuated *spirit mode*. Here with all the pervasive senses of the psyche you are far and away above and beyond the basics usually employed in the physical.

Once free, look about you, observing and absorbing what you see. Be unafraid *knowing* that at will, at any time, you can return to your body. Know too that you are not held to the body as is so often romantically described, tethered by a "physical" silver cord! If this was so then as all of the cords become entangled one with another one can only imagine the utter chaos among all those sleepers and travellers! No, through Natural Law it is only a *metaphorical umbilical cord* spiritually binding you to your physical body during this incarnation. It can only be severed when the soul leaves the body and makes its transition. So if, as I hope, you eventually achieve even a temporary "lift-off" you will become aware of feeling weightless and of seeing light, such as the pink-white iridescence I wrote of in my revelation.

Next go aloft, passing easily through the ceiling and beyond, ever upwards until, on looking down, you enjoy the freedom of a bird's eye view of the landscape below. On looking about you, you may (or not) see others but do not tarry. Simply think where you want to be and almost quicker than the thought you will find yourself there. To return simply reverse the process by thinking yourself back to your body and your familiar bedroom or whatever.

Finally, on reading this back it seems so easy (and it is) but like so many other things our *negative* attitudes make them appear impossible! Like everything else too, it requires the application, desire patience and practise to go the distance!

HAUNTING & EXORCISM. Why are places, often hitherto without the appearance of any kind of phenomenon, suddenly haunted when new owners move in, or even when visitors come to stay? Well, Spirit tells me that if, for example, where "a" is a person or persons has a "d" where "d", etc. is a premises (or any other letter for that matter) then everything remains undisturbed and apparently normal. This is because, though the haunter is in situ, the "formula" is not correct.

If however, "a" moves into an "a" (like vibrations can also, inadvertently, open the "door") premises or "d" into a "d" place, etc. the phenomenon awakens, having been triggered by those particular vibrations. Indeed, any other matching "letters" will bring about the same effect. What happens here is that, uninvited and unwanted, automatically put in motion are "compatible psychic vibrations" between the spirit and human entities and these may promote poltergeist activity or human entity interference or even a combination of these.

Exorcism takes many forms and like all kinds of matters psychic and mediumsitic new methods are constantly emerging. This is basically the result of new discoveries, experimentation and progression in such things by seekers of Light and Truth, both in Spirit and on the earth-plane.

Zarlu and I have also moved on since the incident of his visit to the little boy in Germany for we have both made several other various and similar trips. These, among others, include UK, America and here in Spain. I usually travel astrally if I am needed and he, obviously, travels via his usual method. However, more and more I find that I just ask Zarlu to attend and the follow-up is mostly very positive with the hauntees reporting within a couple of days from contacting me, a cessation of the phenomena! (Logically, these visits are akin to my request of Yu Sin to visit a patient for diagnosis or prognosis, or to intercede with healing.)

Not all can be effected this way however for Zarlu recently visited a flat in England. Knowing that I was shortly visiting the UK, he asked me to attend upon this in person. However, as in many cases, to coin a phrase, it is more a case of exorcism (like justice) being *seen* to be done than that of me personally ridding the place of the unwanted entity - simply being that the hauntee can see me but not Zarlu!

In the past, with a few circle members, I would attend exorcisms and each time, more or less, the same format would be employed. The very first thing we did, in the vernacular, was to "case the joint" for ERNIE! This was another of the "Manna's" sayings meaning Establishing Requirements Normally Indicating Entities! With Zarlu in charge, we would set about the task of investigating the type of phenomena and this might prove to be from a supernormal or merely normal source.

It is amazing how the two can appear to be one or the other and yet, in truth be contra, totally opposite to what is *thought* to be actually taking place, but Zarlu is never mistaken. So if due to normal source, I would explain accordingly. If *supernormal* then, under Zarlu's direction I would seek out the cause, that is poltergeist or human entity activity or a combination of both. It is simply a case of knowing and understanding the quality and strength of the opposition.

Today investigators have access to infra-red film, night and heat sensor cameras, binoculars, magnetic field measuring meters, infra-red video cameras and ultra sensitive sound equipment, etc. (By comparison, Zarlu and my circle members were lucky if we had a tape recorder and a camera loaded with ordinary film!) Sadly though, what most of these experts lack is the very necessary sensitivity (the mediumship capability) for producing phenomena of any kind. These, often referred to as world renowned experts and scientists are mostly parapsychologists or a Ph D's. They are seen going about their work in a very uncaring *(mediumistically speaking)* way, blundering about and often stamping on the clues presented after which they say there is nothing there.

"Empty kettles, etc." but in reality, because they keep in touch with the producers of programmes their reputations grow. It is patently obvious that these associations are built mainly on a sycophantic, fealty-like relationship with their employers, the production companies, accordingly toeing the line. This and the gadgetry used, presents, for the public at large, a more dramatic and histrionic perspective which is, after all, the prime object of programme producers! Mediums it seems are brought in only if a back-up or credibility is somehow thought to be a necessary advantage to that programme.

Perhaps, most frustrating for hauntees, is to get entities to perform or repeat what they claim has previously been happening. The reason is simple; a dog will attack because it smells fear in others for adrenaline smells the same, for fear or fight! Be unafraid, passive and the dog will not attack! In much the same way most entities trade on the fear of the hauntees, using the *fear adrenaline energy* given off to their own advantage. They employ it to affect physical objects, apparitions or whatever! Be unafraid, passive and the phenomena will lessen or disappear!

Entities are also very canny, totally aware of the exorcist's presence and seem to know why they have come, i.e. to get shot of them so they deliberately lie low. It is here that the exorcist medium's experience and a good, solid, exorcist spirit helper come into their own.

There is also a distinct difference between **OBSESSION & POSSESSION**. With obsession, voices of entities, and usually more than one, only *speak* to the person obsessed. They tell them, or more correctly, *urge* them to do things that can vary from the ridiculous to the downright dangerous, from practical jokes to murder! The possessed person differs completely! Meaning what it implies, entities, but only one at a time, actually possess, physically, the bodies of their victims. In both cases however, there is often a cross over of gender, when a male entity speaks to or controls a female and vice-versa.

Aged about twenty-four I was asked to help in a possession case, a lady who became really violent when possessed. I arrived at the house and though she was in a calm state I saw the damage in her aura. Zarlu said to put her into a room devoid of furniture and then go home; I was to return the next morning, when, he continued, the energy levels of both the male entity and the woman would be at a low ebb. Driving home I noticed through the rear-view mirror that the road seemed foggy; then thunderstruck, I realised that the entity was "sitting" in the rear!

Arriving home, I went indoors and straight to bed (I now slept alone in the bedroom; Harry was married and Roy then in the RAF) when he immediately threatened to possess *me*. Telling him that I was neither afraid nor impressed I drew an imaginary line across the floor and dared him to try to cross it! It was not only confidence in Zarlu and Tuan for I was also aware that had he been able to do so he would have executed that move while in the car!

The next morning Mum complained about the bad language during the night and I said it was probably next door arguing. She would not have understood had I told her that it was simply an entity raving mad and that I personally, which was true, had slept soundly throughout.

Back at the house I first checked on the lady and her sister and her husband, looking over my shoulder, boggled at the incredible sight. On the floor by the woman were two piles of one inch square, neatly torn wallpaper and linoleum! Looking up the entity glared, then gesturing with her hands and chuckling "he" said that the room would require re-papering and new lino. Walking towards her extended hands and fingers I saw no damage to them, incredible in itself, for her fingers at least should have been raw and bleeding. Obviously guessing what I was thinking "he" told me that this showed his power and strength, that he could cause damage or not at will. Noting that she had stayed on the floor (the low ebb) making no threat to attack me, I retorted that while it was somewhat impressive, it was nothing compared to Zarlu's achievements!

To cut a long story short Zarlu exorcised the entity, very forcibly I might add, and the lady made a full recovery. Two small amounts of lino and wallpaper were kept and later mounted on wood under a glass dome; this she called her "Altar of Trust" and whenever she felt low (depression can quickly lead to both obsession and possession) she would place it on her lap. Concentrating on Zarlu, the mood would lift but after about six months she no longer felt the need of this "crutch" and it became an ornament and, for all I know, it may well still be around somewhere in her family.

Interestingly, Zarlu has just checked and told me that she recently made her transition and had had no further trouble! Much like the six-monthly check-ups by specialists, the healing, exorcist and other helpers also tend to keep up to date with their patients, etc. until such time as they can safely discharge them.

In that instance I worked alone but soon after I took others with me. Forming a circle Zarlu controlled me and at the same time Tuan and the spirit team set their trap. Using adrenaline to the exorcist's advantage and, thinking the group was afraid, the entity, lulled into a false sense of security, entered the circle. Immediately feeling trapped it looked for escape. Zarlu would leave my body and for a brief moment a "hole" or "break" appeared and, seeing it, the entity would run slap bang into my body.

Talked to by the circle members, he or she was usually persuaded to go to their own place but if it was too belligerent and refused all efforts to leave, Zarlu would then expel the entity. A psychic vortex previously prepared enabled Zarlu and the spirit team to "suck them out" of my body *and* the premises as, if and when required. Passed to a waiting soul-force-group dedicated and qualified in persuading even the most resistant of entities of their mistakes or folly, they would then be helped toward their spiritual destiny.

N.B. The psychic vortex "going up" (in the old days called the veil or door) so often spoken of is actually a metaphoric structure, stemming from the idea that all the good go up to Heaven and the bad down below! In fact, the Spirit world is above and below, about, around, without and within, simply another dimension that most folk can neither see, hear, feel or appreciate.

Coral Polge ranks among the foremost of PSYCHIC ARTISTS to day and after he made his transition she comfortably stepped into the shoes of the late, great and famous Frank Leah. However, such as these are not just psychics - they have moved up a gear and are mediums in their own right. The term psychic artist is purely a matter of convenience, falling off the tongue easier than a medium who draws pictures of spirit people! It is also more convenient and less confusing for all mediums "draw" spirit people!

I have not seen Coral for many years except on television when she admirably acquitted herself. I have seen her drawing in the past though with both individual sitters and in public. She still works sometimes with a clairvoyant by her side who passes names, messages and so on as she sketches. Although this makes for interesting experimentation, like many of the ilk, she does not *have to* as these, herself included, have developed the clairvoyant talent too.

These do not necessarily have to be trained artists either, although to have the skill initially, not mention an interest in art must obviously be an advantage. There are "psychic artists" producing faces, landscapes, seascapes and so on, who speak of being inspired or guided from somewhere outside of themselves.

It is said though that all artists, be they musicians, writers painters or whatever need inspiration from the various muses before they can *even begin* their work. I have to ponder therefore, asking whether many of these just believe that there is some spirit intervention in their work? If they do then perhaps a necessary prerequisite is not only to *believe* it but to *prove* it! Hence my placing the quotation marks, as above, around the words psychic artists.

For me the real psychic artist is one who can produce a portrait, drawing, or a sketch even, from what is "seen" by them or described by another clairvoyant. Further that the person is identified by the recipient at the time or at a later date. I will also accept those who can produce a landscape, seascape, etc. of a place that is being shown to them clairvoyantly which can also be recognised by the sitter within the same parameters, i.e. that proof is forthcoming. I do not take what appears to be this narrow view lightly. In qualifying it I merely reiterate the ever present necessity for proof of Spirit, rather than having self delusion, or even fraud of any kind.

So if you are artistically inclined of course draw what you are "seeing" and use your sketch pad as a focal point, but as with all development do not run before you walk: do not claim to be a psychic artist until your pictures are proven.

Footnote! Worthy of mention are the Bang sisters whose spirit picture talents stand unique in mediumship and Spiritualism. Obviously a physical rather than a mental talent their spirit pictures were achieved by a precipitation process. They neither touched the canvas during the production of the paintings nor were physical brushes, paints nor crayons present. Many of their works survive today and some can still be seen I believe at the Temple of Spiritualism in Portsmouth, while others are on display at Camp Chesterfield, Indiana, USA.

Incredibly they were produced first in a closed box but taking too long this method was discarded. Pictures were precipitated under test conditions, in full view of the sitters and in normal light too! An extraordinary feature was that, in an instant, if the spirit artists felt it was wrong, the whole thing would simply disappear and reappear as quickly, quite different to that previously "drawn" by them! One might well ask where is such talent to be found today - indeed will it ever come again?

AUTOMATIC WRITING is another talent that requires a much closer investigation but this cannot be done here. Many have attempted and claim to have achieved the production of it and perhaps their results would stand examination. However I suggest to the novice generally hearing of this phenomenon from others (most of whom are themselves novices or dabblers) to be very wary indeed. It is just another of the "easy" ways to connect, probably second only to contacting spirit after the ouija board or planchette.

Simply taking up pen or pencil and sitting comfortably with the writing pad on their lap or on a table they request somebody to "write" through their hand. To the uninitiated this may seem quite in order but where is the vitally important protection?

At the start, (especially using the "Is anyone there?") writers mostly receive only scribbled gobbledegook. This can mean that the entity is endeavouring to adjust your brain to their hand (the way you hold the pen, etc.) or applied writing style. Adapting to your hand is much more difficult too if you are right-handed and your spirit communicator is left-handed or vice-versa. But it can also point to self delusion and wasting of your time into the bargain!

After some practice if you begin to receive legible script on various topics note the style. This should not be in your own hand, nor even a scrawl resembling it, as if, for instance, you had written very fast. Others will often tell you that speed is an essential part of automatic writing. I assure you that it is not, it is simply a cop-out in an effort to disguise it, another case of self-deception or at the least unconscious, or worse, even conscious fraud.

If written by a spirit entity through your hand and brain, the writing will be quite foreign to your own style. Subject matter should at least be of real interest and import, bearing at least a modicum of validity! Recognition of the hand-writing and content of a communicator also presents its own problems for unless and until that person's hand-writing is known to you or to others, how can it be verified?

After all, it could still be an extension of you, the writer's, imagination or simply your calligraphy talent!

However, if this *is* a path you wish to tread so be it. I have to state though that the only *real* automatic writers never hold the pen in a conventional manner! These use another talent, the closest relative being a type of psychokinesis, though not exactly the same as such mediums do not touch the objects when demonstrating this. The fingers and thumb are usually extended and kept together parallel to the paper. The pen is positioned vertically to the paper simply resting against the forefinger and the top of the thumb. Thus there can be no doubt that the pen actually writes without the normal physical aid of the medium (holding it) especially in any conventional way.

This type of automatic writing requires an enormous amount of patience, time and trust. For me the use of this method cannot be anything else than authentic! However, take warning! This talent being so hard to develop forces most students to give up the attempts after a very short time!

In the pioneer days of Spiritualism a well known and respected medium, the late Grace Rosher, used this method and though very thoroughly tested, no fault was ever found in her application. How I wish that I had been privileged to witness this truly awesome phenomenon, actually watching the pen write by "itself". I am sure that she will be well documented so if you want to read up on this very individual medium it would be well worth the effort. I believe her to be the only one who demonstrated thus, tending to show that, by any standard, one would find it hard to fill her shoes. So count yourself very fortunately blessed if you are able to achieve anything like the mediumistic level this great lady reached.

Varied and many are the **PROPHETS** who have predicted coming events and just as varied and many are the erroneous results achieved by them. Writers on prophets too, especially in more modern times, have laboured long and hard to make head and tail of these prophecies. The proponents you see seem mostly to have set their prophesies out couched in mysterious terminology. Maybe though much is just garbled verbiage; whatever, researchers run in those proverbial ever decreasing circles trying to make the prophesies fit a time-scale and or date.

Other prophets have had visions and revelations appertaining to more immediate events. However, with few exceptions these are generally seen and experienced individually and not by crowds of people, though there exists records showing that on occasions, thousands of people have witnessed the same vision!

Some individual visionaries claim celestial guidance to places or objects resulting in a complete change of their thinking and lifestyle. One such, apart from Moses and well documented, is Joseph Smith, founder of the Mormon religion. He claimed many visions including a series that led him to a secret place where he found gold tablets covered in ancient hieroglyphic-type symbols. Apparently, he was the only one who could translate these (Surprise, surprise!) and today his writings are the basis of the Mormon Bible. A charismatic young man he was just

273

seventeen when the visions began. True visionary or not the translations contain facts well beyond his imagination, education and indeed his comprehension. Today Mormonism is firmly on the map and they are a very wealthy, powerful and thriving church.

Another young prophet and visionary was the now canonised Joan of Arc. Buddhism, Brahmanism, Islam, the Benedictine Order, the Franciscan Friars and many other religious groups have all benefited from their original visionaries. The same kind of prophets and visionaries are found in the old testament in the Bible, exhorted by the church as being God inspired. Yet this same church abounds with anathema denouncing as witchcraft and sorcery any who practise these things!

Among the most famous of the all-time riddle writers are Nostradamus and Mother Shipton. More recent equally famous prophets are the late Edgar Cayce and late Jeane Dixon; there are many others but I do not want to catalogue already known facts. Such prophets as these tend to receive their predictions mentally through impressions clairvoyantly or clairaudiently, or, as in the case of Edgar Cayce, known as the sleeping prophet, in an hypnotic trance state, often induced by his wife. The Biblical and other religious visionary types tend to be told what is about to happen or what they are to do by apparitions or visions.

Curiously perhaps, these visions appear to be connected totally to each visionary's beliefs insofar as they see the Virgin Mary or similar figures if they are Christian. The Jewish visionaries of old saw previous leaders of *their* faith. Mohammed, Buddha and Brahma too saw only "angels" of their particular beliefs. The theory is that it is wrong to see an "angel" of another faith and is probably a tempter (the devil). This becomes plausible for visions are also a support to the mental picture or voice received. *This* bolsters the prophet's confidence, assuring him that he is not simply imagining the whole thing. So it does not bode good to see a wrong 'un! And somehow, the fact that any vision accepted as a true sighting of miraculous proportions might still well be a product of the imagination seems to have escaped the "vision" of the religious pundits!

Curiously too, there are those who only seem to have one or two predictions throughout their lives, these coming about by way of a dream. I am sure that readers could name a friend or relative who dreamed of a future happening and I also "predict" that many reading this would own to having had premonitions, or at least a feeling that something was about to happen.

A distinction may be drawn twixt modern prophets and ancient ones; the yawning gap between say Jeane Dixon and Nostradamus for instance. Nostradamus wrote secret and disguised words open to the many varied interpretations proffered. Jeane Dixon though, glaringly exposed to the media, had no such safety valve! Just the same, unerringly she told, before the events, not only dates and times, but also the places where these would occur. (It has to be said though, that like many others many predicted events never happened!) Classically, her predictions about the Kennedys display a very strong psychic connection with the family here; more than pure prophesy – possibly more of a karmic link to them.

The distinction is self-evident therefore for any aspiring prophet. This is that unless the predictions specifically state time, place *and* date and are backed up by recording them before the event with a lawyer or similar, they have no real validity. By definition one's predictions have to be a hundred per cent accurate before one can bestow upon oneself such a lofty title! So take care and be sure that your predictive mind is in gear before your mouth works!

Finally, I submit that most "predictions" are often only a careful and intelligent recognition and weighing up of cause and effect thus allowing the "prophet" to offer a balance of probability as to its outcome. So, never put miracles and mystery on a par with moral forces, karma or obligations! Remember too that to foretell the future is not, by any means, always the best way to prepare people to meet or to deal with theirs; indeed probably, more often than not, the reverse is true!

Our spirit helpers or other discarnate intelligences, perhaps the sitter's family or friend, etc. will sometimes dispense information on the future. But they can only see a little further ahead than ourselves, which many times is the way that Spirit answers *our* questions.Therefore since this is the answer at the time, it might change. So even if time, place and date are stated the information may not automatically be simply taken as read! As with all things psychic, we must challenge the substance and reflect on the issue, bearing in mind also the effects of karma per se and not just our own little world of activity! Then and only then can we make a balanced judgement!

During private sittings mediums, including myself, make kinds of predictions, either by request or because we "see" it, especially when they concern personal issues, e.g. prognosis of an illness, the outcome of a divorce, job prospect, business and other affairs, etc. However, I reiterate! These are mostly, at the time, only the *probable turn of events* as seen in that particular "what is, is" period! So many other things hang in the balance, not the least of which is the way that the sitter acts afterwards! So unless the medium possesses the very rare talent of pure prophesy, the proviso of qualifying the advice must always be addressed, weighed up and explained fully to a recipient.

The Manna Group, answering a question on advice of this sort, said: "Although it appears to be so, a juggler never really has all the balls in the air at the same time, so do not suffer the delusion of believing that they are!" This I think, is self explanatory!

Perhaps the nearest I get to prophesy is when **DOWSING WITH THE PEN-DULUM, DIVINING RODS**, or both, although of course, this too is not true prophesy. The predictions come via question and answer, arrived at mainly through deduction. In many cases, as in my own, other facets, e.g. clairvoyance is also employed. So do not draw too fine a line here for various psychic abilities as needed are still often employed by operatives on both sides of the veil.

I am certain that most persons with very little practice can dowse pretty accurately and easily with copper rods. On the other hand, the pendulum is much more complicated requiring more time, energy and patience, not to mention greater talent, to develop. It is also imperative, in most cases, to use the right kind (material content) best suited to oneself.

My experiments consistently show that the copper rods, even in the hands of novices and ignorant of psychic matters almost always react more rapidly than the y-shaped twig employed by many dowsers. In the last test, twenty-three out of twenty-five totally inexperienced persons found various hidden items within minutes. Previously, I had buried or hidden water, metal, plastic, and leather, etc. Again rod use excelled whereas the twig, by comparison, produced little or nothing with almost abysmal results. The obvious reason seems that the rods are easier to hold but I feel that the electro-magnetism in and around our bodies has more of a bearing here and too, that copper is a good electric conductor whereas wood of course, is not! I mean here that the twig-diviner has that extra something that escapes most folk.

The copper-rod operation is quite simple, as is the making for any good, stiff copper wire or rod will suffice! You will need a pair, each one measuring about sixty centimetres in length. Bend each one at a point of about twelve cms. making the bend follow a natural more than an acute ninety degree angle. This allows them to follow, ring-like, the contour of your fore-fingers making for an easier swivel movement.

Place one in each hand, catching the bottom of each short end loosely, but firmly by the little finger. Leave the other fingers together, more or less at right angles to the palms so that the bend of the rod lays at right-angles over the fore-fingers. Some dowsers, myself included, also place their thumbs very lightly on the top of the bend, thus ensuring non-slip of them as they swivel. Similar to the hand-rubbing exercise mentioned previously you will very soon find how far apart the rods (and therefore the hands) have to be for you to operate successfully. Remember to "open" asking for guidance and protection while you work and to thank your God and Spirit, by "closing" afterwards.

Have a friend or family member on hand who can place say, a small plastic bottle of water, a bit of glass, a piece of iron, silver or other metal and so on under cloths, blankets or rugs, etc. in the garden. They might even know of a water source below ground unknown to you. They may of course *only tell you* the kinds of materials hidden. Walking steadily over the area holding the rods as stated you will mostly find what you are searching for. With no conscious movement by you the rods will swivel and form a cross one over the other. Directly below will be the item or whatever and I know that you will be delighted, even amazed, at how quickly you become adept at discovering what and where objects are hidden.

Once you feel confident move onto unfamiliar plans, maps or drawings of areas and "ask" that you may indicate a spot where there is perhaps a bus shelter, a tree, drinking trough or whatever. Obviously only pick things that you are unaware of and ask your associate to find something perhaps that they know and you do not. It will be easily seen that to have these rods waving about, particularly over a small plan, makes pinpointing very difficult. The pendulum here is by far much more practical, particularly for instance, when working over and asking about, a patient.

Experiment in different ways and you too may find that, like me, you are able to work with both, a very valuable talent to achieve. With a pendulum for example the reverse of the above occurs for its difficulties become painfully obvious, e.g. watching it, keeping it steady and still trying to see your way over difficult terrain, especially in windy conditions! I have even seen "clowns" (there is no other word) on TV in cars using a pendulum yet even with rods this is virtually impossible!

Having found the water-table or whatever, you then have to discover how deep it lies, whether you have to bore through rock, clay or other obstacles. Is it just a deposit or a constantly filling lake? Is it the kind of water you are searching for, e.g. drinking or irrigation? Is it an underground stream or river and how far does it extend, etc.? Are you legally entitled to tap into it? (I owned land here in Spain and a clause in the deeds stated that all the water rights below ground belonged to the water company and I was not allowed, by law, to sink a well.) By now you will see that getting the rods to move and find what you are looking for is, therefore, only the beginning! The foregoing also exposes some of the limitations of rod dowsing and this is when the pendulum can be of great help.

Experiment with various pendulums or, better still, if possible, have a good dowser to discover for you which material will produce the best response, i.e. wood, glass, crystal, ceramic, porcelain, granite, stone (precious or common). Also, when checking on metal it is as well to eliminate as many as possible, e.g. lead, brass, copper, bronze, aluminium, alloys, gold, silver, platinum and so on until you perhaps discover "yours." The weight is also important and should feel both comfortable and, for want of a better word, balanced when in use.

Enthusiasts have had foisted upon them by overzealous, but unqualified shopkeepers, the most cumbersome pendulums which might well be more suited in a grand-father clock! Bought at a psychic fair or "in this *fantastic* witch's shop" and very overpriced, it is totally far too cumbersome for a sensitive to use. On explaining that I too would find it difficult to use, they then, in assuring me that they paid a lot of money for it, invariably say that the sellers really knew their business. I normally reply that this is true - they conned them easily enough! At this point I usually show them mine, a "crystal" that was once a part of a key-ring, but it works admirably and cost, by way of comparison to the foregoing, peanuts!

Here let me explain why heavy pendulums are harder to work with. It is, in simple terms, that power (energy) used to move it is taken from both the sensitive and Spirit and the larger it is, obviously, the more is the power needed, a simple demonstration of the law of mechanics. So why make problems for yourself? You will not only find that a smaller one moves more readily but also that the responses are more accurate and easier to recognise. This also applies to the length of the suspended pendulum, the shorter the chain, the quicker the response!

Fortunately I can use pretty-well anything as a pendulum and have, on more than one occasion, answered a query using a pencil attached to string in the hair-dressers, post office, etc. It is very amusing too in seeing the incredulous looks and nudges when I check on something in a supermarket or other outlet. Funnier still is when, on the rare occasion as I round a corner, I see another "nut" using a pendulum. The "motley crowd" look on as if it is a convention or that the whole world has flipped!

Having got your material sorted, now ensure that the pendulum hangs free, absolutely plumb, when suspended between your thumb and fore-finger. If right-handed (otherwise reverse the instructions) rest your left hand and forearm comfortably on a surface. Make sure that there is no pressure on the elbow; let it hang over the edge of the table or whatever. This is done to make sure that you do not cause it to jerk or give pain as the Ulnar Nerve, (the funny-bone) is closer to the surface of the skin than any other and passes across the elbow.

After "opening" suspend the pendulum as above but never work initially for more than fifteen minutes, not more than once a day and never ever let *any work* become obsessive. Ask always at first for a positive and a negative response; most times this will follow the same pattern but not necessarily mine. For me, positive is anti-clockwise circular and negative is backwards and forwards. Maybe is an oval movement, also in an anti-clockwise direction. Also, if, for whatever reason, your polarity is reversed then the positive and negative responses may well change places. So constantly, even when working, update this or you could find your answers "drifting" or even totally wrong.

Next arrange mentally a signal with your door-keeper, even if you are unaware who yours is at this stage. This will brook immediate attention and action from him or her to protect you and, once established, the d/k will ensure that the protection is 100% and subsequently take overall control. It may take some time so keep constant checks on answers and eventually "the proof of the pudding, etc." Important this, for like the ouija board you can, unless there is good, strong control, be led up the proverbial! My signal of control by Tuan is the pendulum turning just three revolutions in a clockwise direction, after which it stops dead and remains completely still. It is easy for me to always get a positive and negative response. However, unless I get confirmation of my d/k's control I will not proceed, even with, or more accurately, *because of*, my long experience.

Before going on realising logically that answers received can only be yes, no, or maybe, you may be conscious that, of the three, maybe is not so definitive. Therefore if the answer is held in question, it may be that it needs re-phrasing, perhaps even splitting into two or more parts. After all, it is impossible to hold a normal conversation when the replies are so clinical, with no discussion as such. It follows therefore that the questions must be put very succinctly but *correctly*, the enquirer, before asking, thinking them through so as to get the correct yes, no or maybe response. It also falls to the dowser to clarify, if necessary, certain confused answers.

Remember too that, as in all phenomenon, forces are in play here. I personally also "talk" mentally with Spirit as I work through a session and this is very helpful when clarifying points. Often too an answer comes before the pendulum responds but be careful it is not your own mind for even I do not expect such premature answers as a matter of course! And even so, enormous amounts of practice, both in the three "clairs" and dowsing to achieve really positive, unshakeable results is required. Even then, as with all things, it is only as it stands at that time, the "is" factor!

Never will it to move either for if you are capable of psychokenesis your talent lies elsewhere for the last thing you want to do is to make it do your bidding! Unless you are a natural and take to dowsing like a duck to water you must needs act somewhat like a detective, asking questions and then questioning that question until you are sure. Try to develop a rapport with your sitters but maintain a certain distance too. In this way you are not persuaded into "answering" emotionally when, with genuine endeavour to assist them you might, albeit unwittingly, commit fraud of some kind.

Finally, do not forget to close your session and to support my earlier statement about becoming obsessed with your work I offer the following for your perusal and guidance:-

I answered some very important personal, family and business questions for someone I will call Vi. A very good healer she thought, quite rightly, that if she had dowsing powers this would greatly assist her. She "knew all about it as me Mam's friend used to do it with cotton tied to a wedding ring!" Explaining that it was far more than just a party game or for fun, I carefully instructed her, especially stressing the important points as above and sorted out the best kind for her to use.

Not unusually though her enthusiasm overrode her better judgement and quarter-hour sessions became one hour then two and eventually she was asking stupid questions to see if she could catch it out - questions like what time it was or should she buy bread, knowing she had none! In other words, an obsessiveness had set in and she of course began to make mistakes.

A lady friend said that she thought she was pregnant and rushing to her aid Vi "diagnosed" a no! Very relieved the lady went away happy only to find two days later that her pregnancy test was through and showed positive! However, Vi's trusty pendulum disputed this, saying the test was wrong; she still got no! The lady had a spontaneous abortion three weeks later - so much for Vi's dowsing she thought! Calling me, very unhappy at her failure, I acted the detective and went through her questions. I soon discovered that she had never once asked if the woman was pregnant and if she was carrying a healthy baby. Her question each time was only was she going to have a baby? Well, of course she had the right answer but, due to her lack of definitive questioning, she caused her enquirer a great deal of avoidable worry. Mentioning that her helpers were a little dismayed at the way she was employing the pendulum and, quietly reading the riot act, I reiterated my original instructions.

Vi is now a much wiser person, has relinquished her pride, is off her "ego wagon" and today is more responsible in her work. She takes both time and care with her questions and has a far more serious approach to her dowsing. She has realised that this phenomenon is far more than just a game to play around with and also that mums do not always know best!

You will know by now the importance I place on logic in all my psychic work. Using a pendulum is no exception. With the co-operation of Spirit, the pendulum can bring forward answers to most problems and situations. From cooking to electrical faults to motor-cars to healing; indeed almost anything you name. Of course the correct use and application has to be strictly observed. Remember to only ask one clear question at a time, which same must, by definition only require a reply of yes, no or maybe.

Equally logically, it follows that since there is a wealth of talent in all fields in Spirit, you may request help from a healer, car mechanic or whatever! The same as here on earth there is always, if you can but reach them, someone ready, willing and able to assist you in solving your problem. Ask and ye shall receive!

Another "secret" is to ask not only for specifics, but to also ask how long it will take to link with that information. Sometimes I have to wait as long as a quarter of an hour to link in after my initial contact with Tuan (my door-keeper). With this in mind I always use a kitchen timer so that I can set the time-lapse. This way you can ask your door-keeper for a "suspension" while you wait. In the event however, make sure that you still have control this end by repeating the link-procedures mentioned above. This will ensure that your door-keeper is still in charge and not tut-tutting because you have not stuck to the rules! More importantly though it also ensures that you will not find yourself up the proverbial without a paddle!

Hopefully, you will reach an advanced state of communication such as I enjoy when questions may be asked mentally or aloud and in any language by my sitters. I am also able to receive answers to questions put over the telephone mentally or aloud and on behalf of another person unknown to me. This method is also invaluable in diagnosis, but remember too so is a knowledge of anatomy, for without this what questions can you authoritatively ask? I am not boasting of my helpers' and my prowess; I am merely pointing out what can be achieved with talent, a forthright, positive attitude and a willingness to learn and progress.

Earlier within these pages I touched on the possibility of encountering harm in using **OUIJA BOARDS AND PLANCHETTES**. In the early days of modern Spiritualism, this type of phenomenon followed hard on the heels of table-rapping because, like the former, it is comparatively easy to practice. This is because (a) more combined energy of the sitters is utilised in the operation and (b) it is the easiest and quickest way to reach through the veil. I chose those last words deliberately as "reaching through" is all one can do.

A problem here, though sounding like a contradiction in terms was that it was so easy to make contact; indeed, I would bet that most folk have "played" with one at some time even without using (not a prerequisite anyhow) a proper board. Sitting around a table at a party, for example, they begin the "spooky-spirits" game, totally ignorant of what a can of worms they might open up; and foolish folk are still "playing" today!

By spreading the letters in a circle and placing an upturned glass in the centre, acting as the pointer, they are ready for action! They begin by asking if "the spirit of the glass is there" a ludicrous question this, for, as with all things, though an energy does exist within the glass the snag is that the only form of "communication" with it is through the power of psychokinesis! So, in the event, "talking" to invoke its "power" results, strictly speaking, in the impossibility of communicating with human soul-level entities anyway! After all, the only active spirit found in a glass comes out of a bottle and it ain't never a genie either!

All too often the "game" is played with spirits in both hands, i.e. in a glass held in one with the other on the glass in the table centre, cajoling, with all kinds of banter, spirits of the other kind! Such "players" though invariably are blithely unaware of the powers they might and can invoke and of the dangers that can follow.

Some problems are (a) controlling who is contacting and the language used, which can sometimes be very ripe and abusive. Then the more inebriated in the "game" often reposte with gusto increasing the already unsavoury entity's intrusion (b) controlling both sitters and length of sessions which often drag on, leaving people tired and vulnerable (c) people accusing one another of pushing the glass around simply for effect and (d) closing down at the end when all too often the lower sphere entities are not willing to return to their "place" and will attach themselves to one or another of the "players." This imposition can lead to obsession and or possession, creating all sorts of mayhem both in their homes and relationships!

I have conducted many exorcisms including obsessions, possessions and hauntings. *Know* that there are many who rue the day when first they "played" with what can sometimes prove to be an awesome phenomenon! Simply because of their wrong approach, the unseen forces *"played"* with *them*! True, a hard lesson is learned by many, but sadly the wrong one, for they are mostly afraid to tread *any* psychic path again.

Yet had they had the right help and guidance many might well have become really good mediums and such loss is of itself a pity. Knowing personally the strength of such individual potential, I feel that this loss may well have contributed to a slower progression of things psychic per se. Nevertheless, a lack of many a medium's psychic education (quite apart from that of the masses) together with many of the more enlightened psychics not speaking out against all types of lower phenomena methodology must also take a large share of the blame.

The problem is to be aware of and be *able to overcome* what is encountered here and worse what can "take hold" of one, since, in general, only the lowest type of entities are contacted. So was it ever so? No, it is just that more people have encouraged more entities into our dimension with little or no thought of the consequences. What distinguished those early pioneers from the "players" then? It was the right conditions prevailing throughout; in a few words, prayers and dedication!

Today in order to maintain, without deviation and interference good quality, consistent communication, one has to be very psychically advanced and preferably a strong medium. So leave such things behind forever and try to become more finely attuned to your d/k and helpers and to reach for and stay *beyond* this level. However, if a student *is* so advanced the whole thing becomes academic for, having moved on to higher things, they will no longer desire to even consider never mind employ this type of phenomena!

The conclusion then obviously is that unless you do have a trained medium on hand who can really, through experience and attunement with Spirit, control the proceedings then do not even begin to operate such devices. If such a medium is in your company then he or she will, in all probability, refuse to conduct such a séance. The exception here is perhaps when, as a part of a circle training session, they might properly demonstrate their ability. Even then they should extract a promise from their students that they will not indulge in this phenomenon out of the circle until or unless they are thus qualified. (See e. of ch. on physical talents!)

Finally, I have explained ouija here only to show the pitfalls and this like any other project in an attempt at communication should *never* be entered into lightly! Experimentation notwithstanding, since there are so many other more productive paths to travel, my advice is that you do not even entertain the idea of this form of communication, never mind attempt it.

(Some will recall how shocked the psychic world was in seeing the market flooded with the ouija board "game". At the time others and I protested, seeking its withdrawal from sale but the protest was not solid, nowhere near enough - where were the movement pundits then?)

Interestingly my writing has just been interrupted by a neighbour with an invitation to coffee! Asked how the book was coming I told her I was writing about the danger of mis-using ouija boards. She then said that many years ago she innocently bought one of these "games" for her son aged thirteen at the time and at boarding school on the coast in England.

After just two sessions (her words follow, not mine!) typically-clad ghosts of smugglers and pirate types, from scarves around their heads, down to their thigh boots began to appear to the lads in their ground-floor dormitory! Cursing audibly, these threw the beds (often with the occupants in them) and other objects around the room. Needless to say the kids were terrified!

Having stirred up this hornets nest of previous occupiers and with teachers, kids and priests witnessing the phenomena but unable to remove it, finally a medium was asked to help. She was, thankfully, able to close the door they had opened and, probably for the boys' psychological benefit more than any actual psychic effect, and or to ensure its destruction, the board was publicly burned.

Prior to the above anecdote I thought I had finished but once again Spirit sure moves and nudges us sometimes in strange, off-beat ways - I could not have asked for a better example of such a misinformed use of a ouija board!

HELPFUL NOTES!

(On physical talents!) *Today table rapping is very rarely practised, considered by many to be old hat but there are other reasons too, notably that it takes too long to develop this to any real level so one can never really be sure who is actually communicating! Nowadays, with time at such a premium, those people who want to develop and research desire to push ahead far quicker than the Victorians. So when sitting for "physical phenomena" these folk want to get into the more advanced talents of, for example materialisation, independent and direct voice, etc. The results, in most cases, also produce far better communication and evidence. Healing though, itself on the red end of the psychic spectrum and, therefore, a physical talent, finds healers emerging from these circles far more commonly than voice, materialisation or transfiguration mediums. For whatever reasons, impatience, desire, or whatever they have, sadly in very many cases, shelved, or even stunted their potential physical mediumship.*

Chapter 6
OTHER PSYCHIC (NOT SPECIFICALLY MEDIUMSHIP) TALENTS AND ACTIVITIES

A biding throughout the psychic spectrum are other, not strictly mediumistic talents as such but they still have their place in one's development. If I have missed out or glossed over your particular hobby-horse it will not be because I do not accept its existence nor is it an oversight on my part. It will be that I am either unaware of it or have little or no experience of it and anyway if you have read this far into the book you will know that I do not pretentiously write on anything I know nothing about. At best therefore I can only *hope* in offering an open-ended opinion for consideration that it may prove to be of some intrinsic value to students.

Many would argue that these should not even be in a book on mediumship. Nevertheless, functional as they undoubtedly are in the right hands, I am obliged to respect them and feel that they are worthy of mention, especially as many enquirers begin here and move on to mediumship later.

Among those mentioned are Palmistry, Tarot Cards and Numerology, this last being basically split into two types, one using the English alphabet and the other the Hebrew version, based on their own and the Greek alphabets.

Clacking, likened somewhat to the effect that drums have upon, among others, the Native American Indians' psyche. (Discotheques actually play very loud beat music because it has been proved that it makes folk drink more) Clacking needs two stones and one must be naturally (This is old magic - opposites coming together!) light and the other dark. Banged rhythmically together, like the drums they are said to lead to concentration and an awakening of the spirit forces. (Well, they say one can make enough noise to wake the dead!)

Although I encourage students both to demonstrate and trance while people carry on talking, etc. (simply because today our world *is* noisy) that is one thing. Clacking and drums are OK too, (as far as I am concerned) so long as one is born into it for one accepts the ways and basic tenets of one's "tribal" customs. Catholic kids, for instance, are taught from the word go not to talk while awaiting their turn in the confessional! From then on, even when adult, they never speak above a whisper in church. But step outside of these confines and it becomes a question of what "accompaniment" suits one on the pathway. For me, clacking and such are no-no's, though I have no problem at all with even *loud* conversation, dogs, cats, telephones, etc., about me.

For me too meditation and healing tapes are no-go areas. As a composer myself, I lose concentration. My mind wanders more to the recognition of this or that piece or identifying the notes as being close to some other melody line, phrasing or chord structure! Hm, very distracting!

Generally outmoded, although some still practise, is *Phrenology*, the art of reading the bumps on the head. Strange too that at one time it was virtually the *most* popular of all psychic talents! There are also those who also read the *moles on the body*, the *lines on the forehead* and yet others who read *the feet* and I am not referring to Reflexology either! Even more surprising is the art of *Myomancy* - divination arrived at through the movements of mice! And believe me, this is in no way a complete list; many other obscure and equally eccentric divining methods exist and are used throughout the world!

Worthy of mention too is an excellent weapon in the arsenal of the charlatans, used by them to great effect! It is that all of us, to some extent, psychic or not, consciously or unconsciously, *read* faces!

Some psychics use a *crystal ball*; others using a *bowl of water* on a dark background work equally as well. There are *tea-leaf* and *coffee grout* readers (this last popular in Iceland) and others who read *a candle* or other flames, etc. But no longer having the need to cling to a concentration "crutch" as they become more "aware" (progressed) they put these aside. The realisation dawns that there is a better route to elevate them from psychic to medium.

The exception is possibly the crystal ball, used sometimes in readings and in healing. I do not have sufficient knowledge or experience on the power or otherwise of the use of crystals in healing so I hold no *valid* opinion. If interested, access to reading matter on these is prolific so study can be simplified - but remember to be a sieve, as all and sundry, like any author rides their own hobby horse! Certainly many practitioners and patients swear both to being healed or to have effected healing with crystals and the use of them seems to be more common than hitherto. So perhaps if the "gazers" possessing a pure crystal ball and not just the more common glass one, may well have the edge on some of their healer friends! After all, by comparison, very few of the multitude of healers are clairvoyant!

There are also other "arts" employed by some people *solely* for fortune-telling but they still deserve a mention. After all, to have discovered or been told how to, if the novice was not actually psychic, the starting point must have stemmed from an interest in psychic matters

For the record I mention two that are used by both the expert and the novice. Each item, by the way it falls or feels gives an "answer" that is usually looked up in an accompanying book (in olden times on parchment sheets and much earlier on stone tablets) showing diagrams with text to delineate the "pattern" formed. First, the Chinese sticks (50 in number) and the more complicated coins (hexagrams). Both of these are types of *I Ching*, used, curiously enough, for a very long time by the Japanese samurai to plan their campaigns!

Confucius, the great Chinese philosopher studied these in detail, endeavouring to unlock the mysteries hidden in them, but he died before achieving this. Over the centuries many others have also tried to unravel the secrets, said to be bound up in enigmatic puzzles and all have failed! Another system, similar, is *Runic Stones*, said by some researchers to have originated with the Druids, although others say this is not so. Actually a Nordic word, it *could* have "landed" in England with the Vikings! But because I do not know, I leave this discussion and argument to the scholars of such things. These too have much of their origins lost to time and are, like *I Ching*, surrounded in mystery and legend.

An exception perhaps to thrown objects being a "game of fortune-telling" are *the bones*, cast in much the same way as the runes. I make the distinction because they are not only used just to tell the future but for a multitude of applications. Whereas the *I Ching* and the *Runes* method trusts simply to chance, *the bones*, when put to work are revered as being spiritually and Spirit influenced, guiding the hands of their operators.

Shamans of many nationalities employ these daily throughout the world and use these and other related forms in delineating just about everything from diagnosing and healing the sick (which medicines to use, etc.) to advice from Spirit, to prayers, meditation and trance-states. In effect, one might say that a shaman almost considers them to be an extra appendage of his body!

The uncanny accuracy achieved suggests that either a sixth sense is used when throwing them or that the bones possess some incredible power of their own! I dismiss this last however, simply because it is the shaman who has to interpret them, the bones themselves obviously being unable to convey anything to the uninformed! It is well known that a shaman has the so-called sixth sense so if this is the only talent they use, then is it reasonable to assume that the bones are simply a prop! Whatever, they have been around for thousands of years and are still widely in use today. No book is in use either since shamans never learn how to read or write.

The best bones in use are *human* and a top shaman will always, once having obtained a set, keep and jealously guard his, passing them on together with all of his secrets (passed by word of mouth only) to his chosen one. He or she will become the next shaman on the shaman's transition or retirement. Apprentice shamans, meanwhile, use the much more readily available but much less "powerful" animal bones. However, possessing no true shaman magic, the ordinary native would never dare to *handle* shaman bones of either variety, never mind contemplate *using* them!

As mentioned earlier I set down the explanation of precious and semi-precious stones and jewels. However, it should be understood that much of the significance of these is only legend. Jewels however do contain secret psychic powers but I am not at liberty to dispense this knowledge and can only say that it involves far more than just looking at them and knowing what they are meant to represent! So this section is written from an interest angle and point of view only.

As do all things, colours and crystalline give off magnetic forces that can refresh both the physical and spirit self. Through the eye a kaleidoscope of vibrations of light and heat is absorbed and this is in proportion to the varying levels of this magnetism. Indeed as mentioned previously on focal points, clairvoyants sometimes use highly polished ones (for example crystal balls and obsidian mirrors) to receive visions.

The sapphire is paramount in producing tranquillity and concentration of mind; a sapphire ring is said to possess great moral power. If doing something you should not be, then you must not wear it, for your actions could be known by your nearest and dearest! When worn by pure mediumistic individuals who commune with higher intelligences, it protects them, warning of hidden dangers; it will also keep away many diseases. Solomon in communion used the sapphire, for it impels one to wisdom, silence, justice and love. It is also the sacred stone of the inner temple of the Eastern S.S.S. - in the west the Z.Z.Z.

The Greeks used a lodestone to assist both memory and to give access to angels and heavenly things; they also believed that that the opal possessed great power. Provided it was not used for selfish gain it could give the owner the light of prophecy. When misused however, the owner became unlucky and had disappointment as his travelling companion.

Opals, the most sacred stone in ancient Mexico was said to contain the soul of truth, indeed the soul of fire that created worlds and men! It is the gem of gods and hermits because both live alone. It is also fateful to love and separates friends.

Rubies are said to hold to the owner all the passionate love of those they desire! The Burmese, on the other hand, believe it is a most sacred human soul about to enter the revered precincts of Buddha in the last stage of transmigration before entering the embrace of Divine Love. In the days of chivalry it was supposed to lead knights to conquest, inspiring bravery and zeal, when obstacles would melt away. It also kept his honour and character unblemished. Health-wise, rubies are supposed to quicken the blood, increasing the will of the physical body, thereby bringing vivacity!

Pearls, emblems of purity, represent virtue, but they will bring tears if given to your true love.

The emerald typifies the purest and highest love. Representing growth and progression it promotes constancy of mind and true friendship but will also give the power of discovering treachery or ingratitude in false friends. The Romans believed that if a serpent just looked at one it would become blind and all other objects of contempt or detestation would fall when in its presence, completely overwhelmed! Some cultures also claim it brings harmony and joy into the household.

The Hebrews claimed the diamond cancelled out the lodestone, for being the most powerful of all gems and stones, it deprived it of its virtues. It was therefore considered the strongest in the school of the Prophets for promoting high concentration and Spiritual ecstasy. Also seen as the Sun's emblem and the charm of the invisible fire, it could be, to its possessor, either the giver of light or bring the most profound darkness into them. The Greeks knew it as the Holy Necessity, the Sun, the ethereal fire and the male of being! Some also claimed them as the tears of Gnomes who had lost their best beloved.

Agates are said to cool and allay fever, quench the thirst and quiet the pulse and palpitations. They ensure good health, giving long and prosperous life. Some also believed that they could render their wearer invisible whilst the amethyst promotes chastity, assists in overcoming habits and passions and strengthens the will power. Knights believed these too gave great power in battles, the wearer being rendered brave, far-seeing and honourable.

Red Coral is used in difficulties of the heart, lungs and indigestion, acting as a health-giver but it excites nervous power, brilliancy and gladness too. Amber is good for the fires of the soul, for the eyes and for glandular swelling of the throat and lungs. Garnets are said to bring cheerfulness and ability to hold one's own in the world. Topaz is favourable for rest and good cheer, hearty digestion, nerve strength and health to the physical body.

The onyx contains an imprisoned demon who in his anger turns back on himself so he who is thus and owning one is his own worst enemy! The demon is only able to come out at night, causing terror to all and should one wear onyx, one will have disturbance of both sleep and the mind.

Finally there is colour, visible and invisible, in everything; even ideas and thoughts have colours, the innate strength lying not simply in the colours alone but in the vibrations that produce them. After all everyone knows the difference between, for want of better expression, a "black" look and a "white" one!

In *Palmistry*, the left hand reveals your inherent traits and family history; the right is you, revealing what you have made, or will make of yourself. Depending upon the talents possessed and utilised by the operative they can (and often do) involve a combination of the shape, the lines, various markings (similar to coloured full-stops) on the front and back of the hands, the nails and the fingers.

Some palmists, as I do, are also able to use clairvoyance, psychometry, prophecy and even auric-colours around and "in" the hands. Good operators will indicate certain traits and experiences that are probable in the future.This however, although being directive, remains somewhat speculative, unless the operator has the true talent of prophecy. Even then, unless the recipient acts exactly as predicted, his or her future will accordingly, to a larger or lesser degree, be different from such predictions so they mostly stand little or no chance of materialising. In my own experience total conformity is virtually non-existent anyway! For instance if the details are not tape-recorded at the time, the sitter is sure to forget most of what was said within days or even hours! And good 'ol freewill and the "what is, is!" will play their part, somewhat throwing the whole thing to the wind anyway!

In the right hand, palm side up, the past traumas and emotional changes, how a person came into the world and so on are all there to be seen. Certain things seen will also show emotional change or upheaval at a point (age of the sitter) in the future, especially with the use of measuring callipers. This can be a move from home, a new love, a marriage, separation, divorce; even the loss of a loved one or whatever. It can also be a new career, a change of, or improvement in, business affairs and so on. But it cannot be seen in the hands alone which of these it will be, for again exactness here requires the pure talent of prophecy and that talent is extremely rare!

The backs of the hands show the family health guide and inherited health conditions, the right one being the father's side and the left the mother's. Chronic rheumatism or arthritis is rarely passed from the father's side, such conditions are mostly passed on from the mother's. Here too we see such things as longevity and circulation problems; whether a person is psychic, has a love of animals and also how tidy and or secure they are at home.

Do not let anyone read your hand in public, unless it is just a brief look, for the past is in the hands! To give your hands to a good operative, telling him you have no secrets from the loved one by your side may be asking for trouble. If the reader is not extremely responsible and holds back on what is seen (when their talent is restricted, placing them at an unfair disadvantage) they will tell you things about yourself that you would never tell anyone, especially your loved one!

Examples of things seen in the left hand, palm side up, are special family traits of the sitter's forebears, musical or other artistic abilities, luck and whether there is, or was, money in the family. It also shows family travel, perhaps that some live abroad or that the family no longer lives in just one area. It can indicate a father to son or daughter continuance of trades or professions, the health, deaths, particularly tragic, violent, or early ones and artistic and passionate characteristics.

Do not allow unpractised persons near your hands either, unless it is purely so that the operator may use you as a guinea-pig and then only if you trust the person. Note fully the details but only take the reading on face value. Tape-record and examine every aspect of the reading; do not be persuaded that this is your hard and fast future. The lines alone, the point at which most students begin, tell the reader very little!

Any *genuinely honest* reader will assure you that *no fixed destiny* exists in the hands and will probably suggest, or even argue that there is doubt that such a fixed one exists at all! In the end as with all decisions we make in our lives the choice we make is ours! Depending on how much the sitter takes to heart, the destiny part will perhaps be "bent" slightly one way or the other. Having said that I support and endorse the value one can gain from a good, honest palmist, the advice given by genuine psychics usually is sound, so it is worthy of consideration. Watch their face though and see whether they are studying yours - the best readers will not even look at you they will be looking at your hands! And also try hard not to respond with movements of your fingers or hands as, like the facial expressions, these are other responses picked up and used by charlatans.

I reiterate; the sitter finally makes the choice, since they mapped out their life prior to coming to earth anyway! There are those, and I count myself among them, who know that destiny has constant variables which we can apply throughout our earthly journey. Having freewill alone proves that we are not obliged to undertake or even think about a compulsory, fixed destiny. We all know that we have to be born and we have to "die" but exercising our prerogatives we may or may not, according to the decisions taken, travel a more flexible path than the more apparent alternatives.

Palmists, like practitioners in any field can, in reality, only gain experience of their craft by experience. I once scanned through a book on palmistry by Cheiro, reckoned by wiser heads than mine to be the Daddy of 'em all. Save for the lines alone, which are basically, always the same, i.e. life, love, health, career, etc., I confess I did not find much in it that agreed with my studies and experience. The contents conflicted with much of what I had already learned and demonstrated, so it was, for me, of little value.

So I went back to the metaphorical drawing board and as always, that meant putting my trust in the guides and helpers to show me the way forward. I make no apology when I say that I do not intend to tell you how to read hands! There are more than enough books on the subject already and my job here, should you be so inclined is to simply whet your appetite!

However, I do not want the foregoing to make students ignore, out of hand, all reading matter. I have always been able to link in with little or no effort to my teachers in Spirit and unless and until you can do likewise one of the best ways to learn is through the writing of others, which of itself gives your brain a chance to exercise.

So unless like me, you are a natural psychic, look into the wealth of knowledge that, to the intrepid seeker, is there. Recognise, absorb and use it! In any event, if you are interested in palmistry, I sincerely recommend that you at least read the works of the very skilled Cheiro who successfully demonstrated and proved beyond doubt, his outstanding ability. I still think though that under his psychic belt he must have had, as well as just the lines, other talents too. These at the very least must surely have been prophecy and clairvoyance but he probably had others yet!

On the *Tarot* I will also say little because although basically sticking to the known methods, I have, over the years, developed my own system, reading the cards esoterically and not as a fortune teller. Though the basic meanings are of course relevant I combine many different talents that have emerged and merged during that time. I have actually also found it necessary to update some of the cards! The reason is that, although intrinsically retaining their form over more than four thousand years, they now require and demand that the meanings should be more in step with today. The justification for this is self-demonstrated! About a hundred years ago mankind was taking halting haphazard steps in technology but since then discoveries and progress in medical knowledge, transport, communication and electronics, to name but a few have, as it were, turned the world on its ear! For me the Wheel of fortune has a much stronger bearing on karma than many of my contemporaries indicate being of a profound nature and not merely indicative of ups and downs in one's life. The XX card (Major Arcana) displays that bad karma is now paid back, balanced and that good karma is immediately forthcoming.

The travel cards indicating dangers (recklessness) relate more to us driving on the roads, or arriving in time for a flight, boat or train than to being aware of the dangers of highwaymen on the stagecoach route! Message cards too no longer refer only to letters which, until comparatively recently, was the only way of sending a private communication to someone else! Today we have telegrams (also rapidly becoming obsolete) the fax, telephone and computer-links that send messages, etc. almost instantaneously and at reasonable costs, to virtually anywhere in the world!

Other examples:- In olden days short journey cards meant perhaps travelling (walking?) to the next town or village, a time scale of say two hours. Today in the same time we can be more than a thousand miles away, a journey that would, almost certainly, have taken perhaps weeks, or even months to conclude then!

The three of pentacles indicates a marriage (or business) for money or where money is important but what partnership does not require this, whether it is business or marriage? The five of pentacles assures abundant wealth or good health but abundance, like beauty, is in the eye of the beholder! Legacy can also mean a health condition inherited, for instance and does not mean therefore, just money! I have listed but a few of the cards I have re-vamped, but once again I urge students to employ logic in their studies and see the cards basically for what they are - simply an indication of the probable turn of events!

I only offer the cards to sitters who do not want a purely spiritual sitting, but that does not detract from their usefulness or their accuracy! In essence, the basic interpretations having altered little over thousands of years, tarot cards, palmistry and astrology must surely be more than just a party trick! It is unfortunate that there are so many (as the ladies of the oldest profession in the world would say) amateurs trying to muscle in, pretending that they too are professional, when often they are only doing it for kicks or pin-money, or both!

There are other misnomers that need putting into perspective. Some "authorities" say that the reader must allow nobody to touch their cards! How then does one get the recipient, unless they are skilled in psychokinesis, to shuffle them? Some say to shuffle them in any of the conventional ways shocks the cards, affirming that they must only be turned, face down and mixed in a circular motion! So which is worse do you think, shocked or giddy cards? Others yet state they must be kept in the dark, wrapped in black silk and or under the reader's pillow, and so it goes on! These are old wives' tales, belonging only to the time when superstitious belief outweighed sensible, logical thought!

I retired my old cards because they are too sticky, badly bent and many of the surfaces almost rubbed away. Given these some forty years ago, they were already then over seventy! They served well until quite recently and the previous owner and myself together clocked up well over a hundred years, never stalling a moment in power-potential! (I only bought new ones because the existing set had worn out!) Therefore, if the foregoing on precautions, none of which were taken is true, they ought to have lost their "power" long ago but the only real difficulty was replacing them with a set of the same design!

Many different versions are available and although they more or less adhere to the trends, they all have a slant as to the ideas or beliefs of the designers. For example the true Egyptian set portrays the original High Priest card whereas the Christianised version of the same set displays the V as the Pope and Nordics prefer one of their ancient gods! Designers too have their own way of illustrating the cards, particularly with the Major Arcana. There are others who lean towards a romantic design; others yet who base their pictures on their country of origin, integrating ideas and scenery into their portrayal.

Some attempted to hide the definitions, by designing a "mystical" set, like the one by Aleister Crowley. Possibly the most famous self-confessed black magician of recent times, he believed that his set and images held more magical powers. To date we even have a round, female oriented set, the designer harping on that all previous cards had, in the designs, a male dominance about them. So even the feminists have jumped on the band-wagon! Perhaps someone will now produce the eternal triangle set! Whatever the design it matters little, so long as the reader knows the definitions must, for good readings, remain basically as they were aeons ago.

I reiterate; I read cards not as a fortune teller but esoterically using the set I have always used, so my advice is as follows. Work with a set that you feel comfortable with and in due course your own little idiosyncrasies will evolve, built into the way that you work and interpret same.

Like the books on palmistry, reading matter on this subject too is, in my opinion, already an overgrown mountain. The advice in these gives various and plentiful ways on the different methods. Therefore I consider it a pointless exercise to add my two-pennyworth on how to! So if this is your thing work through your public library, local book-shops, etc. and find a system that you feel comfortable with. Or realising on the way that *Tarot* is not for you, you may well give up any further study or research.

However, one small piece of advice I will pass on; write on the backs of the cards a form of short-hand of the definitions. This serves several purposes among which are (1) it assures the consultee that definitions given are what you say they mean; (2) it reminds you of your obligation not to twist meanings to make what you say fit the situation, a tool employed by other less honest consultants; (3) it allows you to practise at the start without referring to a book as each card unfolds, giving smoother flow and continuity to your divination. Finally write the definitions in pencil, for, at a later date you may wish to change your short-hand or even dispense with the writing on the backs of the cards altogether!

I have many times tried looking into the *crystal* endeavouring to see what others claim to see, i.e. the crystal ball clouding over and pictures appearing within it. I confess to never once having been successful, but as I have already said within these covers not to have experienced something oneself does not automatically mean that it is not possible!

In the beginning it can be perhaps a good point of concentration but since I receive images, etc. in the purely clairvoyant sense, it was academic, proving it to be unnecessary in my case. Impressions were received whether or not I was crystal gazing! Mind you, although unaware of it at the time, I, perhaps not wanting to become like Aunt Millie, simply put up a mental block making myself a non-starter anyway!

For those wanting to use a crystal I urge you to think about it most carefully. To begin with a genuine one is very expensive; do not be fobbed off with cheap imitations! A ball of some three inches in diameter, usually offered at a "give-away" price by some shops stocking psychic items is of little use. It will probably be glass and is much too small to see into anyway! This type is used by some people who work at psychic fairs, etc. employed for very practical reasons. One, it sits easily in the palm of a sitter's hand and this (they tell them) helps to build up the necessary magic. Two, should they happen to drop it, it can easily and quite cheaply be replaced at very short notice!

A effective ball should be genuine crystal and a minimum of six inches (15 cms.) in diameter. In considering the price of un-worked crystals used by some healers you will quickly realise that a beautifully, absolutely perfectly formed, polished sphere cannot be cheap! So unless you intend to make this your career or you can afford to lay out the money without worrying in any way (should you be unsuccessful) I advise you to exercise extreme caution.

Remember there are not that many really genuine crystal readers out there so whilst at first sight this may prompt the thought that one could become a big fish in a little sea, I reiterate my words of caution! There are but few who stay with it throughout their career, possibly because it is so limited in its expression and others move on because they find they have more than just the one narrow talent!

Remember too that if you fail or need to move on to other facets of development you may wish to sell it. This can present its own problems for you will find that you have to virtually give it away! Indeed you would be hard put to it to find a novice prepared to pay anything like the price you paid and genuine operators would not want a second-hand one anyway!

My conclusions are that I think, through the genuine operator, there is a lot of merit in the crystal method. But there are also far too many charlatans who, using only a glass "crystal" consistently defraud a gullible public. In the end the choice, as always is yours - may you choose wisely.

Chapter 7
AND FINALLY...

Signals, (vibrations) from Spirit that are impressed on the brain are interpreted and put into operation by the psyche within. Each of us has a "radio" but when we purchase one from a shop we have to tune it in. It is the same with our "soul" one for we are *all tuned differently* and, like the shop radio, even though it is capable of receiving the programme, unless the wavelength is correct, we will not receive it! If we do not tune absolutely onto the programme we wish to hear, we can sometimes still receive it, but the reception is distorted. We then have a choice; re-tune or put up with what we have.

Having decided (and this should constantly shift gears) on the type of study you wish to undertake be it physical, mental, philosophical, or an all-round seeking of knowledge, there are certain paths to travel. The first prerequisite however is not to rush into it simply for the sake of getting started! Use the advice given earlier in this book and combine it with common sense and logic.

Try to align yourself with other like-interested persons, people who at least appear to think along the same lines as yourself. This is necessary, for above all, to obtain good results you need to feel good, totally at ease, and comfortable with the other personalities involved. You must also feel that you can rely on the reciprocity of the other group members to help in your development. In the same way you also need to offer your support and effort to shove the wheel in whatever direction is determined. The primary object of sitting is to progress and gain knowledge as unselfishly as is possible. However, it naturally follows that there is little value in sitting in a circle or group where you feel that you are neither learning nor passing on knowledge and therefore achieving nothing! If that is the case I reiterate! It is not right for you and you must seek out new pastures!

Therefore the modus-operandi and one that I have always applied is first, establish the ground rules! Be led, if you have a medium in charge, as to what form these should take but do not simply follow sheep-like what the medium says. Full discussion must be the order of the day so get him or her to explain the reasons for this or that condition and *anything else* you do not understand as well!

Remember, as I have already said that what you cannot accept from within you will not (at least not honestly anyway) accept from without. Be reasonable yes, but make your logic work too! Ensure that whatever you agree to sits well with you, even if tomorrow (which indeed may well be the case) it needs a re-think. Do not vegetate; allow your mind to expand, seek out the grand adventure of True Knowledge for it is yours by right - God and Spirit have always held it thus!

In concluding this narrative normally one might say I have reached the end but for me as ever this is a new beginning! I have so much more to write about, for example reincarnation, self analysis and disciplines, the Spiritual Halls of Learning that are open to all. Red white and black magic, sacred symbols, sin, the elementals and the elements, the animal versus the human soul, the practice of healing and much much more! I pray therefore that I shall be given the time, the strength and opportunity to do so before I make my last transition from this dimension.

Finally, do not be as the centipede! A frog asked him how on earth did he manage to control so many legs? He himself had enough trouble with just four! It was then that the centipede became confused and stumbled, for up until then the thought as to how he did so had never occurred to him! The moral is not to worry about trying to find the pathway to Truth and Light; just *know* that you are on it already! In accepting this in a childlike, trusting way, you will automatically progress towards your spiritual destiny and will draw towards you others, both the seen and the "unseen" who will readily assist you in your search.

AMEN - SO BE IT!